OUTSMARTING THE NEXT PANDEMIC

This book examines the role of law and policy in addressing the public health crisis of COVID-19 and offers reforms that could improve pandemic preparedness for future outbreaks.

Focusing on a number of countries most expected to provide agility and organization in their crisis response – the United States, Canada, Australia, the United Kingdom and Taiwan – the book shows how failures in leadership from governments, executives, and institutions created a vacuum that was quickly filled by naysayers, conspiracy theorists, vaccine hucksters, and fake news generators. Through the key themes of healthcare, leadership, security, and education, the chapters address critical questions: Why have masks become such a polarizing force? How do you self-isolate if you don't have a home? How should equitable triage models for overwhelmed frontline healthcare workers be developed? Can we utilize artificial intelligence to educate the public about manipulated information they access concerning the pandemic? The book was written during the pandemic and weaves into each chapter vignettes with personal revelations from a broad range of countries, including some also grappling with poverty, war, natural disasters, or revolution.

It will appeal to academics, professionals, and policymakers interested in how law and health policy can converge on solutions for global infectious disease. It is suitable for use in upper-level courses.

Elizabeth Anne Kirley is a professor in the Master of Laws program at Osgoode Hall Law School, York University, Toronto. She holds JD (Western), LLM (Osgoode), and PhD (Osgoode) degrees and is called to the Ontario Bar. Elizabeth has served as Assistant Crown Attorney, Children's lawyer, and criminal defense counsel. Her research involves reputational privacy, digital crime, and pandemic law.

Deborah Porter holds an LLB from the University of Western Australia and was previously a registered nurse. She is passionate about health law and was a lecturer in the School of Medicine and the School of Law, Deakin University. Deborah is Legal Educator in end-of-life communications for the iValidate program, Barwon Health, Australia.

OUTSMARTING THE NEXT PANDEMIC

What COVID-19 Can Teach Us

*Edited by Elizabeth Anne Kirley
and Deborah Porter*

Routledge
Taylor & Francis Group

LONDON AND NEW YORK

Cover image: The National COVID Memorial Wall along South Bank, London, UK, displays messages to lost loved ones.
© Getty Images

First published 2022
by Routledge
2 Park Square, Milton Park, Abingdon, Oxon OX14 4RN

and by Routledge
605 Third Avenue, New York, NY 10158

Routledge is an imprint of the Taylor & Francis Group, an informa business

British Library Cataloguing-in-Publication Data
A catalogue record for this book is available from the British Library

Library of Congress Cataloging-in-Publication Data
A catalog record for this book has been requested

ISBN: 978-1-032-10531-4 (hbk)
ISBN: 978-1-032-10530-7 (pbk)
ISBN: 978-1-003-21576-9 (ebk)

DOI: 10.4324/9781003215769

Typeset in Bembo
by Apex CoVantage, LLC

Dedication 1: Deb To my family, the most wonderful people in my world. Thank you.

Dedication 2: Elizabeth To Jerry, Liam & Evan – the smartest and most supportive people I know. To the Thursday Zoom crew who kept me energized. And to Deb . . . I've just read that "antipodes" can be translated as "feet to feet," an apt description of how we have stayed connected with each other and our families in both hemispheres throughout these strange times to complete this writing adventure.

CONTENTS

FIGURES

TABLES

BOXES

CONTRIBUTORS

Li-Yin Chien
Taiwan
Li-Yin Chien is Professor at the College of Nursing, Institute of Community
Health Care, National Yang Ming Chiao Tung University, Taiwan.

Michael A. Crystal
Canada
Michael A. Crystal is a trial and appellate litigation lawyer in Ottawa, Ontario,
and is certified as a criminal law specialist by the Law Society of Ontario. Michael
is also an ad hoc professor at the University of Ottawa Faculty of Law, where he
teaches courses in trial advocacy.

Julie Doldersum
Canada
Julie Doldersum is a nurse and midwife at Collingwood General and Marine
Hospital in Ontario, Canada. She also runs her own midwifery business. Julie
gained experience in caregiving when working for Médecins Sans Frontières
during an epidemic in Congo under challenging conditions. She has worked
closely with new mothers throughout COVID.

William H. Dutton
England
William H. Dutton is Emeritus Professor at the University of Southern California. He was the founding director of the Oxford Internet Institute (OII) and first
professor of internet studies at the University of Oxford, where he is an OII Fellow and a Martin Fellow with Oxford's Global Cybersecurity Capacity Center.

David Guida
Canada
David Guida is a high school computer science teacher in Mississauga, Ontario, for Dufferin-Peel Catholic District School Board (DPCDSB). He recently completed his LLM in Privacy and Cybersecurity Law at York University and applies his unique expertise to consulting for Toronto technology startups.

Joseph E. Ibrahim
Australia
Joseph E. Ibrahim is Professor, Faculty of Medicine, Nursing and Health Sciences, Monash University, and Adjunct Professor, Australian Centre for Evidence Based Aged Care, La Trobe University. He is also a senior specialist in geriatric medicine with over 30 years clinical experience and has published extensively in this area with over 300 papers.

Peter Ketcheson
Canada
Peter Ketcheson is a JD graduate, Queen's University Faculty of Law. He worked with the Queen's Prison Law Clinic, winning the Queen's Law Prize in Advanced Clinical Prison Law. Peter is called to the Ontario Bar and has joined the firm of Hicks Adams LLP in Toronto, Ontario.

Elizabeth Anne Kirley
Canada
Elizabeth Anne Kirley is a Professor in the Master of Laws program, Osgoode Hall Law School's Professional Development Program at York University, Toronto. She is called to the Ontario Bar and has served as Assistant Crown Attorney, Children's Lawyer, and criminal defense counsel. Her published research addresses reputational privacy, digital crime, and nonverbal evidence.

Su-Chen Liao
Taiwan
Su-Chen Liao is Supervisor of Nursing at the Nursing Department, Taipei Veterans General Hospital, Taiwan, and a PhD student at the College of Nursing, National Yang Ming Chiao Tung University, Taiwan.

Marilyn McMahon
Australia
Marilyn McMahon is Professor and Deputy Dean at Deakin Law School, Australia. She researches and publishes in the areas of criminal law and procedure. She earned her PhD from La Trobe University, an MPsych (Forensic) and GDLP from Monash University, and a BA (Hons.) in Psychology, and LLB (Law) from the University of Melbourne.

Jacob Medvedev
Canada
Jacob Medvedev is a JD/MBA graduate from the University of Ottawa Faculty of Law and Telfer School of Management. He anticipates being called to the Bar of the Law Society of Ontario in June 2022.

Sharyn Milnes
Australia
Sharyn Milnes is Manager, Clinical Education and Training, Barwon Health, Australia. She is a registered nurse and has qualifications in critical care nursing and in higher education. She holds a Master of Bioethics and is currently a PhD candidate. Sharyn has coauthored a number of journal articles regarding end-of-life communication and ethics.

Lisa Mitchell
Australia
Lisa Mitchell is a geriatrician at Barwon Health, Australia. She has a Master of Bioethics and is a foundational member of the clinical ethics service at Barwon Health. She is Conjoint Clinical Senior Lecturer in the School of Medicine, Deakin University.

Elena Musi
England
Elena Musi is Lecturer in Artificial Intelligence and Communication at the University of Liverpool. Her expertise lies at the interface of theoretical and applied linguistics, communication studies, and artificial intelligence. Elena has worked as the Language Engineer for Alexa in Italian with the Amazon Alexa Applied Modelling and Data Science team in Cambridge, Massachusetts.

Neil Orford
Australia
Neil Orford is an intensive care specialist at Barwon Health, Australia. He is a board member of the College of Intensive Care Medicine, Australia and New Zealand, and has an interest in communication and ethics in clinical practice. He has coauthored journal articles on a range of clinical practice areas.

Deborah Porter
Australia
Deborah Porter holds an LLB from the University of Western Australia and was previously a registered nurse. She is passionate about health law and was a lecturer in the School of Medicine and School of Law, Deakin University. Deborah is Consultant Legal Educator in the iValidate program, Barwon Health, Australia.

Ana Santos Rutschman
United States

Ana Santos Rutschman teaches health law and intellectual property at Saint Louis University School of Law. Her scholarship has appeared in leading legal and scientific publications for which she has received numerous awards. Her book *Vaccines as Technology: Innovation, Barriers and the Public Interest* will be published in 2022.

Nicholas Simpson
Australia

Nicholas Simpson is Deputy Director of the Intensive Care Unit, Barwon Health, Australia. He has coauthored a number of journal articles on a range of clinical practice areas and has an interest in communication and ethics in clinical practice.

Jacky Visser
Scotland

Jacky Visser is Professor at the Centre of Argument Technology at the University of Dundee, Scotland. He has devised a solution to enable students to take disinformation detection into their own hands: he uses chatbots, or argument technology.

Carolyn Whitzman
Canada

Carolyn Whitzman is Adjunct Professor in the Department of Geography, Environment, and Geomatics at the University of Ottawa and an international housing and social policy consultant. Her primary research interest has been in developing a human rights approach to housing and social service policy, informed by a feminist intersectional analysis.

Stephen Wilks
United States

Stephen Wilks is Associate Professor at the University of Detroit Mercy School of Law, where he teaches corporate and commercial law. His cross-disciplinary research has appeared in several scholarly journals and explores themes of governance and regulation within transactional spaces.

FOREWORD

Outsmarting the Next Pandemic: What COVID-19 Can Teach Us was produced with support from the Jack & Mae Nathanson Centre on Transnational Human Rights, Crime and Security at Osgoode Hall Law School of York University in Toronto. The Nathanson Centre seeks to make a leading, cross-disciplinary contribution to the study of the relationships among crime, human rights, and security in the context of transnational phenomena and as informed by normative and theoretical perspectives. This book makes an important contribution to the work of the Centre during the COVID-19 pandemic and will be essential reading for scholars, policymakers, and a general audience interested in holistic and human rights–based approaches to pandemic response, recovery, and prevention.

Taking a multidisciplinary approach to tackling issues in law and policy across a variety of professional settings and in multiple jurisdictional contexts, *Outsmarting the Next Pandemic* zeros in on how our collective failure to proactively manage the pandemic has been the result, in part, of misidentification and sometimes outright denial of contests and contradictions between "rule of law" imperatives and more compassionate, humane, and individualized policy approaches. As this book puts front and center, there is an important tension at the heart of ubiquitous public health messaging that "we are all in this together." The pandemic has exhibited and intensified material inequalities of all kinds within and between states, showing us that, in fact, we are *not* all in this together. This book does not shy away from this reality; instead, it adopts a forward-looking approach that takes seriously the call to solidarity in an effort to explore practical policy solutions to the fractured and unequal impacts of the pandemic.

The 12 case studies addressed in this book weave in and between the three thematic pillars that animate the Centre's work: human rights, crime, and security in transnational context. From decisions around the rationing of medical care to masking mandates, from travel restrictions to online education, from homelessness to supply chain disruptions, this book contributes to legal and ethical debates about the appropriate frame to apply when we seek to manage the collective good while ensuring minimal infringement of individual autonomy and human rights. As the chapter authors continually remind us, this is a balance that must be struck and restruck throughout the duration of an emergency, as both a question of domestic and global governance.

The edited collection is particularly well suited to carrying out this daunting project. Rather than proposing a unifying theory or totalizing substantive orientation to pandemic preparedness, this volume strikes a cautious, exploratory, and tentative tone. In approaching each case and issue its own terms, the authors collectively generate a policy discussion that is as attentive to difference along class, racialized, gendered, and geographical axes as it is to individual lived experiences of the pandemic. This method is present internally in each chapter, as well as across the chapters and the first-person narrative accounts and photographs. In juxtaposing traditional analytical chapters with the innovative "Corona Shorts," which feature writers from the global north and global south and represent all continents, this collection embodies the central question it seeks to take on: how to foster people-first transnational collaborative responses to the global health crisis while charting a way out of the disparities and inequalities that characterize our current institutions of national and international governance, so that we will be better prepared for the next emergency.

The COVID-19 crisis and the upcoming recovery period stand as a powerful opportunity for scholars, policymakers, professionals, and everyday/everynight workers to build a strategic conversation about how to move away from the systems and structures that have generated deep and persistent global inequality. This collection teaches us how the virus capitalized on very human, very contingent power structures to generate its devastating impacts. That the devastation wrought by the virus has affected some more than others is not a natural or deserved reality; it is the result of concrete decisions taken in service of concrete political commitments. All too often, the mechanisms of global governance have been shrouded in secrecy, captured by elites, and hidden from view. Aligned with the long-standing commitment of the Nathanson Centre to combating transnational corruption, this collection urges transparency as an overarching goal as we build our collective future.

To be sure, new policy directions are always embarked upon with a degree of faith: we can never know, in advance, what unintended consequences our well-intentioned decisions may have. Yet in the midst of this uncertainty, and in the face of suffering on the massive scale generated by the pandemic, action is surely required. This book encourages us to act from an informed yet above all humble space, where we are willing to learn from others and yet are intent on systemic change. As such, it is an essential contribution to the sophisticated, human rights–based policy discussion so urgently required of the current moment.

Congratulations to the editors and the authors.

Heidi Matthews,
Assistant Professor & Co-Director, Jack &
Mae Nathanson Centre on Transnational Human Rights,
Crime and Security (2018–2021),
Osgoode Hall Law School, York University

ACKNOWLEDGMENTS

Sincere thanks to everyone who has supported us on this book journey. We are grateful for the ongoing support of the faculty and staff at the Jack and Mae Nathanson Centre on Transnational Human Rights, Crime and Security at York University in Toronto. We thank all of our indisputably generous contributors for taking the time, and making the effort, to write during such testing times. To those who participated in our Corona Shorts – thank you for sharing your stories; they add a unique and poignant quality to our book.

Additional thanks to photojournalist Mas Agung Willis "Yudya" Baskoro in Jakarta and photographer Leysis Quesada Vera of Havana who risked COVID exposure to bring us the heartwarming images of a newborn in Indonesia (Chapter 3) and ballet students in a makeshift rehearsal space in Cuba (Corona Short #17). And special mention to Diane Masschaele for her generous editing support and guidance along the way; to Cathryn McGregor and Watermark Design Decisions for her inspiring design advice and mock-up; to Angela Lescard, Basema Al-Alami, Sunyatta Moos, Frenialyn Abel (Fren), and others who have located the Corona Shorts narrators from every continent (except Antarctica), and to Tina de los Santos for her thoughtful translation services. We also thank Dr Dorothea Burns for excellent resources on the bubonic plague of early modern Europe. Because of all of you, we have a book to be proud of.

Special gratitude as well to Leanne Hinves, Russell George, and Evie Lonsdale at Taylor & Francis (UK).

INTRODUCTION

Elizabeth Anne Kirley and Deborah Porter

This book is an act of faith. It is a compilation of observations and assessments on the pandemic written *during* the pandemic, from March 2020 to June 2021. Before memories grew dim, 21 authors from various fields sat down amidst the chaos and chronicled what they were observing in their daily lives. They recorded the cracks they saw in the systems that, when life ticks along in a normative fashion, provide the infrastructure for our healthcare, education, social welfare, law, governance, and trade.

The authors were asked to be "smart" by focusing on that aspect of their profession that revealed a "defining moment," a clearheaded realization of what needed to be done to ensure a more successful outcome next time. In their writing and thinking, they were asked to assess what went awry and how we must improve on those shortcomings should this happen again. That exercise in "lessons learned" was difficult for our authors who were attempting an overview while in mid-stream. As economies rose or plunged, and with no guarantees of publication for the authors in a flooded market, these professionals stole time from their uncertain lives to focus on one aspect of what they were observing that they believed could be handled better. Their contributions provide an excellent interplay of knowledge and professional experiences. The authors' deliberations have been organized into four central themes: healthcare, leadership, security, and education. The ensuing 12 chapters constitute their findings.

In Chapter 1, our co-editors examine the science of Severe Acute Respiratory Syndrome coronavirus-2 (SARS-CoV-2) as the pathogen moves from creating a local health crisis to a series of deadlier transmutations that had infected more than 245 million people by autumn 2021 across all but eight countries of the world. A healthcare team from Australia discusses the importance of ensuring the patient

DOI: 10.4324/9781003215769-1

remains front and center in end-of-life decisions, which might include choosing a ventilator or accepting the possible end-of-life consequences (Chapter 2). Three midwives and a nurse discuss the best precautions for mother and baby to birth safely in Taiwan, Australia, and Canada during a pandemic (Chapter 3). A professor of business law in the United States examines the causes and possible solutions to supply chain disruptions emerging from a global health crisis (Chapter 4). Two law professors from Australia and Canada examine the ideological disparities in mask wearing in various countries and suggest that an early, collective response lowers the curve faster than holding individuals responsible for their own risk-taking (Chapter 5). An expert of 30 years in long-term care and aging identifies paternalism and a lack of creative responses to security for the more vulnerable as the two main roadblocks to more protective facilities that would improve crisis response (Chapter 6). An intellectual property professor in Missouri encourages collaborative efforts to offset the commodification and nationalistic approaches to personal protective equipment (PPE) and vaccine distribution (Chapter 7). A Canadian expert in social housing policy discusses some of the more inventive and workable examples of independent living for the homeless (Chapter 8). Three legal professionals assess lockdown risks in Canadian jails and urge replacing custodial sentencing with restorative justice as a more human rights–oriented response to global health crises (Chapter 9). A communications expert at Oxford and Leeds universities in the UK suggests that we focus on equitable and diverse access to education when deciding how to integrate online teaching with classroom learning for effective post-pandemic planning in universities (Chapter 10). Two university educators from Dundee, Scotland, and Liverpool, England, share their research into using chatbots to teach students how to identify fake news and disinformation (Chapter 11). Finally, a high school teacher in computer science presents findings from his Master of Laws studies in Toronto to inform us about how to protect children from sexual predators during online education (Chapter 12).

Driving such intelligent choices, however, must be transnational collaboration and ownership of the global tragedy and the debacle caused by unpreparedness, nationalism, politicization of public health priorities, and denial. Those factors revealed a lack of understanding of how to divorce the pandemic from the political. We can learn both rapid response and resilience lessons from smaller states such as Taiwan and South Korea and the city of Hong Kong, each of which had integrated practices into daily life from SARS and MERS as early as 2003. The process of lessons learned has begun with two formal, independent reviews of the World Health Organization's (WHO) handling of the pandemic, as well as assessments of the role of the United Nations (UN) and the G7. We will need informed political will, technological risk-taking, and eagerness to share health data across geopolitical borders. Those reviews are summarized in the Conclusion.

Instruments used to focus the book and connect its various components are the rule of law and public policy. That focus presents a challenge in that law has been "entangled with every aspect of human life for some time,"[1] whereas medical science deals with the ailment or dysfunction that brings each person to the gurney.

Law is a social science of order and precision, rights, and obligations; medicine is a science of probability and, at times, intuition. As epidemiologist and Pulitzer prize-winning author Siddhartha Mukherjee noted about his own efforts to define the laws of medicine during his residency years, "I had never expected medicine to be such a lawless, uncertain world."[2] Fortunately for the patient, one feature connects law and medicine: the professional's devotion to achieving security of the person.

Expanding law's role in times of crisis can bring public order, but it cannot, without more, put masks on faces or serums into arms. For that, we need to convince people that it is medically wise to do so. To engage readers in such debates in this book, we employ three formats: academic analyses (Chapters 1, 2, 4, 5, 7, 8, 9, and 12); interviews with experts (Chapters 3, 6, 10, and 11); and what we call "Corona Shorts." The latter are first-person narratives of key moments on the ground related by individuals living in all continents except Antarctica. Those personal reflections connect north with south and traverse east and west to bring lessons in surviving the coronavirus in various corners of the world. We structure this broad landscape with two questions we have all asked ourselves over the past several months: "who decides?" and "who speaks for us?"

Who decides?

The first year of a pandemic might be the best time to record raw perceptions of our suffering. After the virus has wreaked its unimaginable destruction over several months, we gain time and evidence to assess successes and missteps, to see which countries responded well and why. On a more personal level, as you watch your job become more tenuous, or if you lose your parents or your home, you face the rudiments of how to survive. If you are alone and homeless, in long-term care, on or off a list for ventilator treatment, or frantically searching for intensive care unit (ICU) beds, oxygen, or fentanyl as a hospital frontline medic, you are unwittingly pulled into the outcomes of your government's history of wins and losses in public health policy. When the realization that you are caught in the onslaught of a worldwide disease is making it difficult to breathe, you might find yourself standing at the window that separates you from your child or grandparent or working your way through yet another queue, masked and wondering, "Who decides?"

Whose decisions determine that you will leave the safety of your home each day to find work or food? Who orchestrates supply chains? When ventilators or ICU beds are in short supply, who selects the lucky ones? When vaccines are delayed, diverted, or defective, who dictates that we order more, and from where? Who decides in richer countries that tree nurseries and liquor outlets are essential services while schools are closed; that dying patients in poorer countries will be buried in a plastic box or set afire on a designated pyre without family or ceremony; that university students are either locked into residences far from home or confined to that faraway home with (maybe) a Zoom lifeline to their teacher and classmates; and that detainees in prisons must breathe each other's air because virtual courts struggle with trial scheduling or witness availability?

The rule of law is not the first recourse when a pandemic arrives. In some countries it is the first casualty. Those initial, panicked months likely found you focusing on the acts of governments, not on lawmakers. It is your government that issues money for support payments, bailouts, and small business subsidies. It will oversee mask supply and vaccine distribution and decide that a military base or football field will be converted to servicing rising numbers of critically ill patients. Your relationship with government in this initial stage is less likely built on trust and more on desperate need.

Another aspect of a public health crisis for which the rule of law is not equipped is "the scramble,"[3] for updated information on the nature and behavior of the pathogen and timely responses. To achieve that, we need a game plan, advanced strategies that have been tried and tweaked: in a word, a playbook – or in the UK, a civil contingencies secretariat in the Cabinet Office.[4] The backstory on the elaborate pandemic playbooks and simulations made available for those governing the larger wealthier nations is slowly unfolding and suggests a tragic case of missed opportunities more akin to a Hollywood whodunnit than this volume of contributions.[5] And yet the need for such preparedness cannot be underestimated. As one account warns:

> It is widely known that the former Soviet Union maintained a stockpile of 20 tons of smallpox virus in its biological weapons arsenal throughout the 1970s, and that, by 1990, they had a plant capable of producing 80–100 tons of smallpox per year.[6]

A game plan overseen at the highest levels is mandatory in the face of such threats to humankind.

While the rule of law does not always dominate the headlines in such existential crises and has eroded remarkably in some countries over the past year, it exists to check excessive use of authority, to address human rights abuses and discrimination, to prosecute opportunistic crime and corruption. During a pandemic, those violations feed on public chaos and a rolling barrage of shutouts, lockdowns, shortages, and supply chain screwups that thwart efforts at accountability. You hope law will force transparency in public and private sectors. We have been learning from news accounts and resources such as this book that regulations function in a pandemic to bring public order (through border closures and airline cancelations), reduce health risks (of food and drug hoarding and vaccine contamination), and highlight human rights (access to housing and isolation of the elderly). Laws function to give voice and equal access for a more just solution. When the virus has been either defeated or subdued, you hope the law will be consulted to sort out corners that were cut, promises unkept, or injustices unattended.

As pandemic survivors in richer nations contemplate attending Olympic Games in Japan or their favorite pub down the street, those left on their own in poorer nations are facing a catastrophic third or fourth wave with a profound lack of antidotes, legal identity for treatment, or privacy to mourn their dead. In war-torn countries, armed groups prevail to discredit state institutions and exploit the disenfranchised.

Who speaks?

A necessary question considering those inequities is who speaks out? Government-side, it is the public health researchers and virologists who have been appearing on public bandwidth alongside their head of state to update their nation on the state of pandemic readiness. Presidents and prime ministers have integrated the science into their messages quite deftly. From them we are learning that an epidemiologist seeks answers for the many; medical doctors for the one.[7] They speak of R numbers, comorbidities, and ace-receptors. Some leaders control the public message, such as President Bolsonaro in Brazil and President Duterte in the Philippines. Others defer to their ministers of public security or public health to explain, and to buttress with best scientific evidence, their most recent decisions about strategies for containment, mitigation, and recovery. Trust-building in support of state institutions is the objective of many televised speeches from the podium. Similarly, public vaccinations of leaders and mask wearing in parliamentary sittings can speak volumes on the optics of leadership and solidarity, feeding the "we are all in this together" meme.

In democratic states, constituents can demand decisions that are "necessary, proportionate, legal, and time bound."[8] That demand has not necessarily been met with success in less stable environments, especially in countries where government agencies use excessive force or are motivated by greed. For example, the distribution of emergency aid, medical supplies, and economic stimuli provides ample opportunity for corruption and fraud, as explained by the United Nations Assistant Secretary-General for Rule of Law and Security Institutions. Without effective institutions, that much-needed aid will not reach intended populations, deepening the social, medical, and economic crises and delaying recovery.[9] This is where lawmakers and law enforcers can speak up by legislating oversight and accountability. Unfortunately, the administrative disruptions and dislocation of services during a pandemic also provide opportunities for terrorist organizations to discredit governments and capitalize on public outrage. As security personnel fall victim to the virus, some armed groups are consolidating to control territory. As the scourge of the pandemic wanes or can be mitigated, international law can be invoked to punish transgressors and restore order.

One question that confounds the epidemiologist and lawyer alike is how smaller, less wealthy, nations achieved relatively low rates of infection and death, at least in the first few months of 2020.[10] We wonder how Japan and South Korea or the city of Hong Kong, all water encircled, each within 100 miles of the Wuhan Institute of Virology, achieved such stellar results initially. Was it the "chatter" shared by colleagues on worldwide list serves that informed the scientific community about a devastating coronavirus? Another small country, Denmark with a population of 5.8 million, followed a strategy of "act fast and with force."[11] The reported result by 8 June 2021 when most countries were battling their first, second, or even third wave was 2,521 deaths.[12] Danish leaders were able to harness public trust and reflexive obedience. Several smaller South Asian states with previous firsthand experience with SARS-CoV-1 in 2003 or Middle Eastern states that suffered another respiratory disease, MERS, in 2012 have ensured that those experiences are ingrained in the health culture of their citizens, as seen in the ready use of face coverings or masks and other non-pharmaceutical precautions such as sequestering.[13] As early as May 2020, Taiwan was reporting 759 cases and 7 deaths in a population of 23.5 million. Low cases and mortality figures show they acted quickly and decisively and were able to boast of zero community transmission. This edge unfortunately disappeared with the influx of variants in mid-2021.

The public has spoken with vigor and emotion during COVID, if not always in deference to the common good, as defined across the history of moral and political thought. For example, in the United States, speaking out about vaccine hesitancy or mask denial is tolerated under constitutional protection for free speech unless it incites imminent harm or danger.

In more autocratically run jurisdictions, speaking out has its political price, from COVID-19 ophthalmologist and whistleblower Li Wenliang working in a Wuhan hospital[14] to Swedish epidemiologist Anders Tegnell, who criticized closing borders as an illogical tactic for a government pursuing herd immunity as the state's public health response.[15] Even a former political advisor to Prime Minister Boris Johnson in the UK has found voice to castigate his former boss as "unfit for the job."[16] Dominic Cummings claims that by failing to get a grip on the crisis, Johnson and Matthew Hancock, the health secretary, are responsible for the unnecessary loss of thousands of lives.[17] Concerning Hancock, Cummings commented, "He was telling half the government to 'hold tests back so I can hit my target,' and [he] should have been fired. It was criminal, disgraceful behaviour that caused serious harm."[18]

Finally, a speech-related phenomenon that dominates this pandemic is the infusion of fake news, disinformation, and misinformation in both citizen journalism and leadership campaigns. Examples abound of faulty advice taken to extremes: in Iran nearly 300 people died from ingesting methanol based on social media recommendations; in South Korea, churchgoers were infected with COVID-19 after being sprayed with saltwater by church leaders; and in the United States, social and national media accounts of how bleach might help kill the virus contributed to individuals intentionally ingesting such high-risk products.[19] In response, various organizations such as the WHO and the Centers for Disease Control are speaking out with strategies to educate social media users.

Unfortunately, some measures to criminalize the spread of misinformation about the virus or to censor speech about government mistakes are being used to silence journalists and critics. More generally, the COVID crisis has heightened inequalities and discriminatory practices of lockdown and other restraints based on ethnicity, race, religion, and gender identity.[20] This book offers a nonmedical antidote to those excesses: when the law disappoints, speak out!

Notes

1 Richard Haigh and Dan Priel, *Law in the Time of COVID*, 57:3 Introduction, Osgoode Hall L. J. 533 (2020).
2 Siddhartha Mukherjee, The Laws of Medicine: Field Notes from an Uncertain Science, Simon & Schuster (2015).
3 A word used by author Malcolm Gladwell to describe the response of wealthier nations to the coronavirus global invasion in March of 2020: "Depending on how long this disruption goes on, there is potential for a kind of scrambling of the power structure of the world." See further, *Malcolm Gladwell on the World after COVID-19*, Munk Dialog. (10 Apr. 2020) at 1:32m, www.youtube.com/watch?v=flWtb_3ETIo.
4 David Pegg, *Covid-19: Did the UK Government Prepare for the Wrong Kind of Pandemic?* The Guardian (21 May 2020), www.theguardian.com/world/2020/may/21/did-the-uk-government-prepare-for-the-wrong-kind-of-pandemic.
5 See, for example, Mark Perry, *America's Pandemic War Games Don't End Well*, For. Policy (1 Apr. 2020), https://foreignpolicy.com/2020/04/01/coronavirus-pandemic-war-games-simulation-dark-winter/; Amy Maxmen and Jeff Tollefson, *Two Decades of Pandemic War Games Failed to Account for Donald Trump*, Nature (4 Aug. 2020), www.nature.com/articles/d41586-020-02277-6; Center for Disease Control and Prevention, *National Pandemic Influenza Plans/Pandemic Influenza (Flu)*, CDC (2020), www.cdc.gov/flu/pandemic-resources/planning-prepared-ness/national-strategy-planning.html; World Health Organization, *A Guide for Conducting Table-Top Exercises for National Influenza Pandemic Preparedness*, WHO Regional Office for South-East Asia (SEARO) New Delhi, India (Dec. 2006) 24 p; *The Pandemic Playbook*, Vox (28 May 2021), www.vox.com/22403980/the-pandemic-playbook; and David Pegg, *What Was Exercise Cygnus and What Did It Find?*, The Guardian (7 May 2020), www.theguardian.com/world/2020/may/07/what-was-exercise-cygnus-and-what-did-it-find.
6 Tara O'Tolle, Mair Michael and Thomas V. Inglesby, *Shining Light on "Dark Winter,"* 34:7 Clin. Infect. Dis. 972–983 (1 Apr. 2002).
7 Siddhartha Mukherjee, *How Does the Coronavirus Behave Inside a Patient?* New Yorker (26 Mar. 2020).
8 Alexandre Zouev, *COVID-19 and the Rule of Law: A Dangerous Balancing Act*, U.N. Covid-19 Resp., www.un.org/en/coronavirus/covid-and-rule-law-dangerous-balancing-act.
9 Id.
10 Timothy I. Mellish, Natalie J. Luzmore and Ahmed Ashfaque Shahbaz, *Why Were the UK and USA Unprepared for the COVID-19 Pandemic? The Systemic Weaknesses of Neoliberalism: A Comparison between the UK, USA, Germany, and South Korea*, 7:1 J. Glob. Faultlines 9–45 (June–Aug. 2020).
11 David Olagnier and Trine H. Mogensen, *The Covid-19 Pandemic in Denmark: Big Lessons from a Small Country*, 53 Cytokine Growth Factor Rev. 10–12 (June 2020).
12 That works out as 43.3 deaths per 100,000 population. *See*, Johns Hopkins University of Medicine's Corona Virus Resource Center at https://coronavirus.jhu.edu/data/mortality.
13 Countries with reported MERS exposure include Saudi Arabia, South Korea, the Philippines, and the Netherlands. The coronavirus originates in camels and does not produce asymptomatic cases.
14 Li Wenliang, *Wuhan Whistleblower' Remembered One Year on*, BBC News (6 Feb. 2021), www.bbc.com/news/world-asia-55963896.
15 Marta Paterlini, *"Closing Borders Is Ridiculous": The Epidemiologist Behind Sweden's Controversial Coronavirus Strategy*, Nature (21 Apr. 2020), www.nature.com/articles/d41586-020-01098-x.

16 *Dominic Cummings: Thousands Died Needlessly after Covid Mistakes*, BBC (26 May 2021), www.bbc.com/news/uk-politics-57253578.
17 Stephen Swinford and Chris Smyth, *"Hypocrite" Dominic Cummings Accused of Trying to Rewrite the Past over Covid Response*, The Times (25 May 2021), www.thetimes.co.uk/article/hypocrite-dominic-cummings-accused-of-trying-to-rewrite-the-past-over-covid-response-hjkmg3wwg.
18 Gareth Iacobucci, *Covid-19: How Did the Health Secretary Respond to Dominic Cummings's Allegations?*, BMJ 373, n1505 (11 June 2021), https://doi.org/10.1136/bmj.n1505.
19 Hye Kyung Kim, Jisoo Ahn, Lucy Atkinson, et al., *Effects of COVID-19 Misinformation on Information Seeking, Avoidance, and Processing: A Multicountry Comparative Study*, 42:5 Sci. Comm. 586–615 (13 Sept. 2020).
20 Ted Piccone, *COVID-19 Has Worsened a Shaky Rule of Law Environment*, Brookings Inst. (15 Apr. 2021).

Bibliography

BBC, *Dominic Cummings: Thousands Died Needlessly after Covid Mistakes* (26 May 2021).
Center for Disease Control and Prevention, *National Pandemic Influenza Plans/Pandemic Influenza (Flu)*, CDC (2020).
Haigh, Richard and Dan Priel, *Law in the Time of COVID*, Introduction, Osgoode H. L. J. (2020) 57:3, 533.
Iacobucci, Gareth, *Covid-19: How Did the Health Secretary Respond to Dominic Cummings's Allegations?*, BMJ (11 June 2021) 373, n1505.
Kim, Hye Kyung, Jisoo Ahn, Lucy Atkinson, et al., *Effects of COVID-19 Misinformation on Information Seeking, Avoidance, and Processing: A Multicountry Comparative Study*, Sci. Comm. (13 Sept. 2020) 42:5, 586–615.
Maxmen, Amy and Jeff Tollefson, *Two Decades of Pandemic War Games Failed to Account for Donald Trump*, Nature (4 Aug. 2020).
Mellish, Timothy I., Natalie J. Luzmore and Ahmed Ashfaque Shahbaz, *Why Were the UK and USA Unprepared for the COVID-19 Pandemic? The Systemic Weaknesses of Neoliberalism: A Comparison between the UK, USA, Germany, and South Korea*, J. Glob. Faultlines (June–Aug. 2020) 7:1, 9–45.
Mukherjee, Siddhartha, *How Does the Coronavirus Behave Inside a Patient?* New Yorker (26 Mar. 2020).
Mukherjee, Siddhartha, *The Laws of Medicine: Field Notes from an Uncertain Science*, Simon & Schuster (2015).
Olagnier, David and Trine H. Mogensen, *The Covid-19 Pandemic in Denmark: Big Lessons from a Small Country*, Cytokine Growth Factor Rev. (June 2020) 53, 10–12.
O'Tolle, Tara, Mair Michael and Thomas V. Inglesby, *Shining Light on "Dark Winter"*, Clin. Infect. Dis. (1 Apr. 2002) 34:7, 972–983.
Paterlini, Marta, *"Closing Borders Is Ridiculous": The Epidemiologist Behind Sweden's Controversial Coronavirus Strategy*, Nature (21 Apr. 2020).
Pegg, David, *Covid-19: Did the UK Government Prepare for the Wrong Kind of Pandemic?*, The Guardian (21 May 2020).
Pegg, David, *What Was Exercise Cygnus and What Did It Find?*, The Guardian (7 May 2020).
Perry, Mark, *America's Pandemic War Games Don't End Well*, For. Policy (1 Apr. 2020).
Scott, Dylan et al., *The Pandemic Playbook*, Vox (28 May 2021).
Swinford, Stephen and Chris Smyth, *"Hypocrite" Dominic Cummings Accused of Trying to Rewrite the Past over Covid Response*, The Times (25 May 2021).

Wenliang, Li, *Wuhan Whistleblower' Remembered One Year On*, BBC News (6 Feb. 2021).

World Health Organization, *A Guide for Conducting Table-Top Exercises for National Influenza Pandemic Preparedness*, WHO Regional Office for South-East Asia (SEARO) New Delhi, India (Dec. 2006) 24 p.

Zouev, Alexandre, *COVID-19 and the Rule of Law: A Dangerous Balancing Act*, U.N. Covid-19 Resp.

PART I
Healthcare

1

HOW SMART IS COVID?

Elizabeth Anne Kirley and Deborah Porter

To ask strangers to be smart during a catastrophe might seem an impertinence. To ask colleagues might seem to take advantage. To ask it of yourself is to set yourself up for criticism as too ambitious or a know-it-all.

It has been suggested that the virtue we are looking for to deal with the coronavirus is resilience, not smartness. That notion builds on sister virtues of tenacity, courage, and forbearance. Those qualities have been named in the profuse array of publications on this moment to describe the doers (those involved in governance of infrastructures to keep responses systematic), the sufferers (those who succumb), and the adapters (those who service the sufferers and those who wait and recalibrate). Very little about SARS-CoV-2 is uncontested, however. The non-pharmaceutical interventions of masks, handwashing, and isolation have been proven to bend the viral curve, but without more, such as a vaccine, we keep ourselves at the mercy of a transmutating organism that, as we are learning, can be just as smart as we are.

Law, too, is a non-pharmaceutical intervention. It is a smart response in that it looks for long-term solutions to the uncertainty and chaos global pestilence brings, not to situational cessation of risky behavior. The law's presence has been central in this disease. As one medicolegal study has calculated, in the first half of 2020 alone, more than 1,000 laws and orders were issued by federal, state, and local authorities in the United States to reduce disease transmission.[1] The study's inventory includes various regulations that touch our own lives, such as stay-at-home orders, mask mandates, travel restrictions, and more particularized rules for business operations, alcohol sales, tax remittances, curfews, and healthcare.

Ideally, we look to "the right mix, intensity, and enforcement approaches" in our laws that control transmission with the least intrusive and unequitable harms.[2] That might suffice in autocracies or in smaller, more geopolitically

DOI: 10.4324/9781003215769-3

contained societies. For the rest of us, looking to law as a way out of this economic and social limbo has accentuated the pluralistic nature of our lives, not its uniformity. The imposition of laws also inevitably brings ethical questions with their own debates: should we force our children, students, healthcare staff, or essential workers to get vaccinated? With limited oxygen or fentanyl, who gets priority treatment?

Choosing "smart" for our title is a bold act, signifying a hope that we can muster intelligence, embolden creativity in the hunt for solutions, and come out of this pandemic dilemma the wiser: more wary of infectious invaders we cannot see, more understanding of societal inequities that health crises bring, and more compassionate towards those too vulnerable to go it alone. One response to a calamity is to work out a strategy, a game plan. It has been done before, of course, with disaster simulations and next-step playbooks. But we shall get into that later. A question at this point is whether we dust off those how-to scenarios and recalibrate or rewrite them with the knowledge and wisdom we have gained from this communal tragedy.

But first, we must start with . . .

What we know

We know that COVID kills. It seems to prefer adults, although children have been infected as well, sometimes with medically curious symptoms and side effects.[3] So for the virus to land in a country with a higher median age, such as Spain or Italy with age medians of 44 and 47 respectively, is to award it an immediate advantage. In fact, we now know that after the age of 30, the chance of dying if one contracts COVID doubles roughly every eight years.[4] If we subscribe to the wet-market-in-Wuhan version of events, the virus has invaded an intermediate species, such as a bat, pangolin, or a civet cat that has, in turn, infected a human. That person can begin community spread any time after infection, from a day to two weeks, through airborne organisms or possibly by touching surfaces other humans will then touch.

We don't know, but some suspect either that the virus has escaped the confines of a biomedical laboratory, is a specimen smarter than its creators, or, like birds that enter your open window, is a serendipitous result of opportune circumstances. Right place, right time. Or for the human patient zero, wrong place and time. Either way, it takes up residence inside millions of people in all countries save a few tiny islands of the world. It can duplicate out of sight, undisturbed, for several days.[5]

In any contest with a killer, a human's first strategic step is to size up the comparative advantages of the opponent.[6] That would involve assessing the viral fitness of the coronavirus against the physical fitness of the host; learning the genetic sequencing of the virus considering the patient's genetic viability; and gauging the pathogen's ability to transmutate in light of our human inability to do so. Intelligence and inventiveness also enter the calculus, as does the patient's will to live. A palliative care team from Lausanne, Switzerland, defines the will to live as the knack of existing in the present, of resisting focusing on the future. The team asks, "[D]oes the person, at the present moment, have an existential motivation to live?" That capability is frequently associated with factors such as resilience and quality of life.[7] Again, resilience is not enough: the viral enemy must be routed and undone for the human to prevail.

In terms of virulence, we are told that the novel coronavirus is not as strong as its predecessor SARS or its cousin MERS.[8] The new microbe is also about 10,000 times smaller than the width of a human hair[9] or 5 million times smaller than you or me.[10] So what's the contest, then? First, the pathogen knows to start its onslaught with the human breath of life: it attacks the epithelial layer of cells covering our throat, airway passages, and our lungs. Our Achilles' heel, as it were, is the ACE-2 receptor in that epithelial layer of cells that accommodates the spike formation on the novel virus, pairing much like a key fitting a lock. As well as the lungs, we have recently learned that smoking, or being exposed to second-smoke, increases the receptivity of ACE-2 receptors in the lining of our noses and mouths, thereby increasing the entry points into our bodies for the coronavirus.[11] With an estimated 1.3 billion tobacco smokers in the world, that strategy seems a sound one for the virus.[12] Once the lungs are infected, the virus can similarly infect most other major organs in the torso.[13]

How we are attacked

That entry technique is only the beginning of the destruction. Once inside, the coronavirus induces the production of proteins,[14] an act that can trigger a massive response from our body's immune system, known as a cytokine storm. The virus has now highjacked our body. It has been called a tightrope balancing act, with our body trying to rein in that immune response and at the same time using it to fight the virus. Apparently, either process can kill us.[15]

At the same time, once activated, the ACE-2 receptors expel a hormone that narrows our blood vessels and increases our blood pressure. One of the risks of that action is heart damage and even a stroke. Medical treatment of the ACE-2 receptor either reduces their number and so reduces the available entry points into our cells or increases the number but confuses the virus. Having entered the lungs and replicated, the new virus then spreads to other vital organs as it continues to replicate.

The novel virus can live without sustenance, outside our body, for up to 17 days, according to a study of infestation aboard the cruise ship *Diamond Princess*.[16] That floating laboratory has also taught us that 18% of all infected people on the ship had no symptoms, that quarantine could have reduced the rate of infection from about 7% to less than 1%, but that the rate of infection could work in the virus' favor if we have preexisting vulnerabilities, such as being black or brown in certain societies, being poor, possessing medical conditions, being a smoker, or any combination of those factors.[17]

External factors that can help or hinder

Factors outside our bodily invasion could also contribute to the rate of transmission of the virus. Heat and cold factors in the environment have proven to affect the rate of spread. A recent study found that warmer and humid climates might slow transmission of the SARS-CoV-2 virus. Cold and dry weather conditions, on the other hand, facilitate the spread of all coronaviruses.[18] This is a critical factor when choosing which vaccine to use under certain temperature conditions. For example, the Pfizer and BioNTech vaccine uses a novel tool, strands of messenger RNA held within lipid particles, that can degrade at room temperature and so require doses to be frozen at −70°C (−158°F) for transportation and then thawed for use. The doses can be kept in the freezer for five days before they start to degrade. Newer vials of Pfizer, however, can now be stored at 2°C–8°C (35°F–46°F) for up to one month if undiluted and thawed.[19] While that method provides more flexibility and will reduce the former destruction rate of doses, the ideal time between the first and second shots is still 12 weeks, or three months, as particularly recommended for older people by a UK study.[20]

The Moderna vaccine, also a messenger RNA variety, has a slight edge: it can tolerate a much warmer environment of −20°C (68°F), which is standard for most hospital and pharmacy freezers, and it remains stable at that temperature for up to 30 days.[21] That difference becomes particularly useful in rural areas and lower- to middle-income countries that lack ultracold freezers or have other vulnerabilities that break the cold chain.[22] The fact that Pfizer and Moderna require two shots for highest efficacy is another complicating factor in the effort to encourage uptake by populations and hence reduce our risk of infection. Another vaccine, Johnson & Johnson, does not face those temperature-related challenges and only requires one shot. However, that brand is proving more effective in men as blood-clotting conditions have been diagnosed in a few women as a response to the vaccine.[23] If we subscribe to the suggestion that Johnson & Johnson be restricted to one gender, we are of necessity handing another strategic advantage to the novel virus.[24] On the other hand, the decision to mix the brands between first and second injections could add flexibility and efficiency to the vaccination efforts and increase the availability of vaccines overall.

The good news is that some of us remember SARS-CoV-1. We have internalized its modus operandi, and because of that knowledge we reflexively wear a mask, lie low, distance, and isolate ourselves from other humans to wait it out. That knowledge is the pathogen's Achilles' heel. We can study it more intimately and learn how to outsmart it.[25] The success of that strategy depends on human compliance. It also takes time, a luxury many sufferers do not have.

On the other hand, the high rate of contagion of the disease means sheer numbers of victims cause a drain on vaccine and oxygen supplies while setting further demands on medical staff and politicians. The populace translates that heightened activity as chaos in the hospital and at the top tier of government. As we grow impatient, we are inclined to forego well-advised precautions such as masking and distancing. The biological fact remains that people can catch this disease by merely breathing in airborne droplets from an infected person. Those droplets can also land on objects and surfaces, and the virus in those droplets can last three hours in the air and up to 72 hours on plastic and stainless steel with slightly less viability on copper and cardboard.[26] Infectious droplets from mucus, vomit, or feces were detected during the original SARS-CoV-1 outbreak. For example, in 2003 at Amoy Gardens, a housing complex in Hong Kong, a huge cluster of infected patients was discovered. It was determined that the inefficient sewerage and toilet ventilation systems enabled the virus to spread.[27] A 2021 study concludes that SARS-CoV-2 is "likely to be able to remain infectious in the environment for the longest time regardless of being in feces, mucus, vomit, sweat, or saliva."[28] That is due in part to its relatively hard outer shell that could provide the virus with greater resistance to a hostile external environment, including actions of the digestive enzymes in the host's GI tract. Humans expand their environmental risk of encountering the coronavirus by their high sociability and the density of urban living that facilitates daily interaction with others in tight geographical spaces. The resultant expansion of our human activity further into habitats of virus intermediaries also adds to wildlife exposure and to the risk of our infection.

How digital technology is helping

Working to our advantage is the human ability to sequence the genetic makeup of the novel virus. Sharing our banks of data across countries and using machine learning in artificial intelligence have expanded human knowledge of SARS-CoV-2 and its variants while markedly compressing the time required to put such knowledge into practical use.[29] In the United States, Director Anthony Fauci of the National Institute of Allergy and Infectious Diseases has urged President Biden to scale up genomic surveillance. Globally, however, its use with SARS-CoV-2 has been described as "patchy."[30] The World Health Organization (WHO) has asked all member countries to share at least 20 samples per month to sequencing laboratories. One such project, the European Molecular Biology Laboratory's Bioinformatics Institute, has been banking anonymized genetic data for a few years in preparation for the next pandemic.[31] When COVID-19 first emerged, the Institute was already alerted to warnings from data-mining networks and social media and so completed investigations in a few months rather than a number of years. A few independent research companies have also contributed knowledge by sharing online "chatter" about a pneumonia-like disease as early as December 2019.[32]

Many high-income countries, such as Canada, Australia, Scandinavia, Iceland, Japan, and South Korea, have sequenced the most viral genomes per 1,000 cases. Other countries, especially in Africa, have no sequencing data at all. We are told that the Gambia, Equatorial Guinea, and Sierra Leone have a higher rate of sequencing than France, Italy, or the United States, suggesting that wealth is not necessarily the key determinant of capacity.[33] Human and artificial intelligence have contributed immensely to a comparatively rapid discovery of simple detection methods for the virus. For example, a research team has determined that a patient's breath can be a strong signifier of infection with COVID. So, the incorporation of highly sensitive and cost-efficient detection devices installed in masks that change color with the intensity of infection could represent a "portable and non-invasive point-of-care diagnosis."[34]

Similarly promising are canine programs that could employ trained dogs to screen people for COVID-19 infection at airports, hospitals, or sports venues. Training techniques are illustrated in Figure 1.1. While researchers caution that peer-review processes and large-scale studies are still required, canine sniffer programs are being developed in a variety of countries such as Russia, England, Chile, Australia, Iran, and Finland.[35]

The London School of Hygiene and Tropical Medicine has also been testing whether the dogs can be retrained from other disease detection to provide a rapid, noninvasive diagnosis of COVID-19. In determining their deployment advantage, regulators also need to address issues of cost, standardized training, and quality control.

Finally, one of the dominant public uses of digital technologies during this pandemic has been the phone applications devised to track and trace spreaders and their victims. The results have raised such debates as whether centralized or

FIGURE 1.1 A dog trains for COVID-19 sniffer exercise at Milton Keynes, England.
Source: Getty Images.

decentralized data collection is most efficient and also protective of our medical privacy. Such devices have also advanced considerably the virus containment efforts of governments.

Who prevails?

Having the right strategies from the onset

If you follow professional tennis, you might be aware of an article suggesting that Rafael Nadal, a contender in the 2021 French Open men's single competition, has been perfecting an excellent defense strategy over the past several years. For each game as he readies for his serve, Nadal is believed to mark with his shoe the spot in front of the baseline where he needs to return after the serve to give himself the best advantage against his opponent's return shot.[36] In Paris, Nadal's strategic use of foresight has had one opponent on the run, who later commented, "At some point he was playing and I was only running."[37] Similar tactics could provide a ready defense against the coronavirus: prepare in advance what your best position will be from which to deflect the onslaught.

Two features of SARS-CoV-2 meant that larger nations would spend the initial months scrambling for knowledge and without a sound strategy: the virus in Wuhan turned out to be far more infectious than its SAR-CoV-1 predecessor, and it spread largely by carriers who showed no symptoms. In terms of the first feature, the inability of Western countries to follow their suspicions and investigate the Wuhan situation in person, when rumors spread in December of 2019, meant that the virus existed outside of China well before the announcement of America's first case on 20 January 2020. European countries did not have surveillance capability through the WHO until a week later, 27 January 2020.[38] A few weeks before the WHO declared the outbreak a Public Health Emergency of International Concern (PHEIC) on 30 January, there was evidence the virus was spreading all along the west coast of the United States.[39] Right about that time, patient zero in England was discovered on a university campus in the city of York.[40] The lag in imposing travel bans from China and from one European country or American state to another strategically set Western countries on their back foot regarding testing, tracing, and isolating, a tragic misstep from which they are only now slowly recovering.

Another equally fateful occurrence was the wane in preparedness vigor that wealthier countries experienced the further they moved from the 2003 SARS event. Although playbooks had been devised in the United States, particularly during the presidency of George W. Bush and during the Obama years, the Trump administration seems not to have been guided by its contents.[41] Even politicians in the intervening years, over the first decade of this century, let other demands on funding dominate.[42] As pandemic author Lawrence Wright has commented, "Politicians seemed to have a short attention span . . . infectious disease slipped in budgetary priority, treated more like a nuisance than a mortal threat."[43]

Some countries created their playbook on the spot, like South Korea. As one journalist reports of the stellar system:

> It was a three-step protocol: test, trace, and isolate. And it worked . . . the country was performing the most Covid-19 tests in the world; it implemented perhaps the most elaborate contact tracing program anywhere; and it set up isolation centers so thousands of patients could quarantine.[44]

South Korea and other more flexible smaller countries conducted those steps with admirable agility, although primarily without questioning the state's authority to collect and store anyone's location data without a warrant or consent.[45]

The second setback, the comparatively late discovery that spreaders could be asymptomatic, was also a negative game changer. As one source put it, people could be contagious before developing symptoms, and some infected people would never manifest illness at all. Somewhat perversely, infected people could show symptoms *before* the person who had given it to them. Due to this situation, the scientific community advised politicians that contact tracing, isolation, and quarantine would likely not be enough. As Dr. Robert Redfield, then head of the Centers for Disease Control and Prevention in the United States, began to see the full impact of that strategic imbalance, he commented, "That whole idea that you were going to diagnose cases based on symptoms, isolate them, and contact-trace around them was not going to work. You're going to be missing fifty per cent of the cases."[46] From the number of reported cases and fatalities, larger countries simply failed to anticipate the crisis, despite assumptions about their preparedness. To apply the tennis analogy, from the first announcement, while COVID has been strategizing, most nations have simply been running.

Having missed that opportunity, a growing faction of medical specialists is predicting that the virus is here for the long term. Three developments have influenced that opinion: the emergence of variants that are several indices stronger than the original; the growing list of 'long COVID' sufferers without general acknowledgment of the condition; and the unpredictable surge in vaccine hesitancy. To overcome each hurdle and move the dial from mitigation to eradication of SARS-CoV-2, an intelligent response would be to maximize the sharing of sequencing information and to step up research.

To that end, researchers are culturing human organ cells or "organoids" in the laboratory and then infecting them with the coronavirus and its mutations. The aim is to better understand how and why the virus and its variants selectively target human organs, a viral strategy that hastens the systemic disabling of the patient. The principal aim is to understand whether human organs are intelligently sought out by the virus as part of an attack on the body's systems.[47]

The best defense is a good offense

Our immune system is a powerhouse when it comes to defense tactics. Its mission is threefold: to memorize and then archive the features of dangerous microbes that invade our bodies; to launch an attack to bring them low; and then to build intelligence to quash future invasions.[48] A year into this pandemic, our immune systems are facing a new challenge: numerous and powerful variants. The coronavirus has been mutating its genetic structure, and that boosts its ability to hop from human to human, despite quite able performances by our antibodies.

Some days, the protection offered by vaccines appears riddled with cracks. In our race with the virus, it frequently seems to be overcoming us. However, we are expanding knowledge of variants almost as quickly as they emerge. For example, we have discovered that the Alpha variant, first observed in Britain and now dominant in the United States, has tested as 50–100% more potent than its 2020 predecessor and has quickly learned to evade our immune responses.[49] It has done that by avoiding using the Spike structure (remember the key-and-lock analogy earlier?) and disabling our ability to produce interferon, buying time for the variant to multiply. We are finding that it is possible that other variants, the Beta B.1.351 that first appeared in South Africa and the Delta, first discovered in India, can disable our host cells in a somewhat similar way.[50] We now need to understand variants' ability to reinfect people who have recovered from earlier versions of the coronavirus.[51]

Data sharing between laboratories in various locations can highlight idiosyncrasies of such variants and their shape-shifting. For example, knowing that the Delta variant is the most common type to escape hotel quarantine in Australia suggests to other countries how to direct their vigilance in tracking down that mutation and its tendencies.[52]

The puzzle of variants

A significant challenge to governments and their public health advisors has been that, as each variant arises, there is an immediate need to understand the molecular structure of the mutated virus to work on a treatment. Other facilities must devise a test contemporaneously to identify infected people so they can be isolated and their recent contacts can be traced.[53] That test–trace–isolate task has been part of the winning strategy of a host of smaller countries in South Asia that, according to the first Global Health Security Index (GHSI) in 2019,[54] were not rated very highly in pandemic readiness before the outbreak of SARS-CoV-2: Singapore, Vietnam, and South Korea, for example.[55] Taiwan, a country that was excluded from the GHSI rankings altogether, initially showed a stellar response that depended extensively on the formula of testing, tracing, and isolation, applied early and aggressively. Lockdowns were swift and firm, technology companies were pressed into service to provide mobile phones and apps to infected persons for tracing, and teams of trackers were assigned to follow up by phone with possibly infected persons and those under state-imposed quarantine. The military was involved in enforcement in several countries with impressive results. Transgressors were fined and/or made to pay for their own hotel quarantine expenses.

Human genes have their own variant history that digital technologies can unlock to provide helpful information. For example, researchers at the Max Planck Institute have published results of a study of DNA samples from the inner ear bones of victims of bubonic plague outbreaks in the sixteenth and seventeenth centuries found in a mass grave in the German city of Ellwangen. They wanted to know whether the bubonic plague experience caused victims to cultivate a stronger immune response to the *Yersinia pestis* pathogen that could be passed on to future generations. They compared those samples with the DNA of 50 current residents of the town. Among the latter group, the team found evidence that a pathogen did, indeed, cause chromosomal changes that signify potential for directing an immune response to infection.[56] That is important to illustrate that pathogens can exert selective pressure on human populations.

Long COVID

The scientific community is also beginning to tackle the condition known as long COVID, a debilitation that persists after the initial disease abates. Symptoms include fatigue, labored breathing, rashes, and heart problems. It creates a constant cycle of disappointments that victims cannot return to work or fully recover. Complications from the infection can linger for over a year. According to one Australian study, it appears in 10–30% of COVID-19 patients.[57] A further complication is the distortion in the senses of smell and taste that affects a growing number of long haulers, as sufferers of long COVID have come to be known. They complain of such distortions as onions, garlic, and meat tasting putrid, and coffee smelling like gasoline.[58]

A problem with studying long haulers is that most have not been tested in hospitals or clinics, so data are lacking and health systems cannot contribute information. Sufferers are beginning to demand attention: out of the 3,000 patients involved in a National Health Service study in England, 300 report symptoms lasting more than two months.[59] One long-COVID sufferer comments:

> This is a very bizarre disease; it is like being repeatedly battered over time. . . . Getting help is really difficult, partly because you are muddled in your own head. The NHS is appalling in its guidance of fatigue.[60]

Without a valid diagnosis, treatment cannot proceed. Further knowledge of the condition is needed for a realistic assessment of COVID's long-term damage and protocols for convalescence.

Conclusion: building better next time

To the unprepared, SARS-CoV-2 has been unpredictable at every turn. Having lost any advantage in the first weeks of disease spreading out of Wuhan, larger Western nations have paid a staggering price in human lives.[61] Smaller, smarter nations have been more flexible and responsible. With the loss of faith in leadership, fissures have appeared in communal efforts to unite in opposition to the pathogen. Nationalism has grown at the cost of international cooperation. Finding a better way does not include that strategy in the long term. Global disease calls for global cohesion. One key setback has been vaccine resistance that populations display. For some, the justification is religious, an apostasy or abandonment of religious or political belief. Others are hedging their bets, a cagey delaying strategy to await more trials and post-vaccine revelations of side effects. Some are wary of human error: a contaminated batch that is withdrawn from the war chest due to improper manufacture or misguided storage can foment vast waves of resistance.[62] Still others rely on constitutional arguments, a legally dubious conflation of the right to security of the person and free speech at the expense of the common good. Law must find a way out of that ideologically boggy ground.

Law can address our feeling of powerless in the face of this pandemic. We would first have to acknowledge that, in its revelation of persistent racial and socioeconomic inequities, law has a chance to point out changes that will help make our society more just and, if we are very lucky, more prosperous. Those changes can start right away if we learn from many of the political and administrative mistakes made in the first year of COVID. One compromise would be to acknowledge that infectious disease on a global scale does not defer to individualism. You cannot negotiate with a virus. The collective response for the common good will be to adopt the rationale behind laws that regulate the three steps to fast containment: test, trace, and isolate. The adverse, how the pandemic will change the law, depends very much on how we individually and collectively choose to behave. In the long term, the pandemic, as any crisis, can also offer opportunities if we have the wisdom to recognize them.

BOX 1.1 CORONA SHORT #1: MEXICO VERONICA, A MORTGAGE BROKER AND MOTHER, FINDS HER HOME LIFE IS UPSIDE DOWN

We had a lot of advanced warning because it started in China, then it went to Europe, Canada and the United States, and we knew it would make its way to Mexico. At first, I thought we were going to be ready for it because we had the time to prepare. At the end of March 2020 when the schools closed, businesses closed, and we were told to stay in our houses and not go out. That was when I knew that this was something unprecedented. It was something that no one of my age had ever experienced in our lifetime.

I'm a mother of two kids (12 and 5) and they couldn't go to school. My house turned into me doing everything; I'm their mother but now also their teacher, cook, and I still had to run my business. I know that we're lucky because my kids have space in our house to do their schoolwork with a reliable internet connection. But my life was turned upside down. My work effectively doubled because I was with my kids all morning helping them with school and trying to run my business doing mortgages and bank loans at night. Jose Carlos is only 5, so he needs me there to help him do the online schooling. Maria Ines is 12, so she's more independent. It's crazy. Keeping a kid connected and engaged on a computer is impossible. It seems to be that everything is landing on one parent. In my case it's me because my partner is a lawyer and has had to be in the office throughout the pandemic, so I have been in sole charge of the home, and that work in the home has increased exponentially.

The isolation, staying inside, and doing the same thing over and over again each day have been the most difficult. Plus, not seeing the people you want to see and care about. I think this is particularly hard for Mexican people. Mexicans are very social. You could have a very long and difficult week Monday to Friday but you know over the weekend you'll go out to eat with your friends, visit family, and in Mexico this is something we do constantly because it changes up your routine and gives meaning to your week. It was so tedious to do the same thing every single day, and there was no relief or change at the end of the week because we couldn't go out and socialize with friends and family. It was very depressing. It impacts culture. The emotional damage has been huge for everyone.

Our government did not do a good job. And there are no safety nets for those who have lost a business or a job. The reason we have such an incredibly high mortality rate is because the government never reached an agreement or a strategy to fight the virus. For the first few weeks the government continued to say that it was just a virus that was no more dangerous than a flu. They said there was no reason to worry nor lock ourselves inside. They still say that masks are unnecessary. Now that everything is opening again it's for economic reasons, not because it's safe. And the government has not helped the people. People who lost jobs or their businesses were promised by the government a laughable amount of money, but even still it never materialized. We have the deaths we deserve because we didn't handle it well.

After I contracted COVID I felt calmer, partially because I survived, and it would increase my immunity. I was in hospital on a ventilator for ten days. But now that we have the vaccines, I'm feeling much better about everything. It's funny because I don't worry as much about my kids as I thought. Children are incredibly resilient.

**BOX 1.2   CORONA SHORT #2: AFGHANISTAN
HOSAY, AN IMMIGRATION CONSULTANT,
SPEAKS OF WAR AND MEDICAL SHORTAGES**

I deal with immigration matters to Canada and the United States. So for our staff it's mentally exhausting. Its taking a toll. Some have taken mental health leave because it's just too much to deal with. We're constantly on edge. Clients calling saying what's going on. If they come here as a domestic or caregiver and had to leave their children back home, they cannot travel to see them or their sick parents.

I got laid off. Along with my mom and dad. I tried to hide it from my parents. I am the eldest child. But I couldn't hide it from them. I was doing well and suddenly I wasn't doing well. Mentally. It was depression. I started therapy, but it was costing way too much. Anxiety . . . the family . . . being the oldest. It still hits you even if your parents are great, which mine are. It really affected my physical health. Just because you cannot see what's wrong with me does not mean I'm OK. I'm not OK. But I am getting the treatments I need now.

Mom was working at a dry cleaner, but they don't have business right now. My dad is self-employed. It's very tough. If you think about the way COVID has affected our country and we are so developed, just imagine underdeveloped countries. My aunt in Afghanistan has TB and then she got corona. They had to travel to India to get decent healthcare. It was really hard for them to get airline tickets to India, but when they went they couldn't stay too long because COVID was getting so bad. My aunt had an oxygen tank so could not stay for a few weeks. When she returned to Afghanistan COVID was spreading enormously. Now she can't walk. The doctors cannot treat her; they tried to but the results are not that great. So we work with the doctor in India who tells the doctor in Afghanistan what to do. Our other option is Pakistan, but we fear they will mistreat her. But India where the health system is so much better they have stopped taking visas. An India hospital is US$400 per night. The GNP is US$430. It's unbelievable. When they get COVID, the test costs them too much.

The only person who's been vaccinated is my grandmother. There's not enough to go around. With Afghan culture you are always together, my aunts, their kids, so when one person got it, everyone got it, including the children. It acted more like the flu but with a lot of pain. For the adults it was hard to breath. So they took home remedies. To be honest, who's going to take care of them?

My uncle's wife was pregnant and she got rushed to the hospital because there was a chance she would lose their baby. We were so far from them. They said, "We are OK" so as not to worry us. If they don't answer the phone we worry.

> And now the whole bombing is going on. A war within a pandemic. They are bombing universities. About a month ago they caught somebody at a vegetable cart on the street, where food is a bit cheaper. A man was dressed as a woman. With bombs strapped around him. They caught him, but this is just one of many. There's been so many of these still going on. A part of me wishes the Americans had stayed. The Taliban are more in the villages. They are not afraid of anything now. How else can the government catch them?
>
> Suicide bombing happens daily. If people go out because they have to work it's such a risk.
>
> For schools online teaching is happening but only for the private schools. One of my uncle's sons just started private school this month and within two weeks they closed it again because people who travel to India brought the variant back.
>
> You hear on the news, "You are locked down you have to stay home." But how can you do this and feed the family? There are large families where only one works. How does that work? It's really hard to watch. In Afghanistan you don't find a middle class. It's extremes. Those who have families abroad who can send money can survive.

Notes

1 Scott Burris, Evan D. Anderson, and Alexander C. Wagenaar, *The "Legal Epidemiology" of Pandemic Control*, 384 N. Engl. J. Med. 1973–1975 (27 May 2021).
2 Id.
3 This virus and its disease are currently known as Severe Acute Respiratory Syndrome coronavirus-2 (SARS-CoV-2) and coronavirus infectious disease 2019 (COVID-19), respectively. The US Centres for Disease Control and Prevention are reporting children who have been exposed to COVID-19 presenting with symptoms of Multisystem Inflammatory Syndrome in Children (MIS-C) associated with COVID-19. Symptoms include fever, abdominal pain, vomiting, diarrhea, neck pain, rash, bloodshot eyes, and feeling uncharacteristically tired. A study in June 2021 found that incidence was higher among Black, Hispanic or Latino, and Asian or Pacific Islander persons compared with White persons and among people under 21 ($n = 248$). *See* Amanda B. Payne, Zunera Gilani, and Shana Godfred-Cato, *Incidence of Multisystem Inflammatory Syndrome in Children among US Persons Infected with SARS-CoV-2*, 4:6 JAMA Netw. Open. (June 2021). The symptoms resemble those of a condition in children labeled Kawasaki syndrome in Japan when first discovered in the 1960s. Since the start of the pandemic, children, ages 18 and younger, have accounted for about 4 million, or 14%, of all COVID-19 cases in the United States, according to an estimate by the American Academy of Pediatrics.
4 Siddhartha Mukherjee, *Why Does the Pandemic Seem to be Hitting Some Countries Harder Than Others?*, The New Yorker (22 Feb. 2021).
5 Countries with zero reported community spread include several islands in the Pacific Ocean. Turkestan and North Korea have also not reported any infections.
6 To characterize COVID as an enemy that must be overpowered is a view not uncontested. As Ed Yong posits in *What Strength Really Means When You're Sick*, The Atlantic (9 Oct. 2020), "Equating disease with warfare, and recovery with strength, means that death and disability are linked to failure and weakness." A similar view is provided

by Yasmeen Serhan, *The Case against Waging "War" on the Coronavirus*, The Atlantic (31 Mar. 2020).

7 Marc-Antoine Bornet, et al., *Assessing the Will to Live: A Scoping Review*, 61:4 J. Pain & Symptom Mgmt. 845–857 (Apr. 2021).

8 Wentao Ni, et al., *Role of Angiotensin-Converting Enzyme-2 (ACE-2) in COVID-19*, 24 Crit. Care. 422 (13 June 2020).

9 Markian Hawryluk, *The Scientist Behind Some of the World's Best Coronavirus Images*, Time (20 May 2020), citing Dr. Elizabeth Fischer.

10 Heidi Ledford, *How Does COVID-19 Kill? Uncertainty Is Hampering Doctors' Ability to Choose Treatments*, Nature (9 Apr. 2020).

11 This account is informed by *The Science Behind the Coronavirus, Part I*, LATimes (20 Jan. 2021).

12 World Health Organization, *Tobacco*, WHO.int/News, (26 July 2021). The website offers an AI companion to assist those looking for cessation aids.

13 Secondary infection causing organ dysfunction is quite common in severe cases, such as acute respiratory distress syndrome (ARDS), acute cardiac injury, acute hepatic injury, and acute kidney injury.

14 Known as chemokines and cytokines, this response can also happen in the fight against the HIV virus.

15 Ledford, *supra* n 10.

16 Smriti Mallapaty, *What the Cruise-Ship Outbreaks Reveal about COVID-19*, Nature 580, 18 (26 Mar. 2020).

17 Id.

18 Paulo Mecenas et al., *Effects of Temperature and Humidity on the Spread of COVID-19: A Systematic Review*, Plos One (22 Sept. 2020), https://doi.org/10.1371/journal.pone.0238339.

19 Jane Greenhalgh, *Pfizer Vaccine Can Stay Longer at Warmer Temperatures before Being Discarded*, NPR (19 May 2021), as authorized in May 2021 by America's Food and Drug Administration.

20 Siladitya Ray, *12-Week Gap Between Pfizer Vaccine Doses Generates Higher Antibody Response, Study Finds*, Forbes (14 May 2021); the study, from Birmingham University researchers, found that delaying the second dose to 12 weeks led to an antibody response that was three and a half times larger than when vaccine doses were kept to the standard recommendation of three weeks apart. However, the study conclusions are not that straightforward. The three-week intervals between the doses "generates a higher peak T-cell response compared to the longer dosing strategy and scientists believe T-Cells may be a marker for long-term immunity."

21 Katie McCallum, *Why Some COVID-19 Vaccines Need to Be Kept So Cold (& What This Means for Availability)*, Houston Methodist (3 Dec. 2020).

22 "Temperature mistakes are mostly due to inappropriate shipping procedures in the cold chain, and these losses are estimated at US$34.1 billion annually," according to Anna Nagurney, *The Challenges of Vaccine Cold-Chain Distribution Must Be Met to End the Pandemic*, Global BioDefense (5 Oct. 2020).

23 Both Johnson & Johnson and Astra-Zeneca vaccines are of the adenovirus type, used to prompt an immune response against the coronavirus. Some experts say that it could instead, in rare cases, prompt an immune response from certain components in the blood that can cause clotting. *See further*, Andreas Greinacher et al., *Thrombotic Thrombocytopenia after ChAdOx1 nCov-19 Vaccination*, 384 N. Engl. J. Med. 2092–2101 (2021).

24 BBC, *Johnson & Johnson Vaccine Paused over Rare Blood Clots*, BBC.com (13 Apr. 2021). The clotting disorder is called cerebral venous sinus thrombosis. The Johnson & Johnson (known as Janssen in parts of Europe) and AstraZeneca vaccines work in very similar ways and their clotting side effects appear "comparably rare" according to this BBC report.

25 Dr. Patrick Soon-Shiong, *Introduction to the Science Behind the Coronavirus, Part III, Mutations*, LATimes (20 Jan. 2021), www.latimes.com/politics/s4yhqvshcng-123.

26 Neeltje van Doremalen, et al., *Aerosol and Surface Stability of SARS-CoV-2 as Compared with SARS-CoV-1*, 382 N. Engl. J. Med. 1564–1567 (16 Apr. 2020).

27 Gerard Kio-Meng-Goh, et al., *Shell Disorder Analysis Predicts Greater Resilience of the SARS-CoV-2 (COVID-19) Outside the Body and in Body Fluids*, 144 Microb. Pathog. 104177 (July 2020).

28 Id. *See also*, World Health Organization, *Water, Sanitation, Hygiene and Waste Management for the COVID-19 Virus*, Tech. Brief (3 Mar. 2020). Reasearchers' debates over the infection risk of fomites continues as of this writing.

29 Editorial, *Genomic Sequencing in Pandemics*, 10273 Lancet 445 (6 Feb. 2021).

30 Id.

31 Chris Edwards, *Coalition of the Willing Takes Aim at COVID-19*, 54:1 Comm. of the ACM 19 (Jan. 2021).

32 Canadian company BlueDot serves as example.

33 GISAID, *Global Sequencing Coverage*, CovidCG, https://covidcg.org/?tab=global_sequencing.

34 See Figure 5.1 infra at p. 120. See further, Giorgia Giovannini, Hossam Haick, and Denis Garoli, *Detecting COVID-19 from Breath: A Game Changer for a Big Challenge*, 6:4 ACS Sens. 1408–1417 (23 Apr. 2021); *Smart Mask: Rapid COVID-19 Identification of Infected Populations*, Sci. Animated (19 June 2021).

35 Alan Taylor, *The Dogs Trained to Sniff Out COVID-19*, The Atlantic (27 Jan. 2021). *See also*, James Gorman, *Covid-Sniffing Dogs Are Accurate But Face Hurdles for Widespread Use*, NYTimes (12 June 2021) discussing issues of cost, standardized training, and quality control; *see also*, C.M. Otto, et al., *The Promise of Disease Detection Dogs in Pandemic Response: Lessons Learned from COVID-19*, 183 Disaster Med. Pub. Health Preparedness 1–19 (2021), indicating further research is needed to measure their effectiveness and feasibility and to ensure public and political support.

36 Matthew Futterman, *In Paris, Rafael Nadal Is the Same as Always, and Yet He's Different*, NYTimes (8 June 2021).

37 Id. BlueDot (at https://bluedot.global/covid-19-control/) promotes the test–trace–isolate approach to detection and containment and has prioritized methods that have proved most effective in various countries: (1) decentralization of laboratory testing (e.g., Uruguay, Rwanda), (2) domestic development and production of tests and supplies (e.g., Uruguay, Singapore), (3) pooled testing (e.g., Uruguay, Rwanda, China, Viet Nam), (4) mass testing campaigns (e.g., Hong Kong S.A.R., China, Viet Nam), (5) early engagement with the private sector (e.g., South Korea), (6) wastewater testing (e.g., Canada, Australia), and (7) community-based health volunteers (e.g., Thailand).

38 Gianfranco Spiteri, et al., *First Cases of Coronavirus Disease 2019 (COVID-19) in the WHO European Region, 24 January to 21 February 2020*, 25:9 Euro. Surveill. (5 Mar. 2020).

39 Lawrence Wright, *The Plague Year*, The New Yorker (Dec. 28, 2020).

40 Oliver Wright, *Coronavirus: How the UK Dealt with Its First Covid Case*, BBC (29 Jan. 2020).

41 Executive Office of the United States President, *Playbook for Early Response to High-Consequence Emergency Infectious Diseases, Threats and Biological Incidents*, 69 pp. It was a meticulous guide for combatting a "pathogen of pandemic potential," and a directory of government resources to consult the moment things started to convert to a real crisis. *See further* Lawrence Wright, *supra* n 39.

42 Dylan Scott, et al., *The Pandemic Playbook*, Vox (28 May 2021).

43 Wright, *supra* n 39.

44 Dylan Scott and Jun Michael Park, *South Korean's Covid-19 Success Story Started with a Failure*, Vox (19 Apr. 2021).

45 Id.

46 Wright, *supra* m 39. Wright particularly notes diminished budgets given to institutions, the closing of hospitals, and the deterioration of stockpiles of emergency equipment.

47 Smriti Mallapaty, *Mini Organs Reveal How the Coronavirus Attacks the Body*, Nature (22 June 2020), www.nature.com/articles/d41586-020-01864-x#ref-CR3. While the use of

organoids saves time and avoids the ethical and practical issues of animal experimentation, testing will ultimately need to be conducted on animal models and in clinical trials where researchers can observe "the crosstalk between organs that happens in the body," according to Bart Haagmans, a virologist at Erasmus MC in the Netherlands.

48 Katherine Wu, *The Body Is Far from Helpless Against Coronavirus Variants*, The Atlantic (12 Feb. 2021).

49 Lucy G. Thorne, et al., *Evolution of Enhanced Innate Immune Evasion by the SARS-CoV-2 B.1.1.7 UK Variant*, bioRxiv (7 June 2021), not peer-reviewed.

50 Carl Zimmer, *How the "Alpha" Coronavirus Variant Became So Powerful*, NYTimes (7 June 2021).

51 Robert Bollinger and Stuart Ray, *New Variants of Coronavirus: What You Should Know*, Johns Hopkins Medicine (22 Feb. 2021).

52 Liam Mannis, Mathew Dunckley, and Aisha Dow, *What We Know about the Delta Variant Now in Melbourne*, The Age (4 June 2021).

53 The Delta variant has been found to have two defining mutations in its spike protein that can bind with the host cell more strongly and attack the host's immune system more aggressively.

54 In October 2019, the first Global Health Security Index appeared, a sober report of a world largely unprepared to deal with a pandemic. "Unfortunately, political will for accelerating health security is caught in a perpetual cycle of panic and neglect," the authors observed. "No country is fully prepared." Yet one country stood above all others in terms of readiness: the United States.

55 GHS Index, *Building Collective Action and Accountability* (2019). The test–tract–isolate function in the United States has been the weakest administrative link in the institutional effort to combat the virus, as detailed in Lawrence Wright, *supra* n 39.

56 Alexander Immel, et al., *Analysis of Genomic DNA from Medieval Plague Victims Suggests Long-Term Effect of Yersinia Pestis on Human Immunity Genes*, Molecular Bio. & Evol. (18 May 2021).

57 Vanessa Bryant, Alex Holmes and Louis Irving, *The Mystery of "Long COVID": Up to 1 in 3 People Who Catch the Virus Suffer for Months: Here's What We Know So Far*, The Conversation (6 June 2021).

58 Valentina Parma, et al., *More Than Smell: COVID-19 Is Associated with Severe Impairment of Smell, Taste, and Chemesthesis*, 45:7 Chem. Senses 609–622 (Sept. 2020). Chemesthesis is defined as the chemically initiated sensations in the mouth (such as a burning sensation instigated by hot chilies or cooling sensation when ingesting peppermint leaves). Long COVID: diagnosis, management, prognosis.

59 BJM, *Long Covid: Diagnosis, Management, Prognosis*, YouTube Webinar (4 Sept. 2020).

60 Id.

61 As of 24 June 2021, 180 million reported cases and 3.89 million reported deaths. Sources include NYTimes, Johns Hopkins University, and Our World in Data.

62 Dhruv Khullar, *Why Are So Many Health Care Workers Resisting the Covid Vaccine?*, The New Yorker (2 Feb. 2021), www.newyorker.com/science/medical-dispatch/why-are-so-many-health-care-workers-resisting-the-covid-vaccine (summarizing justifications for hesitancy among health workers that includes not knowing "how long vaccine-generated immunity lasts, about how serious the long-term side effects might be, and about what could happen if the virus mutates further").

Bibliography

Bollinger, Robert and Stuart Ray, *New Variants of Coronavirus: What You Should Know*, Johns Hopkins Medicine (22 Feb. 2021).

Bornet, Marc-Antoine, et al., *Assessing the Will to Live: A Scoping Review,* J. Pain & Symptom Mgmt. (Apr. 2021) 61:4, 845–857.

Burris, Scott, Evan D. Anderson and Alexander C. Wagenaar, *The "Legal Epidemiology" of Pandemic Control,* N. Engl. J. Med. (27 May 2021) 384:1973–1975.

Gorman, James, *Covid-Sniffing Dogs Are Accurate But Face Hurdles for Widespread Use,* NY Times (12 June 2021).

Greinacher, Andreas, et al., *Thrombotic Thrombocytopenia after ChAdOx1 nCov-19 Vaccination,* N. Engl. J. Med. (2021) 384:2092–2101.

Kio-Meng-Goh, Gerard, et al., *Shell Disorder Analysis Predicts Greater Resilience of the SARS-CoV-2 (COVID-19) Outside the Body and in Body Fluids,* Microb. Pathog. (July 2020) 144:104177.

Mecenas, Paulo, et al., *Effects of Temperature and Humidity on the Spread of COVID-19: A Systematic Review,* Plos One (22 Sept. 2020).

Mukherjee, Siddhartha, *Why Does the Pandemic Seem to be Hitting Some Countries Harder Than Others?,* The New Yorker (22 Feb. 2021).

Nagurney, Anna, *The Challenges of Vaccine Cold-Chain Distribution Must Be Met to End the Pandemic,* Global BioDefense (5 Oct. 2020).

Ni, Wentao, et al., *Role of Angiotensin-Converting Enzyme-2 (ACE-2) in COVID-19,* Crit. Care. (13 June 2020) 24:422.

Otto, C.M., et al., *The Promise of Disease Detection Dogs in Pandemic Response: Lessons Learned from COVID-19,* Disaster Med. Pub. Health Preparedness (2021) 183:1–19.

Payne, Amanda B., Zunera Gilani and Shana Godfred-Cato, *Incidence of Multisystem Inflammatory Syndrome in Children among US Persons Infected with SARS-CoV-2,* JAMA Netw. Open. (June 2021) 4:6.

Spiteri, Gianfranco, et al., *First Cases of Coronavirus Disease 2019 (COVID-19) in the WHO European Region, 24 January to 21 February 2020,* Euro. Surveill. (5 Mar. 2020) 25:9.

Thorne, Lucy G., et al., *Evolution of Enhanced Innate Immune Evasion by the SARS-CoV-2 B.1.1.7 UK variant,* bioRxiv (7 June 2021).

van Doremalen, Neeltje, et al., *Aerosol and Surface Stability of SARS-CoV-2 as Compared with SARS-CoV-1,* N. Engl. J. Med. (16 Apr. 2020) 382:1564–1567.

Yong, Ed, *What Strength Really Means When You're Sick,* The Atlantic (9 Oct. 2020).

2

NOTHING ABOUT ME WITHOUT ME

Rationing and shared end-of-life decision-making during a pandemic

Sharyn Milnes, Lisa Mitchell, Neil Orford, Deborah Porter and Nicholas Simpson

Editors' introduction: Imagine you are 75 years old and dangerously ill with COVID-19. You are at the hospital alone – your family is not allowed to visit. As you struggle to take each and every breath, the doctor tells you the treatments you are being given don't seem to be helping and you will most likely die soon. The doctor says:

> We could try to ventilate you, this means we would put a thick tube down your throat, attached to a machine, which will force your lungs to breathe. You will remain awake and aware of what is going on around you, but you will not be able to talk or move around.

With this horrific picture in your mind, the doctor goes on to tell you,

> The most likely outcome is that you will live a little longer but ultimately die while you are being ventilated. If, against the odds, you do survive, it is very unlikely you will have the quality of life you had before you caught COVID-19. You will probably have a very long road of illness ahead and it is unlikely you will ever make a full recovery. You will likely struggle with ongoing breathing problems and have other complications, including chest and joint pain, relentless tiredness, headaches, memory loss and poor concentration.

What would you choose?

During the pandemic many countries have experienced overwhelming patient numbers at hospitals together with insufficient resources, such

DOI: 10.4324/9781003215769-4

as hospital beds and ventilators, to meet the needs of escalating patient numbers. We've seen heart-wrenching stories of families unable to be at the bedside of their loved ones as they die from COVID-19 – the tragic accounts of suffering and death are endless.

We have also seen heartwarming stories of the empathy and the fortitude of healthcare workers endeavoring to provide the best care and treatment they can in these relentless, wretched working conditions. And we know this is taking a significant toll.

But what of the hospital processes and procedures that underlie all of this? Surely it is important to understand how decisions are being made. For example, how are patients being triaged in these circumstances? Where the usual process of deciding the order of treatment is based on the degree of medical urgency, how does this translate where the number of desperately ill patients surge well beyond the hospital's capacity? How is it decided which patients get the limited resources? Who makes this decision? And, most importantly, is the patient front and center in the treatment decisions that are being made? We have heard of shocking cases of discrimination in decision-making, such as "not for resuscitation" orders being made in relation to patients' with a disability, without their knowledge. How can we prevent this from happening?

This chapter considers these issues. The contributors, based in Victoria, Australia, comprise health professionals, an ethicist, and a lawyer. All are involved in training health professionals in the importance, from a clinical, ethical, and legal perspective, of shared decision-making between doctor and patient, and strong communication skills to promote this.

The authors propose a range of practical strategies that promote shared decision-making during a pandemic. They also advocate for the development of a transparent triage model that facilitates ethical rationing of scarce health resources. And finally, for healthcare workers, they recommend consideration of legal risks, and provision of appropriate legal protections, that will support these workers. Ultimately, the authors' aim is to ensure the resilience of hospitals and health services to function effectively, and ethically, in these most dire of times.

Introduction

During the early stages of the COVID-19 pandemic, there was a frenzy of action toward accessing and manufacturing more ventilators, together with sensationalist headlines asking "who gets the ventilator?" However, there was little discussion regarding the patient's choice in the matter. It is important to remember that not every patient will want to be ventilated in the event it is clinically indicated, even if this means he or she will die. This chapter aims to put the patient front and center in the discussion of access to, and allocation of, health resources: a discussion based on sound ethical, legal, and clinical principles.

Health systems internationally have been overwhelmed by the rapid escalation of the COVID-19 pandemic, the largest global infectious disease event in over a century. The ensuing public and professional discussion has dominated 2020 and included a focus on resource scarcity and the need to ration hospital beds, ventilators, and other essential services. This debate turned quickly to the complex and emotive principles of triage and rationing of scarce resources, and associated ethical, legal, and societal implications. Although important, this discussion presents a gap between patient choice and the conflict of usual ethical models of care to that of the ethics of triage and rationing.

This chapter will address the gap in our discussion of pandemic ethics: why, and how, we must ensure shared decision-making (SDM) occurs during a pandemic and the necessity for a considered ethical model for triage (prioritizing patients) and allocation of limited health resources during a pandemic.

We aim to first outline the ethical and legal principles and framework for pre-pandemic clinical care, best described as shared decision-making. We will then explain the preparatory actions that can be taken to support and maintain SDM during a pandemic. Finally, we will discuss the need for development of an ethical model for triage and rationing of scarce resources – a model for implementation in hospitals and health services in the event of an overwhelming surge in patient numbers.

Pre-pandemic SDM

The mix of an aging population with increasing complexity of healthcare needs has led to the recognition that improving end-of-life care is an urgent priority in developed countries. Twenty percent of deaths in the United States occur in an ICU, or shortly after an ICU stay,[1] and an increasing proportion of older Americans spend time in an ICU during the last month of life.[2] In Australia one-third of patients in acute hospitals are in their last year of life.[3]

In medical treatment decision-making, the guiding legal and ethical principles are respect for patient autonomy, justice, beneficence, and non-maleficence. However, it is autonomy that dominates the ethics of clinical interaction. It is vital to ascertain the meaning of autonomy in this context, as it goes beyond pure self-determination and recognizes the patient as an individual with particular values and preferences, and in the context of their significant relationships. In this way, patient autonomy is conceptualized in medical treatment to include values the patient considers necessary for living well and deciding preferences for care.

A balance of integrating patient autonomy and medical advice and expertise is required to achieve high-quality person-centered care (PCC). This is operationalized through the framework of SDM. In SDM, patients' values, preferences, and goals are elucidated and integrated into their medical care in order to assist clinicians and improve patient experience and outcomes. This is recognized as the best practice in health standards worldwide.

Unfortunately, while we may know this,[4] the gap between our knowledge and practice of SDM is highlighted in academic publications, government announcements, media, and personal stories. Evidence indicates that health professionals do not participate in person-centered end-of-life care and may provide non-beneficial, unwanted, and expensive interventions:

> Although talk about patient-centered care is ubiquitous in modern health care, one of the greatest challenges of turning the rhetoric into reality continues to be routinely engaging patients in decision-making.[5]

SDM in the clinical environment – ethics and law

There are clear legal and ethical imperatives for patient-centered decision-making. The law has long recognized a person's right to autonomy, acknowledged in the oft-quoted statement of Justice Cardozo in a 1914 US case:

> Every human being of adult years and sound mind has a right to determine what shall be done with his own body; and a surgeon who performs an operation without his patient's consent commits an assault, for which he is liable in damages.[6]

This means, in many Western societies, an adult with decision-making capacity has the right to make decisions as to which medical treatment they will accept or reject and the right to make decisions regarding future medical treatment that might become clinically appropriate.[7] Failure by a health professional to respect a patient's autonomy might result in civil, disciplinary, or criminal proceedings, even where the health professional believes they are acting in the patient's best interests.

The importance of the concept of autonomy is also recognized in most Western theories of ethics.[8] In the Kantian conception, to be autonomous is to be "governed by the will itself so far as it is determined by reason alone,"[9] that is, self-rule.[10] Contemporary legal definitions of autonomy emerged out of that Kantian idea.[11] Madrid medical historian and ethicist Diego Gracia demonstrates how these contemporary legal definitions of autonomy are commonly used as the basis for the bioethical consideration of autonomy. Gracia goes on to point out that in medicine and bioethics informed consent is the touchstone topic in any discussion of autonomy.[12]

Given the complex nature of healthcare, careful consideration is required as to how "autonomy" is defined, constructed, and respected by clinicians. The justice-based definitions of autonomy, common to arguments for libertarian paternalism, offer little in the way of action guidance for medical practitioners and are contrary to the desired outcomes for PCC and SDM.[13] A care-based ethic that operationalizes autonomy in a connected sense is applicable, in that it considers the dynamic influence of individual values of the doctor and patient separately, as well as the relative power imbalance within the actual doctor–patient relationship at the time of the interaction.[14]

Relational frameworks of autonomy consider the agent (or decision-maker) as fundamentally interconnected with other people. This understanding of autonomy posits that "autonomy emerges within and because of relationships."[15] Proponents of this framework assert that the preferences, values, and decisions made by individuals are formed from their position within their complex web of relations, rather than as isolated rational actors. Further, our power to be in charge of our own decisions (to be autonomous) emerges out of social relations, norms, and positions: it is not a static moral good bestowed on individuals who exist in a vacuum. The idea of a relational autonomy emerged out of feminist philosophy, as a challenge to the liberal conception of the autonomous individual acting in isolation. As Anderson and Honneth explain, our values, preferences, and conceptions of what a good life is are all "bound up with webs of social recognition"; hence, our ability to make decisions about our lives is facilitated by, if not formed upon, social relations.[16] Further, "within a relational understanding of autonomy, self-identity and decisional capacities are dynamic in nature, changing with the meanings and structures of people's relationships and their world."[17]

Webster identifies that in addition to relationships, patient preferences, values, and goals of the patient are a core element of the PCC process.[18] It is relevant, therefore, to consider how health professionals construct these patient processes in what we could call "patient autonomy." Intuitively, patient autonomy is crucial in decision-making processes, but finding this balance can be challenging. Therefore, it is unsurprising that communication and decision-making with patients has been a focus of medical ethics, professionalism, and education literature in recent times.[19]

What does SDM require of doctors and patients?

It can be broadly stated that SDM is a model in which the process of making decisions about a patient's care is shared between doctor and patient.[20] The degree of responsibility for certain decisions (and aspects of certain decisions) can be said to operate on a sliding scale between completely patient-directed decisions and completely doctor-directed decisions, with most falling somewhere between these two poles and all involving some discussion.[21] In this model, doctors and patients provide information to each other: patients provide information about their "circumstances, goals and preferences"[22] and doctors provide information about a condition, a test, or a treatment and the advantages, disadvantages, and risks of having (or not having) a certain treatment or test. From this point, consensus is built between doctor and patient, and an agreement is then reached through a dynamic process. Patient autonomy is often said to be afforded respect via the use of the SDM model.[23] As Sandman and Munthe note, application of the SDM model can go some way toward "the aim of making patients continuously more skillful at taking care of their best interest themselves."[24]

SDM is an approach in which clinicians and patients communicate using the best available evidence when faced with the task of making decisions. Patients are supported to deliberate about the possible attributes and consequences of options, to arrive at informed preferences in making a determination about the best course of action that respects patient autonomy, as well as ethical and legal norms.[25]

Operationalization of PCC through SDM

The US Institute of Medicine (IOM) defined PCC as "[p]roviding care that is respectful of and responsive to individual patient preferences, needs, and values, and ensuring that patient values guide all clinical decisions."[26] Put more simply, "nothing about me, without me."[27] Globally, there are a number of communication models that operationalize PCC in end-of-life decision-making:

> Communication models provide an alternative framework and list of skills that detail the means by which doctors conduct the medical interview, develop rapport, obtain the required information described in the traditional medical history, and then discuss their findings and management alternatives with patients.[28]

The Calgary Cambridge Model for communication in the clinical interaction has been researched extensively in the healthcare setting. This model is the basis of many communication education programs, including those teaching SDM. The Calgary Cambridge guide to the medical interview[29] provides a structure for the conversation between clinician and patient, including the information to be provided to the patient and, with the patient's active involvement in the conversation, the development of a shared understanding. Ultimately, by employing SDM and encouraging the patient to contribute their ideas, suggestions, and preferences, this results in a mutually acceptable plan for the patient.[30]

The guides have been well received globally:

> [A] number of organizations at all levels of medical education and across a wide range of specialties hav[e] adopted the guides as the underpinning to their communication skills teaching programs. Institutions in Australia, Canada, Norway, South Africa, Spain, the United Kingdom, the United States, and elsewhere have used the guides as a primary resource for teaching, assessment, or research.[31]

North American applications of the model include VitalTalk (previously Onco-Talk)[32] and Harvard Serious Illness Care Program (SICP), both developed to address known and proven gaps between patient goals/preferences and the care given.[33]

At the heart of the SICP is the Serious Illness Conversation Guide – a list of patient-centered questions designed to assist clinicians in gaining a more thorough understanding of their patient's life in order to inform future care decisions. The questions address

- a patient's understanding of their illness;
- their preferences for information;
- their personal goals;
- their fears and worries, as well as their sources of strength;
- the abilities they find most important to their daily life and tradeoffs they are willing to make for the possibility of more time; and
- how much their loved ones know about their wishes.[34]

An Australian example is the "iValidate" program (based on the Calgary Cambridge and Harvard models) – Identifying Values, Listening, and Advising High-risk Patients in Acute Care.[35] This model is used for patients with a life-limiting illness (LLI) – the cohort of patients at a very high risk of acute infection and death from diseases such as COVID-19.

The iValidate program, which the authors are involved in delivering, adopts identification of individual goals and values as the threshold test for PCC. The course is offered to health professionals, with aims including "encouraging earlier conversations with patients and families while they are competent, establishing goals, values and treatment plans and improving shared decision making with patients and families."[36]

The process is reinforced in teaching, a purpose-developed Goals of Care (GOC) form, and in day-to-day practice through clinical support. The model includes the following components:

1 **Identification** of patients with an LLI using a trigger checklist, based on the Gold Standard Framework (GSF) criteria.[37]
2 **Establishing capacity and surrogate:** Ensure patient has capacity and ensure the surrogate decision-maker is known and available as needed.
3 **Establishing personal goals and values:** Discussion using skills acquired through communication training.
4 **Providing medical advice** to relative to patients, disease, goals and values, and formulating a plan.
5 **Consensus:** Ensuring all health teams and carers are aware of, and understand, the plan.
6 **Document:** Documenting the process on the GOC form.[38]

The iValidate course also teaches the fundamentals of ethical and legal principles related to medical treatment decision-making. This includes the right of a person to make an advance care directive in relation to future medical treatment. For example, in Victoria, Australia, under the Medical Treatment Planning and Decisions Act 2016 (MTP&D Act), an advance care directive comprises an instructional directive and a values directive. A person with decision-making capacity may make either or both of these, and they become effective at any time that a person lacks capacity.

An instructional directive provides specific instructions about medical treatment a person consents to or refuses, either entirely or in particular circumstances. Importantly, where an instructional directive provides consent to a particular medical treatment, a health practitioner is only required to administer that treatment if they are of the opinion it is clinically appropriate to do so. A values directive contains statements of a person's preferences and values.

The MTP&D Act also provides for a person to appoint a medical treatment decision-maker who has the power to make decisions for the person who lacks capacity. They must do so in accordance with any known values and preferences of the person, such as those set out in a values directive.

Further, the MTP&D requires reasonable efforts to ascertain whether, for an incapacitated patient, there is an advance care directive or a medical treatment decision-maker. If so, any end-of-life conversations must incorporate the content of any advance care directive[39] and be undertaken with the medical treatment decision-maker instead of the patient.

SDM – at baseline and in preparation for a pandemic

The COVID-19 pandemic was predicted to affect more than 50% of the population,[40] with a daily caseload of affected patients requiring either hospital or critical care admission that exceeded surge capacity. People with LLI such as frailty, dementia, metastatic or untreatable cancer, or severe organ failure are among the most vulnerable to COVID-19-related illness. The development of moderate to severe respiratory disease in this population is associated with high mortality.[41] Given this, it is considered crucial to discuss escalation of cares that are invasive, potentially unsuccessful, and often unwanted.

In pandemic conditions the volume of patients with LLI and severe respiratory distress presenting to hospital and ICUs might overwhelm resources. These circumstances have the potential to produce rushed, lower-quality discussions and distressing end-of-life care for families, patients, and staff. This has been reflected in international scientific and media reports describing the experience of discussions about "rationing" access to critical care where patients with pre-morbid conditions associated with poor outcomes are not offered certain levels of care.[42]

Before health systems are overwhelmed, there is a role for SDM. Systematic engagement of patients with an LLI in SDM, with information specific to COVID-19, could lead to

- majority of patients with LLI choosing comfort care in their accommodation;
- reduction in hospital and critical care presentations and admissions; and
- increased satisfaction for patients and families.

Systematic delivery of high-quality comfort care and support in usual accommodation is a crucial component of this model. In addition, there is an important secondary effect of SDM. Widespread engagement of patients with LLI in end-of-life planning will result in pre-emptive, planned decisions to not undergo invasive life support in the event of COVID-19-related deterioration. The primary benefit of high-quality PCC, allowing people to die or experience care at home, also reduces demand on critical care resources[43] and improves access for those who are likely to benefit from and choose critical care–level treatment. Given this, enhancing SDM systems in key areas, particularly for vulnerable subpopulations such as those with LLI, should be prioritized during pandemic preparation.

The optimum pandemic preparation model is based on institutional experience.[44] Preparations should begin by ensuring all hospital inpatients have a completed, documented, values-based, GOC discussion. Specific resources may need to be dedicated to the provision of SDM to achieve this. Executive support is crucial, as is training of groups of skilled communication experts. These groups may be mobilized in order to support inpatient ward staff and staff in residential aged care in having structured, values-based conversations about decision-making in the event of a critical illness.

Formation of a broad-based working group might assist utility. This could involve geriatricians, community and aged-care practitioners, palliative care, advanced care planning (ACP) counselors, and intensive care specialists. This group would ideally work collaboratively and report to an institutional executive or incident management team. Such a reference group has the ability to provide advice and oversight to an SDM program.

Consideration should also be given to operationalizing inpatient SDM processes in tiers of support. A list of trained communicators, reviewed for skill mix, is helpful in supporting targeted mobilization of support for inpatients. A graded level of support may be provided during the pandemic period. For example:

- In *Tier 1* trained communicators support clinicians in having GOC conversations with their own patients with LLI. This should involve the provision of COVID-19-specific information and critical care advice and/or direct clinician support with difficult conversations.
- In *Tier 2* trained communicators have GOC conversations directly with patients with LLI. This might be in the context of treating clinicians whose capacity is limited by experience, confidence, or time constraints.
- In *Tier 3* other staff are supported in having GOC conversations with patients with LLI, with the provision of clear guidelines, including the use of a series of preformatted "scripts" or conversation aids.

The combination of these three levels of support should provide access to a support pathway for all clinicians, in order to have values-based conversations about goals of care, using up-to-date, pandemic-specific information. An escalation pathway should be designed for those engaged in SDM where conflicts occur: for example, where there are requests for care which are inconsistent with the care being offered and where there are complex family or interdisciplinary team environments.

In addition, disease-specific advice and treatment options for those patients with LLI should be developed. Many patients, both in residential aged care facilities and in hospital, may elect to have treatments which are less interventional or may be provided in their own environments.[45] These preferences require consideration of care which is safe, effective, patient-centered, timely, efficient, and equitable. This care needs to meet the physical and emotional needs of patients and supporting family members. The ability to provide care should be assessed by members of the cross-disciplinary team, including the treatment and care options within residences and outside critical care settings. Those resources should be augmented where necessary. This includes simple considerations (provision of oxygen, antibiotics, or morphine) and those that are more complex (cohorting, access to telehealth communication with families, and palliative care).

To ensure effective and accurate communication, clear, centralized messages should be developed, forming the basis of SDM for patients with LLI. The messages should be ethical, patient-centered, specific to the circumstances and environment, and endorsed by the organization. These messages must include information to advise patients of choices and SDM; up-to-date prognostic information regarding COVID-19; and tailored information for groups such as hospital inpatients with LLI and residents within nursing homes and subacute care. A core message should be the continuation of SDM processes within pandemic periods, with this being seen as one of the most efficient ways to deliver appropriate care and allocate resources. Consistent communications to the public, including the central messages of the ethic of care and SDM, are also important.

An emphasis should be placed on the identification of residential aged care and hospital inpatients with LLI. A dedicated audit might assist with the identification of patients in hospital with LLI, including the adequacy of current GOC, in order to notify inpatient teams or skilled communicators as appropriate. Subsequent GOC progress and patient outcomes should be recorded, with feedback to clinical leaders in order to continually improve the provision of SDM. Similarly, all residential aged care and nursing home patients who meet criteria for LLI should be identified and offered the opportunity to participate in SDM.

Consideration should also be given to having a dedicated ACP team to support SDM in residential aged care and subacute facilities. This team might assess the adequacy of current GOC documentation, as well as providing discussion and further documentation of GOC as necessary. Importantly, this process should be conducted along with consultation with the local primary care workforce. GOC preferences should be audited and recorded in order to tailor resources, including for those who wish to receive care in their own residences.

The outcomes of ACP and SDM communication team discussions with patients should be documented on GOC forms which are readily available. GOC forms should be utilized for inpatients, as well as subacute, and residential clients.

ACP forms and other values-based directives might also be completed and/or used to inform GOC forms.

Ideally, in terms of SDM, pandemic periods should be seen as an augmentation of business as usual. In some healthcare settings there is not enough time or warning to institute these systems. However, where there is a lead time to pandemic responses, it is important to emphasize the conditions which contribute to SDM in vulnerable populations. Indeed, perhaps some of the most effective strategies to best utilize resources will synergize with the best methods of providing person-centered healthcare.

Ethics – triage preparation for COVID-19

The COVID-19 pandemic has taught us a sobering lesson in health system preparation. At various stages of pandemic activity our hospitals and ICUs become overwhelmed, and we are faced with rationing, a reality that challenges our usual ethical framework. In the United States this was the near immediate recognition of insufficient PPE; in Lombardy, Italy, the lack of ventilators and ICU beds; in Daegu, South Korea, hospital beds; and in the United Kingdom downgrading of protective equipment requirements.

In these circumstances the ability to provide systematic and universal SDM becomes impossible, despite preparatory steps, and requires efforts to maximize capacity and reduce demand. When this occurs, a superimposed ethical rationing model is required, with the alternative being a system of access to scarce resources that is biased, inequitable, or random.

It is important to note that lessons relating to ethics of triage and rationing have been learnt in recent history. The SARS epidemic in 2003 overwhelmed the Toronto healthcare system. Subsequently, Singer et al. (2003) formed an expert working group that identified ten key ethical values and five major ethical issues faced by health decision-makers.[46] The key ethical values were individual liberty protection of the public from harm, proportionality, reciprocity, transparency, privacy, protection of communities from undue stigmatization, and the duty to provide care, equity, and solidarity. The key ethical issues were the ethics of quarantine; healthcare workers' duty to care and the duty of institutions to support them; privacy of personal information and public need to know; collateral damage; and epidemics in a globalized world.

During the current COVID-19 pandemic, a number of publications in major medical journals have described ethical frameworks for rationing and triage decision-making. Emanuel et al.[47] discussed allocations of values according to four fundamental values:

- Maximizing the benefits produced by scarce resources: saving the most individual lives or saving the most life years by giving priority to those likely to survive longest after treatment.
- Treating people equally: random allocation; lottery; first come, first served system.

- Promoting and rewarding instrumental value: giving priority to those who can save others or who have saved others in the past.
- Giving priority to the worst off: giving priority to the sickest or younger people who will have lived the shortest lives if they die untreated.[48]

For Emanuel et al. (2020), these values yielded six prima facie recommendations. The first is to maximize benefits through saving more lives and more years of life. This is a consensus value across expert reports and is consistent with both utilitarian and non–utilitarian views.[49] There are reasonable ways to do this; however, they must be consistent and there are specific issues that should be considered. These include determining years of life as subordinate to saving more lives; avoiding the use of future quality of life due to the limited time and information available in these circumstances; and supporting the consideration of the removal of ventilatory support to allow treatment of a patient more likely to survive. In particular, the risk of trying to predict long–term survivability and assigning value to quality of life should be avoided, as these subjectively bias against groups with disability or chronic illness. In comparison, predicting near–term survivability is more feasible, although the relative merits of scoring systems designed for large groups, not individuals, versus expert opinion are debated.[50] The second way is to prioritize health workers, not because they are more worthy, but because they have instrumental value in saving future lives. This is subject to a warning against abusing this privilege to include wealth and power. The third is to not allocate on a first come, first served basis, as it discriminates against those who do not have the means to attend hospitals, and it encourages crowding of healthcare facilities and might disadvantage those who adhere to social distancing policy and who then get sicker later when resources are exhausted. The fourth way is to be responsive to evidence. As an example, if older populations are at increased risk of dying due to COVID-19, vaccine should be directed preferentially to them, not younger patients. The fifth is to recognize research participation, as this cohort accepts risk in order to help future patients. Finally, these principles should be applied to all COVID-19 and non-COVID-19 patients.

It is unreasonable to expect overwhelmed clinicians and health systems to systematically, consistently, and transparently implement an ethics rationing system of values and recommendations during overwhelmed pandemic conditions. To achieve this, an expert group comprising a mix of clinicians, ethicists, consumer representatives, and public officials is required. In practice, these groups require preparation and training, with developed prioritization guidelines. They should be activated as required and should undergo a regular quality cycle of audit and reflection. Importantly, this group should take on the responsibility of communicating with patients and families about rationing decisions.[51]

Since the COVID-19 pandemic started, attempts to operationalize these values, issues and, recommendations have emerged. For instance, the "Australian and New Zealand Intensive Care Society (ANZICS) guiding principles for complex decision making during the COVID-19 pandemic 2020" provides a framework aimed at supporting clinicians to make decisions during conditions where demand exceeds capacity. In that case, a triage and rationing model is required. By necessity these types of documents reflect regional practice and culture. The ANZICS document explicitly warns against the use of illness severity scores to prognostic individual patient outcomes and to make allocation decisions based on this. It supports the use of expert senior clinicians, reflecting the nature and regard for critical care as a specialty in Australia and New Zealand. It focuses heavily on the benefit of universal engagement in SDM to ensure patients goals, preferences, and values are understood prior to triage and rationing. Importantly, the document considers approaches to tiebreaker situations and emphasizes the importance of communication and provision of high-quality comfort care for all patients and families. Other institutional and regional guidelines are similar, with some providing additional advice on self-awareness for triage decision-makers. Those factors might impair sound ethical decisions, ways to support clinical decision-makers, models of governance and bench-marking, and implementation of increasing levels of triage and rationing as the pandemic escalates through phases.[52]

In relation to tiebreaker situations, it is necessary to develop a method of choosing between patients of equal clinical priority when demand for resources exceeds supply. Tiebreakers are only utilized after a full assessment of the patient's goals, clinical situation, and capacity to benefit from the resource has been made and it has been identified that there are a number of patients of similar clinical priority. A brief overview of tiebreaker options, together with the relevant pros and cons, is set out in Table 2.1.

The benefits of implementing a system that combines all the principles, values, recommendations, and operational issues described are many. Patients and surrogates receive a fair, unbiased, consistent approach to scarce resource allocation, and the risk of bias and discrimination is minimized. Physicians are relieved of the emotional toll of "the terrible task of improvising decisions about whom to treat or making these decisions in isolation."[53] Finally, as discussed next, the possible adverse legal ramifications of rationing are arguably reduced through

TABLE 2.1 Tiebreaker options

	PROS	CONS
First come/first served	Consistent with ordinary clinical care of waiting rooms and waiting lists	Waiting longer is not necessarily morally significant Could lead to early/ unnecessary referrals for scarce resources Generally not recommended in pandemic

(Continued)

TABLE 2.1 (Continued)

	PROS	CONS
Frontline healthcare workers/ other first responders	Survival and ability to return to workforce can contribute to overall healthcare in future (probably not during pandemic unless lengthy) Instrumental value = maximizing benefit of the resource Attempt to mitigate the harm caused by higher risk of exposure recognizes risk taken to care for others (reciprocity argument) Caring for staff important consideration for health organizations (reciprocity argument)	May be viewed as unfair by public and valuing some occupations/people higher than others If using reciprocity as an argument, then should ideally apply to any essential service worker who has been exposed to COVID in line of work (incl first responders, teachers, supermarket workers etc.) Means of contracting COVID shouldn't be morally significant
Aboriginal and Torres Strait Islanders/First nations people (ATSI)	Overcoming systematic health disadvantages Prioritizing those who are worse off	Could lead unintentionally to greater hostility toward ATSI people.
Socially disadvantaged groups	Overcome systematic health disadvantages (B/J) Prioritizing those who are worse off	
Pregnant women	Maximizing number of lives saved	
People with caring responsibilities	If they survive, can continue caring role (instrumental value)	Discriminatory for people without dependents
Life-cycle considerations (*beyond comorbidity/ frailty which would have been factored into earlier assessment of clinical likelihood of survival/benefit*)	Younger people have not had opportunity to get to the next phase of life (fairness argument), worse off than an older person if they die A younger person might have a longer survival time and therefore possibly greater benefit. More problematic than the fairness, life cycle argument (*maximizing years of life saved*)	Discriminatory for older people.
Lottery	Each eligible person has equal opportunity, treating people equally	Can lead to resources not being directed to person most likely to benefit; less efficient, wasteful

Source: Adapted from Emanuel et al. 2020; Dawson et al. 2020; and Rogers and Carter 2020

the implementation of a system based on deliberate implementation of rationing ethics values and recommendations.

Triage during a pandemic – a legal perspective

Where rationing is required because health services and resources become over-whelmed, the absence of a triage and rationing ethical model ("triage guidelines") is likely to lead to a system of access to scarce resources that is biased, inequitable, or random. This creates potential legal liability for health services on grounds such as discrimination and unreasonableness and raises concern regarding the potential legal implications for health professionals involved in triage decisions and their implementation.

In usual practice, health professionals are expected to exercise reasonable care and skill, and failure to do so will leave them susceptible to a range of legal actions. For example, in civil law, sub-standard care or treatment may result in liability for negligence due to failure to meet the required standard of care,[54] possible human rights breaches, and the potential for a complaint and consequent disciplinary proceedings. In more serious cases, criminal liability may also arise.

In circumstances of overwhelmed capacity, there is arguably an increased legal risk to health professionals making and implementing triage decisions. One example is withholding or withdrawing potentially life-saving treatment, such as a ventilator, from one patient in preference for another patient. How is the standard of care to be determined in these circumstances? Generally, the law looks to the hypothetical actions of reasonable practitioners in the same circumstances. It has been recognized that, in circumstances of overwhelmed capacity, there is "substantial change in usual healthcare operations and the level of care it is possible to deliver."[55] That is, "the standard of care against which clinicians and health care entities will be judged in a pandemic is not the same as the standard of care under normal circumstances."[56] Despite this, where "decisions are made by doctors on a case-by-case basis, without reference to an agreed and detailed policy, they may be inconsistent, arbitrary, unfair and/or discriminatory – and thus, potentially illegal."[57] A means of reducing the legal risk to health professionals working in these circumstances is to provide well-developed triage guidelines which support triage decision-making. As has been recognized, "[a]dherence to well-recognized triage guidelines . . . will likely constitute strong evidence that the standard of care was satisfied."[58]

From a health service perspective, it is likely that triage guidelines could be challenged on the basis of administrative law principles, such as judicial review on the grounds of unreasonableness or bias. However, "[a] public that is aware of and has the opportunity to participate in a forum addressing these very difficult issues will be less likely to view the decisions as unfair or motivated by suspected partiality."[59] This suggests that triage guidelines developed through a robust and transparent process would be less likely to be subjected to, or indeed succumb to, an action for judicial review. In addition to incorporating all the principles, values, recommendations, and operational issues described earlier, the guidelines must have a high level of authority;[60] ensure broad consultation of stakeholders[61] including the public; and preferably be developed prior to the circumstances in which they will be implemented.[62]

More broadly, it has been suggested that

> [c]ommunities that have developed, disseminated, and adopted well-thought-out *crisis standards of care* will be more resilient in the face of health emergencies. Developing such standards brings disparate groups of people together to address issues, including the allocation of scarce resources, ethical obligations, and legal concerns (such as health care workers' liability during a disaster), and ensures these questions are preemptively considered in an open, transparent manner [emphasis in original].[63]

In order to further reduce legal risk for health professionals working in circumstances of overwhelmed capacity, some jurisdictions have enacted specific legal protections. In the United States, states provide specific protection for health professionals during a relevant declaration of emergency or disaster. For example, legislation in Maryland provides that "a health care provider is immune from civil or criminal liability if the health care provider acts in good faith and under a catastrophic health emergency proclamation."[64] Nevertheless, there remains concern in the United States that some states might not have sufficient protections in place, and there is a call for more to be done.[65]

During the current pandemic, the UK enacted the Coronavirus Act 2020. As outlined in its Explanatory Notes, the Act relevantly provides "indemnity coverage for clinical negligence of health professionals and others carrying out NHS activities connected to care, treatment or diagnostic services provided under the arrangements for responding to the COVID-19 outbreak."[66] However, concerns remain regarding potential liability, in particular in relation to triage and decisions regarding withholding and withdrawing of ventilation.[67]

In Australia, it has been recognized that allocation of scarce resources has potential legal implications,[68] and yet, there is very little literature or other publicly available evidence of discussion regarding this matter. Furthermore, there are no specific legislative protections for health professionals working in accordance with triage guidelines in circumstances of overwhelmed capacity.

It might be that the current law in some jurisdictions would provide the appropriate protections for health professionals; however, in the interests of their appropriate support, this requires clarity. If, following careful consideration, it is determined that a particular jurisdiction has sufficient protections in place, then this should be clearly and publicly articulated. In the absence of adequate existing legal protections, consideration must be given to legislating appropriate measures: for example, immunity for health professionals from civil and criminal liability provided they comply with relevant triage guidelines and act in good faith and in the absence of willful misconduct.

Failure to provide clarity around triage guidelines and legal protections for health professionals working in circumstances of overwhelmed capacity is counterproductive for everyone. In addition to the potential increased risk of bias or discrimination in the allocation of scarce resources, uncertainty heightens stress and burden for health professionals and might, contrary to the interests of society, foster reluctance or refusal by health professionals to work in the healthcare environment.

Conclusion – where to from here?

We have witnessed the global sentiment of appreciation and support of health professionals during the pandemic, as evidenced by displays of applause and cheering as health workers come and go from work. They are our heroes. It is time for governments, with the support of relevant experts in each jurisdiction, to consider, consult, and, where necessary, develop a clear public stance and strategy in relation to triage guidelines. Associated legal protections for health professionals working in circumstances of overwhelmed capacity must also be available. Clarity is essential.

In this chapter, we have seen the ethical and legal imperative for SDM in medical treatment and strategies to, and the benefits of, facilitating ongoing SDM during a pandemic. We have discussed the ethical, legal, and clinical benefits of well-developed triage guidelines supported by specific legal protection for health professionals working in accordance with such guidelines during times of overwhelmed capacity.

In an ideal world we are prepared. We see the wave coming and take time to consider ethical principles, discuss emotive issues, and create workable models that can be operationalized in an environment where clinicians are overwhelmed and require support. In the real world we are rarely prepared. A colleague from a major London ICU shared some details of what it looked like from the front line during the first wave of the pandemic:

> To begin with, the numbers are daunting. A tertiary ICU that usually has 42 beds, and 4 extracorporeal membrane oxygenation (ECMO) referrals per week, found itself with over 70 ECMO referrals per week, up to 15 simultaneously, and up to 100 ICU patients. All this with a significant part of the senior medical workforce sick or furloughed. The triage issues grow quickly. Insufficient capacity for demand, with decisions about access made using scoring systems. Resources directed towards nightingale hospitals, with major concerns about PPE and workforce. The most striking is the effect this has on clinicians, who describe feeling haunted thinking of the patients they did not provide care for, the burden of making rationing decisions alone, all compounded by fatigue.[69]

Ultimately, the argument supporting a triage and rationing ethical model and system is compelling. What is missing is evidence. We might still be in the early days of this pandemic, and we will wait and watch for descriptions of implementation and experience of these models clinically. In time, we must ensure we learn from the pandemic experience, and we must be better prepared.

BOX 2.1   CORONA SHORT #3: AUSTRALIA KARLEEN, A WIFE, MOTHER, GRANDMOTHER AND GREAT GRANDMOTHER, LOOKS FOR GOOD CANCER CARE

I've been married to my husband for 58 years. We've raised four children and we live in our own home. I've had good health most of my life, but my husband has struggled with heart problems since he was a policeman in his 20s, so I've recently become my husband's carer.

The year 2020 was a particularly difficult year for us. First, we had news of the pandemic which came as a shock. My husband and I are both in our late 70s, so we were concerned because we fell in the high-risk age category. We did what we could to stay safe by following precautions: we wore a mask when we left our house and sanitized our hands regularly. We limited our visits to the shops for groceries and made sure we followed the lockdown rules.

Then more bad news came – my husband was diagnosed with lymphoma. I was already worried about him because of COVID, but the cancer diagnosis made me even more concerned. I was worried my husband might not survive. The cancer diagnosis also meant we had to be out in the community for doctors' appointments, tests and treatments. Of course, this raised our stress levels and we also had further frustration because I was not able to attend some of his medical appointments with him due to COVID restrictions. I had to drop him off at the oncology center for his chemotherapy treatments but couldn't walk in with him or stay for a while.

Even appointments with our local doctor became more complicated. Sometimes we had to wait outside the clinic in our car and the receptionist would ring to let us know when we could come in. I remember one day we waited for the best part of an hour in the car, it was a warm day and my husband started to feel quite sick. Some appointments were by phone, and I didn't mind those – the doctor seemed to prepare really well and to know our background health information before we got started. And it meant we could have a list ready and make sure we covered all the issues we wanted to discuss.

We had noticed a change in the attitude of some doctors from when we were in our sixties. It seemed at times our medical complaints were brushed off and not taken seriously. It makes me feel like the doctor thinks we are old and we don't really matter. I have a friend in her late 80s and she says sometimes the doctors make her feel like she's past her use-by date. When her daughter attends appointments with her, the doctor tends to speak to her daughter rather than to her, like she can't keep up or something. Just because we're getting older doesn't mean we don't know what is going on.

On a brighter note, we have a close family and have all helped and supported each other through this tough year. And we have been really touched by so many people who have reached out to us. We live in a small regional town with a population of about 5,000. People in the community knew something wasn't right because my husband usually goes shopping with me but wasn't able to because he was even more at risk of COVID while he was having chemotherapy. They would ask how he was and when I told them he had cancer, they would always have some kind, supportive words.

And there were also some amazing acts of thoughtfulness that really lifted our spirits, like a friend of our daughters who sent a beautiful book of photography for my husband to enjoy while he was undergoing a long day of treatment. And our neighbor who told us to please let her know if there was anything she could do to help us – a widow who is 88 years of age, no less!

All in all, it has been a difficult year, with lots to think about and work through. But still I feel very blessed – by the end of 2020 my husband's treatment for lymphoma was successful and, shortly into 2021 my first great-grandchild arrived!

BOX 2.2   CORONA SHORT #4: AUSTRALIA
JOSEPH IS A GERIATRICIAN IN MELBOURNE
AND FINDS MUCH TO CRITICIZE IN AGED CARE
FACILITIES

What surprised me most, especially in Australia, was the paternalism of the country's leaders in how to address the pandemic. They were saying "we know what to do" but I was thinking

> You don't know what to do, you've never lived through a pandemic before. Don't come telling me this is well thought out, when in fact this is your best guess. Tell me how you are making these decisions.

If you look at who made the decisions, it felt a bit like a boys' club. I would have loved to have seen a citizen's jury involved. I also would have liked two groups working on the same issues; the groups are isolated from each other, given the same relevant information and we could then objectively assess options. In this way, the decision-making is structured with a validation process which is what we need during times of uncertainty. This could have happened pretty quickly. It seems that we haven't learned anything from the science of risk-perception, human factors, how the decision-making processes and an individual's potential for cognitive bias.

This knowledge should have been used to gather and appraise information and to critique and evaluate decisions. We relied on a small number of content experts in a limited range of health disciplines. What we neglected was wisdom from other disciplines of medicine and fields of knowledge in law, human rights, anthropology and psychology.

> Ultimately, instead of doing something different that addresses the unique once in a century event, we just did the same thing we do in usual circumstance, we did it faster and more often! So, I think we could have achieved a better outcome by being collaborative and innovative and bringing the community with us.

Notes

1 Steven A. Trankle et al., *Are we making progress on communication with people who are near the end of life in the Australian Health System? A thematic analysis.* Health Communication. 2020:35(2) pp. 158–167.

2 Id.

3 Id.

4 For example, this was recognized by the American Institute of Medicine in 2001 in the context of improving quality in health care. Institute of Medicine, *Crossing the quality chasm: A new health system for the 21st century*, National Academy Press 2001. See also, Michael J. Barry & Susan Edgman-Levitan, *Shared decision making: Pinnacle of patient-centered care.* N Engl J Med. 2012:366(9) pp. 780–781.

5 Michael J. Barry & Susan Edgman-Levitan, *Shared decision making: Pinnacle of patient-centered care.* N Engl J Med. 2012:366(9) pp. 780–781.

6 Schloendorff v Society of New York Hospital 105 NE 92, 93 (NY 1914).

7 For example, by way of an advance care directive pursuant to legislation or common law.

8 Thomas L. Beauchamp & James F. Childress, *Principles of biomedical ethics*, Oxford University Press 2001.

9 Diego Gracia, *The many faces of autonomy.* Theoretical Medicine and Bioethics. 2012:33(1) pp. 57–64 and Immanuel Kant, Allen W. Wood & J. B. Schneewind, *Groundwork for the metaphysics of morals*, Yale University Press 2002.

10 J. Andrew Billings & Eric L. Krakauer, *On patient autonomy and physician responsibility in end-of-life care.* Archives of Internal Medicine. 2011:171(9) pp. 849–853.

11 Gracia, supra, note 9.

12 Id. Thank you to Jack Turley for his contribution to this research.

13 Marli Huijer & Evert van Leeuwen, *Personal values and cancer treatment refusal.* J Med Ethics. 2000:26(5) pp. 358–362.

14 Robert D. Truog, *Patients and doctors: Evolution of a relationship.* N Engl J Med. 2012:366(7) pp. 581–585.

15 Carolyn Ells, Matthew R. Hunt & Jane Chambers-Evans, *Relational autonomy as an essential component of patient-centred care.* International Journal of Feminist Approaches to Bioethcis. 2011:4(2) pp. 79–101.

16 Joel Anderson & Axel Honneth, *Autonomy, vulnerability, recognition and justice* in *Autonomy and the challenges to liberalism: New essays*, Cambridge University Press 2005.

17 Carolyn Ells et al., supra, note 15.

18 Fiona Webster et al., *Where is the patient in models of patient-centred care: A grounded theory study of total joint replacement patients.* BMC Health Services Research. 2013:13 p. 531.

19 Bijan Fateh-Moghadam & Thomas Gutmann, *Governing [through] autonomy: The moral and legal limits of "soft paternalism".* Ethical Theory and Moral Practice. 2014:17(3) pp. 383–397; and Philippe Thompson-Leduc et al., *Shared decision-making behaviours in health professionals: A systematic review of studies based on the Theory of Planned Behaviour.* Health Expectations. 2015:18(5) pp. 754–774.

20 Tammy C. Hoffmann et al., *Shared decision making: What do clinicians need to know and why should they bother?* Medical Journal of Australia. 2014:201(1) pp. 35–39; and Alexander A. Kon, *The shared decision-making continuum.* JAMA. 2010:304(8) pp. 903–904.

21 Tammy C. Hoffmann et al., *Shared decision making: What do clinicians need to know and why should they bother?* Medical Journal of Australia. 2014.

22 Glyn Elwyn, Jon Tilburt & Victor Montori, *The ethical imperative for shared decision-making.* European Journal for Person Centred Healthcare. 2013:1(1) pp. 129–131.

23 Hoffmann et al., supra, note 21; and Glyn Elwyn et al.; and Cathy Charles, Amiram Gafni & Tim Whelan, *Shared decision-making in the medical encounter: What does it mean? (or it takes at least two to tango).* Social Science & Medicine. 1997:44(5) pp. 681–692.

24 Lars Sandman & Christian Munthe, *Shared decision-making and patient autonomy.* Theoretical Medicine and Bioethics. 2009:30(4) pp. 289–310.

25 Jonathan Lewis, *Getting obligations right: Autonomy and shared decision making.* Journal of Applied Philosophy. 2020:37(1) pp. 118–140.

26 Institute of Medicine, Committee on Quality of Health Care in America, *Crossing the quality chasm: A new health system for the 21st century*, National Academy Press 2001.

27 Id.

28 Suzanne Kurtz, Jonathan Silverman & John Benson et al., *Marrying content and process in clinical method teaching: Enhancing the Calgary: Cambridge guides.* Academic Medicine. 2003 Aug.:78(8) pp. 802–809.

29 Jonathan Silverman, Suzanne Kurtz & Jon Draper, *Skills for communicating with patients*, CRC Press 2016.

30 Id.

31 Kurtz et al., supra, note 28.

32 Anthony L. Back et al., *Efficacy of communication skills training for giving bad news and discussing transitions to palliative care.* Archives Intern Med. 2007:167(5) pp. 453–460.

33 Id.

34 Ariadne Labs, *Serious illness conversation guide*, www.ariadnelabs.org/areas-of-work/serious-illness-care/ (last visited Jul. 5, 2020).

35 Nicholas Simpson et al., *iValidate: A communication-based clinical intervention in life-limiting illness.* BMJ Supportive & Palliative Care. 2019.

36 Id.

37 Sharyn Milnes et al., *A prospective observational study of prevalence and outcomes of patients with Gold Standard Framework criteria in a tertiary regional Australian Hospital.* BMJ Supportive Palliative Care. 2019:9(1) pp. 92–99.

38 Labs, supra, note 34; and Neil R. Orford et al., *Effect of communication skills training on outcomes in critically ill patients with life-limiting illness referred for intensive care management: A before-and-after study.* BMJ Supportive & Palliative Care. 2019:9(1) pp. e21-e.

39 In the case of an instructional directive, this must be complied with if it is relevant in the circumstances.

40 Robert Verity et al., *Estimates of the severity of coronavirus disease 2019: A model-based analysis.* Lancet Infect Dis. 2020 Jun.:20(6) pp. 669–677.

41 Pavan K. Bhatraju et al., *Covid-19 in critically ill patients in the Seattle region: Case series.* N Engl J Med. 2020:382 pp. 2012–2022; and Graziano Onder, Giovanni Rezza & Silvio Brusaferro, *Case-fatality rate and characteristics of patients dying in relation to COVID-19 in Italy.* JAMA. 2020:323(18) pp. 1775–1776.

42 Douglas B. White & Bernard Lo, *A framework for rationing ventilators and critical care beds during the COVID-19 pandemic.* JAMA. 2020:323(18) pp. 773–774.

43 Nicholas Simpson, Sharyn Milnes & Daniel Steinfort, *Don't forget shared decision-making in the COVID-19 crisis.* Intern Med J. 2020:50 pp. 761–763.

44 Id.

45 Neil R. Orford et al., *Effect of communication skills training on outcomes in critically ill patients with life-limiting illness referred for intensive care management: A before-and-after study.* BMJ Supportive & Palliative Care. 2019:9(1) pp. e21-e.

46 Robert Verity et al., supra, note 40.

47 Ezekiel J. Emanuel et al., *Fair allocation of scarce medical resources in the time of Covid-19.* N Engl J Med. 2020:382 pp. 2049–2055.

48 Pavan K. Bhatraju et al., *supra* note 41.

49 Douglas White et al., supra, note 42; Peter A. Singer et al., *Ethics and SARS: Lessons from Toronto*. BMJ. 2003:327 pp. 1342–1344.
50 Douglas White et al., id.
51 Peter A. Singer et al., supra, note 49.
52 Ezekiel J. Emanuel et al., supra, note 47.
53 Pavan K. Bhatraju et al., supra, note 41.
54 Kathleen Liddell et al., *Who gets the ventilator? Important legal rights in a pandemic*. J Med Ethics. 2020:46 pp. 421–426; and I. Glenn Cohen, Andrew M. Crespo & Douglas B. White, *Potential legal liability for withdrawing or withholding ventilators during COVID-19: Assessing the risks and identifying needed reforms*. JAMA. 2020:323(19) pp. 1901–1902.
55 Institute of Medicine, *Guidance for Establishing Crisis Standards of Care for Use in Disaster Situations: A Letter Report*, The National Academies Press 2009, www.ncbi.nlm.nih.gov/books/NBK32749/ (last visited Aug. 19, 2020). See also National Academies of Sciences, Engineering, and Medicine, *Rapid expert consultation on crisis standards of care for the COVID-19 pandemic*, The National Academies Press 2020.
56 I. Glenn Cohen et al., supra, note 54, p. 1901.
57 Kathleen Liddell et al., supra, note 54, p. 422.
58 I. Glenn Cohen et al., supra, note 54, p. 1901.
59 Eleanor D. Kinney et al., *Altered standards of care for health care providers in the pandemic influenza*. Ind Health L Rev. 2009:6(1) pp. 11–12.
60 For example, government or National Health Service level for the United Kingdom – see, e.g., Kathleen Liddell et al., supra, note 54.
61 Institute of Medicine, *Guidance for establishing crisis standards of care for use in disaster situations: A letter report*, The National Academies Press 2009, www.ncbi.nlm.nih.gov/books/NBK32749/ (last visited Aug. 19, 2020).
62 Eleanor D. Kinney et al., supra, note 59.
63 Serena Vinter, Dara Alpert Lieberman & Jeffrey Levi, *Public health preparedness in a reforming health system*. Harv. L. & Pol'y Rev. 2010 Summer: 4(339) pp. 353–354.
64 MD Code, Public Safety, §14–3A-06.
65 I. Glenn Cohen et al. supra, note 54.
66 Explanatory Notes relevant to the Coronavirus Act 2020 (UK). See, e.g., section 11 of the Act.
67 Kathleen Liddell et al., supra, note 54.
68 See, e.g., Wendy Rogers & Stacy Carter, *Ethical considerations regarding allocation of ventilators/ICU beds during pandemic-associated scarcity* of the Australian Centre of Health Engagement, Health and Values, Wollongong University (2020), www.uow.edu.au/the-arts-social-sciences-humanities/research/acheev/ (last visited Aug. 15, 2020), which was prepared "to assist Local Health Districts working to produce guidance for resource allocation." See also Angus Dawson et al., *An ethics framework for making resource allocation decisions within clinical care: Responding to COVID-19*. J Bioethical Inq. 2020: pp. 1–7, where questions that raise legal implications are asked and, given the document is an ethics framework, discussed from an ethical, but not a legal, perspective. For example, "Should the standard of care for patients change in an epidemic?"; "What are the obligations of organisations?" and "What are the obligations of individual clinicians?"
69 Many thanks to Dr. James Doyle and Mrs. Nanci Doyle for sharing their experience.

Bibliography

Table of legislation

MD Code, Public Safety, §14–3A-06.
Coronavirus Act 2020 (UK) & explanatory notes.
Medical Treatment Planning and Decisions Act 2016 (Victoria, Australia).

Table of cases

Schloendorff v Society of New York Hospital 105 NE 92, 93 (NY 1914).

Bibliography

Anderson, Joel & Honneth, Axel, *Autonomy, vulnerability, recognition and justice* in *Autonomy and the challenges to liberalism: New essays*, Cambridge University Press (2005).

Ariadne Labs, *Serious illness conversation guide*, www.ariadnelabs.org/areas-of-work/serious-illness-care/ (last visited Jul. 5, 2020).

Back, Anthony L. et al., *Efficacy of communication skills training for giving bad news and discussing transitions to palliative care*, Archives Internal Med, 2007;167(5):453–460.

Barry, Michael J. & Edgman-Levitan, Susan, *Shared decision making: Pinnacle of patient-centered care*, N Engl J Med., 2012;366(9):780–781. doi:10.1056/NEJMp1109283.

Bhatraju, Pavan K. et al., *Covid-19 in critically ill patients in the Seattle region: Case series*, N Engl J Med, 2020;382(21):2012–2022.

Billings, J. Andrew & Krakauer, Eric L., *On patient autonomy and physician responsibility in end-of-life care*, Archives Internal Med, 2011;171(9):849–853.

Charles, Cathy, Gafni, Amiram & Whelan, Tim, *Shared decision-making in the medical encounter: What does it mean? (or it takes at least two to tango)*, Soc Sci Med, 1997;44(5):681–692.

Cohen, L. Glenn, Crespo, Andrew M. & White, Douglas B., *Potential legal liability for withdrawing or withholding ventilators during COVID-19: Assessing the risks and identifying needed reforms*, JAMA, 2020;323(19):1901–1902.

Dawson, Angus et al., *An ethics framework for making resource allocation decisions within clinical care: Responding to COVID-19*, J Bioethical Inq, 2020,1–7.

Ells, Carolyn, Hunt, Matthew R. & Chambers-Evans, Jane, *Relational autonomy as an essential component of patient-centred care*, Intern J Feminist Appr Bioethics, 2011;4(2):79–101.

Elwyn, Glyn, Tilburt, Jon & Montori, Victor, *The ethical imperative for shared decision-making*, Euro J Person Centered Healthcare, 2013;1(1):129–131.

Emanuel, Ezekiel J. et al, *Fair allocation of scarce medical resources in the time of Covid-19*, N Engl J Med, 2020;382:2049–2055.

Fateh-Moghadam, Bijan & Gutmann, Thomas, *Governing [through] autonomy: The moral and legal limits of "soft paternalism"*, Ethical Theory and Moral Practice, 2014;17(3):383–397.

Glass, Katherine Elizabeth et al., *Shared decision making and other variables as correlates of satisfaction with health care decisions in a United States national survey*, Pat Educ Counselling, 2012;88(1):100–105.

Gracia, Diego, *The many faces of autonomy*, Theoretical Med Bioethics, 2012;33(1):57–64.

Heyland, Daren K. et al., *The seriously ill hospitalized patient: Preferred role in end-of-life decision making?* J Crit Care, 2003;18(1):3–10.

Hoffmann, Tammy C. et al., *Shared decision making: What do clinicians need to know and why should they bother?* M J Austr, 2014;201(1):35–39.

Institute of Medicine, *Guidance for establishing crisis standards of care for use in disaster situations: A letter report*, The National Academies Press (2009), www.ncbi.nlm.nih.gov/books/NBK32749/ (last visited Aug. 19, 2020).

Institute of Medicine (US) and Committee on Quality of Health Care in America, *Crossing the quality chasm: A new health system for the 21st century*, National Academy Press (2001).

Kant, I., *Groundwork for the metaphysics of morals* (A. W. Wood, Trans.), With essays by J. B. Schneewind, Marcia Baron, Shelly Kagan, & Allen W. Wood. Yale University Press (2002).

Kinney, Eleanor D. et al., *Altered standards of care for health care providers in the pandemic influenza*, Ind Health L Rev, 2009;6(1):11–12.

Kon, Alexander A., *The shared decision-making continuum*, JAMA, 2010;304(8):903–904.

Kurtz, Suzanne, Silverman, Jonathan & Benson, John et al., *Marrying content and process in clinical method teaching: Enhancing the Calgary: Cambridge guides*, Academic Medicine, 2003;78(8):802–809.

Lewis, Jonathan, *Getting obligations right: Autonomy and shared decision making*, J Appl Philosophy, 2020;37(1):118–140.

Liddell, Kathleen et al., *Who gets the ventilator? Important legal rights in a pandemic*, J Med Ethics, 2020;46:421–426.

Milnes, Sharyn et al., *A prospective observational study of prevalence and outcomes of patients with Gold Standard Framework criteria in a tertiary regional Australian Hospital*, BMJ Supportive Palliative Care, 2019;9(1):92–99.

National Academies of Sciences, Engineering, and Medicine, *Rapid expert consultation on crisis standards of care for the COVID-19 pandemic*, The National Academies Press (2020).

Onder, Graziano, Rezza, Giovanni & Brusaferro, Silvio, *Case-fatality rate and characteristics of patients dying in relation to COVID-19 in Italy*, JAMA, 2020;323(18):1775–1776.

Orford, Neil R. et al., *Effect of communication skills training on outcomes in critically ill patients with life-limiting illness referred for intensive care management: A before-and-after study*, BMJ Supportive Palliative Care, 2019;9(1):e21.

Rogers, Wendy & Carter, Stacy, *Ethical considerations regarding allocation of ventilators/ICU beds during pandemic-associated scarcity* of the Australian Centre of Health Engagement, Health and Values, Wollongong University (2020), www.uow.edu.au/the-arts-social-sciences-humanities/research/acheev/ (last visited Aug. 15, 2020).

Sandman, Lars & Munthe, Christian, *Shared decision-making and patient autonomy*, Theoretical Medicine and Bioethics, 2009;30(4):289–310.

Silverman, Jonathan, Kurtz Suzanne & Draper Jon, *Skills for communicating with patients*, CRC Press (2016).

Simpson, Nicholas et al., *iValidate: A communication-based clinical intervention in life-limiting illness*, BMJ Supportive & Palliative Care, 2019;0:1–7. doi:10.1136/bmjspcare-2018-001669.

Simpson, Nicholas, Milnes, Sharyn & Steinfort, Daniel, *Don't forget shared decision-making in the COVID-19 crisis*, Internal Medicine Journal, 2020;50:761–763.

Singer, Peter A. et al., *Ethics and SARS: Lessons from Toronto*, BMJ, 2003;327(7427): 1342–1344.

Solomon, Mildred Z., Wynia, Matthew K. & Gostin, Lawrence O, *Covid-19 crisis triage: Optimizing health outcomes and disability rights*, New England Journal of Medicine 2020.

Thompson-Leduc, Philippe et al., *Shared decision-making behaviours in health professionals: A systematic review of studies based on the Theory of Planned Behaviour*, Health Expectations, 2015;18(5):754–774.

Trankle, Steven A. et al., *Are we making progress on communication with people who are near the end of life in the Australian Health System? A thematic analysis*, Health Communication, 2020;35(2):158–1567.

Truog, Robert D., *Patients and doctors: Evolution of a relationship*, N Engl J Med, 2012; 366(7):581–585.

Truog, Robert D., Mitchell, Christine & Daley, George Q., *The toughest triage: Allocating ventilators in a pandemic*, New England Journal of Medicine, 2020;382(21):1973–1975.

Verity, Robert et al., *Estimates of the severity of coronavirus disease 2019: A model-based analysis*, Lancet Infect Dis, 2020 Jun.;20(6):669–677.

Vinter, Serena, Lieberman, Alpert & Levi, Jeffrey, *Public health preparedness in a reforming health system*, Harv. L. & Pol'y Rev, 2010 Summer;4(339):353–354.

Webster, Fiona et al., *Where is the patient in models of patient-centred care: A grounded theory study of total joint replacement patients*, BMC Health Services Research, 2013;13:531.

White, Douglas B., & Lo, Bernard, *A framework for rationing ventilators and critical care beds during the COVID-19 pandemic*, JAMA, 2020;323(18):1773–1774.

3

DECISIONS IN THE MATERNITY UNIT

Containment in Taiwan and Canada

Li-Yin Chien and Su-Chen Liao with Julie Doldersum

Editors' introduction: This interview is based on the article "The maternity response to COVID-19: An example from one maternity unit in Taiwan," which appeared in *Midwifery,* a journal published by Elsevier.[1] To that point, Taiwan had prided itself in avoiding any reported cases over most of 2020 due to its reliance on masking, testing, and community self-restriction that made lockdowns unnecessary.

On Wednesday, 23 December 2020, within days of this interview, Taiwanese officials announced the first community transmission of COVID-19 since April of that year, ending 253 days of a coronavirus-free island. Two people were treated for the virus, a 60-year-old pilot with EVA Airlines who was originally from New Zealand and his friend, a woman in her 30s. On 28 December 2020 Health Minister and Central Epidemic Command Center (CECC) head Chen Shih-Chung announced eight new imported COVID-19 cases, raising Taiwan's total number of infections to 793 in a country with a population of 23.5 million.[2]

Taiwan brought this outbreak under control and went on to achieve over three months COVID-free before a further outbreak occurred in late April 2021. This was connected once again to flight crews and to hotel quarantine issues, following some relaxing of the quarantine rules. By mid-May, Taiwan was reporting 333 new cases, mostly in Taipei city and New Taipei city. This is yet another tragic reminder that while we seek some normality by easing restrictions, the virus never rests.[3]

DOI: 10.4324/9781003215769-5

Interview with Taiwan Staff in the maternity unit, Taiwan – 18 December 2020

Editor Elizabeth Kirley (EK): Are you very busy now with the pandemic or have matters in Taiwan settled down?

Li-Yin Chien (LY): A little bit more intense than usual but we are getting used to it. It's just wearing masks right now, so pretty close to what we describe in the article in terms of the preventative measures. The government has not changed much, so we are doing well.

EK: Does that mean that there are not as many pregnant women or that COVID numbers are not high?

LY: No there are no pregnant mothers with COVID right now.

EK: You work in the maternity unit, not any other part of this hospital, is that right?

LY: Su-Chen is the Nursing Supervisor. She's in charge of the maternity unit. At this time all supervisors convene together to talk about COVID . . . preventative measures, those kinds of things.

EK: OK, so Su-Chen Liao, is there any COVID in the hospital generally?

Su-Chen Liao (SC): *[with LC interpreting]* During the pandemic, in September only, there was one imported pregnant mother with COVID so she delivered and that was the only case in the hospital. In Taiwan it's all centralized, so we don't have community infections. We do have imported cases because of people traveling. What we do is, if you have been traveling, then our Central Epidemic Command Centre will order you to go to the hospital. But they will keep each hospital with only a very few number of cases. So, they will evenly distribute them to hospitals. But they will keep each hospital with very few cases.

EK: Your hospital is one of many hospitals with a maternity unit in Taipei?

LI: Yes, but our hospital is one of the biggest.

EK: In Taiwan, your numbers were so low – 429 cases – what was the date for that?

LI: In May 2020. And now we have had a total of 759 cases and seven deaths in the whole country. So still a very low number of cases.[4]

EK: By comparison, in Canada in May 2020 we had a total of more than 58,000 cumulative cases and over 4,500 deaths in a population of 37 million.[5] A startling difference. We were flattening the curve but now we are in the midst of a second wave. In your article you say the reason your numbers are low is because you have a national program.

LI: Yes, it's centralized. So, the government convened experts and they met every day or at least every week during July to September 2020. And now it's pretty calm. Only during the harsh time is the meeting every day. They discuss what measures they will take and they give their policy guidelines to every hospital, and the hospitals have a meeting every day to discuss how they will follow the guidelines and how we can control the virus.

EK: **So when this group of experts meet, are their conclusions presented on television?**

LY: Yes, because in Taiwan information communications are distributed quite well – computer, television, radio, internet. You can always get access to that information. And they also have short talks concerning their conclusions that are broadcast everywhere.

EK: **Do they speak about numbers?**

LI: Yes, and you can update it everywhere.

EK: **Do you find there are more cases in the urban centers? Are there certain hot spots?**

LI: No because we don't have community infections. Most of the numbers are from imported cases.

EK: **How is it possible to have "imported" cases? We don't have international travel in Canada – we aren't allowed to leave the country, and sometimes we cannot leave the province**.

LY: Well now their minds are open. For example, in yesterday's news a dance group from Russia wanted to perform in Taiwan. Forty people in the group but during quarantine four of them had the fever. They tested positive for COVID and so were sent back. The performance was canceled. But we are a low-risk country so they want to perform here. Those kinds of activities are still allowed here.

Editor Deborah Porter (DP): **How long is your quarantine?**

LY: Fourteen days.

DP: **With your quarantine, with flights coming in, do you have the crew on the plane going into quarantine as well?**

LY: They are under "self-control," the quarantine does not apply to pilots or flight attendants.[6] They have temperature measures in the airport so they are asked to monitor their own health situation but are not required to quarantine.

DP: In Australia, we had aircrew from South America fly in last week and they did not self-isolate like they were supposed to before going out into the community. So now we have community transmission and now aircrew must quarantine as well.

LY: Not here, but the mask policy is being strictly enforced.

EK: **Are there masks on the street? For everyone outside?**

LY: Indoors yes, but most people also wear them on the street. A few don't wear them outside. But if they need to go indoors it's mandated or security won't allow them to come in. On the street the majority of people wear masks.

DP: I have a daughter who is due to have her first baby in three weeks. So, I am about to be a grandmother for the first time.

LY and SC: Congratulations!

DP: Thank you. One of the changes in areas near where I live is that they have moved antenatal classes online. They create Zoom classes. Some of the mothers say they would like to be in the room with other pregnant women so they can talk and be with them. But being online is not the same. They comment that they are missing out to some extent.

EK: What's happening in Taiwan with antenatal classes?

LY: Before the pandemic we also had those types of group classes. But from early periods, from January to June of 2020, our group classes were canceled. Now we only do face to face. I think most hospitals did the same, moving to individualized service.

DP: That's interesting – different from what's happening here. The other change is that for antenatal checkups doctors have done some face-to-face visits but most are by telephone. Not even by video link. So, pregnant women are not getting their blood pressure checked, not being physically observed, and not getting fundal measurements or even bedside ultrasound. So, some moms are getting anxious, feeling they are not getting checked as they normally would. **What's happening to antenatal checks in Taiwan?**

LY: Nothing new. As usual, no mother misses her antenatal chats because of the pandemic.

DP: That's great, well done.

LY: That's why she [points to Su Chen] cannot have a normal life. Too busy. [laughter]

EK: Is this the antenatal programming for the entire country?

LY: Yes, for the entire country. Also, we have the data checked and no mother is missing her antenatal chats because she is afraid of COVID, no.

DP: With the screening for postnatal depression after birth in Australia they do that in the antenatal phase, during pregnancy, to see if the mother is prone to develop depression.

That is normally done at a face-to-face meeting but during this pandemic it's being done by telephone. The comment I've heard so far is that that is really good because it means the discussion is being slowed down. Now everything is being read out and the conversation happens more fully. Whereas normally with the face-to-face meeting on this issue there are boxes to be ticked, you know, just a series of questions rather than a fuller conversation allowing the woman to open up and talk about her past and her concerns. So interestingly that's one area that seems to be done better by telephone. **How do you conduct the antenatal discussion?**

LY: I think in the prenatal check they ask about how you are feeling, about your mood. But they do not do the full screening checklist because the post screening questions are in the mother's handbook that we distribute so she can see the questions. Unless the healthcare worker suspects you have antenatal depression, we don't do active screening regarding that. But if there's a suspicion of course they will do it. And for postpartum depression, even before this pandemic, hospitals do telephone conversations with those women. So nothing's changed there.

EK: **Your published article "The maternity response to COVID: An example from one maternity unit in Taiwan," outlines practices in birthing during a global pandemic. Do you have midwives in your maternity unit to assist?**

LY: Actually in Taiwan we have a midwife license but in hospitals there are fewer with just a midwife license. Very, very few people with only a midwife license. Most times a nurse has both qualifications. More than 99% of births are being delivered in hospitals, and by obstetricians in hospitals, so midwives are only to accompany women and sometimes provide a little bit of ante and postnatal education.

EK: In Canada that has changed, so in most provinces midwives can actually come into the delivery room and assist with the mother. In the province of Ontario, there has been some anxiety among maternity teams due to a lack of uniform COVID guidelines across all hospitals. Now those guidelines are available to obstetricians, nurses, and midwives and allow the mother to have one support worker in the delivery room if that person has tested negative for the coronavirus, there's enough PPE for that person, and the hospital has provided for adequate physical distancing between patients.

Before the guidelines, one doctor commented, "The biggest challenge for all of us is there is no playbook for this virus."[7] Some families have reportedly been "shopping around" for hospitals with more permissive policies in terms of visiting guidelines. That practice can result in babies being delivered without medical records on hand, leading to an increased health risk for mother and the baby.[8]

LY: Home births with the assistance of midwives are still allowed here. But most of the women here prefer the hospital setting because they feel safer. If they choose home delivery, it's more likely they will be delivered by a midwife who is licensed by the government.

DP: **We've heard stories that, in the United States, women have to wear masks even when they are in labor because of the COVID risk. Is that happening in Taiwan?**

LY: Yes, we practice the same. The only exception is the caesarian delivery because we put the anesthetic mask on the mother's face. So only that time is without the mask. You need to wear the mask. Our women do not say "no" to that. No problems about that. Sometimes the delivery time is very long. So, if the mother says she needs air, everybody else needs to wear the mask.

EK: **When there was COVID in Taipei, there was some virus in the hospital . . .**

LY: But we don't have community disease.

EK: Right but I refer to when you had those numbers you quoted earlier.

LY: The central government would distribute the cases so there were not too many in one hospital. Through our screening stations we could test for COVID before allowing anyone to enter.

EK: For those numbers, **did you follow their progress after they left the hospital? Because there was no vaccine.**

LY: Because we have sufficient resources and low number of cases, they were distributed to all those hospitals and kept hospitalized until they had two negative test results. So, the risk was very low. They were advised to self-monitor. Even then the public health nurse would call them to check their progress. But at the time of discharge, they were already virus-free.

EK: **Are there precautions for family members who are visiting the mother?**

LY: During the pandemic we kept our regular routine. Only two visitors allowed at one time. But during the hospital stay, for the mother it's three days, for Caesarian it's six days. We hope during that time the visitors will be limited to those two people. They also need to report their TOCC (travel, occupation, contact, and cluster) and APN (a brief health check) to us to see they are OK. And every time they go to the hospital they are checked.

EK: **How do you know they are not asymptomatic, but still carriers?**

LY: Because we don't have community infection. And because we have a national health insurance system. It's like an information system in that it is pretty connected. And we can use it to check if their information is correct. So . . . it's government checked and also self-reporting. If it says "all clear" we assume they are clear.

DP: We are doing the same in Australia with limiting visitors to two people for now, and they have to do the temperature check and complete the form. But we don't have a VPN check so we have to rely on people being honest.

EK: **So no problems with holidays? Family get-togethers?**

LY: It's pretty normal now. In the beginning of the year people were more nervous, in January and February. But even at that time people still kept together with their families because it was the Lunar Chinese holiday. But people were more cautious about going out to restaurants and department stores even though they were kept open. After July it was very normal besides wearing the mask.

EK: **And tourists are allowed to come into the country?**

LY: I think we have a country list and if you are on it you are allowed to come in. But not for high-risk countries. But no matter where you come from, you need to go into quarantine for 14 days when you arrive. The same for domestic people or foreign travelers.

DP: **Is that quarantine policed?**

LY: Yes, by public health workers. You can choose if it is a separate room in your house or in a hotel. But every day a public health worker will come to you no matter where you are. The government will give you a hand phone so they're checking where you are. If they call that number and you don't answer, they will ask police to find you.

DP: That's a good system. That's where Australia had problems, with people breaching quarantine. Getting out and going to shopping centers and we had an outbreak and fairly significant second wave because of that. So now they are much stricter about quarantine.

LY: Our community leader works with the public health nurse to keep checking and calling to see if they are in quarantine.

SC: [*with LC interpreting*] Here's something very interesting. According to previous experience, people in quarantine would become depressed about the 7th or 8th day so on the 7th or 8th day a retired nurse who is working as a volunteer would call them and ask about their emotions and feelings and try to get them talking. And hopefully help with their depression.

DP: That's terrific. Sounds like a good measure. In Australia there's a lot of talk about the mental wellbeing of people in quarantine. Perhaps people were not thinking about it before but are starting to address that now. It sounds like a good measure, making contact and having a discussion.

EK: **For someone who does not obey quarantine, is there any involvement with the law?** In Canada there have been cases of steep fines or being put in jail and charged criminally. I understand this has happened in England as well. Has that happened in Taiwan?

LY: Yes, they will be fined and put in jail if they resist.

DP: I think every country is having that problem. Again, in Australia, we actually fined 12 members of a plane crew from South America. I was looking at a couple of articles and in Germany they had a large outbreak in a maternity facility. One of the things they were having trouble with was getting staff to social distance during their breaks. When they were having their lunch they would forget. The article said they had to train them as to the importance but they also had other staff come in and promote that behavioral change so when they were more relaxed they wouldn't forget their social distancing. **Is that something you have had to address?**

LY & SC: In the maternity unit the measure is that we arrange different times for each staff person's lunch. Also, in the sitting area they each have to face the wall. So due to seating restrictions they are also assigned to different times.

DP: That's good.

LY: But in smaller centers we are not so sure.

DP: The article I read was in a large perinatal center. There was another article I read about Australia where they actually simulated an emergency in a clinical environment and they would work out what would be required in a real emergency. One of the things they tested was how staff would put on PPE appropriately and how to take it off without transmitting the virus. The simulation was for an emergency caesarian section so they had to get dressed quite quickly. What they found was that to get people to put on equipment properly they had to have them buddy up with another staff member to watch each other. There was also not enough room for staff to get ready and the time they took was too long. So, making sure equipment was put on properly and that there was enough time and room. **Have any of those problems occurred in Taiwan?**

LY & SC: Because we did not encounter a large number of cases that are emergencies, we do have training classes both online and in person. And in the hospital the Infectious Disease Prevention Unit will go to each unit and check if you know how to properly put on and take off PPE. Only those with post graduate training for more than two years will have to put on PPE and to deal with suspected cases. Because in that scenario, after they put on their PPE, usually the leader of the ward or the nursing leader will check the person to see they are wearing PPE properly before they go into the infected area.

DP: Sounds like there are checks in place. Hopefully you will never have to encounter that in a COVID situation.

LY: Yes, but the only difference is that we don't know how we would perform in a case of emergency because we don't have them. We don't have any community cases.

DP: One other thing that has to do with the mask and PPE is that in simulations we heard staff had trouble communicating with other staff and with the patient. What they ended up doing was using baby monitors and walkie-talkie radios and even speaker phones so they could communicate more clearly. **Have you had experience with that?**

LY: [*conferring with SC*] She does not think that even with PPE on talking is a big problem, only that it is very hot. Probably it is because of the emergency.

DP: Maybe because of the number of people talking at the same time and rushing in an emergency, yes.

EK: Did you have any shortage of PPE at any time?

LY: No, I think not, no concern because we have a low number of cases. So, no concern over lack of PPE, no.

EK: A related question: when we first heard of COVID but it was not in our country yet, people were very fearful. Some people began to buy a lot of some goods like toilet paper. [*laughter by LY and SC*] And flour, to cook. Deb, what else did people hoard?

DP: Rice and pasta. They sold out very quickly.

EK: Before there was even a case. I remember looking at the television news about Italy and China as well and other countries that were experiencing the virus. The streets were bare. And the mood was very fearful. **Did you go through anything like that? Any hoarding behavior?**

LY: I think you know rumors will spread anywhere. Yes, we did hear "toilet paper will be out soon." But in a very short period of time, the Prime Minister shot an advertisement saying "see, you don't need to buy that much toilet paper. Everything is fine." It only lasted a short time because I think our government acted well and quick in terms of those things. Even in terms of the mask, the government acted quickly. I think they were the first government in the world to ban freely buying masks and they central-ized buying masks and rationing the mask to each person.

Because of that they showed that they had the ability to deal with the situation. They said "you don't have to buy these things. We are well under control" and we believe them during this pandemic. I think it was only for one week. About the toilet paper, some people were saying "the price is going to go up," not that it would be out of stock. But at all times every-thing was normal for us. In every shop there is still lots of merchandise so no people are worried.

EK: Thank you. How about you, Deb. I seem to remember you saying at one point you could not get certain cuts of meat. Or hand sanitizer.

DP: Yes, initially we had a real rush for toilet paper and items like rice and hand sanitizer. There was a lot of panic so they quickly put rationing on the number of these items you could buy. Pretty shocking.

But then, when we had the second wave, we again had a rush. They reduced the number of workers in some of our meat businesses dealing with beef and chicken and that reduced the risk of transmission . . . but this time the State government leaders spoke to us on television, updates every day, and said, "There will be less, but there will be enough if you just buy what you need." And we didn't have any problems because people understood that it was OK. People were fine, even if they couldn't get their favorite cut of meat. It just goes to show if you keep people informed what a difference it can make.

EK: So it will be the same for the vaccines, right? Of course, Taiwan doesn't have community cases so **will you distribute the vaccine?**

LY: We probably want to keep open to all visitors and to resume normal life so we still need vaccine, right? People can feel safe to travel anywhere.

EK: I understand there are different practices and COVID policies in various countries about feeding the newborn and isolating the infant from the mother immediately after birth.[9]

LY & SC: It's for mothers with suspected symptoms for infection that we will prefer separation and pumping of breast milk. But without the infection risk of course we would go for rooming in and breastfeeding as the norm.

EK: OK. In Canada, it appears "rooming in" and "breastfeeding" are still sup-ported during a positive COVID test in the spirit of "shared decision-making" between families and healthcare providers, as recommended by the Canadian Paediatric Society.[10]

What about in Australia, Deb?

DP: Same. But we are in the situation where we currently have no community transmission in the state where l live (Victoria) and so things are easing up as well.

EK: So do you know what the situation was when numbers were higher?

DP: I think the visiting restrictions were much tighter, but from what I am hearing, they still did the breastfeeding and business as usual for the way the baby was managed.

EK: So is it pretty well accepted that COVID can be transmitted through breastmilk?

DP: I saw an article recently that said there is no evidence that it can be transmitted through breast milk but they did not feel they had a large enough sample.[11] I would be interested to hear what you think, Li-Yin?

LY & SC: I think for safety reasons here we all agree there is a possibility that COVID will appear in breast milk so we do take precautions.

EK: And which precautions do you take? To test the milk?

LY: No, to ask the mother to pump the milk and give the baby formula milk when there is a suspicion the mother has COVID.

DP: That the baby will be bottle fed and the mother will be tested.

EK: If you go into a second wave would you change anything?

LY: No, we would not do anything different because we think what we did for the first wave was effective so we will just keep going.

EK: I cannot speak for all of Canada, but what the media finds confusing is the amount of resistance to precautions that science tells us are wise. Even wearing the mask – still highly contentious. The vaccine? In Chapter 5 of this book we try to understand that. **Do those sorts of stories about resistance reach your media as well?**

LY & SC: [*laughter*] Of course, everywhere in the world there are just a few people who don't like to follow the rules. But in Taiwan, no, resistance is not a big problem. And also, those people who think differently from others they will not broadcast their message on TV like in the United States. Here, at least with these measures, the government's voice is bigger. So, no opposite voices appear.

EK: Any other questions?

DP: No, but I'd like to say I've found this discussion fascinating. So, thank you.

LY & SC: Yes, "nice to meet you." Everybody stay safe.

DP: That's a good plan.

   Update via email on 10 May 2021

DP: Did Taiwan experience a second and third wave of COVID?

LY & SC: We have not experienced a big pandemic, though two cluster infections since our interview occurred. There were 21 cases in the cluster incident at the Ministry of Taoyuan Hospital and one death (in February, 2021). One is now ongoing which was from pilots of the China Airline and regarding hotel quarantines there are 31 confirmed cases up to now.

DP: Have the COVID precautions in maternity services changed at all since our interview? And if they have changed, what are the changes?

LY & SC: Since the epidemic has eased, the prenatal parenting classroom has been restored. But it is now closed again.

DP: What do you think is the most important policy or policies in maternity services that have been effective against COVID?

LY & SC: Mask wearing and limited visitors through stringent APN or the virus could enter the hospital.

Interview with Canadian Midwife

At this point, we are joined by registered nurse Julie Doldersum, who offers a comparative look at birthing practices during COVID-19 in Canada. As a practicing partner in Midwife Nottawasaga Practice Group, Julie works as a frontline healthcare worker at Collingwood General & Marine Hospital in Ontario Canada where she is the head midwife. Midwifery in Ontario is managed by practice partners with associates who are involved in maternity health both in hospitals and private homes. They are autonomous healthcare providers that are independently employed and bill their services through the provincial Ministry of Long-Term Health. They are regulated by the Ontario Association of Midwives, mandated to carry professional insurance, and provided with oversight by the Ontario government regarding their standards of care and continuing education. Under all circumstances, pandemic or not, they have the same admitting privileges as physicians. The mother is the "boss", but midwives are responsible for her case and outcomes.

EK: In our interview with the Taiwanese nurses, it seems midwives in Taiwan also hold nursing or obstetrics degrees.

Julie Doldersum (JD): There are tiers of midwifery care in some countries and perhaps the system in Taiwan has nurses that might be better trained for natal care. We are much like the UK in that we are registered as a nurse and a midwife simultaneously.

EK: How many midwives practice in Canada?

JD: In the 2,000s.

EK: I've noted some policy changes in Ontario since COVID's arrival that limit the mother to one support person in the delivery room.

JD: Yes so that's probably the biggest panic. I remember I caught a baby on March 14th and then the pandemic was declared the next day in Canada and that was my first concern: am I allowed to have a support person with me? In parts of urban centers like Toronto, Oakville, I believe, they were excluding support people. In Collingwood [approximately 1.5 hours north of Toronto] we were always allowed to keep one support person with us.

It really came down to PPE initially. There was an acute shortage and it felt suffocating to not know if we were going to have sufficient PPE for ourselves and for the support person and for clients. Also, we wanted to make sure we were not inviting possible infectious persons into the same room.

EK: To be clear, is that the term of art, to "catch a baby"?

JD: Well, I think it's a bit obnoxious to say "I delivered a baby." The mother delivers it, it's her baby. Sometimes she catches her own baby. I just help that along.

EK: **Such a different perspective than the historical hospital delivery experience.**

JD: Yes, it's about empowering the woman. She is our client, not our patient, and we are there to meet her needs. In our area 90% of the time babies are born without complications and that is why the mother can often catch her own baby.

EK: **So the whole business about PPE . . . it's now coming out in the news that our government had originally spent a lot of money on N-95 masks that were faulty in the way they were stored . . . so not up to standard and they had to be discarded. Did that happen in your practice?**

JD: I don't have any direct experience, I was just aware that that was the situation in March of 2020. Warehouses of PPE were not stored appropriately and had to be destroyed. It was affected by moisture and therefore their integrity was damaged. It was really scary – one thing that definitely made me cry – was that I was responsible for acquisition of PPE and I didn't think I was going to pull it off. And I have friends who were responsible for PPE and had to take a leave of absence because of the stress of not being able to do their jobs because they just couldn't get access to the resources they needed.

EK: **How did the administration ensure you had enough?**

JD: We all have our private suppliers, and the supply went to the hospital initially because that's where the most acutely ill were being treated. We couldn't access it at first for our own clinic. People in the community were incredibly generous, donating masks and gloves to our clinic. But they were not N-95 standard for sure.

   I remember filling out spread sheets at two in the morning to apply to the Ministry of Health to say how many sets of equipment I needed for clients. In the wake of a pandemic, I had to develop a whole new skill set – immediately – no heads up. You had to keep learning computer programs overnight, at the same time you were involved in the delivery of babies. And babies didn't stop coming!

EK: **Does Canada have its own vaccine or is it imported?**

JD: I actually don't know yet. Just this week a few nurses and doctors in Collingwood have received the vaccination.

EK: **So you are front line?**

JD: Absolutely. 100%.

EK: **And your hospital is managing?**

JD: We've come a long way. We held our breath about a second wave – its' upon us now. We have been lucky that our numbers have been manageable.

I cannot speak for the ICU staff. We've opened up a field hospital at the Legion to be our secondary hospital, for people who are booked for long-term care. I continue to have great faith in the professionalism of our medical staff. They are doing a great job of following the rules and protecting people.

EK: **And how has all this affected the mother's interaction with her new baby?**

JD: Infants are encouraged to remain skin to skin with the mother who has COVID, as long as she is stable. And whoever is caring for the baby and is COVID positive should wear a mask.

EK: **Our Taiwanese nurses spoke about the difficulty of mothers keeping the mask on when they receive anesthetic.**

JD: In Canada if you have a Caesarean birth you receive a spinal injection, not anesthesia so you are awake and able to wear a mask. If mothers ask, the answer is "Yes, you have to wear a mask." If it falls off will we stop and insist they put it on? No, but we as staff are all wearing a mask.

EK: **How about classes for mothers?**

For the group activity they prefer video. That's received the most comment, though, in that most healthcare clinics are only inviting those receiving direct care into the clinic but not the support person – to support contact tracing.

EK: **Is your PPE being thrown away?**

JD: Everybody wore disposables at first and that was a huge environmental problem. Eventually, we got reusable PPE and good quality plastic eyewear that could be sterilized. And face masks. The face masks we were using at first had to last for a 12-hour period. Now, I hate to say, we throw them away. I don't have sterilizing equipment in my house or car. So, for home labor, I gown and mask in my car and carry my equipment into their house. I don't eat or drink or use the bathroom in their house. Difficult for the longer births.

We ask that they confine their numbers to the parents. Most respect that. So, the grandmother exclusion issue was a huge heartache but people are just getting used to it and not complaining so much. Occasionally I have been asked to call grandparents and ask that they stay a distance. I don't take that on – it's not my responsibility.

EK: **Do you have rules for the parents in handling their baby?**

JD: We trust they are taking on that responsibility.

EK: **What about handling discussions about postpartum depression?**

JD: Maternal health is a major component so we ask a new client to detail their history, including care by a psychiatrist. We check into their mood. We give referrals to mental health specialists. Two of my colleagues have that specialty.

There is an Edinburgh Postnatal Depression Scale (EPDS) that's a tool for indicating depression or anxiety and the woman fills out a survey about herself. Our main tool is checking out the woman in person. There is an exposure risk in that situation because how long can you sit with someone before you increase your risk if they are COVID-positive? We have to check her belly and touch her in a few ways for examination and delivery purposes. In the past we would sit for an hour or more with a mother, but we are tightening up that time frame.

The pandemic has brought a few positive changes including rates of breastfeeding and length of breastfeeding, mainly because the mother is forced to stay inside and so has more time to do it. And also, people's partners are working from home. So, lots of support. People are doing better as a result. Fewer women are struggling.

EK: **Are those things you can take into post COVID time?**

JD: Long term we are going to keep the virtual groups going where transportation or other issues mean they can't meet face to face. People have embraced postpartum virtual meetings. They love them.

EK: **Any surge in births during COVID?**

JD: Yes, definitely. We have a Mennonite population here and all the pandemic babies arrived at once.

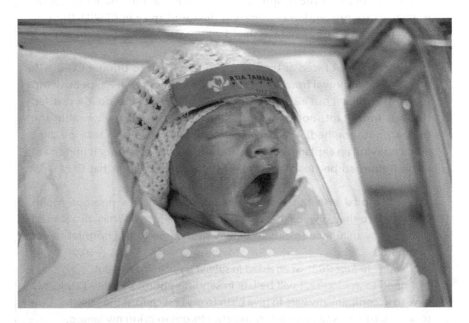

FIGURE 3.1 A newborn wears a face shield as protection against the coronavirus in Thailand.

Source: Yudha Baskoro

BOX 3.1 CORONA SHORT #5: INDONESIA MAS AGUNG WILLIS YUDHA BASKORO, A PHOTOGRAPHER IN JAKARTA, DESCRIBES HOW HE OBTAINED THE PHOTOGRAPH IN FIGURE 3.1 ABOVE

As a photojournalist, I just tried to read the situation on the field. I thought the pandemic has had an impact on the maternity process. To answer this question, I contacted Rumah Sakit Ibu dan Anak Tambak hospital (RSIA).

The hospital's Public Relations said that the management prepares a faceshield for every newborn. RSIA, a children's hospital in Menteng, Central Jakarta, has been putting on mini face shields on newborn babies to protect them from the coronavirus infection. The mini face shields are made by nurses at the hospital from thin plastic attached to a DIY headband made from soft foam rubber and an elastic.

Because the birthing process is a private matter, the hospital only gave me permission to take pictures of the newborn who was wearing a face shield.

A pediatrician at the hospital, Dr. Eveline P., said the mini face shield is a necessary precaution considering the rapid spike in COVID-19 cases all over the city. The mini face shield will protect the baby's respiratory tract.

The difficulty I faced at that time was that I had to bring a COVID-19 medical test approval from a laboratory. It wasn't only very expensive (up to 400 US dollars) but also rare because not every lab can do it. I realized this was important, not only for me but also for the baby's health -the baby I photographed. The baby's parents allowed me to take pictures after receiving an explanation from the hospital that this story is important to be published because it can make Indonesians aware that COVID-19 is real.

The hospital also put would-be mothers through a rigorous health check before they give birth at the hospital. The hospital has also started giving away mini face shields to babies who come to the hospital to get vaccinated.

Update 30 June 2021 when asked to submit a photo to this book:

I need to apologize. I will be late in sending photos because I suddenly have to accompany my wife to give birth to my first child at the hospital. Due to an emergency situation unfortunately, I forgot to bring my laptop.

As the COVID-19 cases is in spike at Central Java, I have to follow the hospital health protocol guidelines so I can't leave the hospital yet. I want to protect my wife and the baby too.

BOX 3.2 CORONA SHORT #6: COSTA RICA
STEVEN, A NURSE IN SAN JOSE, DESCRIBES
ACUTE SHORTAGES OF OXYGEN AND FENTANYL

(*Using Google translate for certain parts*) It is difficult to see the reaction of the family and patient. But the most difficult thing now is we are seeing very young people, some who don't have any risk. Then you see later that patient's case is very complicated so we must fight very hard to keep them alive.

Another thing that is very hard is when your patient dies. It is a different protocol. Before the pandemic when a patient died it was very hard for us but the patient could stay with their family members. Now, we use a plastic box to put them in. It feels really, really, really bad. It is not normal for us. We say it is like an animal.

Costa Rica has three levels of care: country clinics, medium clinics, and general hospitals. All the specialties are in the hospital here in San Jose. I'm a general nurse working in emergencies. I love emergencies with the pandemic because we can give fast treatment. But they have to be admitted to the hospitalized area to get more treatment.

We have a shortage of fentanyl. It is the most important medication with a machine because obviously the patient must be sleeping without pain. I think it is a world problem. We are a poor country so we don't have the same access to fentanyl like Canada or the United States. We are now using morphine. It is the biggest problem today.

Actually, we have two problems now, the pandemic and the economy too. They closed everything. People need to work. They need to eat. Now the government does not have resources to help everybody like they did at the beginning. They gave economic help. Now they don't have the money to help. They are trying to make some changes so people can go into the city. For example, I can go out with my car, but only Monday, Wednesday and Friday. And Sunday. The same every week. I have a special letter, a permit, to go to the hospital and drive back to my home. But my life since the pandemic is this: go to the hospital, come back to my home and do it all over again. People don't like this now.

The pandemic has been very hard for us. For the patients because it is new for us so we are not accustomed to that kind of patient. Secondly, our family and friends must make changes in our social life. In my case I had to find another thing to do because the pandemic can make you crazy. In my case I decided to make changes in my life. To make a gym in my house to distract me. Every day is the same, but I am living. My mom is here. And the hospital becomes like your second home. We try to keep things good with our co-workers. What else can we do? We are waiting for a normal life, but we don't know when. You must look to do something different. I painted my house. I was thinking of planting trees. I have three cats so I have something waiting for me when I come home.

At the beginning they closed all schools but then we had maybe three or four months we were doing well so they decided to open the schools again and the children were very happy. But now with this 3rd wave education has been closed completely. Not even virtual school. It is because here in Costa Rica some people have access to a computer but older students have a problem getting virtual.

Social life is nothing now. Now we are living the most difficult part of the pandemic. I was reading about Latin America. They say Costa Rica will be the first country of Latin America to finish the pandemic. I hope it is going to be like that. We are doing a good job with the vaccines. We are six million, not too many. We are poor so the government made us the 3rd country to have the vaccine beside Mexico and Chile. We are now giving vaccines to young people. Our vaccines come from the UK, I think. Our government had a conversation with Biden to give us some vaccines, so we are waiting for that.

Notes

1 Shu-Chen Liao, Yan-Shing Chang, and Li-Yin Chien, *The Maternity Response to COVID-19: An Example from One Maternity Unit in Taiwan*, Midwifery (2020), DOI: 10.1016/j.midw.2020.102756. The lead author works at Imperial College, London.

2 Keoni Everington, *3 Passengers from UK flight to Taiwan test positive for COVID*, Taiwan News (28 Dec. 2020), www.taiwannews.com.tw/en/news/4088482. "Out of the 793 officially confirmed cases, 698 were imported, 56 were local, 36 came from the Navy's "Goodwill Fleet" [and] two were from the cargo pilot cluster."

3 Heather Davidson, *How did Covid slip through Taiwan's 'gold standard' defences?*, The Guardian (17 May 2020), www.theguardian.com/world/2021/may/17/how-did-covid-slip-through-taiwans-gold-standard-defences?CMP=Share_iOSApp_Other.

4 With a population of 23.7 million, Taiwan has 32.88 confirmed cases per million and 0.29 deaths per million population as of 26 December 2020, according to Johns Hopkins University, which relies on data collected by the European Center for Disease Control and Prevention (ECDC). The website Our World in Data notes that comparisons of testing data across countries are affected by differences in the way the data are reported at https://ourworldindata.org/search?q=canada+covid+cases+per+million+population. *See further* Hannah Ritchie, Esteban Ortiz-Ospina, Max Roser, and Joe Hasell, *COVID-19 Deaths and Cases: How Do Sources Compare?*, Our World in Data (19 Mar. 2020), https://ourworldindata.org/covid-sources-comparison.

5 With a population of 37.7 million Canada has a total of 80.35 million confirmed cases (149 confirmed cases per million) and 390.7 deaths per million population as of 26 December 2020. As reported by Johns Hopkins University as of 26 December 2020 at https://ourworldindata.org/coronavirus/country/canada and https://ourworldindata.org/covid-sources-comparison.

6 This policy is now under review by government authorities since the announcement of new cases on 23 December 2020, according to Helen Davidson, *Taiwan imposes New regulations after first Covid case since April*, The Guardian, (23 Dec. 2020), www.theguardian.com/world/2020/dec/23/taiwan-imposes-new-regulations-after-first-covid-case-since-april.

7 Megan Ogilvie, *Ontario doctors, midwives welcome updated guidelines for women giving birth during pandemic*, The Star, (3 May 2020), www.thestar.com/news/gta/2020/05/03/ontario-doctors-midwives-welcome-updated-guidelines-for-women-giving-birth-

during-pandemic.html (accessed Dec. 30, 2020). As Dr. Mark Walker, co-chair of the provincial Maternal-Neonatal COVID-19 Task Force and chief of obstetrics, gynecology and newborn care at Ottawa Hospital, has commented, "In everything else we're trained to do we have evidence, textbooks and published articles. For the first time in our lives, we are facing a situation where the answers aren't always known."

8 *Id*, according to Dr. Jon Barrett, co-chair of the task force and head of maternal fetal medicine at Toronto's Sunnybrook Health Sciences Centre.

9 Munish Gupta, John A.F. Zupancic, and Dewayne M. Pursley, *Caring for Newborns Born to Mothers with COVID-19: More Questions Than Answers*, Pediatrics (Aug. 2020), https://pediatrics.aappublications.org/lens/pediatrics/146/2/e2020001842#content/contributor_reference_1. Numbers after countries indicate resources used by authors.

10 Michael Narvey et al., *Breastfeeding When Mothers Have Suspected or Proven COVID-19*, Can. Paed. Society (6 Apr. 2020), www.cps.ca/en/documents/position/breastfeeding-when-mothers-have-suspected-or-proven-covid-19.

11 C. Chambers et al., *Evaluation for SARS-CoV-2 in Breastmilk from 18 Infected Women*, 324:13 JAMA 1347–1348 (2020). *See contra*, K.F. Walker et al., *Maternal Transmission of SARS-COV-2 to the Neonate, and Possible Routes for Such Transmission: A Systematic Review and Critical Analysis*, 127:11 British J Obst. & Gyn. 1324–1336 (2020).

PART II
Leadership

4

DESIGNED FOR DISRUPTION

Fractured supply chains and politicized global trading

Stephen Wilks

Editors' introduction: As the pandemic spread across the globe and people became aware of the realities of lockdowns and other restrictions on normal movement, hordes rushed to stock up on toilet paper, pasta, hand sanitizer and other essentials. In a short space of time, we saw footage of supermarket shelves stripped bare and even arguments and physical jostling over who got the last available jumbo pack of toilet paper.

Was there merit to the perceived necessity to stock up on essentials? How reliable are our supply chains during a pandemic, where international flow of goods slows significantly, thereby impeding normal movement of goods? Is there good reason to be concerned about a country's capability to ensure supply within their borders of essential goods, including food?

As noted by this Chapter's author, Dr. Stephen Wilks, the issue of competing for goods is not restricted to private citizens. We have witnessed competition between governments across the globe and between governments and the private sector, over coveted medical equipment. As the author suggests, state power should labor to protect citizens or, at the very least, avoid undermining them.

As Associate Professor of Law at the University of Detroit Mercy, Dr. Wilks suggests the current state of international trade might well be the logical result of a globalized economy experiencing a mix of factors including competitive deregulation, falling trade barriers, and the strategic expansion of manufacturing footprints outside the developed world. He notes that supply chains require recalibration to improve their agility and resilience in a global marketplace where other structural problems have been afoot prior to COVID-19's arrival.

DOI: 10.4324/9781003215769-7

Introduction

Imagine that you are a wholesale purchaser of processing chips, with a longstanding relationship with three suppliers in Wuhan, China. Over a five-year period, you and your Chinese suppliers develop a recurring transaction: processing chips made in Wuhan are sent to a plant you own in Lincoln, Nebraska, where dozens of your workers are employed assembling video game consoles. You sell these consoles to a wide variety of video game enthusiasts on a wholesale and retail basis. Inexplicably, your orders stop and the contacts you normally reach out to when minor logistical issues arise are not answering emails, text messages, telephone calls or faxed letters. You are not in arrears on payments, and the seller offers no reason for the stoppage of orders. After reaching out to trade associations and other shared networks, you discover your Chinese suppliers have also stopped shipping goods to other US buyers without any explanation.

Several days later, you learn of a mysterious virus in Wuhan, but State censorship makes it impossible for people outside China to get any information about what is going on. Given China's dominance in the production of processing chips, locating suppliers in other countries proves impossible for various reasons. Alternative suppliers lack production capacity and cannot meet the sudden increase in demand from buyers now racing to reconfigure their supply chains. Downstream, unfilled orders from impatient customers are piling up – and the virus that has disrupted your suppliers has now entered your plant, forcing a complete shutdown of your operations. Anxious to protect your business, you begin to search for medical supplies and other equipment that might help your workers return to work. Your search quickly leads you to realize the global marketplace for such goods has become a kind of Wild West, where government and private buyers are competing for lifesaving equipment amid completely upended medical supply chains. Those shortages are personally noted in Box 4.1 and 4.2 (below) and in Box 12.1.

To unknowing observers, the early days of the COVID-19 pandemic must have created the impression that conflict between governments, or between governments and the private sector, over coveted medical equipment, were new to global supply chains already coping with other pandemic-related burdens. One disaster response expert described the scenario as "Lord of the Flies: PPE Edition."[1] These contests also seem at odds with Hobbesian social contract theories as normally expressed through state power. At a minimum, this power should work to protect citizens or, at the very least, avoid undermining them. After all, we are used to governments across the ideological spectrum demonstrating fealty to this principle during natural disasters, plane crashes, large-scale industrial accidents, or other events where societies anticipate a role for the state in bringing stability to disorder. But other features of the social contract have eroded in developed countries, particularly those centered around labor-management relations, which have coincided with the hardening of working-class attitudes toward migrant labor and internationalism more broadly.[2] The current state of international trade might well be the logical result of a globalized economy accelerating core features of this devolution, most notably through a mix of competitive deregulation, falling trade barriers, and the strategic expansion of manufacturing footprints outside the developed world. But it is just as plausible that supply chains require recalibration to improve their agility and resilience in a global marketplace where other structural problems have been afoot and which precede COVID-19's arrival.

The international trading system is a quintessentially politicized environment. Through the World Trade Organization (WTO) and other multi-lateral bodies, this global system produces a set of aspirational ideas designed to guide the behavior of parties involved in cross-border commerce. At a governmental level, involvement is inherently political insofar as countries inevitably argue over competing national interests while projecting power on the global stage. Both the structure and function of supply chains grow out of state priorities and relationships – the business, institutional, and policy environments that determine where, when, and how international production occurs.

COVID-19's entry into the world's supply chains

Fractures exposed by a pandemic

A "supply chain" is the shorthand phrase used to describe the processes and structures used to source, distribute, integrate, and transform raw materials into end products for sale in commercial or consumer markets. Now the subject of training and research across a wide variety of institutional settings, supply chains are complex, highly dynamic, and carefully coordinated to account for the wide range of potential disruptions that complicate domestic and international production. In a globalized economy, a broad range of events can disrupt supply chain management. In the normal course of business, supply chain participants rely on trade usage, case law, commercial agreements, and insurance policies to mitigate or allocate risks arising from natural disasters, piracy, or trade tariffs.

The global COVID-19 pandemic has produced immediate and severe effects on global trade. Governments have tried slowing the spread of the coronavirus by imposing social distancing measures, which range from strict lockdown measures to closing public spaces. These forced changes in human activity have ceased production and supply chain functions across most sectors, with some industries closing entirely. Dramatic changes to the consumer and commercial pathways connecting manufacturers, wholesalers, retailers, and buyers are now playing out alongside cut-throat competition for scarcely available PPEs, ventilators, and other medically relevant supplies. United States government agencies have infamously stood out among global competitors. At a national level, they have "poached" shipments bound for state and local buyers as part of their response to the health crisis.[3] This strategy has extended into international markets, where countries and civil society groups historically accustomed to American cooperation have been forced to compete with the United States for medical supplies.[4] Between seeing their supplies diverted en route from Chinese factories to American representatives outbidding them for goods on the open market, the fight over access to needed goods has strained international relations while diminishing prospects for the degree of cooperation historically required to fight global health crises.[5]

Private firms throughout the pharmaceutical, biotechnology, and healthcare supply sectors have struggled to meet demand for their products and services while trying to avoid unwanted political attention. Neither task has been easy. President Trump reportedly offered a private German lab $1 billion in exchange for exclusively American access to its vaccine research.[6] He also invoked powers under the Defense Production Act to compel multinational conglomerate The 3M Company ("3M") "to send to the United States [N95] masks made in factories overseas and to stop exporting masks the company manufactures in the United States."[7] This decision was especially controversial because it entailed using power to control a private actor's supply chain in ways that transcend prioritizing government orders over all others.[8] Such strategies also complicate relationships between suppliers and buyers, service providers providing logistical support, and the public-private relationships inside developing countries where much of our global supply chain input begins. The cumulative effect is to contaminate these relationships by undermining basic commitments to good faith and fair dealing normally conducive to market efficiency.

This intense clamoring for limited medical supplies has eclipsed preexisting contract-based commitments in a global market where highly coveted medical supplies are now sold to buyers showing up at manufacturing sites with suitcases full of cash.[9] Public officials have also taken extraordinary lengths to covertly transport and guard medical supplies in an effort to keep them from falling into the hands of US federal agencies. Illinois Governor Jay Pritzker secretly orchestrated a supply flight carrying medical supplies directly from China.[10] After arranging a similarly clandestine flight carrying 500,000 test kits from South Korea, Maryland Governor Larry Hogan deployed the National Guard to a secret location to prevent anyone – including the federal government – from taking them.[11] When officials in Massachusetts had their order of three million masks confiscated by the US government in the Port of New York, New England Patriots' owner Robert Kraft used the team's plane to locate and ship a million masks from China.[12] Hospital systems in Florida, California, Washington, Oregon, and Alaska have also reported federal government seizure of their medical supplies.[13]

Politicization from government, the private sector, civil society, and soft law mechanisms

Politicized conflicts have long been among the many pressures brought to bear on global trade and on the movement goods in particular. In this regard, current COVID-19-related tensions over medical supplies join disputes centering on national security, tariffs, human rights, environmentalism, fair trade, and other considerations intersecting arrangements designed to choreograph the global movement of goods. Studying these arrangements offers insights into partici- pant motives and priorities in any given moment – especially governments that insert themselves into global commerce often to wield power over contested issues, protect national interests, or otherwise influence behavior in a manner that accords with important priorities.

As a starting point, cost and quality will often dominate decisions about where businesses source materials, labor, and transportation arrangements in a global- ized marketplace.[14] To meet these needs, Western manufacturing has primarily relied on China, which has emerged to become a dominant supply chain actor.[15] But the complexities are more than a matter of geography, given the dizzying variety of raw or intermediate goods moving through a fragmented produc- tion process – disbursing and sequencing tasks locally, regionally, or around the world. These features function less like a "chain" – which connotes linearity – and more like a "spider," pulling together inputs from multiple directions as part of a carefully choreographed exercise that culminates in final assembly.

A large body of cross disciplinary scholarship has evolved alongside the glo- balized supply chain, some of it criticizing its animating motivations – a quest for low-cost production – and the resulting effects. These writings offer up impor- tant insights into the behaviors that develop between buyers and sellers, such as: the treatment of human labor, particularly in regards to women and human trafficking,[16] consideration of environmental standards;[17] geopolitics;[18] agricul- tural sustainability;[19] conflict minerals;[20] conscious consumerism in developed countries;[21] corporate social responsibility;[22] and developing country control over economic development more broadly.[23] These writings reveal the extent to which supply chain practices function as incidents of globalization while attracting responses from government, the private sector, civil society, and trans- national institutions. They also help to account for the wide sweep of formal, voluntary, transnational, and consumer-driven practices penetrating all phases of the supply chain. Domestic regulation, voluntary participation in certification regimes, civil society engagement, human rights controversies, and consumer demand have all played a role.

Global trade's structural and social effects in the wake of China's economic ascent

An end to thirty years of expansion

Prior to the pandemic, global trade faced a confluence of disruptive forces originating from three arenas of activity: technological disruption, shrinking commitments to trade liberalization, and a revising of cost calculations shap- ing international production. Global trade increased fivefold in the two decades between 1990 and 2010, with much of this activity producing considerable supply chain movement among multinational firm (MNF) affiliates or through processes MNFs otherwise controlled.[24] Although investment in cross-border production slowed significantly in the wake of the 2008 global financial crisis, degrees of country interdependence remained in place.[25] This was evident in the increased input of intermediate goods, particularly in China, which remained a key global supply chain actor.[26] While Western MNFs turned to contracting out production as an alternative to direct foreign investment, they used private ordering to retain control over operations while maintaining a presence in overseas markets.[27]

The advent of "asset-light" firms (ALF) complemented these developments. ALFs use a mix of human and technological assets to control outsourced production. Apple Inc.'s experience in the 1990s offers an instructive example of how this strategy extends through its supply and retail chains to control and harmonize participant behavior.[28] Then Chief Operating Officer Tim Cook outsourced most production, reduced inventory, and embedded its engineers at supplier locations during intensified production periods.[29] Apple stores use similar strategies to push retail standards throughout its network of third-party retailers,[30] and through control of its App Store.[31] Apple's asset-light approach to its operations illustrates the potential to reshape supply chains by changing where products are designed, manufactured, and assembled.[32] This approach is one of the ways technology has helped MNFs transform their supply chains into highly sophisticated production networks – expanding their global footprint in the process.[33] Artificial intelligence (AI), algorithms, blockchain, smart contracts, and other disruptive innovations will impact demand for human labor while raising questions about resulting social dislocation among those working in sectors awaiting massive structural change.[34]

Structural changes have also produced shifts in sentiments that have historically underpinned liberal democracies, which are under pressure. This is most apparent in changes to the way government, civil society, and the private sector position themselves in response to globalization's social effects. Americans have experienced these trends, most significantly in the declining fortunes of workers across America's industrial heartland and in the corresponding deterioration of their communities due to shrinking tax bases.[35] Growing wealth gaps and the social cleaving along the lines of education – particularly among white, middle-aged men – are producing attitudinal changes within electorates that are increasingly receptive to political strategies that openly court affinity for racism, xenophobia, and a hardening of attitudes toward legal and illegal immigration.[36] To varying degrees, some Western governments have exploited the shifting socio-economic zeitgeist by expressing interventionist sentiment on the international stage. A mix of national policies, protectionist rhetoric, disengagement from multi-lateral agreements, politicized trade disputes, and the equivocating of commitment to existing multi-lateral trade relationships have all been noticeable features of this declining faith in trade liberalization.[37]

The spirit of interventionism was already starting to have impacts on the number of major cross-border mergers and acquisitions (M&A) before the pandemic's arrival. These transactions are relevant to supply chain discourse in at least three respects. First, businesses can disburse their operations across a network of subsidiaries to exploit respective benefits available in different jurisdictions.[38] Such strategies have important supply chain implications in manufacturing, logistics, or sectors governments consider strategically significant, all of which are determinants of planning where goods are designed, assembled, and shipped. Second, broadening governmental interest in M&A transactions reveals new ways in which politics, national security concerns,[39] and geopolitical maneuvering now find their expression in the denial of regulatory approvals – especially from developed country regulators.[40] Third, national regulators will influence both their foreign counterparts[41] and private actors in strategically important industries.[42]

In 2018 alone, 22 proposed transactions representing a value of $50 million or more were withdrawn for regulatory or political reasons – double the 2017 figures.[43] In 2019, 13 major cross-border M&A transactions exceeding values of $100 million failed to close – three for national security reasons and another three on anti-trust grounds.[44] In most instances, regulators objecting to these transactions were in developed country jurisdictions.[45] Western regulators were, and remain, prepared to oppose deals they believe involve foreign powers working through state-owned firms to acquire strategically important Western assets or otherwise increase their market share in key industries. This is evident insofar as a proposed deal's subject matter, the industry involved, and the transacting parties' beneficial owners combine to figure prominently in American regulatory objections. The most scrutinized transactions have been in financial services, high-tech manufacturing, digital mapping services, telecommunications, and security services.[46]

Responses to China's rise

Between 2009 and 2016, Chinese firms executed 2715 cross-border M&A transactions, up from 1250 such deals in the period between 1990 and 2008.[47] Estimates of China's outbound foreign investment in the United States were $1.1 billion in 2011, jumping more than 800% to $10.3 billion in 2016.[48] These figures inform part of the concern about China's role in sponsoring state-controlled firms in the global marketplace, which have figured prominently in US regulatory posturing – much of which is playing out against the backdrop of wider geopolitical tensions that continue to strain Sino-American relations.[49]

China's decades-long trajectory of economic expansion has fueled some of these tensions – along with shifting approaches to trade in both public and private arenas.[50] China's Gross Domestic Product has grown steadily since the late 1970s when Den Xiaoping embarked on a series of ambitious reforms to open up his country's economy.[51] This strategy included re-establishing participation in the General Agreement on Tariffs and Trade (GATT) more than thirty years after the Communist Revolution prompted its 1948 withdrawal from the multilateral treaty;[52] negotiating investment treaties with 37 GATT/ WTO countries over a 15-year period ending in 1999;[53] and becoming a full member of the WTO in 2001.[54] China's accession to the WTO transpired at a time when it was experiencing growth and pivoting toward producing the kinds of commercial inputs that allowed Chinese firms to compete with their American counterparts.

America's response to a global trade challenger and the inconsistent approach to WTO compliance

On their face, bilateral commitments made during these negotiated processes seemed promising. China's entry into the WTO required undertakings to open its market, improve protections for intellectual property, adopt a most-favored-nation (MFN) protocol that would end differential treatment it extended to developing countries,[55] and agree to an extensive list of terms under accession protocols.[56] Just over a year before China's accession to the WTO, the United States enacted Section 421 of the Trade Act of 1974 (Trade Act).[57] This provision mimicked language in Section 406 of the Trade Act designed to target imports from "Communist countries" and to prevent them from disrupting US markets.[58] Section 406 owes its origins to Section 201 of the Trade Act, under which the President might impose import controls or take other action where the US International Trade Commission (ITC) determines certain imported goods are a "substantial cause of serious injury, or threat" to a domestic industry producing similar or competitive products.[59] Section 421 codified terms timed to coincide with China's entry into the WTO and created presidential authority to grant MFN tariff treatment once accession was complete.[60] Taken together, these domestic and international provisions were expected to have liberalizing effects on China's economy by putting it on a path to toward better integration with Western markets.

Expectations that China's government would eventually abide by the spirit of WTO rules did not materialize. While China did lower tariffs and eliminate import quotas, it embarked on a program of state intervention that included manipulating its currency,[61] exerting influence over the governance and operation of heavily subsidized state-owned entities,[62] and resorting to a range of rent-seeking behaviors – such as requiring foreign firms to handover technical expertise and intellectual property as a condition of entering its markets.[63] Additionally, there were forty-four WTO complaints against China between 2006 and 2015.[64] During the same period, complaints between the United States, Japan, and Europe declined considerably.[65]

It is inconceivable that parties negotiating China's WTO accession anticipated the extent to which it blurred the lines separating state-financed commerce and fully free enterprise – both inside China itself and beyond its borders. Organized in 2003, China's state-owned Assets Supervision and Administration

Commission of the State Council (SASAC), assumed control over government shares in 196 of the largest state-owned entities.[66] This level of ownership gives the SASAC control over more than 50% of the Chinese companies on the Fortune Global 500's list of the world's biggest corporations – some of which have shares traded on major stock exchanges.[67] The Chinese government works through SASAC and its share ownership to control private firm management composition and shape business judgment.[68] The resulting structures constitute what Curtis J. Milhaupt and Li-Wen Lin have called a "networked hierarchy," consisting of corporations, banking institutions, and universities operating beneath the SASAC.[69] They have also coined the phrase "institutional bridging" to capture how the SASAC horizontally links entities around issues of mutual interest.[70] This organizational strategy has produced important structural and functional outcomes:

> These mechanisms create networks among businesses and other organs of the party-state, promote information flow, and provide high-powered incentives to actors in the system by linking corporate performance and political advancement. Together, these features can be thought of as means to assemble what Mancur Olson called an "encompassing organization" – a coalition whose members "own so much of the society that they have an important incentive to be actively concerned about how productive it is.[71]

In addition to forming SASAC, Chinese officials have also established the National Development and Reform Commission (NDRC) – a modernized iteration of the Mao-era's State Planning Commission (SPC).[72] Tasked with carrying out China's five-year plan, the NDRC controls the pricing of commodities, including oil, water, natural gas, and electricity – all of which serve to impact production costs.[73] The NDRC is also the ultimate approval authority for investment and infrastructure projects for state and private applicants.

While state-owned entities and economic planning are not unique to China, it stands alone in the way it has used such entities to exercise unusual degrees of control over its market and actors within it. In addition to the SASAC and NDRC, the Chinese Communist Party (CCP) has found other ways to insert itself into China's economic life. It requires entities with three or more CCP members to have Party committees. While the internal affairs of these committees are unclear, they have been known to wield considerable power over the corporate governance of firms – either locally or in response to the CCP's central authorities. In 2013, for example, the CCP made an overnight decision to change the leadership at three of China's major telecommunications firms, all of which were publicly traded companies.[74]

Capturing the extent of state-driven influence over its economy demands recognizing where it has left room for free enterprise. In 2017, for example, the Federal Reserve Bank of New York published a study in which it concluded Chinese industries where there were significant input tariff reductions experienced the largest increase in exports.[75] Tariff reductions lowered production costs, making Chinese manufacturers more competitive.[76] Major infrastructure projects such as highways and shipping ports reduced delivery times.[77] The resulting period of remarkable growth reveals the extent to which disentangling state and private interests in China remains difficult.

Against the backdrop of these developments, American politicians and trade diplomats were inconsistent in holding China to its commitments. George W. Bush, the first American president to contend with China as a WTO member, repeatedly rejected ITC recommendations when US businesses brought Section 421 complaints challenging Chinese trade practices. The rationale for these rejections – which occurred twice in 2003,[78] once in 2004,[79] and again in 2005[80] – was that the President needed to consider the effect these decisions had on the entire economy rather than the complaining party's particular industry.[81]

Although United States Trade Representative (USTR) delegates appeared willing to bring complaints directly to the WTO, their efforts also produced mixed results. There were seven Bush-era complaints before the WTO between 2004 and 2008.[82] Both Bush and the private sector were more inclined to encourage informal dialogue and dispute settlements rather than pursue full-blown litigation,[83] reflecting a decidedly political approach:

> Bush's advisors . . . worried that if one industry got protection under the safeguard, virtually every U.S. manufacturer competing with Chinese imports would be clamoring for similar treatment. That would put the entire U.S.–China trade relationship at risk, and U.S. multinationals – which were reaping big profits in the Chinese market – lobbied heavily to avoid any major disruptions.[84]

Bush institutionalized his strategy of preferring high-level talks instead of adjudication by creating the Senior Dialogue and the Strategic Economic Dialogue as forums for discussing issues of mutual interest in the United States–China relationship.[85] This project became less of a priority with the onset of the 2008 financial crisis, effectively creating more strategic opportunities for China.[86] Chinese trade practices continued to trigger complaints from the United States. As of 2020, the USTR has initiated nearly two dozen complaints against China at the WTO – fourteen during President Obama's two terms in office.[87] Despite prevailing in most of these actions, the USTR maintains that China continues to disregard WTO panel or appellate rulings.[88] The USTR has also alleged that China abuses WTO remedies, such as antidumping and countervailing duty investigations, as a strategy to dissuading WTO countries from exercising rights under existing rules.[89]

By the end of Bush's presidency, America's legacy of half-hearted, or insufficient, efforts to confront China's noncompliance exposed complex interdependencies. Americans enjoyed cheap consumer goods and billions flowed back to China, where millions were able to escape poverty. Chinese reinvestment in capital markets around the world included buying US Treasury Bonds as well as investing in Fannie Mae and Freddie Mac (which helped Americans access afford-able mortgages). Neither country in the US–China relationship wanted a trade war that would put supply chains at risk. But the parties pursued different paths with the onset of the 2008 recession, which ravaged major Western markets and altered perceptions of Western capitalism in China. In contrast to governments that struggled to address the financial crisis, China worked through the NDRC to issue a $586 billion stimulus, which was directed to various domestic projects in areas such as education and healthcare.[90] China's central bank also stepped in, cutting interest rates and requiring that banks generously extend credit to their state and private clients.[91] Both of these activities were fundamentally at odds with China's WTO commitments.

The Obama administration tried neutering China's regional and global influ-ence through the Trans-Pacific Partnership (TPP). Signed on 5 February 2016, the ill-fated TPP marked an attempt to design a trade system that would require China to accept new trading terms and submit to additional demands as a condi-tion of congressional ratification.[92] Obama deliberately excluded China from the rulemaking process while making it the TPP's primary target.[93] TPP negotia-tions gave signatory states better trade privileges than those available to WTO members. The Obama administration also crafted the TPP's rules in an effort to address WTO member grievances, most of which revolved around the view that China had used its WTO membership to access foreign markets without honoring rules – particularly the presence of trade barriers, the ongoing subsidy of state-owned enterprises, and the violation of intellectual property rights.[94]

The timing of Obama's efforts was such that they could not outpace the rising disaffection prompted by massive job losses, community erosion, and the percep-tion that governments had failed to protect their interests in the global trading system that seemed especially cruel to working-class communities in the United States and throughout the developed world. The result has been the growing allure of politicized nationalism mixed with attitudes about the market that dif-fer among 80s-era conservative moments. David Frum put it this way:

> The rise of these nationalist parties is forcing a rearrangement of the politi-cal grammar of the developed world. The conservative parties of the 1980s defended markets and were skeptical of economic redistribution. The nationalist movements of the 2010s are skeptical of markets and defend economic redistribution, provided that the redistribution benefits people of the correct ethnic stock and cultural outlook.[95]

These class-based frustrations were the seedbed for Donald Trump's successful presidential campaign, which tapped into grievances about feeling left behind in the global economy. Trump's supporters were reassured by promises to be tough with China. He made good on his promise a day after his inauguration by issuing a Presidential Memorandum announcing the United States' withdrawal from the

TPP on 23 January 2017.[96] In August of the same year, the Trump administration commenced an investigation into China's trade practices under Section 301 of the Trade Act.[97] Sections 301 through 310 are often collectively described as "Section 301." These provisions authorize the imposition of trade sanctions on countries that violate trade agreements with the United States or that resort to conduct deemed an "unjustifiable" or "unreasonable" burden on American commerce. Before the advent of the WTOs resolution dispute mechanism, the United States used Section 301 to pressure countries to lower barriers and open their markets.[98] The decision to use this statute, rather than initiate another WTO complaint, signaled a turning point in America's relationship with the WTO and fits within a pattern of disengagement from multi-lateral processes that has been a defining feature of Trump's presidency.[99]

After a seven-month investigation, the USTR made several key findings in a lengthy report focusing on China's unmet commitments to change its technology transfer strategies.[100] These commitments included refraining from conditioning market access on technology transfer, agreeing not to insert technology transfer decisions into negotiations with foreign businesses, and undertaking not to work through regulatory or administrative mechanisms designed to compel disclosure of trade secrets.[101] Among the report's finding, four areas of interest stand out as relevant to the present discussion: (i) the Chinese government works through foreign ownership restrictions to require or pressure the transfer of technology from US companies to Chinese entities;[102] (ii) China uses technology regulations to interfere with American firms' freedom to bargain for terms of technology transfer without Chinese government intrusion;[103] (iii) China has heavily invested in Chinese entities as part of a large-scale outbound direct foreign investment strategy to acquire or invest in US firms in an effort to expand its market share and to secure technology assets – especially in Europe and the United States;[104] and (iv) China has resorted to industrial espionage through a program of cyber intrusions into American commercial networks. This activity aims to access trade secrets, sensitive internal communications, and other forms of business information.[105] Two examples below, one brief and another more detailed, outline the effect of the challenged conduct on practices inside China and in operations beyond its borders.

Two case studies and their lessons about rent-seeking power's effect on compliance demands

Gamesa's foray into China's wind farm industry

The experience of the Spanish firm Grupo Auxiliar Metalúrgico (Gamesa) demonstrates how the NDRC operates to extract foreign technological expertise, configure production practices in favor domestic firms, and ultimately influence the footprint of foreign firms in any given market in relative terms. Founded in 1976 as a machine-making company, Gamesa pivoted toward wind turbine production in 1994. By 2010 it was the third-largest wind turbine maker in the world.[106] Gamesa owed part of its success to sales in China when its government developed an interest in clean energy and eventually captured 35% of the Chinese market by 2005.[107] Bidding on state-run wind farms gradually increased domestic production quotas – the proportion of turbine equipment that had to be produced in China.[108] That same year, the NDRC formally set that quota at 70%.[109] Anxious to cash in on a growing Chinese market, foreign firms obliged. They built factories, hired local workers, and built relationships with domestic suppliers by showing them how to build components needed for production. With access to cheap, municipally supplied land and low-interest, government-backed loans, Chinese firms eventually acquired 85% of China's market. Gamesa's share fell to 3%.[110] Whether or not these events form the basis of WTO complaints, China gambled on the assumption that foreign firms were unlikely to complain because their profits were still increasing given the size of China's market.[111]

Trade and security concerns arising from Huawei's global dominance of 5G installations

Founded in 1987 by Ren Zhengfi, Huawei Technologies Co., Ltd. (Huawei) is China's largest telecommunications manufacturer and has surpassed Apple to become the world's second largest smartphone maker as of 2017.[112] In addition to pursuing partnerships throughout Asia and Europe, Huawei is emerging as one of the world leaders in 5G deployment.[113] The company's global operations employ 194,000 employees in more than 170 countries.[114] In 2019, the telecom giant's revenues reached US$123 billion, 15% of which was devoted to research and development carried about by almost half of all employees.[115] It also held more than 85,000 patents worldwide as of December 2019 – most of which were issued from countries outside of China.[116] Huawei uses this vast network of human and technical assets to provide a range of services and products. Its clients include 35 carriers, more than 700 municipalities, and over 200 Fortune Global Fortune 500 companies.[117] Huawei has also played a role in helping to develop technical standards for 5G networks.[118]

The scale and nature of Huawei's operations have attracted national security concerns, not least of all because of the company's relationship to branches of the Chinese government. Modern communications networks have evolved to become a vital common good and a critical feature of our modern economy. But these networks that connect us, support commercial activity, and transmit private information carry out these functions using features that make them vulnerable to misuse.[119] With the arrival of 5G networks, telecommunications networks will increase in speed and responsiveness.[120] National security concerns arise from the risk that these networks are designed with technological features enabling surveillance, fraud, theft of information, or other forms of commercial or military espionage.[121]

National security fears as they pertain to Huawei's operations are well-founded. The history of Huawei's leadership and its ties to the Chinese military have worried US officials, given its business activities outside China. Huawei's founder was a member of the People's Liberation Army and remains a member of the CCP. Huawei's current rotating Chairman of the Board is also a CCP member. US lawmakers awoke to Huawei's possible security risks after the release of a 2012 House Intelligence Committee Report detailing how its hardware and software applications could support a wide range of industrial and military spying.[122] FBI Director Christopher Wray reiterated these concerns at a 2018 Senate Intelligence Committee Hearing, pointing out that Huawei might use its infrastructure to collect intelligence on the United States at the Chinese government's behest.[123]

Actions against Huawei quickly escalated. In August 2018, Congress passed a law banning Huawei from participating in contracts with any agency of the U.S federal government.[124] Over the next two years, US officials stepped up pressure on Huawei by discouraging use of the company's handsets and by pressuring other countries to exclude it from 5G projects.[125] These efforts produced mixed results. So far, Australia, New Zealand, and the UK have adopted the American position, while Canada is also under pressure to do so.[126] Countries in Europe and elsewhere were not so keen to follow suit.[127]

American posture toward Huawei hardened into a mix of criminal prosecution and coercive international pressure when Meng Wanzhou – Huawei's Chief Financial Officer and the daughter of its founder – was arrested at Vancouver International Airport on 1 December 2018, following an extradition request by the United States.[128] According to the request's underlying allegations, Meng made a series of false statements to HSBC in 2013, effectively understating the extent of Huawei's relationship with Skycom Tech. Co. Ltd. (Skycom), a company based in Iran, and the ongoing nature of their relationship.[129] These misrepresentations facilitated the execution of a $1.5 billion syndicated loan orchestrated by HSBC and the clearance of dollar transactions by its US subsidiaries over a ten-year period.[130] Some of these transfers led to transactions between Huawei entities and Skycom, causing HSBC to violate The International Emergency Economic Powers Act.[131] Between 2010 and 2014, US financial institutions cleared more than $100 million worth of Skycom-related transfers.[132]

Meng's arrest put Canada in a difficult position, given its treaty obligations to the United States and China's demands to release Meng.[133] Months of pressure ensued, including the arrest of two Canadians by Chinese police, the blocking of Canadian imports to China, and Beijing's denial of entry visas for trade delegates trying to negotiate an end to the conflict.[134] Despite these problems, US officials remained unbowed. On 28 January 2019, the Department of Justice unsealed a thirteen-count indictment against Meng, Huawei, and its affiliates.[135] The press release was telling insofar as it connected criminal law concerns to unaddressed trade grievances:

> "These charges lay bare Huawei's blatant disregard for the laws of our country and standard global business practices," stated FBI Director Wray.

"Companies like Huawei pose a dual threat to both our economic and national security, and the magnitude of these charges make clear just how seriously the FBI takes this threat. Today should serve as a warning that we will not tolerate businesses that violate our laws, obstruct justice, or jeopardize national and economic well-being."[136]

At the time of this writing, the extradition proceedings continue, but US pressure on Huawei has continued – most recently in the form of decisions to block outbound shipments of semiconductor chips bound for Huawei-affiliated facilities.[137] In addition to being frozen out of federal contracts, the Federal Communications Commission (FCC) has also made Huawei a named entity – effectively banning the company from participating in contracts funded by the Universal Service Fund, a federal program created to subsidize access to telecommunications infrastructure across the United States.[138]

US tariffs between the United States and China, which began in 2018, would ratchet up over the summer of 2019 in a series of tit-for-tat retaliatory measures, undoubtedly destroying supply chain relationships that took years to develop.[139] A surge in imports from Canada, Mexico, and other countries diminished any expectation that imposing tariffs on Chinese goods would somehow repatriate American jobs lost during the preceding thirty years.[140]

Conclusion: how unsavory bargains in government and the private sector helped create the current crisis

Before and after China's entry into the WTO, its use of state power to suppress dissent and limit personal autonomy garnered little concern to international business until it was systematically deployed to exert control over the marketplace.[141] But the combined effects of being a one-party system presiding over a population of 1.4 billion people have endowed China with a labor force to support massive, government-sponsored outputs and a growing consumer base with immense buying power. This is a potent combination in a global economy where China enjoys the kind of rent-seeking power to incentivize Faustian bargains that undermine WTO compliance. The willingness to strike these bargains has shaped government and private business behavior. While economic incentives made US MNFs anxious to avoid full-blown trade disputes with China, American trade diplomats feared a wave of Section 421 challenges would put pressure on the federal government to re-establish tariffs and hinder the cross-border flow of goods.[142] Private businesses operating inside of China could still expect to reap major profits despite being forced to surrender their intellectual property, technological know-how, and much of their share of the Chinese market.

Beyond the size of China's labor pool and consumer markets, reluctance to enforce trade rules on a more regular basis, is consistent with the desire to protect supply chain structures.[143] Trump's trade war with China exposed how little time it took to undermine years of effort put into developing relationships needed to support international production.[144] But the COVID-19 pandemic has exposed the legacy of competing economic interests and varied commitments to international trade rules and has produced larger structural failures.[145] Thanks to many of the Chinese trade practices describe above, China now dominates the world's market for PPEs.[146] This dominance grew out of generous Chinese state subsidies, requirements that China's hospitals buy domestically made medical supplies, and the CCP working with Sinopec to build facilities for producing the special fabric used in masks and respirators.[147] Meanwhile, American firms have pursued an entirely different calculus, operating on the basis that demand for PPEs will not last long enough to justify retooling their factories.[148] Yet each of these positions results from decades of choices that now leave the country that mobilized so impressively during prior national crises – including years of wartime activity – unable to produce enough seventy-five cent masks to protect its own citizens.[149]

Recommendations for law reform

Although the global supply chain system was designed for disruption long before the pandemic's arrival, perhaps it is time to leverage aspects of this fragility. International trade has reached a point in its evolution where warnings appear whenever the mobility of goods, people, and capital deviate from well-established patterns of activity. This capacity to monitor trade practices – be they grounded in colorable claims of concern for trade compliance or in contests for the balance of global power – evinces the pathways that complement existing forms of trade-based scrutiny. Such complementary forms of surveillance already exist, such as the kind carried out by the US military's National Center for Medical Intelligence (NCMI). In the fall of 2019, NCMI issued an internal report warning that an unknown virus was sweeping through the Wuhan region.[150] The report's precise date of authorship is unclear, but its release came sometime between November 2019 and January 2020.[151] The result of covert surveillance, the NCMI report described wholesale changes to life patterns and business activity in the Wuhan region.[152] This surveillance took place around the time a 55-year-old patient from Hubei was being treated for what would later become known as the first recorded case of COVID-19.[153]

The wholesale purchaser mentioned at the opening of this chapter is a critical actor in the trade surveillance paradigm. His position within a broken supply chain raises several important questions for future policy planners: With whom should he share information about his disrupted business operations? When should he share it? Does his industry association have a role in this information sharing? Who should be tasked with collecting this data? Assuming data collection should exist at the interface between government, the private sector, and civil society, when do public health experts enter such information exchanges? Be they formal or informal, reporting systems designed around capturing critical information would help buy valuable time to prepare when, not if, signs of the next pandemic appear on the horizon.

BOX 4.1 CORONA SHORT #7: DENMARK
CHRISTINE, ON WORK LEAVE IN ODENSE
WHEN COVID FIRST EMERGED, SPEAKS OF
HOARDING BEHAVIOR

Q: You were living in Denmark when COVID first emerged?

A: Yes. I went over because my husband was doing a post-doc there. I was going to spend a fun year traveling and living a fun life but eventually it fell apart because I couldn't travel anywhere. He was applying to all these academic conferences and I was planning our travels around those. We went to a lot of great places like Lisbon in 2020 and before we left my parents called and said "Are you sure you want to go? There's this COVID thing, you know." And I said, "You're just retired and you are watching too much TV – we'll be fine."

By the time we got back from Lisbon we were thinking, "No, this is very serious."

Q: It was not being taken seriously in Portugal?

A: Not then. When I was coming back to Denmark I saw one person wearing a mask in the airport and I thought, "This silly person, there's no need to wear a mask."

And that night I went to a 200-person concert and everything seemed fine. Within two weeks of that I thought, "Oh no, this *is* serious," and by 10 March they did their first lock down.

Q: You had to recalibrate quickly because I read that when Denmark announced they were shutting down, teachers and other groups actually started the lockdown four days early.

A: Yes, but it was a stressful time. My Danish was not good enough to watch TV and understand the news. There was a lot of panic buying – really intense. For months yeast was extremely difficult to find. In the supermarkets if they ran out of something there would be a posted sign telling people not to worry, there would be more tomorrow with a little "we're all in this together" comment to discourage hoarding.

There was also a practice put into place in most stores where your first item, such as hand sanitizer or toilet paper, sold for one amount, but your second and beyond was much more expensive, sometimes like $100 more, to discourage people from buying more than they needed.

I also saw this sign from time to time which (I think) is a war-time reference to hoarding: "Hamsters, shame on you." The Danes love wordplay and their word for hamster and hoard is similar.

And then everybody was talking about what a great job Denmark was doing and it felt like we were in control. But later in November the minks with COVID were culled [Denmark has the largest mink farming industry in the world]. Public opinion went to "Oh, no," we are not doing well at all.

Q: Did that unnerve you?

A: The minks made me think, "This is not going well." That and the news from back home in Canada. The thing about Denmark that's different is that people really trust the government. And follow the rules. So if the government says, "Just stand 6 feet apart and we're going to shut you down," I would think, "OK, Denmark will take care of me." Unlike my parents who were suggesting I get a hazmat suit to go to the drug store. Even the mink culling caught me off guard. But the Danes would be thinking, "Well, they are doing this to protect us." Danes are such a monoculture and have a strong sense of what being Danish means. They have this Scandinavian exceptionalism, like "We're Danish and we're doing it better than everywhere else."

BOX 4.2 CORONA SHORT #8: INDIA
A MEDICAL RESIDENT STRUGGLES WITH
FRONT LINE CARE PRESSURES IN THE STATE
OF TAMIL NADU

I'm in my first year of a two-year medical residency at a private hospital in India. I plan to specialize in internal medicine but I've been transferred to the front line for COVID patients as the numbers have reached crisis proportions in my country.

Our course has changed dramatically to critical care at this time. We are now manning the emergency wards due to a second wave. We really feel we are missing out on the learning we were supposed to do this year, although we understand the emergency situation. The pandemic has changed everything: the residents from last year had their exams postponed and they had to work for longer to qualify. I am just not sure how it will affect my residency.

I had a patient arrive with symptoms with COVID the other day. He was very far from where he lived. The government has set up a system for patients to check on their phones to see which hospitals in their area would be best to go to. But lower-income patients don't always have phones or don't know how to download that information. So the people it's meant to help are not getting access to the information they need.

In this state the government has socialized medicine. Anyone can get treatment. The difference is in the quality of care. We started off vaccination for healthcare workers. Everybody was to get the vaccine but not everybody I work with is getting it, for various reasons. In the hospital, all patients above 60 got it but now we are not able to get enough for those younger. The vaccine comes from the government so they work out the distribution. But we don't have AstraZeneca or Covishield at this time, nor Covax or Covaxin (Indian made) either. Covishield is both made here and imported.

I have lived in the same room and gone to the same hospital for the past three years. It's a hostel with shared bedrooms and facilities. You are living in close quarters. You cannot wear a mask in the showers. If someone gets sick, they go elsewhere so they won't infect the rest of us. There are hundreds of people living in this building so there's no way to avoid it. But in the second wave it has become more personal. I remember saying to my friends "It's going to get personal," meaning it was not just a disease we are treating in others. Nobody can be sure if there will be an ICU bed for themselves. It feels very personal and scary right now. At this time people around me are getting sick in other departments.

Our hospital has had an instance of critical oxygen shortage. One day we were going to lose our oxygen supply to the ICUs by the end of the day. It felt unreal because we had never thought it would happen to us, with our region manufacturing most of the medical oxygen for the country. We had to be terribly conservative with oxygen, sometimes contrary to what would be best for the individual patient's recovery. There was an 18-year-old boy who was being given oxygen from one cylinder after another in the government hospital till they all ran out and then he ended up with us. He made it to the ICU – it was a close call and it showed that we were not prepared to deal with this sort of disease burden. I have seen multiple patients come to the ER very sick because they ran out of oxygen in the ambulances on the way to the hospital.

For most patients older than 60, severe COVID is practically a death sentence. They might or might not get beds, and they certainly are unlikely to get ICU care if they need it. Preference is given to younger patients. But there is still the aftermath – invasive fungal infections of the sinuses – to deal with. The situation is infuriating because so many of these deaths and this injury was avoidable – and we still don't have close to adequate vaccine coverage. The only good thing I can see coming out of this is that governments or their voters in developing countries finally realize that they need to properly invest in healthcare.

Notes

1 Nahal Toosi, *"Lord of the Flies: PPE Edition": U.S. Cast as Culprit in Global Scrum Over Coronavirus Supplies*, Politico (3 Apr. 2020).
2 James F. Hollifield, *Migration, Trade, and the Nation-State: The Myth of Globalization*, 3 UCLA J. Int'l L. & Foreign Aff. 595, 597, 623 (1998).
3 Nathaniel Cline, *Feds Intercept a Loudoun County-Bound Order of PPE*, Loudoun Times–Mirror (7 May 2020); Marianne Goodland, *Gov. Jared Polis: FEMA Took Our Ventilators Out from Under Us*, Colorado Politics (4 April 2020).
4 Toosi, *supra* note 1.
5 Jeanne Whalen et al., *White House Scrambles to Scoop Up Medical Supplies Worldwide, Angering Canada, Germany*, Wash. Post (4 Apr. 2020).
6 Katrin Bennhold & David E. Sanger, *U.S. Offered "Large Sum" to German Company for Access to Coronavirus Vaccine Research, German Officials Say*, NYTimes.com (15 Mar. 2020).

7 Anna Swanson et al., *Trump Seeks to Block 3M Mask Exports and Grab Masks from Its Overseas Customers*, NYTimes.com (26 May 2020).

8 *Id.*

9 Nicholas Frew, *Suitcases Full of Cash Offered at PPE Factories Overseas Affecting Global Supply*, CBC.ca (18 May 2020).

10 Sergei Klebnikov, *Illinois Gov. Pritzker Secretly Bought Medical Supplies from China and the White House Is Not Happy*, Forbes.com (18 Apr. 2020).

11 Ariel Shapiro, *Maryland Gov. Hogan Takes Extraordinary Steps to Keep Feds from Confiscating COVID Tests*, Forbes.com (30 Apr. 2020).

12 *Id.*

13 Noam N. Levey, *Hospitals Say Feds Are Seizing Masks and Other Coronavirus Supplies Without a Word*, Latimes.com (7 Apr. 2020).

14 Philipp Harms et al., *Offshoring Along the Production Chain*, 45 The Canadian J. Econ. 1, 93, 94 (2012).

15 Ronald C. Brown, *Up and Down the Multinational Corporations' Global Labor Supply Chains: Making Remedies That Work in China*, 34 UCLA Pac. Basin L.J. 103, 107 (2017). *See also Still Made in China*, Economist (12 Sept. 2015).

16 Anita Chan, *Labor Standards and Human Rights: The Case of Chinese Workers under Market Socialism*, 20 Hum. Rts. Q. 4, 886, 889 (1998) (discussing China's mistreatment of its "rural-to-urban migrants who are subject to tight controls excluding them from access to social welfare benefits, schooling for children, or rights to property ownership"); Dong-Sook S. Gills, *Globalization of Production and Women in Asia*, 581 The Annals of the American Academy of Political and Social Science 106, 111 (2002) ("Asian women workers in global production are a special category of labor that is not only different from men in general but also different from women workers in the developed economies."); Jennifer Gordon, *Regulating the Human Supply Chain*, 102 Iowa L. Rev. 445 (2017) (critiquing the use of employer-sponsored visa programs to import and exploit low-wage foreign workers in the U.S.). *See also* Zehra F. Arat, *Analyzing Child Labor as a Human Rights Issue: Its Causes, Aggravating Policies, and Alternative Proposals*, 24 Hum. Rts. Q. 1, 177 (2002); Denis G. Arnold & Laura P. Hartman, *Worker Rights and Low Wage Industrialization: How to Avoid Sweatshops*, 28 Hum. Rts. Q. 3, 676 (2000); Greg Asbed & Steve Hitov, *Preventing Forced Labor in Corporate Supply Chains: The Fair Food Program and Worker-Driven Social Responsibility*, 52 Wake Forest L. Rev. 497 (2017); Elliott Brewer, *Closed Loophole: Investigating Forced Labor in Corporate Supply Chains Following the Repeal of the Consumptive Demand Exception*, 28 Kan. J. L. & Pub. Pol'y 86 (2018).

17 Daniel Berliner & Aseem Prakash, *Signaling Environmental Stewardship in the Shadow of Weak Governance: The Global Diffusion of ISO 14001*, 47 Law & Soc'y Rev. 2, 345, 368 (2013) (arguing that firms in low-regulation jurisdictions are more likely to participate in voluntary environmental certification processes).

18 Frederick Cooper, *What Is the Concept of Globalization Good for? An African Historian's Perspective*, 100 African Aff. 189 (2001) (critiquing constructions of globalization in the African context that gloss over historical and spatial relationships. "Africanists . . . should be particularly sensitive to the time-depth of cross-territorial processes, for the very notion of 'Africa' has itself been shaped for centuries by linkages within the continent and across oceans and deserts – by the Atlantic slave trade, by the movement of pilgrims, religious networks, and ideas associated with Islam, by cultural and economic connections across the Indian Ocean."); Peter Knorringa, *Responsible Production in Africa: The Rise of China as a Threat or Opportunity?, in* The New Presence of China in Africa 177–198 (Amsterdam: Amsterdam University Press, Van Dijk Meine Pieter ed., 2009).

19 Tim Bartley, *Institutional Emergence in an Era of Globalization: The Rise of Transnational Private Regulation of Labor and Environmental Conditions*, 113 Am. J. Soc. 297, 299 (2007) (arguing that "political conflicts about the regulation of global capitalism – and the embeddedness of these conflicts in neoliberal rules and scripts – generated institution-building projects that

proved crucial to the rise of certification" as part of a process labeled "political construction of market institutions"); *see also* Peter Debaere et al., *Greasing the Wheels of International Commerce: How Services Facilitate Firms' International Sourcing*, 46 The Canadian J. Econ. 1, 78 (2013); Travis Miller, *The Evolving Regulations and Liabilities Entwined in Corporate Social Responsibility*, 46 Tex. Envtl. L.J. 219 (2017); Thi Mai Yen Pham & Thi Minh Khuyen Pham, *The Factors Affecting Green Supply Chains: Empirical Study of Agricultural Chains in Vietnam*, 7 J. Mgmt. & Sustainability 135 (2017).

20 Franziska Bieri & John Boli, *Trading Diamonds Responsibly: Institutional Explanations for Corporate Social Responsibility*, 26 Soc. F. 501 (2011) (discussing the origins of the Kimberley Process Certification Scheme used to certify rough diamonds as "conflict free"); Remi Moncel, *Cooperating Alone: The Global Reach of U.S. Regulations on Conflict Minerals*, 34 Berkeley J. Int'l L. 216 (2016) (discussing how portions of the Dodd-Frank Wall Street Reform and Consumer Protection Act required companies traded on the U.S. Stock Exchange to undertake due diligence assessments to identify the presence of conflict minerals in their international supply chains). *See also* Jasper Humphries, *Resource Wars: Searching for a New Definition*, 88 Int'l Aff. 1065 (2012); Ingrid J. Tamm, *Dangerous Appetites: Human Rights Activism and Conflict Commodities*, 26 Hum. Rts. Q. 687 (2004).

21 Tim Bartley & Curtis Child, *Shaming the Corporation: The Social Production of Targets and the Anti-Sweatshop Movement*, 79 Am. Soc. Rev. 4 (2014) (discussing, generally, how transnational actors become targets of "naming and shaming" activism); Damani James Partridge, A*ctivist Capitalism and Supply-Chain Citizenship: Producing Ethical Regimes and Ready-to-Wear Clothes*, 45 Current Anthropology S3, 597 (2011) (linking the cumulative effects of "ethnical production from design houses to factory floors, from showrooms to department stores, and from NGO monitoring agencies to consumer protest networks" in the formation of "Supply-Chain Citizenship"). . *See also* Michele Micheletti & Deitlind Stolle, *Sustainable Citizenship and the New Politics of Consumption*, 644 The Annals of the American Academy of Political and Social Science 88 (2012).

22 Robert Neil Mefford & Payson Johnston, *The Evolution of Sustainability in a Global Firm and Its Supply Chain*, 6 J. Mgmt. & Sustainability 77, 79 (2016) (discussing how multinational entities are pushing expressions of corporate social responsibility imperatives through their supply chains).

23 Larry Cata Backer, *Are Supply Chains Transnational Legal Orders: What We Can Learn from the Rana Plaza Factory Building Collapse*, 1 U.C. Irvine J. Int'l Transnat'l & Comp. L. 11 (2016) (discussing a new theory of developing country governance in response to the collapse of the Rana Plaza garment factory building, which killed over a thousand workers). *See also* Kenta Goto, *Competitiveness and Decent Work in Global Value Chains: Substitutionary or Complementary?*, 21 Dev. Prac. 7, 943 (2011).

24 U.N. Conference on Trade & Dev., World Investment Report 2020: International Production Beyond the Pandemic, at 123, U.N. Sales No. E.20.II.D.23 (2020) [hereinafter WIR2020].

25 *Id.* at 125.

26 *Id.*

27 *Id.*

28 Nicolas Kachaner & Adam Whybrew, *When Asset Light Is Right*, Boston Consulting Group, (30 Sept. 2014).

29 *Id.*

30 *Id.*

31 *Id. See also App Store Review Guidelines.*

32 WIR2020, *supra* note 24, at 127.

33 *Id.* at 123.

34 For example, see Ma Huimin, *The Influence of the Virtualization of the Global Market on Traditional Foreign Trade Companies in China*, 8 J. WTO & China 87 (2018).

35 For example, see Robert Ginsburg, *What Plant Closings Cost a Community: The Hard Data*, 1 Lab. Res. Rev. 22 (1994); Wendy Patton & Zach Schiller, *Hard Times at City*

Halls: Localities Struggle with Damaged Tax Base, State Cuts, Policy Matters Ohio (7 Jan. 2015).

36 Stephen C. Wilks, *A Complicated Alchemy: Theorizing Identity Politics and the Politicization of Migrant Remittances under Donald Trump's Presidency*, 50 Cornell Int'l L.J. 285 (2017).

37 *See infra* discussion in Parts II & III.

38 U.N. Conference on Trade & Dev., World Investment Report 2016: Investor Nationality: Policy Challenges, at 124–125, Sales No. E.16.II.D.4.

39 For example, see Greg Roumeliotis, *U.S. Blocks MoneyGram Sale to China's Ant Financial on National Security Concerns*, Reuters.com, www.reuters.com/article/us-moneygram-intl-m-a-ant-financial/u-s-blocks-moneygram-sale-to-chinas-ant-financial-on-national-security-concerns-idUSKBN1ER1R7 (Jan. 2, 2018) (describing how Ant Financial – a subsidiary of Chinese internet conglomerate Alibaba Group Holding Ltd. – withdrew its offer to buy MoneyGram, a major American money services provider in the wire transfer industry after the Committee of Foreign Investment in the United States (CFIUS) gave notice it would not approve the proposed transaction).

40 Liana B. Baker, *Trump Bars Chinese-Backed Firm from Buying U.S. Chipmaker Lattice*, Reuters.com (13 Sept. 2017).

41 For example, see William Wilkes, *Germany Withdraws Approval of Chinese Takeover of Aixtron*, wsj.com (24 Oct. 2016) (describing how CFIUS influences its German counterpart to withhold approval of a transaction in which the acquiring party was a Chinese firm).

42 84 Fed. Reg. 40,216 (13 Aug. 2019), at 39, 959–940, 224 (rule prohibiting Chinese firms Huawei Technologies Company, ZTE Corporation, their subsidiaries or affiliates from bidding on U.S. federal government contracts). *See also* Siladitya Ray, *Report: Trump Administration Poised to Ban Companies That Use Huawei Devices from Federal Contracts*, forbes.com (July, 9, 2020); David Shepardson, *Exclusive: U.S. Finalizing Federal Contract Ban for Companies That Use Huawei, Others*, Reuters.com (9 July 2020).

43 U.N. Conference on Trade & Dev., World Investment Report 2019: Special Economic Zones, at 89, U.N. Sales No. E.19.II.D.

44 WIR2020, *supra* note 24, at 103.

45 *Id.*

46 *Id.* at 85.

47 U.S. Trade Representative, Exec. Office of the President, 2020 Report to Findings of the Investigation into China's Acts, Policies, and Practices Related to Technology Transfer, Intellectual Property, and Innovation Under s.301 of the Trade Act of 1974, 6 (22 Mar. 2018) [hereinafter S.301 Report].

48 *Id.*

49 For example, see Sara Dillon, *Getting the Message on Free Trade: Globalization, Jobs and the World According to Trump*, 16 Santa Clara J. Int'l L. 1 (2018) (discussing how the pursuit of foreign labor made American workers valuable in a globalized economy, all of which U.S. politicians largely ignored despite the erosion of communities, identities, and ways of life. "While displaced workers could be told that they would ultimately have better jobs and higher skills as a result of free trade, or that they were being displaced by automation every bit as much as by globalization, the subterranean unhappiness at this state of affairs created the potential for explosive political capture."); Frank J. Garcia & Timothy Meyer, *Restoring Trade's Social Contract*, 116 Mich. L. Rev. Online 78 (2017); Alexis Littlefield, *Exploring the Security Dimension of Sino: US Trade Asymmetry: Implications for the International Trade System*, 4 Source: Strategic Studies Q. 90, 92 (2010) ("[R]egarding the role of a hegemonic power, what impact does an emerging China have upon world order? In other words, as US leadership erodes and Chinese leadership increases, what effect will this have on the global community, and what security issues arise, if any?").

50 Huiyun Feng & Kai He, *China's Institutional Challenges to the International Order*, 11 Strategic Studies Q. 23 (2017) (arguing that China's institutional challenge to the international order will be more peaceful than widely predicted).

51 Simon Lester & Huan Zhu, *The U.S.-China Trade War: Is There an End in Sight*, 40 Cato J. 15 (2020). Unfortunately, the scope of this discussion leaves insufficient time to discuss China's seventeenth- and eighteenth-century experience with western powers forcing their way into Chinese markets. For a useful discussion of how this history overshadows China's contemporary trade negotiations with the U.S., see Alan Rappeport, *19th Century "Humiliation" Haunts China-U.S. Trade Talks*, NYTimes.com (27 Mar. 2019).

52 Henry Gao, *China's Participation in the WTO: A Lawyer's Perspective*, Singapore Year Book of Int'l L. 11, 41 (2007).

53 Lester & Zhu, *supra* note 51, at 16.

54 *Member Information: China and the WTO*, World Trade Org.

55 Under the WTO rules, a most-favored-nation (MFN) clause requires signatories to grant concessions, privileges, or immunities granted to one nation in a trade agreement to all member countries. *See Principles of the Trading System*, World Trade Org.

56 *Accession: Explanation: How to Become a Member of the WTO*, World Trade Org, www. wto.org/english/thewto_e/acc_e/acces_e.htm (accessed July 11, 2020) ("The Protocol of Accession of the new entrant a Protocol of Accession annexed to the Report which states that the country accedes to the WTO Agreement, defines the Schedules and outlines final provisions for timing of acceptance of the Protocol and full membership of the WTO."). The Accession Protocols generated in connection with China's WTO entry can be found at: World Trade Organization, Annex 8 (Revised) to the Draft Protocol on the Accession of China of 18 June 2001, WT/ACC/CHN/42 (2001).

57 Trade Act of 1974, § 423(c), 19 U.S.C. § 2451b(c) [hereinafter Trade Act].

58 *See* 19 U.S.C. § 2432(a).

59 *See generally* S. Rep. 93–1298, at 210–213.

60 Trade Act, *supra* note 57.

61 Paul Blustein, *The Untold Story of How George W. Bush Lost China*, Foreign Policy (2 Oct. 2019).

62 *Id.*

63 *Id.*

64 Mark Wu, *The "China, Inc." Challenge to Global Trade Governance*, 47 Harv. Int'l L.J. 262–263 (2016).

65 *Id.*

66 Blustein, *supra* note 61.

67 Wu, *supra* note 64, at 271.

68 Blustein, *supra* note 61.

69 Curtis J. Milhaupt & Li-Wen Lin, *We Are the (National) Champions: Understanding the Mechanisms of State Capitalism in China*, 65 Stan. L. Rev. 697, 701 (2013) ("*Networked hierarchy* is our term for the way top-down governance features within individual state-controlled corporate groups are coupled with extensive linkages to other state-controlled institutions.").

70 *Id.* "*Institutional bridging* is our term for the pervasive use of personnel-rotation systems, linked equity-ownership structures, and strategic forms of cooperation, such as joint ventures, which serves to unite separate components of the state sector." *Id.*

71 *Id.* at 702.

72 Wu, *supra* note 64, at 276.

73 *Id.* at 277.

74 *Id.* at 281.

75 Mary Amiti et al., *How Did China's WTO Entry Affect U.S. Prices?*, no. 817 Fed. Res. Bank N.Y. Staff Rep. 23 (June 2017).

76 Blustein, *supra* note 61.

77 *Id.*

78 Pedestal Actuators from China, Inv. No. TA-421-1, USITC Pub. 3557 (Nov. 2002); Memorandum on Pedestal Actuator Imports from the People's Republic of China, 39

Weekly Comp. Pres. Doc. 82 (17 Jan. 2003); Certain Steel Wire Garment Hangers from China, Inv. TA421–2, USITC Pub. 3575 (Feb. 2003); Memorandum on Wire Hanger Imports from the People's Republic of China, 39 Weekly Comp. Pres. Doc.492 (25 Apr. 2003).

79 Certain Ductile Iron Waterworks Fittings from China, Inv. TA-421–4, USITC Pub. 3642 (Oct. 2003); Memorandum on Imports of Certain Ductile Iron Waterworks Fittings from the People's Republic of China, 40 Weekly Comp. Pres. Doc. 331 (3 Mar. 2004).

80 Circular Welded Non-Alloy Steel Pipe from China, Inv. TA-421–6, USITC Pub. 3807 (Oct. 2005); Presidential Determination on Imports of Circular Welded Non-Alloy Steel Pipe from the People's Republic of China, 41 Weekly Comp. Pres. Doc. 1921 (30 Dec. 2005).

81 Blustein, *supra* note 61.

82 Request for Consultations by the United States, *China: Value-Added Tax on Integrated Circuits*, WTO Doc. WT/DS309/1 (23 Mar. 2004); Request for Consultations by the United States, *China: Measures Affecting Imports of Automobile Parts*, WTO Doc. WT/DS340/1 (3 Apr. 2006); Request for Consultations by the United States, *China: Certain Measures Granting Refunds, Reductions or Exemptions from Taxes and Other Payments*, WTO Doc. WT/DS358/1 (7 Feb. 2007); Request for Consultations by the United States, *China: Measures Affecting the Protection and Enforcement of Intellectual Property Rights*, WTO Doc. WT/DS362/1 (16 Apr. 2007); Request for Consultations by the United States, *China: Measures Affecting Trading Rights and Distribution Services for Certain Publications and Audiovisual Entertainment Products*, WTO Doc. WT/DS363/1 (Apr. 16, 2007); Request for Consultations by the United States, *China: Measures Affecting Financial Information Services and Foreign Financial Information Suppliers*, WTO Doc. WT/DS373/1 (5 Mar. 2008); Request for Consultations by the United States, *China: Grants, Loans and Other Incentives*, WTO Doc. WT/DS387/1 (7 Jan. 2009).

83 Lester & Zhu, *supra* note 51, at 18.

84 Blustein, *supra* note 61.

85 *Id.*

86 *Id.*

87 U.S. Trade Representative, Exec. Office of the President, 2019 Report to Congress on China's WTO Compliance 7 (2020) [hereinafter USTR 2019 Report] ("The United States . . . has brought nearly two dozen cases against China at the WTO covering a wide range of important policies and practices, such as: (1) local content requirements in the automobile sector; (2) discriminatory taxes in the integrated circuit sector; (3) hundreds of prohibited subsidies in a wide range of manufacturing sectors; (4) inadequate intellectual property rights (IPR) enforcement in the copyright area; (5) significant market access barriers in copyright-intensive industries; (6) severe restrictions on foreign suppliers of financial information services; (7) export restraints on numerous raw materials; (8) a denial of market access for foreign suppliers of electronic payment services; (9) repeated abusive use of trade remedies; (10) excessive domestic support for key agricultural commodities; (11) the opaque and protectionist administration of tariff-rate quotas for key agricultural commodities; and (12) discriminatory regulations on technology licensing."); Lester & Zhu, *supra* note 51, at 19.

88 USTR 2019 Report, *supra* note 87, at 7.

89 *Id.*

90 Blustein, *supra* note 61; Wu, *supra* note 64, at 277.

91 Blustein, *supra* note 61.

92 Daniel C. K. Chow, *How the United States Uses the Trans-Pacific Partnership to Contain China in International Trade*, 17 Chi. J. Int'l L. 370, 370 (2016).

93 *Id.* at 374.

94 *Id.*

95 David Frum, *Faith, Reason, and Immigration*, theatlantic.com (21 Mar. 2019).

96 Withdrawal of the United States from the Trans-Pacific Partnership Negotiations and Agreement, 82 Fed. Reg. 8, 497 (23 Jan. 2017).

97 Title III of the Trade Act of 1974 (Sections 301 through 310, 19 U.S.C. §§2411–2420).

98 Andres B. Schwarzenberg, Cong. Research Serv., IF11346, Section 301 of the Trade Act of 1974, 1 (2020).

99 Martin Finucane & Jeremiah Manion, *Trump Has Pulled Out of International Agreements Before: Here's a List*, bostonglobe.com (1 Feb. 2019); Alex Pascal, *Against Washington's "Great Power" Obsession*, theatlantic.com (23 Sept. 2019).

100 S. 301 Report, *supra* note 47. This was not the USTR's first report canvassing pathways to engineer China's compliance with WTO rules. *See* U.S. Trade Representative, Exec. Office of the President, U.S.-China Trade Relations: Entering a New Phase of Greater Accountability and Enforcement (Feb. 2006).

101 *Id.* at 7.

102 *Id.* at 19 *et seq.*

103 *Id.* at 48 *et seq.*

104 *Id.* at 62 *et seq.*

105 *Id.* at 153 *et seq.* For a scholarly perspective on these arguments, see Emilio Iasiello, *China's Three Warfares Strategy Mitigates Fallout From Cyber Espionage Activities*, 9 J. Strategic Security 45 (2016) ("China is engaged in longstanding cyber espionage against the U.S., as well as other nations, to collect sensitive public and private information in support of national objectives laid out in its 12th Five Year Plan."). *See also* Teng Jianqun, *Trump's America First Security Strategy: Impact on China-US Relations*, 70 China Int'l Stud. 116, 122 (2018).

106 Keith Bradsher, *To Conquer Wind Power, China Writes the Rules*, NYTimes.com (14 Dec. 2010), [hereinafter, Bradsher, *To Conquer Wind Power*].

107 *Id.*

108 *Id*

109 *Id.*

110 Blustein, *supra* note 61.

111 Bradsher, *To Conquer Wind Power*, *supra* note 106.

112 Rob Davies, *The Giant That No One Trusts: Why Huawei's History Haunts It*, The Guardian (8 Dec. 2018).

113 "5G" is shorthand for the telecommunications industry's fifth generation of technical standards for cellular networks. Telecommunications firms around the world began deploying 5G networks in 2019.

114 Huawei, Building a Wonderfully Connected, Intelligent World, 2019 Annual Report ii (2019).

115 *Id* at 84.

116 *Id* at 64.

117 *Id* at 3.

118 *Id* at 80.

119 *In re* Protecting Against National Security Threats to the Communications Supply Chain Through FCC Programs, 34 FCC Rcd. 11423, 11424 (2019) [hereinafter, FCC Statement, 2019].

120 *Id.*

121 *Id.*

122 Mike Rogers & Dutch Ruppersberger, Investigative Report on the U.S. National Security Issues Posed by Chinese Telecommunications Companies Huawei and Zte 3, 31, 42, 44 (2012). Similar comments have come from academics. For example, see Report Part Title: Much Ado about Huawei (part 1) Report Part Author(s): Elsa Kania Report Title: Huawei and Australia's 5G Network Report Author(s): Australian Strategic Policy Institute published by: Australian Strategic Policy Institute (2018) ("At a time when Huawei is actively pursuing commercial opportunities and collaborations worldwide, any deliberate introduction of vulnerabilities into its products or networks

would clearly contradict its own corporate interests. However, it's clear that Huawei's global expansion, in and of itself, can serve as vector for Beijing's influence.").

123 Open Hearing on Worldwide Threats: Hearing Before the S. Comm. on Intelligence, 115th Cong. 64–65 (2018) (statement of Christopher Wray, Dir., Fed. Bureau of Investigation).

124 John S. McCain National Defense Authorization Act for Fiscal Year 2019 § 889(a), (f(3)(A), 132 Stat. at 1917–1918.

125 Grace Sullivan, *The Kaspersky, ZTE, and Huawei Sagas: Why the United States Is in Desperate Need of a Standardized Method for Banning Foreign Federal Contractors*, 49 Pub. Cont. L.J. 323, 334 (2020).

126 Matthew S. Schwartz, *In Reversal, U.K. Will Ban Huawei Equipment from Its 5G Network*, NPR.org (14 July 2020); *Huawei and ZTE Handed 5G Network Ban in Australia*, bbc.com (23 Aug. 2018); Ian Young, *Canada Faces New Pressure to Block Huawei from 5G, after UK Ban Risks Marooning Ottawa from Five Eyes Intelligence Allies*, scmp.com (14 July 2020).

127 Nikos Chrysoloras & Natalia Drozdiak, *EU Spares Huawei from Blanket 5G Ban, Defying Trump*, Bloomberg.com (29 Jan. 2020).

128 United States v Meng, 2019 BCSC 2137, at para 9 (CanLII).

129 United States v Meng, 2020 BCSC 785, paras 7–19 (CanLII).

130 *Id.*

131 *Id.*; Title II of Pub. L. 95–223, 91 Stat. 1626.

132 Press Release, U.S. Dep't of Justice Off. of Pub. Affairs, Chinese Telecomm. Conglomerate Huawei & Huawei CFO Wanzhou Meng Charged with Fin. Fraud (28 Jan. 2019).

133 Davide Cochrane, *Canada Had No Choice But to Arrest Huawei Executive at Washington's Request: Expert*, cbc.ca (7 Dec. 2018).

134 David Ljunggren, *Fed Up Canada Tells U.S. to Help with China Crisis or Forget about Favors*, reuters.com (5 May 2019); Young, *supra* note 126.

135 Press Release, U.S. Dep't of Justice Off. of Pub. Affairs, Chinese Telecomm. Conglomerate Huawei & Huawei CFO Wanzhou Meng Charged with Fin. Fraud (28 Jan. 2019).

136 *Id.*

137 Export Administration Regulations: Amendments to General Prohibition Three (Foreign-Produced Direct Product Rule) and the Entity List, 85 Fed. Reg. 29849 (19 May 2020).

138 FCC Statement, 2019, *supra* note 119, at 11433.

139 Brown, *supra* note 15.

140 Lester & Zhu, *supra* note 51, at 21.

141 Blustein, *supra* note 61.

142 *Id.*

143 *Id.*

144 For example, see, Emma Newburger, *"Trump Is Ruining Our Markets": Struggling Farmers Are Losing a Huge Customer to the Trade War: China*, cnbc.com (10 Aug. 2019); Jesse Newman, *Farmers Built a Soybean Export Empire around China: Now They're Fighting to Save It*, wsj.com (4 July 2019).

145 Keith Bradsher, *China Dominates Medical Supplies, in This Outbreak and the Next*, NYTimes.com (5 July 2020).

146 *Id.*

147 *Id.*

148 *Id.*

149 Timothy Egan, *The World Is Taking Pity on Us*, NYTimes.com (8 May 2020).

150 Josh Margolin & James Gordon Meek, *Intelligence Report Warned of Coronavirus Crisis as Early as November: Sources*, ABC News (8 Apr. 2020).

151 *Id.*; *see also* Eric Lipton et al., *He Could Have Seen What Was Coming: Behind Trump's Failure on the Virus*, NYTimes (updated 2 Oct. 2020).

152 Margolin & Meek, *supra* note 150.
153 Josephine Ma, *Coronavirus: China's First Confirmed Covid-19 Case Traced Back to November 17*, scmp.com (13 Mar. 2020).

Bibliography

Books

Aggarwal, Vinod K. & Govella, Kristi (eds.), Linking Trade and Security: Evolving Institutions and Strategies in Asia, Europe, and the United States (2013).

Nau, Henry R., Trade and Security: U. S. Policies at Cross-Purposes (1995).

Scholarly journals

Bin, Sheng, *The Impact of COVID-19 on Global Value Chains and Its Policy Implications*, 10 J. WTO & China 16 (2020).

Carreno, Ignacio et al., *The Implications of the COVID-19 Pandemic on Trade*, 11 European J. Risk Reg. 2, 402 (2020).

Gantz, David A., *North America's Shifting Supply Chains: USMCA, COVID-19, and the U.S.-China Trade War*, 54 Int'l Law. 121 (2021).

Hongjian, Cui, *The Dual Role of COVID-19 in Changing International Landscape*, 82 China Int'l Stud. 71 (2020).

Jones, Kevin W., *Managing Critical Infrastructure during the COVID-19 Pandemic*, 60 Infrastructure 1 (2020).

Meyer, Timothy, *Trade Law and Supply Chain Regulation in a Post-COVID-19*, 114 Am. J. Int'l L. 4, 637 (2020).

Nied, Mathew & Hindi, Andrew, *Frustration of Contract in the Era of COVID-19*, 51 Advocates' Q. 3, 421 (2020).

Pache, Gilles, *The "Day after" Covid-19 Pandemic: Logistical Disorders in Perspective*, 12 Rev. Eur. Stud. 1 (2020).

Rongjiu, Xue, *COVID-19's Impact on and Damage to International Trade and China's Coping Mechanisms*, 10 J. WTO & China 3 (2020).

Teremetskyi, V. I. & Duliba, Ye V., *Role of the WTO in Regulating World Trade in Medicinal Products and Equipment during the COVID-19 Pandemic*, 2020 Law & Safety 146 (2020).

5

LEADERSHIP VACUUM AND MASK DENIERS

Elizabeth Anne Kirley and Marilyn McMahon

Editors' introduction: As US president and COVID-19 patient Donald Trump circled a Maryland hospital in a dark SUV in early October 2020, he appeared intent on assuring his audience on the street and online that he was still a contender in the 2020 election. The optics of his breach of hospital protocol were ironic: the ultimate mask denier, compromised as he had become by the virus, was sporting a face mask. This defining moment capped nine months of Trump's taunting of his political opponents who wore face coverings in public. Uniquely targeted was presidential candidate Joseph Biden, whom Trump derided for his "blue state wimpiness" in broadcasting his campaign messages from his house and wearing a mask in public.

Trump's conversion to the mask was short-lived, however. Within 24 hours, he would stage a dramatic mask removal on the South Portico balcony of the White House. With what was to become a highly politicized mask resistance meme, the Mask-Denier-in-Chief had reverted to full denunciation as a campaign strategy.

In this chapter, Professors Elizabeth Anne Kirley in Canada and Marilyn McMahon in Australia examine their observations at the six-month mark to get a better understanding of the rationale and sentiment that has fueled mask resistance worldwide. To assess the psyche of vast numbers of potential coronavirus victims who refuse this protective device that offers them safety and mobility, the authors consult three prototypical professions: the medical historian, the epidemiologist, and the social scientist. The authors find that early shortages of personal protection equipment caused equivocation over the mask choice among public health and

DOI: 10.4324/9781003215769-8

government authorities when a clear "yes" or "no" was the direction the public primarily sought. The result in many countries was that denial and politicization of mask wearing quickly filled that information gap.

The cost of such partisanship has been profound. People have died for calling out those who refuse to mask-up; others have been spurned for wearing masks into business premises of deniers. Tensions have reached ignition over the mere act of wearing a niqab while Muslim or a face covering in white neighborhoods while Black. Incontrovertibly, the mask has become a politicized meme for the gas-lighting of well-intentioned wearers and a trigger for anger, racism, and violence. We have seen resistance to non-pharmaceutical intervention in past public health crises, such as the condom for HIV-AIDs, and the mask during the 1918 influenza. This time, however, some international law scholars see the mask phenome as a move away from a pluralistic world political system under an impartial global rule of law to a populist denouncement of the goals of sovereign equality and collective security.[1] Among its calls for reform, this chapter asks for a re-consideration of the unifying potential of seeking the common good.

Introduction

Pandemics pose unpredictable global public health problems. One of the most divisive to emerge with COVID-19 is the lack of public and political cohesiveness over the prophylactic merits of face coverings. Eighteen months into COVID-19, as global case counts surpass 178 million with 33 million dead,[2] the pandemic science community has converged on a partial solution to viral spread: the unassuming face mask, 4-ply if possible, worn indoors when treating the afflicted and in public when not social distancing. While the debate continues well into the second year of the pandemic over whether the mask, properly worn, most benefits the wearer or those in proximity, studies have emerged that affirm the coronavirus is transmitted by aerosol bursts from the mouth,[3] that pathogens can linger in indoor environments for hours,[4] and that mask wearing can function as a physical barrier to such dangers of contagion. Gone, however, are blanket statements from public institutions that the mask, unattended by other non-pharmaceutical interventions, can stop community transmission.

There has been sufficient scientific research from reliable sources, however, that wearing a mask reduces risk, particularly in super-spreader situations. Why, then, is there ongoing, persistent denial of the effectiveness of the mask when the data is medically persuasive and the precaution so cheaply accomplished? This chapter examines this incongruity from three sources: the medical historian whose accounts show the gradual understanding of the role of the mask; from the epidemiologist whose role is to amass best evidence; and from the social scientist who can expand on what the mask can signify to the wearers, to the deniers, and to those caught in the stand-off. Our findings are complex: as French anthropologist Claude Lévi-Strauss has noted, "The mask is not only what it displays but also what it transforms . . . it is not just what it means, but also what it denies."[5]

Denial was a recurrent theme in the politicization of the mask from the beginning of the rumors in January 2020: by Xi Jinping of China, state presidents like Bolsonaro in Brazil, Obrador in Mexico, Putin in Russia, and Trump in America. Within the UK, Prime Minister Boris Johnson shook hands with medical hospital staff just before falling victim to the virus, one minister breached lockdown protocol,[6] and the chief medical officer of Wales defined masking-up as a "personal choice" as there was only a "marginal public health case" for wearing them.[7] Such missteps in the pandemic response by nations of great wealth or populations were followed by the initial hesitation of institutional authorities such as the Centers for Disease Control and Prevention (CDC), the Surgeon General in America and the WHO to urge politicians to consider a mandate for mask wearing and the backtracking on that messaging later on. In some respects, changing official positions aligned with the newest science illustrates that researchers work with mutable facts, not *the* facts.[8] For those not fastidiously following the research, or unschooled in the health sciences, reversals in policy can create confusion and skepticism of authorities who direct life and death decisions. Public feelings of exposure to uncertain risks have left us to inform ourselves from the misinformation blogosphere, mediated through our personal beliefs and biases.[9]

More broadly, the politicization of the mask at the highest levels breeds unpreparedness and has rendered us vulnerable to both known and unknown hazards of the emerging disease.[10] Rather than taking a precautionary stance while health researchers were building an accurate bio-immunological profile of the coronavirus, public health authorities responded to the supply chain shortfalls of PPE by minimizing the containment value of properly fitted face coverings.[11] This missed completely the core rationale, adopted in relation to other preventive measures, that precaution and saving lives was better than inertia.[12] The reasons given for relegating N95 masks to frontline medical workers left civilians losing trust that governments and their institutions had their backs. It resulted in many people resorting to their own devices, sometimes adopting the questionable protections of cottage industry face coverings such as repurposed bras, flannelette pajamas, turtleneck sweaters, and even plastic shopping bags.[13]

The failure of Western heads of state to heed lessons learned from various pandemics over the twentieth century has rendered them unprepared and panicked. Civilian denial stems from that leadership shortfall at a moment in America and similarly constructed democracies where "ideas of supranational organization and post-national sovereignty are increasingly resisted."[14] One can look for causes to the confluence of the coronavirus crisis and a global populist movement "which has brought a generation of political 'hard men' into power."[15] The result has been a veneration of the economy over public safety, the devaluing of membership in globalist institutions like the WHO, the rejection of big government policies, and an entrenched refusal to consider scientific explanations. Masks have become the most recent totem of that movement.[16]

In the United States, the "playbook" assembled by previous presidents George W. Bush and Barack Obama has become the biggest casualty in global public health preparedness.[17] On the ground, the broader result has been the individualization and politicization of every citizen's decision-making.[18] We are ultimately left to our own altruistic or self-focused choices, informed by complex personal views about science, religion and economics.

This chapter offers legal and policy changes that should assist us in outsmarting the next pandemic. We propose that the way forward lies in adopting a Janus-like perspective: looking backward to lessons learned from this and past pandemics, and forward to circumstances which require nimble adaptations to emerging science.[19]

The medical historian: theories of disease and containment

The observations of the medical historian can provide general reference points for today's theories of contagion and methods of containment. This is what social and cultural historian Dr. Julie Livingston calls learning "the prehistory and long aftermath" of infectious disease rather than focusing solely on each discrete pandemic event.[20]

More generally, contemporaneous record keeping during past pandemics can reveal the extent to which the people understood the risk of the pathogen and the local officials knew their duty to respond. Peste chroniclers and plague doctors might have identified the moment when mask wearing entered normative public health practice. The totemic significance of masks across the ages suggests that face coverings have always, for one reason or another, served to "transport and transform the user and the observer."[21]

The Marseilles plague (1720–22)

The epidemic that began in Marseilles in 1720 marked the last outbreak of the bubonic plague that had been ravaging Western Europe for over four centuries.[22] French medical historian Jean-Noel Biraben has studied the awareness of local authorities that disease was transported into France through merchant goods conveyed across key water and land routes. While not necessarily aware of the *biological* causes of infection at that time, city authorities knew of the susceptibility of porous and absorptive materials like cloth and paper to act as surfaces for carrying pathogens.[23] Within days the stricken among the ninety thousand inhabitants of Marseille included those who had carried the wares, those who had purchased them, neighbors of the purchasers, and sailors who had traveled with the cargo. By the tenth week of infestation, nearly 10,000 residents had fled the city before soldier-patrolled sanitary zones were erected and municipal officials could close all travel into and out of the city. Biraben speaks of lockdown that put commerce and livelihoods in jeopardy as food merchants and slaughterhouse workers grew overwhelmed. Orphaned babies were dying at a rate of thirty-to-forty a day, and volunteer gravediggers were overcome by the disease. As historian Colin Jones commented about the rapidity of plague poison: "In the twinkling of an eye, plague turned the quick into the dead."[24]

Other outbreaks of the *peste* in early eighteenth-century Europe had been attributed to a miasma or disease-sodden air, although records indicate a general understanding that contaminants could spread by human touch. Tobacco smoking was recommended to fend off such vapors from the earth, even for children. Smoke was also suggested, in addition to vinegar washes, to fumigate paper that might have served as a template for the pathogen.[25] Homes and possessions of the departed were routinely burned to kill residual miasmic traces.[26] Those still alive were barred from leaving their homes, resulting in infection of their entire families.[27]

The degree of mask acceptance during pandemics of that period is not definitively agreed among researchers. Medical historians Bruno Strasser and Thomas Schlich speak of "nose and mouth coverings" as part of traditional sanitary practices against infectious diseases.[28] That account speaks of mask-wearing in the time of the Marseilles 1720 outbreak as "marginal."[29] Historian William Eamon suggests face coverings were worn primarily by medical caregivers who were exposed to a patient's breathing, sneezing, or coughing.[30]

The image of the "plague" or "beak" doctor, originating in a sixteenth-century copper engraving from Rome, has been linked to the Marseilles plague in several accounts. While there is no verification of his therapeutic presence at plague sites, such a curious figure from masked and beaked head to long leather coat and boots would almost certainly have evoked alarm at that shadow of looming death.[31] Some accounts particularly note that the beak in those masks was filled with cloves, cinnamon, and other herbs and liquids, reputed to fend off all smell from, and contact with, the miasma.[32] Biraben mentions the eye holes of the head-covering were filled with a layer of crystal for protection.[33] A doctor in such costume would attract attention, holding a stick to distance himself from a patient as he points out the symptoms of the disease and explains to those in attendance how he proposes a cure.[34] That image suggests a professional approach to social distance between one human and another, but again only the figure of the doctor is masked.

Plague tracts are another source of rich detail about the Marseilles plague. Colin Jones has examined 264 medical volumes from France that point out the "extraordinary measures of quarantine and exclusion" that ultimately drove the plague from France during the second decade of the eighteenth century.[35] The entries promoted a regimen of sobriety, moderate sexual behavior, and spiritual rituals to ensure a balanced urban life.

Historian Frank Snowden has noted the widespread "evasion, resistance, and riot" that met public health efforts at plague control in Marseilles. He speaks of many cases being concealed from the eyes of city health officials due to "the fear of being separated from loved ones" and the lack of interest in protecting the public on the part of those charged with enforcing the rules.[36]

The third sector influencing the popular psyche was the civil magistrate[37] whose ordinances were strictly enforced: streets were to be cleared, drains cleaned, rubbish removed, animals culled, food supplies organized and, once it was deemed safe to do so, trade resumed, infirmaries opened for the sick and dying, and all necessary rituals reinstated to move the community toward normalization.[38] Behavior reinforcement could be strict: soldiers stationed at *cordones sanitaires* were recorded as using their rifles to butt heads of those refusing to obey state ordinances.[39]

Superstition provided another explanation for resistance to state regimens. Astrology and dark arts infused the belief among the masses that precious stones and rare metals held "talismanic properties."[40] Those beliefs led to driving out unnatural elements in the population, identified at the time as any foreigners, Jews, and physically vulnerable people. Such resistance to state ordinances fuelled belief that to heal one must identify human outliers and drive out the culprits.[41] That attitude can be seen in COVID times in the xenophobia and other biased behaviors displayed when citizens are instructed to mask up.[42]

Medical historians, then, note the perception of mask wearing in early modern Europe as a protection relegated primarily to medical doctors against poisonous air. For the masses with no access to such finery, available preventive measures included fleeing the plague-ridden city, inhaling tobacco, exposing paper to herbal smoke or a vinegar bath, or placing one's faith in clean living or the occult. By the time of the influenza pandemic of 1918, the use of masks was more science-based but resistance was still rampant, emerging most notably among medical professionals.

The great influenza pandemic (1918–20) and after

The story of the normalization of mask wearing in twentieth-century America and Europe follows the evolution of the germ theory of contamination.[43] That discovery evolved in the latter half of the 1800s in tandem with improvements in research equipment such as microscopes.

In 1897 Dr. Carl Georg Friedrich Wilhelm FlÜgge, a prominent bacteriologist and hygienist in Germany, developed the droplet theory of infection built on the idea that microorganisms in droplets expelled from the respiratory tract are a means of transmission. That same year in Breslau, Germany, surgeon Johann von Mikulicz Radecki constructed a surgical mask composed of one layer of gauze.[44] He tied it by two strings to his surgeon's. It covered his nose, mouth, and beard. Mikulicz's mask was intended to avoid disease *spread* rather than *disease infection by the wearer.*[45]

A further development was the practice during the Manchurian plague of 1910 of requiring medical workers, police, and patients to don masks when *outside* the operating room. Such laws were imitated in 1918 in several US cities[46] and the practice was mirrored by governments in the UK.[47]

The practice of using surgical masks as a prophylactic in the operating theatre was receiving only minor notice in medical journals in Europe and North America when the 1918 flu pandemic erupted. It was tied to the British surgeon Joseph Lister's proposal in the late nineteenth century that wound disease was caused by the germs of microscopically small living organisms.[48] While Lister proposed applying antiseptic substances to the body to treat infection, by the 1880s several surgeons were working with the strategy of creating barriers to prevent germs from entering wounds in the first place. A historical account in the Lancet assessed this new practice as "a risky strategy. Hands, instruments, even the operator's exhalations were suspect now."[49]

Mask mandates initially stirred little resistance in America during World War I, primarily due to the patriotic belief that it aided the troops.[50] Masked citizens were viewed as acting with heroism and "accepting their duty."[51] Public health authorities also appealed to people's self interest in good health by urging them in newspaper advertisements to "Wear a mask and safe your life!"[52] More sinister was a San Francisco streetcar poster that warned that "Spit spreads Death," an incivility not possible while wearing a mask.[53]

Complaints and pushback did eventually occur in 1919–20, as seen in the lax requirements by city officials for design and materials,[54] exemptions granted to cigarette smokers for poking holes in masks,[55] efforts to trivialize the role of masks for women by promoting them as a fashion statement,[56] and accounts of resistance because masks were "uncomfortable, ineffective, or bad for business."[57] On the other hand, historian John Barry views favorably the enthusiastic boast in a newspaper advertisement by San Francisco authorities that masks were "99% proof against influenza."[58] He credits such promotion for giving people a sense of control, unlike the "paralyzing fear" that gripped other communities.[59]

Mask elitism was a problem within the medical profession during the Great Pandemic. The rejection of masking by doctors and public health authorities can be seen in several photographs of medical teams where doctors stand barefaced behind their subordinates who compliantly wear gauzy face coverings.

While the mask was making sporadic forays into surgical practice in post-WW1 Germany and America, its prophylactic potential was not always fully appreciated. Masks were almost completely foregone among most surgeons in the first quarter of the twentieth century in Europe and North America. We are told that "the generation of head physicians rejected them, as well as rubber gloves, in all phases of an operation as they were considered 'irritating.'"[60]

By the 1940s, with the discovery of lighter, synthetic materials and methods to germ-proof them, masks gained wider acceptance for surgery across the Western world.[61] Those changes ushered in a throwaway culture, the "progressive replacement of reusable face masks by disposable ones."[62] COVID-19 has amplified that disposable attitude, as masks and gloves have been observed contributing to the plastic glut on land and water.[63]

We will now look at what we have learned over the first year of the coronavirus pandemic from epidemiologists.

The epidemiologist: how does the coronavirus spread?

COVID-19 is an infectious disease caused by a new form of coronavirus. It is part of a large family of viruses that includes the common cold and viruses associated with diseases that triggered previous pandemics, such as Middle East Respiratory Syndrome (MERS) and Severe Acute Respiratory Syndrome (SARS). Epidemiologists study and investigate the causes and sources of diseases in much the same way as medical doctors, but they are not considered actual physicians. They focus on society writ large, not individual cases.

The WHO has maintained that the key source of COVID-19 transmission are relatively large respiratory droplets (usually greater than 5 micrometers in size) propelled from an infected person's nose or mouth when they sneeze, cough, or talk. Due to gravity, those droplets do not travel far before landing; these characteristics underpin the recommendations for social distancing at 1.5–2 meters and for cleaning surfaces to remove recently landed droplets.[64] However, in early July 2020 more than 200 scientists endorsed a paper that identified airborne transmission of smaller droplets, capable of being suspended in the air, as an additional source of infection. This would have major implications for preventative measures: for instance, it would make possible transmission of the virus through air conditioning systems and validate suspicions that microorganisms could reside in corners of a room and other areas with little or no airflow or ventilation, such as an indoor bar or restaurant. With that discovery, the air properties of larger buildings, such as schools and places of worship, as well as factories and hotel rooms, became a source of focused study.

COVID-19 spread quickly as there was no existing immunity in communities. Common symptoms associated with it are fever, coughing, sore throat and shortness of breath. The virus can spread from person to person through close contact with an infectious person; contact with droplets from an infected person's cough or sneeze;[65] or touching objects or surfaces that have droplets from an infected person, and the person then touching their mouth or face.

Asymptomatic cases pose critical difficulties for the epidemiologist. It is challenging to know when such people might be infectious, and the period of active contagion. Early research indicated that up to 40% of cases could be asymptomatic. Now, the figure has been refined to one in five.[66] Without symptoms, there is no incentive to test; some individuals who test positive for the virus never manifest any symptoms. Others have delayed symptoms and can spread the virus for several days with impunity. Given those uncertainties, strategies to contain the coronavirus are challenging. In this context epidemiologists would likely advise a simple strategy of wearing a mask to cover all those risks.

Another initial problem was the limited availability of masks in some countries.[67] While that problem has abated somewhat in the ensuing months as supply is more systematically manufactured for most countries, and public education has clarified what constitutes an effective mask design, there remains the inability of key organizations to convey changes in policy in a clear way. For instance, when wearing a mask in public spaces became legally mandated in certain areas of Victoria, Australia in July 2020, the government recommended that three-layer cloth masks be worn but acknowledged that scarves and bandanas would also suffice. That communication is unclear: if three layers are recommended, does that mean scarves and alternatives must be wound around the face three times? Does it mean wearers are more susceptible with only a two-layer mask? What about thicker materials? Why mandate masks if other materials at hand will do? Such vital communicators should aim the message at non-medical viewers and consider the possible ramifications of loosely identifying public risk.[68]

Over a year later, a similarly confusing message was delivered regarding individual decision-making about wearing a mask. With vaccine rollouts addressing contagion across America, the CDC announced that masks were not needed if people were fully vaccinated.[69] Many epidemiologists were disquieted by the CDC's advice. They perceived a flaw: what about vaccinated people who stopped masking in groups with an unknown number of unvaccinated people? Recent studies confirm that vaccines, while preventing you from getting ill, do not necessarily stop you from getting infected or spreading the germ.[70] Do currently available vaccines protect you from much more virulent variants? The answer from the CDC itself seems to say, not necessarily.[71]

Even worse, what if that comingling is within a contained space, where crowds are breathing the same air? That aspect has particularly worried authorities like the United Food and Commercial Workers union, who represent thousands of grocery store workers. It criticized the CDC for failing to consider how the new policy would impact essential workers who must deal with customers who are not vaccinated. "Millions of Americans are doing the right thing and getting vaccinated, but essential workers are still forced to play mask police for shoppers who are unvaccinated and refuse to follow local Covid safety measures."[72] The question became, whether food and commercial essential workers would have to become the vaccination police as well. The CDC announcement was criticized in countries where variants were creating second, third and fourth waves of infection. The problem seemed to be that its core message was being forgotten, that only when the percentage of vaccine uptake reached near saturation could authorities order the lifting of mask mandates.[73]

Journalist Ed Yong takes a broader view to explain how epidemiologists are, by the nature of their profession, at odds with public health authorities and executives like former President Trump who encourage individual responses. Epidemiologists, unlike medical practitioners, address the collective or communal situation. They deal with infectious diseases which are always collective problems due to their rapid contagion. With a coronavirus, "An individual's choices can ripple outward to affect cities, countries, and continents," Yong observes. "One sick person can seed a hemisphere's worth of cases."[74] That characteristic pattern does not sit well with the individualist approach that Biden-appointed CDC director Rochelle Walensky was taking. While she explained her decision to loosen mask requirements as a reward for vaccine compliance, Dr. Walensky's message that she wanted to "empower people to take this responsibility into their own hands" carried infectious risks that it was not within the power of citizens to manage.[75] Like the chief medical officer of Wales in 2020,[76] the CDC director was framing a public health problem as a matter of personal choice. That approach seemed more in line with Donald Trump's talk about dominating the virus through personal strength and individual initiative.[77] Although the national mythos of America has always been that anyone can succeed by pulling themselves out of adversity by sheer individual will and grit, such independence cannot bring an effective pandemic response. As Yong concludes, "It explains why so many Americans refuse to act for the collective good, whether by masking up or isolating themselves."[78]

Two key justifications have been used by deniers of masking: efficacy and libertarianism. Many officials argued that there was no scientific evidence of the efficacy of wearing masks in preventing transmission of the virus.[79] Others regarded policies that mandated public health measures as unwarranted intrusion in the affairs of citizens.[80]

On the issue of efficacy, the emergence of studies,[81] reviews[82] and meta-analyses that progressively confirmed the value of wearing of masks has led to a change of advice from medical and scientific bodies. Typical of this research was an American study conducted in mid-June 2020 by researchers at the CDC. They investigated an outbreak of the virus on the *USS Theodore Roosevelt* aircraft carrier and reported a lower infection rate among those wearing a face covering (56% infection rate compared to 81% for those who did not wear a mask).[83] The CDC also reported that wearing a mask was as effective as social distancing and increased handwashing in preventing the spread of the disease. In the same month a review of several preventive measures (physical distance, face masks and eye protection) also reported that wearing face masks was associated with a "large reduction" in risk of infection.[84]

Policy and law on masking

By mid-June 2020, more than 50 countries made it mandatory to wear a face mask in some circumstances. In June 2021, many countries or states still impose masking conditions, primarily for unvaccinated citizens. The United States mandates masks for unvaccinated people on trains, planes, public transit, medical settings, prisons and some other specific settings. In China, the authorities subject people to mandatory mask-wearing rules nationwide at hospitals and transport hubs. In Japan, while there's no legal national mask requirement, the government recommends having one on in public where the pace of vaccinations lags behind other global financial hubs just months before the delayed Tokyo Olympics. Earlier in 2021, Germany ruled out cloth face coverings and requiring medical masks in shops, hairdressers, and offices. Masks that filter particles are required in many indoor locations such as public transport. In India almost all states have made mask-wearing mandatory, with several imposing fines for rule-breakers. India's federal government COVID-19 taskforce tightened its guidance late in April and recommended that citizens even wear masks at home, in response to the aggressive spread of the Delta variant.

In Europe, masks were mandatory alongside other social distancing measures in countries including France, Germany, Austria, Hungary, Poland and the Czech and Slovak Republics. Typical situations where a face covering was required included shopping, on public transportation and in other public spaces where social distancing was not possible.[85] In the United States, 38 states passed laws requiring the wearing of masks in some circumstances. The requirement was usually limited to specific groups (such as hospitality workers) in particular locations (areas with high numbers of coronavirus cases) or circumstances (restaurants, gyms, etc.).[86]

Countries did not impose masking in unison. For example, Singapore enacted regulations at an early stage. More commonly, mask wearing was mandated when other strategies had failed to sufficiently slow down transmission of the virus. In Australia, for instance, there was an initial low infection rate and, after an early period of lockdown, authorities mainly relied on other preventive measures.[87] However, after a second wave of infection in the state of Victoria that jeopardized control and recovery, face masks in public areas became mandatory. Interestingly, New Zealand had a low infection rate and a highly successful strategy of going into lockdown at a very early stage. Mask wearing was never part of the New Zealand response as the government determined that there was "no convincing evidence" that the use of face masks prevented community transmission.[88]

The role of face masks in the COVID-19 pandemic was not determined simply by their function in limiting transmission of the virus, however. They also had a communicative role that was invested with individual, cultural, historical, and political dimensions.

The social scientist: socio-cultural signifiers

> Mask-wearing affirms that social responses to disease are rarely driven by scientific evidence alone . . . historically, symbolic dimensions can be more important.[89]

Cultural influences

Individual decisions about wearing or resisting a mask are, like other decisions, located within social and cultural values. As the sociology team reminds us with their epigraph above, understanding those values often means reading the symbolic form in which they are expressed. As such, those values can change with time and experiences. The normalization of mask wearing in several countries of South East Asia has been viewed by outsiders as a fixed, collective courtesy to others. Two sociologists contested that perception almost a decade ago with their study of Japanese surgical mask wearing. They determined that, through a combination of commercial, corporate, and political pressures, Japanese people wore masks as a self-protective risk ritual rather than a selfless collective practice.[90] The key impetus was the 2011 tsunami where masks were employed against the threat of radiation from the Fukushima reactor.

There is an experiential memory factor in mask wearing as well. For those geographic regions that suffered the SARS, MERS, and avian flu epidemics of the early new millennium, wearing face coverings as a prophylactic measure came more easily during the arrival of this coronavirus.[91] Those experiences were entrenched in cultural norms and social practices to protect themselves and prevent the transmission of illnesses to others,[92] as well as more diffuse notions of impoliteness associated with coughing and sneezing in public. Thus, in some countries wearing a mask was integrated into everyday life before the COVID-19 pandemic. Indeed, in Japan this practice was embedded in more general understandings of modernization[93] and was so routinized that, for some, it could be done for purely aesthetic reasons.[94] Consequently, in many of those countries government recommendations to wear a face mask were uncontroversial and readily adopted by citizens. But, in other countries, individual understandings of the nature of the health risks presented by the virus were located within more general socio-cultural attitudes that were hostile to government intervention and an unwillingness to subjugate individual autonomy to collective welfare. This had significant implications for the uptake of mask wearing as a public health measure.

Masks and bad faith

One cultural trope that was hostile to the use of face coverings was the wrongdoing their use could signal. Masks have long been worn for the purpose of hiding or disguising the wearer. Sometimes playful, as in the masked balls of Venice, more often face covering is associated with deception and bad faith: lawlessness, deceit and untrustworthiness. The masked bandit or armed robber is a well-entrenched meme and, more generally, covering the face has often been viewed as facilitating lawbreaking. This is reflected in anti-masking laws that can be traced back to New York in the nineteenth century and, at the beginning of the twenty-first century, for prohibiting members of groups as diverse as the Ku Klux Klan in the United States, the democracy movement in Hong Kong[95] and G20 protesters in Canada[96] from wearing masks in specified places.

During the COVID-19 pandemic, racial and religious tensions were triggered by the issue of masks. Some African Americans expressed a reluctance to cover their faces during the pandemic out of fear that they would be perceived as lawbreakers and consequently be more vulnerable to police harassment and brutality.[97] Another aspect of the racial politics of face masks related to religion. Making masks desirable and even mandatory re-ignited controversy over another form of face covering prohibited in some countries – those adopted by some orthodox Muslim women.

More than a decade prior to the COVID-19 controversy about masks, public wearing of the niqab (a veil covering the face below the eyes) and the burqa (a garment covering the entire body, including the face) had been the center point of disputes over national identity and religious freedom. Prohibitions were enacted in several European countries, typically based on the claim that obscuring the face violated the requirements of good citizenship.[98] The generalized wearing of face masks during the pandemic *prima facie* caused the issue to be revisited. The issue was especially significant in France, where in April 2011 the government had banned the public wearing of face coverings. The ban campaign emphasized that "La République se vit à visage découvert" (The Republic lives with its face uncovered).

The French government had justified the public ban on the basis that obscuring the face violated the foundational civic principles of equality, fraternity and civility. However, the mandated wearing of face coverings in public as a preventive health measure in May 2020 generated uncertainty: would this have the spin-off effect of making other (religious) face coverings also lawful? The government's response was quick: face covering for a public health purpose was essential but the prohibition on other face coverings remained. President Macron addressed the issue by wearing a face mask that had the colors of the French flag, literally flagging his commitment to civic principles while adopting a hitherto condemned practice[99] and turning the mask into a symbol of good faith. The continued prohibition on the burqa and niqab, with penalties for wearing those face coverings in public, manifested an asymmetry of law, under which the situational legality of covering the face depended on the context and the person. Some viewed the distinction as "arbitrary at best, discriminatory at worst."[100]

In summary, the mask not only protects the wearer and limits transmission from an infected person but also functions to externalize the wearer, manifesting his many aesthetic, communicative and personal values. Socio-political values were also to become increasingly prominent as the pandemic gained ground, giving a renewed voice to those who were often on the edge of mainstream political discourse. We examine a few of those voices here.

Opposition based on faith in God and distrust of government

Faith in God, combined with distrust of government, meant that the most extreme resistance to wearing masks (and other preventive measures) came from four entwined and overlapping groups: human rights activists, economic conservatives, religious fundamentalists and anti-vaxxers.[101] Two key themes united those groups: hostility to modern science and opposition to intrusion by government. This opposition exploited any confusion and inconsistency in public health information and directives about the efficacy of masking but was rooted in preexisting and deeply entrenched values that valorized individualism, economic activity, and blind faith.

Human rights activists

Objections to wearing a mask sometimes came from those who purported to base their objections in human rights concerns. In Australia, an objector referenced the *Charter of Human Rights 1948*, invoking a claimed right not to be told what to do by government.[102] In Asia, echoing a rights concern, a Japanese newspaper conducted a poll to determine if readers viewed a legal obligation to wear a mask as a human rights violation.[103] And in the United States, some queried whether there was constitutional protection for those who refused to wear a mask.[104]

Human Rights organizations and law associations were quick to point out that directives to wear masks were lawful, grounded in public health concerns and directed toward protecting the fundamental human right to health.[105] But this response was unlikely to influence those whose objections were based on a particular view of the social contract that invested individuals with unqualified rights and absolute autonomy, devoid of any obligations toward others in their community. It was a political view that was also mediated through economic, religious and anti-scientific attitudes.

Economic conservatives

The profoundly adverse economic impact of the pandemic, underpinned by the largest job losses in recent history, ensured that governments had to manage an uneasy tension between restrictive measures to protect the community and policies that would exacerbate a downward financial spiral. Those concerns became the binary around which a mainstream political divide emerged. Conservatives emphasized the negative economic impact of government measures introduced to limit the spread of the coronavirus in the community and were more likely to favor no restrictions and early lifting of any preventive measures. Conversely, liberals were more concerned with health issues associated with the transmission and therefore more supportive of government intervention and restrictive policies.[106]

How this tension related to mask wearing was not necessarily apparent. Mask wearing could facilitate a return to some routine economic activity insofar as it permitted a move away from lockdown, allowing people to interact at closer distances when social distancing was not possible.[107] It could also assuage consumer concerns about the risks involved in accessing the usual goods and services.[108] Accordingly, some conservatives favored mask wearing if it facilitated an early end to lockdown and a return to economic activity. However, those who favored an unfettered return to business as usual frequently rejected face coverings as incompatible with business activity and demonstrative of a lingering health concern that would negatively impact consumer confidence. This seems to have been the attitude of President Bolsonaro of Brazil, who was dismissive of all preventive measures and continuously prioritized economic interests.[109]

Thus, because mask-wearing could, unlike lockdowns and social distancing, actually facilitate the continuance of social and economic activity, economic conservatives were not universally opposed to this measure. This can be contrasted with those whose political and social views were already outside mainstream politics – the survivalists, the religious fundamentalists, the antivaxxers – for the pandemic simply provided them with an opportunity to reiterate their vehement, unconflicted opposition to government and their belief in God.

Religious fundamentalists

There were diverse ways in which religious fundamentalists demonstrated their opposition to limiting the spread of the virus. They were strongly opposed to lockdown as a preventive strategy. They widely opposed closing places of worship. Calling on anti-scientism and conspiracy beliefs, some proclaimed "The virus, we believe, is politically motivated."[110] Consequently, numerous fundamentalist groups defied mask wearing and staying at home directives and came into close physical contact with others not wearing masks. Evangelical Christians in some US states argued that any COVID-19 related restrictions were a violation of their constitutional right to freedom of religious expression and governors in several States acceded to their pressure.[111] The religious group Liberty Counsel contested restrictions in the courts, relying on the protection of religious freedom enshrined in the First Amendment:

> [C]hurches, pastors, and believers have a constitutionally protected right to gather together to worship God and to do so without government interference. Even in a time of crisis or disease . . . the First Amendment does not evaporate. The First Amendment is as applicable during a pandemic, or any other crisis, as it is every other day. There is no pause button on the Constitution.[112]

While support came from courts in Kansas and Kentucky,[113] informed critics pointed out that there was no legal precedent or logic for exempting religious faith-based gatherings from general restrictions.[114]

Logically, agreeing to mask-wearing could facilitate the continuance of religious gatherings. Opposition, however, was embedded within a more general hostility to science that generated opposition to *all* public health measures. Fundamentalist believers accepted that God would protect believers from harm; consequently, preventive measures were unnecessary, went the thinking. This coalesced with the view of another anti-science group: the anti-vaxxers.

Anti-vaxxers

A notable feature of the opposition to mask wearing is the conjunction of religious and anti-scientific views. Fundamentalist religious beliefs promoted a quietism about the impact of the pandemic, as well as a conviction that believers would be protected. Anti-vaxxers adopted a more active, targeted hostility toward science, not necessarily mediated by religious belief. They opposed restrictive measures of all sorts, sometimes preferring the option of developing herd immunity through widespread community infection and always using the pandemic as an opportunity to reiterate their objections to science.

Anti-vaccine protests in Germany began with the introduction of a COVID-19 vaccine but soon expanded to objections to state surveillance and former Microsoft developer Bill Gates.[115] Similarly, in Australia a lawyer gained prominence for his opposition to the mandatory wearing of masks but combined that objection with mandatory vaccination, believing both to be a breach of human rights.[116] In the United States, the conjunction of religious and anti-vaxxer views is clearly evident in the sign painted on the side of a truck at a rally in Pennsylvania opposing the introduction of restrictive public health measures: "Jesus is my vaccine,"[117] Although the purpose of the rally was to object to lockdown policies introduced by the state governor, protesters also demonstrated their opposition to mask wearing: video recordings and photographs of those present reveal that none of them were wearing masks.[118] This broad opposition to any public health measure to deal with the pandemic is similarly manifest in the book *Plague of Corruption*[119] and the video *Plandemic*, made and uploaded to multiple media sites by the discredited medical researcher Dr. Judy Mikovits. Among the endorsement of multiple conspiracy theories (it accuses Bill Gates of using the pandemic for financial and political advantage)[120] and the wholesale rejection of preventive measures (including the development of a vaccine),[121] Dr. Mikovits claimed that wearing a mask made individuals more physically vulnerable by activating the coronavirus. The video was subsequently removed by *Facebook* and *YouTube* on the basis that it made medically unsubstantiated and dangerous claims relating to the coronavirus pandemic.[122] But it had already been very popular; it was viewed more than eight million times in the first week of May 2020.[123]

The hostility of anti-vaxxers to preventive measures was simply a generalization and new application of their deeply entrenched hostility to science. Combined with a fatalist religious belief and a distrust in government, it provided a significant counterpoint to the increasingly anxious interventions of government as the pandemic escalated.[124]

Moving forward

In some ways, the COVID-19 threat is discrete from all previous pandemic events. As medical historians are fond of reminding us: "If you've seen one pandemic you've seen one pandemic."[125] A lot of what we learn in COVID times might not apply to future pandemic threats, even if they are coronavirus related. The key difference in having the mask debate now is the lessons we can learn about access – to mask materials and to knowledge of their effectiveness in fighting this particular disease.[126]

As Part I of this chapter has shown, any material that covers our noses and mouths provides a more effective defense against air-borne or surface residing germs than going without. While N95 and KF94 models and plastic face shields are preferred for frontline medical care staff, various cottage industry models can reduce transmission by air while providing a barrier when our hands touch our faces with germs we have contacted from various sources. It can also reduce transmission of our germ-laden breath to others if we are infected. In Figure 5.1 we see the mask as worn by an uninfected person.

Online media is expanding our access to new knowledge that will enlighten our decision-making. For those of us for whom internet connection is available and affordable, informing ourselves about how to balance the increased mobility of populations, as well as the influence of civil liberties on public health policy, is very manageable.

The challenge is to filter through false and hyperbolic information to get workable knowledge sources we can trust. For the SARS infectious disease threat in 2004, we were advised that increased recognition of the threat posed by emerging infectious diseases within the general population had led to greater international cooperation in reporting and responding to disease outbreaks. The key proposition of this chapter has been the political tailspin away from that

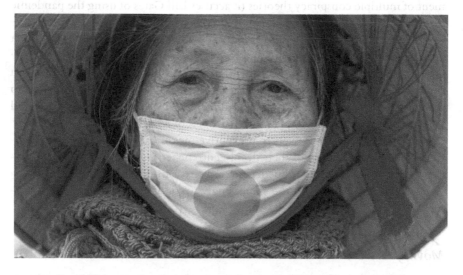

FIGURE 5.1 A Vietnamese woman wears a face mask. The patch will change color if she is infected with COVID-19

Source: Photo permission: Annie Ruimi

collaboration, as epitomized by mask denial initially espoused by political leaders in Western democracies.[127] Going forward with lessons from COVID-19 will involve a recommitment to that international cooperation in reporting and responding to disease outbreaks, as embodied in recent calls for revisions to the WHO's International Health Regulations.[128]

The mask shortage due to supply chain disruptions is another basis of denial, but those economic issues seem to be waning as Covax distribution and certain sources of supply, such as China and Russia, are stepping in to meet shortfalls. It is possible the mask stand-off will only be resolved once the pandemic has abated and we are left to assess the damage and count our communal and global blessings.

This chapter proposes three practices, directed at each of our three professionals, that will move that objective forward. For medical historians, working with verifiable facts and figures from past records can better inform our current and future decision-making. While each pandemic pathogen is, by definition, a novel organism, we are now sufficiently distanced from the SARS-1 and MERS experiences to gleaning lessons about detection, containment, and treatment. For epidemiologists and other medical researchers, keeping a critical eye on scientific developments and rising above the confines of political nationalism can begin to defeat the distrust and chaos that has hampered the COVID recovery. For social scientists, we encourage their acknowledgement that law is as necessary to formulating answers as psychology and sociology. Continuing evidence-based research and policies and shaping a pandemic law specialty can inform and guide our policy deciders and even jurists about steps forward. Among our calls for reform, this chapter asks for a re-consideration of the unifying potential of law to protect the common good.

Conclusion

In ancient Greek culture, masks performed a mimetic function: they were an imitative representation of the real world. Rules governed the types of masks that were worn in theatre and made them intelligible to audiences. In the words of German art historian Hans Belting, "The wearers performed their masks as readable signs."[129] With the modern pandemic, the wearing (or non-wearing) of a mask arguably performs a similar mimetic function: choosing whether to cover our face reflects our individual, many-layered understandings of, and attitudes toward, the pandemic. It represents our understanding of health risks, mediated through individual, socio-political and cultural factors. Thus, while public health authorities stress the value of creating a physical boundary to reduce transmission and infection, our decisions about mask wearing in future can also convey communicative and performative functions that signify other aspects of our identity.

In those first chaotic, fearful months of this pandemic, our most leaden and debilitating moments came with the mounting equivocation of those we expected to trust most: leaders, governments, and health authorities. Masking was their most divisive issue. Some of us have surprised ourselves in how quickly we've learned to adapt to radical disruption. We must now fill that knowledge vacuum with what we've learned.

BOX 5.1   CORONA SHORT #9: HONG KONG NICOLE, A LAW STUDENT IN CANADA, SPEAKS OF TRAVEL RESTRICTIONS IN ASIA

My dad came to Canada from Hong Kong because of the handover in 1997. He didn't trust China to keep Hong Kong a democratic city. Looking back, he tells us we should be grateful given what's happening there now. Also of all the English-speaking countries, my dad felt there was less Asian discrimination in Canada. He works in Hong Kong and China so he flies back and forth.

If you arrive at the Hong Kong airport they put you in a quarantine area just as you land. I saw a picture – it looks like an exam center with desks equally distanced. When Dad went back in July 2020, he had to wait for 4–5 hours for test results. If negative, they put you in a government assigned area for additional testing. It was very confusing in the beginning for him but now the government is getting used to how to handle COVID.

My mom is currently on day 20 of quarantine over there; she's visiting her ill father. Authorities took her to a hotel room with no windows. She hasn't been able to go outside all that time. There's also government designated housing. She paid more money for the hotel because she figured it was safer. They have certain requirements for the hotels. The ventilation system for each room must be individual to ensure germs do not travel through the whole building.

Hong Kong residents are advised to "maintain household draining pipes" by flushing out the pipes every week. That's because back in 2003 when SARS broke there was a large residential building where a lot of people died from the pathogen. They later discovered it was because the SARS virus traveled through the pipes. They are super concerned about it now. There was a recent outbreak of COVID in one of those residential buildings in Hong Kong and so everyone was removed and taken to a government designated quarantine center. Even people who didn't share the same pipes as the infected people. I think that's why the Hong Kong government responded so quickly because everybody remembers SARS.

It would be very hard to get Canadians to live in a certain building just because there's been an outbreak. I remember studying law and economics about how democratic systems are less efficient than authoritarian ones in situations like a pandemic. Societal values affect how decisions are made.

Governments will try to take decisive action, but I just don't see Canadians responding to that. They will argue there has to be "reasonable limits" on their freedoms. But I can see the value in governments restricting everyone to control COVID.

When I go to Hong Kong I see people wearing masks to protect other people from their colds or other illnesses. They are not thinking of themselves but of other people. I asked a friend there if there is social distancing during rush hours and she said, "No, the subway is very busy but everybody, everywhere wears a mask." That's an example of thinking of others.

The people in Hong Kong do not trust the Chinese about vaccines. The first available versions were Sinovac and Sinopharm from China so that's a key reason many people were not vaccinated. And a lot of people just don't want it. My grandparents are scared of the side effects. The media in Hong Kong treats side effects very seriously and out of proportion. When China said "Nothing's wrong" in reply to inquiries of outside countries, that was the reason Hong Kong responded so quickly because they did not believe that. Doctors at hospitals in Hong Kong were already taking precautions. Same in Taiwan. The public health people sent a team to China to check the status of the rumors. They came back and said all the evidence has been destroyed. That's when people in Hong Kong thought "This is very serious."

Notes

1 To paraphrase Peter C. Dancin et al., *The Pandemic Paradox in International Law*, 114:4 American J. Int. L. (2020).
2 Recorded on 21 June 2021 according to Johns Hopkins University of Medicine, *Coronavirus Resource Center*, https://coronavirus.jhu.edu/map.html. The accumulative count for that date in the United Kingdom is 4.6 million reported cases and 128,000 deaths; America reports the highest accumulative counts of all countries at 33.5 million cases with 602,047 deaths. Vaccinations administered by that date are 2.6 trillion.
3 Renyi Zhang et al., *Identifying Airborne Transmission as the Dominant Route for the Spread of COVID-19*, 117:26 Proc. Nat. Academy Sci. (30 June 2020). *See contra*, Umair Irfan, *What a Controversial Face Mask Study Says about the Science in the COVID-19 Era*, Vox (29 June 2020), www.vox.com/2020/6/29/21302489/coronavirus-face-mask-covid-19-pnas-study. *See also* Derek K. Chu et al., *Physical Distancing, Face Masks, and Eye Protection to Prevent Person-to-Person Transmission of SARS-CoV-2 and COVID-19: A Systematic Review and Meta-Analysis*, Lancet (1 June 2020), www.thelancet.com/journals/lancet/article/PIIS0140-6736(20)31142-9/fulltext#%20.
4 The WHO announced in December of 2020 that the use of a mask is only part of a strategy to deter transmission of COVID-19. *See* World Health Organization, *Coronavirus Disease (COVID-19) Advice for the Public: When and How to Use Masks*, www.who.int/emergencies/diseases/novel-coronavirus-2019/. For earlier positions on this debate, *see*, John Lednicky et al., *Viable SARS-CoV-2 in the Air of a Hospital Room with COVID-19 Patients*, medRxiv (3 Aug. 2020); and Megan Molteni and Adam Rogers, *How Masks Went from Don't-Wear to Must-Have*, Wired (2 July 2020), www.wired.com/story/how-masks-went-from-dont-wear-to-must-have/.
5 C. Levi-Strauss, The Way of the Masks, trans. Sylvia Modelski (1982), ISBN: 9780295966366 (with reference to myths and inter-tribal dialogues about status of the Northwest Coast Indigenous tribes).

6 Stephen Castle and Mark Landler, *Dominic Cummings Offers a Sorry-Not-Sorry for U.K. Lockdown Breach*, NYTimes (1 May 2020), www.nytimes.com/2020/05/25/world/europe/dominic-cummings-boris-johnson-coronavirus.html.

7 *Face Masks: How Is Wales' Advice Different to England?*, BBC (27 July 2020), www.bbc.com/news/uk-wales-52631835.

8 Nina Bai, *Still Confused about Masks? Here's the Science Behind How Face Masks Prevent Coronavirus*, Patient Care (26 June 2020), www.ucsf.edu/news/2020/06/417906/still-confused-about-masks-heres-science-behind-how-face-masks-prevent, (advising that "The legitimate concern that the limited supply of surgical masks and N95 respirators should be saved for health care workers should not have prevented more nuanced messaging about the benefits of masking.") Bai also interviewed University of California San Francisco epidemiologist George Rutherford who admitted, "We should have told people to wear cloth masks right off the bat." *See also*, David Shukman, *Big Shift in Guidance*, BBC News (6 June 2020), www.bbc.com/news/health-52945210 (noting that "[the WHO] points to recent research that people can be highly infectious in the few days before they show symptoms and that some people catch the virus but never show symptoms at all.").

9 Jordan Sand, *We Share What We Exhale: A Short Cultural History of Mask-Wearing*, T. L. Supp. (1 May 2020) (reminding us that "It was not until April 2 that the CDC announced that covering the face was in fact advisable. In the long run-up to the recommendation, no expert in the US seemed to know what masks might accomplish. They would not protect you because they could not be expected to fit perfectly, we were told. They might instil wearers with a false sense of security, it was proposed. The most commonly repeated claim was that there was "no data" regarding their effectiveness.").

10 Lawrence O. Gostin, *Our Shared Vulnerability to Dangerous Pathogens*, 25:2 Med. L. Rev. (Spring 2017), http://doi.org/10.1093/medlaw/fwx016.

11 Elliot Aronson and Carol Tavris, *The Role of Cognitive Dissonance in the Pandemic*, Atlantic (12 July 2020), www.theatlantic.com/ideas/archive/2020/07/role-cognitive-dissonance-pandemic/614074/ (suggesting "Because of the intense polarization in our country, a great many Americans now see the life-and-death decisions of the coronavirus as political choices rather than medical ones.").

12 Megan Molteni and Adam Rogers, *How Masks Went from Don't-Wear to Must-Have*, Wired (2 July 2020), www.wired.com/story/how-masks-went-from-dont-wear-to-must-have/.

13 Tara Parker-Pope, *Can You Make a Mask Out of Jeans? Bra Pads? Reusable Grocery Bags?*, NYTimes (21 Apr. 2020), www.nytimes.com/2020/04/21/well/live/coronavirus-mask-materials-jeans-bra-pads-grocery-bags.html. For nations who had endured the SARS pandemic in 2003 and were acculturated to wearing masks to prevent germ spread, compliance was voluntary.

14 Dancin et al., *supra*, n 1.

15 Claudia Pagliari, *What Do World Leaders Really Mean by Refusing to Wear Face Masks?*, U. Edinburgh Covid-19 Response, www.ed.ac.uk/covid-19-response/expert-insights/what-messages-are-world-leaders-giving-when-they-r.

16 *Id.*

17 David Mikkelson, *Did the Obama Administration Fail to Prepare a Pandemic "Game Plan"?*, Snopes (13 May 2020), www.snopes.com/fact-check/obama-pandemic-playbook/. The fact checking website affirms, "Tactics and key policy decisions were laid out in a 69-page National Security Council playbook on fighting pandemics put together in 2016." *See also*, Fred Charatan, *Bush Announces US Plan for Flu Pandemic*, 331(7525) BMJ 1103 (2005).

18 Tara McKelvey, *Coronavirus: Why Are Americans So Angry about Masks?*, BBC News World (20 July 2020), www.bbc.com/news/world-us-canada-53477121 (pointing out American attitudes about mask wearing fall along political party lines).

19 Aronson and Tavris, *supra* n 11.

20 For a historical overview, *see* Alex Langstaff, *Pandemic Narratives and the Historian*, LA Review of Books (18 May 2020), https://lareviewofbooks.org/article/pandemic-narratives-and-the-historian/.

21 J. Foreman, Maskwork (2000).

22 Jean-Noel Biraben, *Certain Characteristics of the Plague Epidemic in France, 1720–22*, 97:2 Daedalus (Spring 1968), Historical Population Studies, pp. 536–545. We now know bubonic plague was caused by a bacillus *Yersinia pestis*.

23 This paragraph is informed by L. Fabian Hirst, The Conquest of Plague: A Study of the Evolution of Epidemiology (1953) (setting out the transition of plague theory from deistic causes to belief in the miasma as causative to the emergence of germ or contagion theory in the 20th century.)

24 Colin Jones, *Plague and Its Metaphors in Early Modern France*, 53 Representations 97–127 at 98 (Winter 1996).

25 *See generally*, S. S. Block (ed.), Disinfection, Sterilization, and Preservation, 4th ed. (1991).

26 Elizabeth Kolbert, *Pandemics and the Shape of Human History*, New Yorker (30 Mar. 2020), www.newyorker.com/magazine/2020/04/06/pandemics-and-the-shape-of-human-history.

27 Sir Richard Evans, *The Black Plague*, Gresham Lectures, YouTube, www.youtube.com/watch?v=_5ImYgBeBS0&t=2847s.

28 Bruno J. Strasser and Thomas Schlich, *A History of the Medical Mask and the Rise of Throwaway Culture*, Lancet (29 May 2020).

29 Id.

30 *See, for example*, William Eamon, *Review: Plagues, Healers, and Patients in Early Modern Europe*, 52:2 Ren. Quart. 474–486 (Summer 1999); and Jones *supra* n 24.

31 Christiane Matuschek et al., *The History and Value of Face Masks*, Eur. J. Med. Res. (23 June 2020), https://eurjmedres.biomedcentral.com/articles/10.1186/s40001-020-00423-4#ref-CR2, commenting "Nevertheless, there is no proof that these 'plague-doctors with beak-like masks' really existed.

32 Joseph P. Byrne, Daily Life during the Black Death (2006).

33 Biraben, *supra* n 22, pp. 23 and 137, Figure 17 with caption in French.

34 *Id.*

35 Jones, *supra* n 24, p. 103.

36 Frank M. Snowden, Epidemics and Society: From the Black Death to the Present (2019).

37 *Id.* p. 69, (noting that magistrates were empowered with full legislative, executive and judicial authority in all things related to public health.)

38 Biraben, *supra* n 22, pp. 541–543.

39 Such actions are echoed in COVID-19 reports that 340,000 police officers have been deployed across Indonesia to enforce masking mandates and those in default are made to read the Koran in public or post apologies on social media: AFP Staff, *Indonesia Rolls Out Public Shaming for Virus Violators*, CTV News (29 May 2020), www.ctvnews.ca/health/coronavirus/indonesia-rolls-out-public-shaming-for-virus-violators-1.4960350.

40 Snowden, *supra* n 36 at 62.

41 Ed Yong, *Everyone Thinks They Are Right about Masks*, Atlantic (1 Apr. 2020), www.theatlantic.com/health/archive/2020/04/coronavirus-pandemic-airborne-go-outside-masks/609235/ (reinforcing the concept in COVID-19 times that masks are "an affirmation of civic-mindedness" as they "could signal that society is taking the pandemic threat seriously." Yong predicts that "their widespread adoption here [the US] could both reduce the stigma of illness and curb some of the racial connotations that have provoked COVID-born xenophobia."

42 Suyin Haynes, *As Coronavirus Spreads, So Does Xenophobia and Anti-Asian Racism*, Time (6 Mar. 2020), https://time.com/5797836/coronavirus-racism-stereotypes-attacks/.

43 The germ theory was first postulated in the latter quarter of the 19th century by Robert Cohn who experimented with the spread of anthrax in laboratory animals; it was then endorsed in practice by British surgeon Joseph Lister.

44 John L. Spooner, *History of Surgical Face Masks*, Sci. Direct, www.sciencedirect.com/sdfe/pdf/download/eid/1-s2.0-S0001209208713590/first-page-pdf.

45 Strasser and Schlich, *supra* n 28. The surgical mask had its critics: the Berlin physician Alexander Fraenkel was skeptical of the "whole surgical costume with a bonnet, mouth mask and veil, devised under the slogan of total wound sterility."

46 Alfred Crosby, America's Forgotten Pandemic: The Influenza of 1918 (2003); N. Tomes, *Destroyers and Teacher: Managing the Masses during the 1918–1919 Influenza Pandemic*, (Suppl. 3) Pub. Health Rep. 48–62 (2010).

47 L. Loeb, *Beating the Fu: Orthodox and Commercial Responses to Influenza in Britain, 1889–1919*, 18:2 Soc. Hist. Med. 103–224 (2005).

48 Most recently identified by French researcher Louis Pasteur.

49 Strasser and Schlich, *supra* n 28.

50 Becky Little, *When Mask-Wearing Rules in the 1918 Pandemic Faced Resistance*, History.Com (6 May 2020), www.history.com/news/1918-spanish-flu-mask-wearing-resistance, citing one Red Cross PSA: "The man or woman or child who will not wear a mask now is a dangerous slacker."

51 John M. Barry, The Great Influenza (2018).

52 *Id* at 374.

53 *Id*, Photo 11.

54 Little, *supra* n 50 (citing Alex Navarro, assistant director of the Center for the History of Medicine at the University of Michigan).

55 *Id*, with reference to a Phoenix, Arizona ordinance.

56 *Id*, citing the Seattle Daily Times (18 Oct. 1918) headline, "Influenza Veils Set New Fashion: Seattle Women Wearing Fine Mesh with Chiffon Border to Ward Off Malady." For a COVID version of mask-as-fashion-statement, *see* Laura Armstrong, *The Great Mask Debate: Which of These COVID-19 Face Coverings Is Right for You?*, The Star (5 May 2020).

57 Id.

58 Barry, *supra* n 51.

59 Barry's later assessment, however, was that masks of the time were "useless," and the city had simply been lucky prior to the devastating third wave that brought the worst death rates on the West Coast of America. *See* Afterward (2004) 457.

60 Strasser and Schlich, *supra* n 28.

61 *Id*.

62 *Id*.

63 Ashifa Kossam, *"More Masks Than Jellyfish"*: Coronavirus Waste Ends Up in Ocean, The Guardian (8 June 2020), www.theguardian.com/environment/2020/jun/08/more-masks-than-jellyfish-coronavirus-waste-ends-up-in-ocean#:~:text=Conservationists/.

64 World Health Organisation, *Coronavirus*, Health Topics, www.who.int/healthtopics/coronavirus/.

65 *See further*, Linda Morawska and Donald Milton, *It Is Time to Address Airborne Transmission of COVID-19*, Clin. Infect. Dis. (2020), https://doi.org/10.1093/cid/ciaa939.

66 Bianca Nogrady, *What the Data Say about Asymptomatic COVID Infections*, Nature (18 Nov. 2020).

67 Yanqiu Zhou, *The Global Effort to Tackle the Coronavirus Face Mask Shortage*, Conversation (17 Mar. 2020), https://theconversation.com/the-global-effort-to-tackle-the-coronavirus-face-mask-shortage-133656.

68 *Face Coverings*, Dept. Health Hum. Serv., www.dhhs.vic.gov.au/updates/coronavirus-covid-19/face-coverings-1159pm-wednesday-22-july. *See also*, Prateek Bahl et al., *Face Coverings and Mask to Minimise Droplet Dispersion and Aerosolisation: A Video Case Study*, Thorax 1–2 (2020). However, there was also imprecision in some of the

scientific discussion of masks; *see* C.R. MacIntyre et al., *A Cluster Randomised Trial of Cloth Masks Compared with Medical Masks in Healthcare Workers*, Infect. Dis. (2015), https:// bmjopen.bmj.com/content/5/4/e006577. *See response*, C.R. MacIntrye, *COVID-19, Shortages of Masks and the Use of Cloth Masks as a Last Resort*, 5:4 Inf. Dis. (2015), https://bmjopen.bmj.com/content/5/4/e006577.responses#covid-19-shortages-of-masks-and-the-use-of-cloth-masks-as-a-last-resort.

69 The White House, *Dr Walenski Announces New CDC Guidance for Vaccinated People*, YouTube (13 May 2021), www.youtube.com/watch?v=rcejFn22cSs.

70 Sanjay Mishra, *Can People Vaccinated against COVID-19 Still Spread the Coronavirus?*, Conversation (25 May 2021).

71 Centres for Disease Control and Prevention, *COVID-19 Vaccines Work*, Covid-19 (20 May 2021) (stating that "some variants might cause illness in some people even after they are fully vaccinated.")

72 Michael Corkery et al., *Covid-19: C.D.C. Guidance Prompts Caution in Some States*, NYTimes (23 May 2021).

73 Ed Yong, *The Fundamental Question of the Pandemic Is Shifting*, Atlantic (9 June 2021).

74 Id.

75 Walensky later used similar language to Twitter followers: "Your Health is in your hands" she messaged.

76 Cf *supra* n 6.

77 Ed Yong, *What Strength Really Means When You're Sick*, Atlantic (9 Oct. 2020). Yong supports his view with two studies that found more individualistically prone countries tended to report more COVID-19 cases and deaths. Another study found that mask wearing was more popular in collectivist countries.

78 Yong, *supra*, n 73.

79 K.K. Cheng et al., *Wearing Face Masks in the Community during the COVID-19 Pandemic: Altruism and Solidarity*, Lancet (16 Apr. 2020), https://doi.org/10.1016/S0140-6736(20)30918-1.

80 Comprising a third group are those who claim health-based exemptions, a challenge for clinicians as discussed in Doron Dorfman and Mical Raz, *Mask Exemptions during the COVID-19 Pandemic: A New Frontier for Clinicians*, JAMA Health For. (10 July 2020), https://jamanetwork.com/channels/health-forum/fullarticle/2768376.

81 *For example*, C. MacIntyre et al., *Face Mask Use and Control of Respiratory Virus Transmission in Households*, 15:2 Emerg. Infect. Dis. 233–241 (2009).

82 *Face Masks and Coverings for the General Public: Behavioural Knowledge, Effectiveness of Cloth Coverings and Public Messaging*, Royal Soc. (26 June 2020), https://royalsociety. org/-/media/policy/projects/set-c/set-c-facemasks.pdf?la=en-GB&hash=A22A87CB 28F7D6AD9BD93BBCBFC2BB24.

83 D.C. Payne et al., *SARS-CoV-2 Infections and Serologic Responses from a Sample of U.S. Navy Service Members: USS Theodore Roosevelt'*, 69 MMWR Morb. Mortal Wkly. Rep. 714–721 (April 2020).

84 Chu et al., *supra* n 3.

85 *Which Countries Have Made Wearing Face Masks Compulsory?*, Aljazeera (3 June 2020), www.aljazeera.com/news/2020/04/countries-wearing-face-masks-compulsory-2004 23094510867.html.

86 Littler Mendelson, *Facing Your Face Mask Duties: A List of Statewide Orders, as of 11 June 2020*, Littler.com (11 June 2020), www.littler.com/publication-press/publication/ facing-your-face-mask-duties-list-statewide-orders.

87 Jeremy Howard and Nick Talley, *Why Are Masks Not Yet Mandatory in Australia?*, Sydney Morn. Her. (8 July 2020), www.smh.com.au/national/why-are-masks-not-yet-mandatory-in-australia-20200708-p55a4k.html.

88 Ministry of Health (New Zealand), *COVID-19: Use of Face Masks in the Community*, Health.govt.nz (12 June 2020), www.health.govt.nz/our-work/diseases-and-conditions/ covid-19-novel-coronavirus/covid-19-health-advice-general-public/covid-19-use-face-masks-community.

89 Adam Burgess and Mitsutoshi Horii, *Risk, Ritual, and Health Responsibilisation: Japan's "Safety Blanket" of Surgical Face Mask-Wearing*, Soc. Health and Illness (2012) 34:8, 1184–1198 at 1185.

90 *Id.*

91 Mika Morishima and Koya Kishida, *Understanding Attitudes toward Hygiene Mask Use in Japanese Daily Life by Using a Repeated Cross-Sectional Survey*, 61:2 Work 303–311 (2018).

92 Nisha Gopalan, *SARS Lessons Inoculate Hong Kong against Epidemic*, Bloom. Opin. (7 Mar. 2020), www.bloomberg.com/opinion/articles/2020-03-07/coronavirus-sars-lessons-reduce-hong-kong-infection-rate.

93 Burgess and Horii, *supra* n 89.

94 Jordan Sand, *We Share What We Exhale: A Short Cultural History of Mask-Wearing*, TLS (1 May 2020), www.the-tls.co.uk/articles/a-short-cultural-history-of-mask-wearing-essay-jordan-sand/ (discussing a 2016 survey reported in Aerodot, an online journal, that found that 53.1 per cent of female respondents in their twenties said they had worn masks for reasons other than hygiene; 30.2 per cent said they wore them to feel secure, while 51.7 per cent said they did so to conceal the fact that they were not wearing make-up).

95 Holmes Chan, *Hong Kong's High Court Rules Anti-Mask Law Unconstitutional*, HKFP (18 Nov. 2020), https://hongkongfp.com/2019/11/18/breaking-hong-kongs-high-court-rules-anti-mask-law-unconstitutional/. The prohibition was subsequently partially struck down by the High Court of Hong Kong. The Chief Executive of Hong Kong reportedly had relied on the *Emergency Regulations Ordinance* to enact the mask ban without bringing the matter before Parliament.

96 Criminal Code of Canada, RSC, 1985, c. C-46, ss 65(2), 66(2).

97 Opinion/ *This Is Why Some Black Men Fear Wearing Face Masks during a Pandemic*, Wash. Post (8 Apr. 2020), www.washingtonpost.com/video/editorial/opinion-this-is-why-some-black-men-fear-wearing-face-masks-during-a-pandemic/2020/04/08/5a897b6a-78bf-4836-94cd-c3446dc06196_video.html; Nathan Woodside, *Men in Masks at Wood River Walmart Think Officer Profiled Them: Chief Asks NAACP, FBI to Investigate*, The Telegraph (7 Apr. 2020), www.thetelegraph.com/news/article/Men-wearing-masks-in-Wood-River-Walmart-think-15185810.php.

98 Quebec's ban of face coverings of any kind in 2017 was forced by the debate over "how traditionally white, Catholic and French-speaking Quebec can absorb and respect the religions and cultures of immigrants arriving to the province, while protecting its own identity." *See*, Catherine Porter, *Behind Quebec's Ban on Face Coverings: A Debate over Identity*, NYTimes (25 Oct. 2017), www.nytimes.com/2017/10/25/world/canada/quebec-ban-face-coverings.html. For a discussion on the effect of COVID-19 on that debate, *see further* Katherine Bullock, *We Are All Niqabis Now: Coronavirus Masks Reveal Hypocrisy of Face Covering Bans*, Conversation (27 Apr. 2020), https://theconversation.com/we-are-all-niqabis-now-coronavirus-masks-reveal-hypocrisy-of-face-covering-bans-136030.

99 James McAuley, *France Mandates Masks to Control the Coronavirus: Burqas Remain Banned*, Wash. Post (10 May 2020), www.washingtonpost.com/world/europe/france-face-masks-coronavirus/2020/05/09/6fbd50fc-8ae6-11ea-80df-d24b35a568ae_story.html. Muslims expressed a particular irony in the duality of mask wearing treatment by authorities: James McAulay, *France Mandates Masks to Control the Coronavirus: Burqas Remain Banned*, Wash. Post (9 May 2020), www.washingtonpost.com/world/europe/france-face-masks-coronavirus/2020/05/09/6fbd50fc-8ae6-11ea-80df-d24b35a568ae_story.html.

100 *Id*, quoting Fatima Khemilat.

101 The typology of three distinct groups is not meant to downplay overlap nor instabilities but simply to highlight key sites of resistance to mask wearing.

102 In the state of Victoria, after wearing a mask in certain public places was legally mandated in mid-July 2020, a woman who was fined by police for refusing to wear a mask

claimed that the requirement was "in breach of the 1948 charter of human rights" and that it was her right "as a living woman to do what I want." *See* Tony Zhang, *Requirement to Wear a Mask Is Legal and Does Not Breach Human Rights, Say Experts*, Lawyers Weekly (27 July 2020), www.lawyersweekly.com.au/biglaw/29031-requirement-to-wear-a-mask-is-legal-and-does-not-breach-human-rights-say-experts. A lawyer, Nathan Bucley, also encouraged people to defy the government order and not wear masks on the basis that it was a violation of human rights and in breach of the Australian constitution; *see* Naomi Neilsen and Tony Zhang, *Sydney Firm "Trolled" for Response to Mask Order*, Lawyers Weekly (21 July 2020), www.lawyersweekly.com.au/sme-law/28980-sydney-firm-trolled-for-response-to-mask-order.

103 *Some People Argue That Mandating Anyone to Wear Face Masks during the Pandemic Is a Violation of Human Rights: Do You Agree?*, Japan Today (6 July 2020), https://japantoday.com/category/poll/Some-people-argue-that-mandating-anyone-to-wear-face-masks-during-the-pandemic-is-a-violation-of-human-rights.-Do-you-agree-.

104 Helena Rosenblatt, *No, There Isn't a Constitutional Right to Not Wear Masks*, Wash. Post (20 Aug. 2020), www.washingtonpost.com/outlook/2020/08/20/no-there-isnt-constitutional-right-not-wear-masks/.

105 See for example, *The Requirement to Wear a Face Mask Does Not Breach Human Rights*, Vic. Equal Opp. Human Rts. Comm. (27 July 2020), www.humanrights.vic.gov.au/news/the-requirement-to-wear-a-face-mask-does-not-breach-human-rights/.

106 A poll conducted in the United States during the 2020 Democratic presidential primary reported that one-third (32%) of Democrat voters chose health care as the most important issue to their vote decision, followed very closely by the coronavirus pandemic in the U.S. (29%). Conversely, Republican voters identified the economy as the most important issue (40%), followed by foreign policy and national security (18%). Significantly fewer Republican voters identified health care (11%) and the coronavirus (6%) as the most important issue. *See*, *KFF Health Tracking Poll*, IFF.Org (May 2020), www.kff.org/coronavirus-covid-19/report/kff-health-tracking-poll-may-2020/.

107 For instance, the Secretary of Health for Washington State in the US mandated the wearing of face coverings in certain circumstances (such as when social distancing was not possible) from 26 June 2020 to facilitate economic activity as that state moved out of lockdown: Department of Health (Washington), *Order of the Secretary of Health: Face Coverings – Statewide*, www.doh.wa.gov/Portals/1/Documents/1600/coronavirus/Secretary_of_Health_Order_20-03_Statewide_Face_Coverings.pdf.

108 Maria Polyakova et al., *COVID19: Can Masks Help with Reopening the Economy?*, Stan. Freeman Spogli Instit. Intern. Studies (5 Apr. 2020), https://fsi.stanford.edu/news/can-masks-help-reopening-economy.

109 President Bolsonaro was himself ordered by a judge to wear a mask when in a public place in Brasilia, the capital of Brazil after a law was enacted in the federal district where the capital is located requiring people to cover their nose and mouth in all public spaces, including public transport, shops and commercial and industrial premises: *Brazil's Jair Bolsonaro Ordered to Wear Mask in Public*, BBC News (23 June 2020), www.bbc.com/news/world-latin-america-53154890.

110 The statement was made by the Apostolic Pastor of Tabernacle Life Church in Baton Rouge, Louisiana, at a church service attended by more than 300 people in violation of a ban on gatherings of more than 50 people: Chrissy Stroop, *Authoritarian Christians Are Deliberately Undermining the Public Health Response to Coronavirus*, Conversationalist (27 Mar. 2020), https://conversationalist.org/2020/03/27/authoritarian-christians-are-deliberately-undermining-the-public-health-response-to-coronavirus/.

111 Chrissy Stroop, *"Jesus Is My Vaccine": Culture Wars, Coronavirus, and the 2020 Eletion*, Conversationalist (30 Apr. 2020), https://conversationalist.org/2020/04/30/jesus-is-my-vaccine-culture-wars-coronavirus-and-the-2020-election/.

112 Liberty Counsel, *Rights of Churches to Meet for Religious Services*, LC.org, https://lc.org/PDFs/Memo-ReOpen-Church.pdf.

113 *On Fire Christian Center, Inc. v. Fischer*, No. 3:20-CV-264-JRW, 2020 WL 1820249 (W.D. Ky. Apr. 11, 2020); *First Baptist Church v. Kelly*, No. 20–1102-JWB, 2020 WL 1910021 (D. Kan. 18 Apr. 2020).

114 Chrissy Stroop, *There's No Legal Reason for Churches to Receive Quarantine Exceptions*, Rel. Dispatches (Mar. 2020), https://religiondispatches.org/theres-no-legal-reason-for-churches-to-receive-quarantine-exceptions/.

115 Loveday Morris and William Glucroft, *Prospect of a Coronavirus Vaccine Unites Anti-Vaxxers, Conspiracy Theorists and Hippie Moms in Germany*, Wash. Post (3 July 2020), www.washingtonpost.com/world/europe/coronavirus-vaccine-anti-vaxx-germany/2020/07/02/da7efc7e-acba-11ea-a43b-be9f6494a87d_story.html.

116 *See further*, the various posts on these issues on the Facebook page of G&B Lawyers, a small law firm in Sydney, Australia: www.facebook.com/pages/category/Lawyer-Law-Firm/GB-Lawyers-197895204117588/.

117 Holly Yan, *Protests Erupt Again over Coronavirus Shelter-in-Place Orders: Here's Why Some Governors Aren't Budging*, CNN Bus. (20 Apr. 2020), https://edition.cnn.com/2020/04/20/us/protests-coronavirus-stay-at-home-orders/index.html.

118 *Jesus Is My Vaccine': Pennsylvania Protesters Demand Reopening*, SBS News (16 May 2020), www.sbs.com.au/news/jesus-is-my-vaccine-pennsylvania-protesters-demand-reopening.

119 Judy Mikovits and Kent Heckenlively, Plague of Corruption: Restoring Faith in the Promise of Science (2020).

120 E.J. Dickson, *Judy Mikovits, Disgraced Doctor at the Center of "Plandemic," Has a Bestselling Book on Amazon*, Rolling Stone (12 May 2020), www.rollingstone.com/culture/culture-news/plandemic-judy-mikovits-plague-of-corruption-998224/.

121 Although Dr Mikovits claims that she is not "anti-vaccine," she has called for an immediate moratorium on vaccine developments, claimed that vaccines have killed "millions" and repeated claims of anti-vaxxers: Martin Ensirink and Jon Cohen, *"Fact-Checking Judy Mikovits, the Controversial Virologist Attacking Anthony Fauci in a Viral Conspiracy Video*, Science (8 May 2020), www.sciencemag.org/news/2020/05/fact-checking-judy-mikovits-controversial-virologist-attacking-anthony-fauci-viral.

122 Elizabeth Culliford, *Facebook, YouTube Remove "Plandemic" Video with 'Unsubstantiated' Coronavirus Claims'*, Health News (8 May 2020), www.reuters.com/article/us-health-coronavirus-tech-video/facebook-youtube-remove-plandemic-video-with-unsubstantiated-coronavirus-claims-idUSKBN22K077.

123 Davey Alba, *Virus Conspiracists Elevate a New Champion*, NYTimes (9 May 2020), www.nytimes.com/2020/05/09/technology/plandemic-judy-mikovitz-coronavirus-disinformation.html.

124 Chance Bonar, *"Jesus Is My Vaccine" Has a Millennium-Long History Rooted in Antisemitism*, Rel. Disp. (19 May 2020), https://religiondispatches.org/jesus-is-my-vaccine-has-a-millennium-long-history-rooted-in-antisemitism/.

125 John M. Barry, The Great Influenza, Afterward (2018). The comment has also been attributed to mathematician and writer Adam Kucharski.

126 The challenge of providing equitable access to health-care resources is dependent on the politics and policies that prevail where you live, a worthy subject examined throughout this book.

127 Pew Research data revealed a breakdown along political party lines regarding how respondents in the United States viewed mask-wearing: "The word 'mask,' however, was the "single most-used term among Republicans and Republican-leaning independents, who were roughly twice as likely as Democrats and Democratic leaners to mention it in the context of negative effects from the outbreak." Patrick Van Kessel and Dennis Quinn, *Both Republicans and Democrats Cite Masks as a Negative Effect of COVID-19, But for Very Different Reasons*, Pew Research Center (29 Oct. 2020), www.pewresearch.org/fact-tank/2020/10/29/both-republicans-and-democrats-cite-masks-as-a-negative-effect-of-covid-19-but-for-very-different-reasons/.

128 Oona Hathaway and Alasdair Phillips-Robins, *Covid-19 and International Law Series: Reforming the World Health Organization*, justsecurity.com (11 Dec. 2020), www.

justsecurity.org/73793/covid-19-and-international-law-series-reforming-the-world-health-organization/
129 Hans Belting, Face and Mask: A Double History (2017) 49.

Bibliography

Aronson, Elliot and Carol Tavris, *The Role of Cognitive Dissonance in the Pandemic*, Atlantic (12 July 2020).

Bahl, Prateek, et al., *Face Coverings and Mask to Minimise Droplet Dispersion and Aerosolisation: A Video Case Study*, Thorax (2020) 1–2.

Bai, Nina, *Still Confused about Masks? Here's the Science Behind How Face Masks Prevent Coronavirus*, Patient Care (26 June 2020).

Barry, John M., The Great Influenza (2018).

Belting, Hans, Face and Mask: A Double History (2017) 49.

Biraben, Jean-Noel, *Certain Characteristics of the Plague Epidemic in France, 1720–22*, Daedalus 97:2 (Spring 1968), Hist. Pop. Studies, pp. 536–545.

Block, S. S. (ed.), Disinfection, Sterilization, and Preservation, 4th ed. (1991).

Bonar, Chance, *'Jesus Is my Vaccine' Has a Millennium-Long History Rooted in Antisemitism*, Rel. Disp. (19 May 2020).

Bullock, Katherine, *We Are All Niqabis Now: Coronavirus Masks Reveal Hypocrisy of Face Covering Bans*, Conversation (27 Apr. 2020).

Burgess, Adam and Mitsutoshi Horii, *Risk, Ritual, and Health Responsibilisation: Japan's 'Safety Blanket' of Surgical Face Mask-Wearing*, Soc. Health and Illness 34:8 (2012) 1184–1198 at 1185.

Byrne, Joseph P., Daily Life during the Black Death (2006).

Chan, Holmes, *Hong Kong's High Court Rules Anti-Mask Law Unconstitutional*, HKFP (18 Nov. 2020).

Cheng, K.K., et al., *Wearing Face Masks in the Community during the COVID-19 Pandemic: Altruism and Solidarity*, Lancet (16 Apr. 2020).

Chu, Derek K., et al., *Physical Distancing, Face Masks, and Eye Protection to Prevent Person-to-Person Transmission of SARS-CoV-2 and COVID-19: A Systematic Review and Meta-Analysis*, Lancet (1 June 2020).

Cohen, Jon, *Fact-Checking Judy Mikovits, the Controversial Virologist Attacking Anthony Fauci in a Viral Conspiracy Video*, Science (8 May 2020).

Corkery, Michael, et al., *Covid-19: C.D.C. Guidance Prompts Caution in Some States*, NYTimes (23 May 2021).

Crosby, Alfred, America's Forgotten Pandemic: The Influenza of 1918 (2003).

Culliford, Elizabeth, *Facebook, YouTube Remove 'Plandemic' Video with 'Unsubstantiated' Coronavirus Claims'*, Health News (8 May 2020).

Dancin, Peter C., et al., *The Pandemic Paradox in International Law*, American J. Int. L. 114:4 (2020).

Dickson, E.J., *Judy Mikovits, Disgraced Doctor at the Center of 'Plandemic', Has a Bestselling Book on Amazon*, Rolling Stone (12 May 2020).

Dorfman, Doron and Mical Raz, *Mask Exemptions During the COVID-19 Pandemic: A New Frontier for Clinicians*, JAMA Health For. (10 July 2020).

Eamon, William, *Review: Plagues, Healers, and Patients in Early Modern Europe*, Ren. Quart. 52:2 (Summer 1999) 474–486.

Foreman, J., Maskwork (2000).

Gostin, Lawrence O., *Our Shared Vulnerability to Dangerous Pathogens*, Med. L. Rev. 25:2 (Spring 2017).

Hathaway, Oona and Alasdair Phillips-Robins, *Covid-19 and International Law Series: Reforming the World Health Organization*, justsecurity.com (11 Dec. 2020).

Haynes, Suyin, *As Coronavirus Spreads, So Does Xenophobia and Anti-Asian Racism*, Time (6 Mar. 2020).

Hirst, L. Fabian, The Conquest of Plague: A Study of the Evolution of Epidemiology (1953).

Jones, Colin, *Plague and Its Metaphors in Early Modern France*, Representations 53 (Winter 1996) 97–127.

Kolbert, Elizabeth, *Pandemics and the Shape of Human History*, New Yorker (30 Mar. 2020).

Langstaff, Alex, *Pandemic Narratives and the Historian*, LA Rev. Books (18 May 2020).

Lednicky, John, et al., *Viable SARS-CoV-2 in the Air of a Hospital Room with COVID-19 Patients*, medRxiv (3 Aug. 2020).

Levi-Strauss, C., The Way of the Masks, trans. Sylvia Modelski (1982).

Little, Becky, *When Mask-Wearing Rules in the 1918 Pandemic Faced Resistance*, History. Com (6 May 2020).

Loeb, L., *Beating the Fu: Orthodox and Commercial Responses to Influenza in Britain, 1889–1919*, Soc. Hist. Med. 18:2 (2005) 103–224.

MacIntrye, C. R., *COVID-19, Shortages of Masks and the Use of Cloth Masks as a Last Resort*, Inf. Dis. 5:4 (2015).

MacIntyre, C. R., et al., *A Cluster Randomised Trial of Cloth Masks Compared with Medical Masks in Healthcare Workers*, BMJ Open 5:4 (2015).

Matuschek, Christiane, et al., *The History and Value of Face Masks*, Eur. J. Med. Res. (23 June 2020).

McKelvey, Tara, *Coronavirus: Why Are Americans So Angry about Masks?*, BBC News World (20 July 2020).

Mikkelson, David, *Did the Obama Administration Fail to Prepare a Pandemic 'Game Plan'?* Snopes (13 May 2020), https://www.snopes.com/fact-check/obama-pandemic-playbook/.

Mishra, Sanjay, *Can People Vaccinated against COVID-19 Still Spread the Coronavirus?*, Conversation (25 May 2021).

Molteni, Megan and Adam Rogers, *How Masks Went from Don't-Wear to Must-Have*, Wired (2 July 2020).

Morawska, Linda and Donald Milton, *It Is Time to Address Airborne Transmission of COVID-19*, Clin. Infect. Dis. (2020).

Morishima, Mika and Koya Kishida, *Understanding Attitudes toward Hygiene Mask Use in Japanese Daily Life by Using a Repeated Cross-Sectional Survey*, Work 61:2 (2018) 303–311.

Nogrady, Bianca, *What the Data Say about Asymptomatic COVID Infections*, Nature (18 Nov. 2020).

Pagliari, Claudia, *What Do World Leaders Really Mean by Refusing to Wear Face Masks?* U. Edinburgh Covid-19 Response.

Parker-Pope, Tara, *Can You Make a Mask Out of Jeans? Bra Pads? Reusable Grocery Bags?* NYTimes (21 Apr. 2020).

Polyakova, Maria, et al., *COVID19: Can Masks Help with Reopening the Economy?*, Stan. Freeman Spogli Instit. Intern. Studies (5 Apr. 2020).

Sand, Jordan, *We Share What We Exhale: A Short Cultural History of Mask-Wearing*, T. L. Supp. (1 May 2020).

Snowden, Frank M., Epidemics and Society: From the Black Death to the Present (2019).

Spooner, John L., *History of Surgical Face Masks*, AORN J. 5:1 (Jan. 1967) 76–80.

Strasser, Bruno J. and Thomas Schlich, *A History of the Medical Mask and the Rise of Throwaway Culture*, Lancet (29 May 2020).

Stroop, Chrissy, *Authoritarian Christians Are Deliberately Undermining the Public Health Response to Coronavirus*, Conversationalist (27 Mar. 2020).

Stroop, Chrissy, *"Jesus Is My Vaccine": Culture Wars, Coronavirus, and the 2020 Election*, Conversationalist (30 Apr. 2020).

Tomes, N., *Destroyers and Teacher: Managing the Masses during the 1918–1919 Influenza Pandemic*, Pub. Health Rep. (2010) Suppl. 3, 48–62.

Van Kessel, Patrick & Dennis Quinn, *Both Republicans and Democrats Cite Masks as a Negative Effect of COVID-19, But for Very Different Reasons*, Pew Research Center (29 Oct. 2020).

Yong, Ed, *Everyone Thinks They Are Right about Masks*, Atlantic (1 Apr. 2020).

Yong, Ed, *The Fundamental Question of the Pandemic Is Shifting*, Atlantic (9 June 2021).

Yong, Ed, *What Strength Really Means When You're Sick*, Atlantic (9 Oct. 2020).

Zhang, Renyi, et al., *Identifying Airborne Transmission as the Dominant Route for the Spread of COVID-19*, Proc. Nat. Academy Sci. 117:26 (30 June 2020).

Zhou, Yanqiu, *The Global Effort to Tackle the Coronavirus Face Mask Shortage*, Conversation (17 Mar. 2020).

6

HARD LESSONS

Long-term care homes as hot spots in Australia

Joseph E. Ibrahim

Editor introduction: As the pandemic got started, we watched in horror as the SARS-CoV-2 virus decimated nursing home after nursing home across the globe. Deaths were catastrophically disproportionate to the rest of the population, families were deprived of seeing their loved ones, even in their last living moments, and staff numbers were insufficient due to sickness and fear.

How could this have happened? Should we have foreseen such a devastating outcome? What preparations and measures could have been implemented to counter the enormity of the pandemics impact in the aged care sector?

We introduce Professor Joseph E. Ibrahim, a professor at the Department of Forensic Medicine, Monash University, Victorian Institute of Forensic Medicine, Australia, where he is head of the Health Law and Ageing Research Unit. Dr. Ibrahim is also an adjunct professor at the Australian Centre for Evidence Based Aged Care, La Trobe University, and a practicing senior consultant specialist in geriatric medicine at Ballarat Health Service with over 30 years of clinical experience.

Dr. Ibrahim's ongoing research investigates approaches to reducing harm to older persons and improving quality of life. Dr. Ibrahim provided evidence at the Royal Commission into Aged Care and, more relevantly here, to that part of the inquiry that produced the "Aged Care and COVID: a special report." He has provided evidence for, and has been cited in, the Australian Law Reform Commission into Elder Abuse, Carnell and Paterson Report, the Commonwealth Senate Inquiry for protecting residents from abuse and poor practices, the House of Representatives Inquiry, and the Royal Commission into Aged Care Quality and Safety.

DOI: 10.4324/9781003215769-9

Dr. Ibrahim was one of three people recognized by the *Sydney Morning Herald Good Weekend's* "People Who Mattered 2019: Health." He has published over 300 papers including 160 articles in peer-reviewed journals and is also a producer, co-writer, and narrator of four short films about ethical issues in persons with dementia and ageing, including "Dignity of Risk" and "To Resuscitate or Not" (see ProfJoe.com.au).

In the following discussion, Dr. Ibrahim shares his insights into underlying reasons for the devastating impact of COVID-19 on residential aged care homes, together with his suggestions for a better way forward.

Interview with Professor Joseph E. Ibrahim, Victoria, Australia – 28 January 2021

Deborah Porter (DP): By way of introduction, what can you tell us about the characteristics of the people living in residential aged care in Australia?

Joseph Ibrahim (JI): Most people think when you get old, you become frail, disabled, and unable to care for yourself. That's not the case.

In fact, in Australia of our total population of about 25 million people, there's about 3.8 million people aged 65 years or older. Those older people are categorized into three major groups. First is the vast majority who are community-dwelling older people and who are generally healthy and independent. The second group also comprises community-dwelling people; however, this group also have a form of physical or mental health disability and require assistance to remain living in the community. There are approximately 800,000 people in this category. The third and final group comprises people who are living in residential aged care facilities, perhaps better known in other countries as social care or long-term care or nursing homes. In Australia, we have approximately 210,000 older people living in residential aged care facilities with another 60,000 people entering the facilities temporarily for respite care, so the total accessing some form of residential care is approximately 270,000 people each year.

We see from this data that about one in three older people need some form of assistance and the vast majority live in the community. Readers should be reassured that they will live a relatively well and healthy life into old age.

DP: What you're saying is about 1% of the Australian population live in residential aged care?

JI: Yes, that's correct. The calculation is an approximation based on a national total population of 25 million people and between 210,000 to 270,000 frail, older people in residential care. Older people living in residential care facilities constitute approximately 1% of the total population in our country.

If we consider it in another way, it is about 7% of all the 3.8 million older persons.

DP: **Is it fair to say those living in residential aged care are defenseless?**

JI: Yes, that is a fair comment. People living in residential aged care facilities are probably the most vulnerable in our society.

Remember, that the very reason people enter residential care is because they have a cognitive, physical, or mental health condition that leads to a substantive impairment in functional capacity. That is, the person is not able to independently manage aspects of personal care, such as eating, toileting, bathing, or dressing.

The typical characteristics an older person living in residential aged care in Australia is of an 86-year-old female, with cognitive impairment due to dementia, an underlying mental health condition such as depression and anxiety, and multiple medical comorbidities such as heart disease and arthritis and typically prescribed nine or more medications. The average length of stay after entry into residential aged care is just under three years with reason for departing being death.

DP: **So, these people are cognitively vulnerable, are they also vulnerable in other ways?**

JI: This group of people represent a high level of vulnerability both physically and cognitively, and they're also socially and emotionally vulnerable. The physical vulnerability is due to the presence of frailty, multiple diseases, and physical de-conditioning, or having hearing or vision impairment. An important aspect to understand is that residents generally have a poor physiological reserve – this means an inability to tolerate or recover from small physical insults or injury. For example, a mild viral infection could rapidly lead to physical decompensation and more severe illness.

The cause of cognitive impairment is typically due to an underlying neurocognitive disorder such as dementia. There is also cognitive impairment due to cerebrovascular disease such as stroke. Cognitive function is also impacted by a high prevalence of mental health illness in older people, particularly depression and anxiety.

Older people are also psychologically and emotionally vulnerable because they have often lost their preexisting social connections on entry into the facility and struggle to continue existing or developing new relationships. Imagine how challenging it must be to develop social connections if you are in pain, struggling to get through the basics of your personal care, and often feeling unhappy. They are also dependent on others for their basic care needs, creating an unequal relationship with the resident feeling disempowered. This then creates an even greater level of isolation from other residents, staff, family, and friends.

So, the end result is we have a group of people that are physically frail, cognitively impaired, and not able to manage as others would; they are vulnerable socially because they are dependent on others for their day-to-day care needs and are therefore not in a position to speak up or challenge what occurs in the care home where they are living.

DP: **That sounds like quite a miserable existence . . .**

JI: All told, it is a pretty bleak picture, especially if we are viewing it from the point of view of a younger, able-bodied, and independent person. Interestingly, most older people manage to cope and keep going, living and enjoying their lives in residential aged care. It is not always so dark or so bleak. Some older people flourish in aged care, especially those who were socially isolated, alone in insecure housing and struggling with their own care. This group often revel in having secure housing, meals, regular presence of caregivers, and the social interactions.

DP: **Who are the main players in the residential aged care sector in Australia, and what are their roles?**

JI: An initiative to improving aged care requires understanding the key stakeholders in the aged care sector. This is straightforward, although it is often presented as a complex web of interactions. The basic model is fairly similar across the world for most human services. In essence, the aged care sector comprises a funder, a regulator, an approved provider, and the resident.

In Australia, the Federal Government is responsible for aged care. The detailed rules and laws of operation are enshrined in the Aged Care Act 1997 (Cth). I'll come back to this shortly.

The Federal Government provides the funding for the care of residents. Funding is determined by using an "Aged Care Funding Instrument" (ACFI) – a national standardized instrument that determines the level of disability an older person has, and in turn the level of assistance required. That is, funding for the resident is allocated according to their level of disability – the greater the disability, the greater the amount of funding.

Once the ACFI is completed, the funding allocated for a resident goes directly to the approved provider for the provision of the care needed by the resident. The resident is not aware of the funding allocated and does not have an ability to direct how the funds are distributed for themselves. The Federal Government provides funding of approximately $12 to $14 billion each year for the care of older people in residential aged care, which is less than 1% of our Gross Domestic Product (GDP).

DP: **So, the government is the funder, who else is involved?**

JI: The next tier is the regulator. There are two parts to the regulation. First, an aged care provider must be registered as an "approved provider," which requires the provider to meet a set of criteria specified by the government. The approval process and how decisions are made are not disclosed to the public.

The regulator is the Australian Aged Care Quality and Safety Commission, which has been renamed or reconstituted at least three times since the Aged Care Act 1997 (Cth). The regulator's central role is to conduct audits of residential aged care facilities according to a set of standards. The Aged

Care Quality and Safety Commission determines whether an approved provider has met the minimum standard and, if so, a facility is accredited.

DP: **How important is accreditation?**

JI: Accreditation is a mandatory prerequisite for obtaining funding from the Federal Government. Without accreditation a residential aged care facility cannot obtain government funding for the care of residents and cannot accept new residents into the facility. As a consequence, the facility is not financially viable.

The regulator has been challenged in its role of establishing care standards, assessing adherence to those standards, and applying sanctions where the required level of care has not been met. In Australia, the independent Commissioner of the regulator (Aged Care Quality and Safety Commission) talks about "soft touch" regulation, that is being supportive rather than punitive. As such, the regulator is seen as being in partnership or collaboration with federal government and the provider, and the goal is to work together for the common interests of the residents.

This creates friction and debate about the optimal role of the regulator: should it be a hard-nosed watchdog that is ensuring compliance without comprise or an amiable advisory body helping approved providers who are considered to be well-intentioned but don't quite know how to meet the required standards. Whatever the view, what it actually does is place the regulator in a conflicted position. This was evident during the COVID-19 pandemic, where the regulator attempted to play both roles and created confusion and disenchantment with approved providers, residents, and their families.

DP: **OK, so we have the funder and the regulator, tell us about those actually providing the service**.

JI: The third stakeholder in the aged care sector is the approved providers. These providers are the business owners of residential aged care services. There are approximately 900 providers in Australia, operating approximately 2,700 facilities to house the 270,000 residents mentioned earlier.

There is enormous diversity in the types of providers: their organizational cultures, business operations, and models of care. The providers are generally divided into three groups:

- public sector or government owned, typically by the State Governments of Australia. The largest of these is located in the State of Victoria, which operates about one-quarter of the facilities in Australia;
- not-for-profit ownership, which has over half the aged care market. These are typically faith-based or community-based charitable organizations;
- private ownership. This form of ownership is growing and holds over one-third of the market in Australia.

DP: **What do these private providers generally look like?**

JI: The private providers are divided into two further distinct categories. One grouping is the small, typically family or cottage style, owners who may operate one facility. The second is the large, often multinational groups that are typically listed on the stock market. The latter group often generates controversy about their role in the aged care with debate about whether their priority to make a profit and satisfy their shareholders is congruent with a human service provider.

  That is essentially the structure of the residential aged care sector in Australia. There are three stakeholders that dominate: the Federal Government which provides the funding; the regulator which assesses every facility every year to determine whether the standards are being met to maintain accreditation; and the approved provider who operates the facility to provide for the care needs of residents. Interestingly, the other two major stakeholders, that is the residents and the health and aged care workforce, have very little influence in the sector.

DP: **What about the residents, do they have a voice?**

JI: The residents have little, if any, voice and virtually no power at all. Their underlying physical frailty, cognitive impairment, and lack of connection limit their ability to self-initiate action or to mobilize as a coherent, sustainable force. As such, they are not able to lobby or advocate for change or to have their views represented to effect change. There are a number of consumer organizations and advocacy services, some of which are funded by the Federal Government, to assist individual residents with a specific complaint or concern. What is missing is an organization that is able to address the views and needs of the residents as a group.

DP: **That sounds quite alarming . . .**

JI: Yes, this is a major gap and one that you don't see in most other human services. For example, consider the consumer advocacy groups seeking to improve care delivery in childcare, schools, and health care. So, the representation of residents' views is not well organized or effective. This creates a vacuum, especially when you consider, for the reasons outlined earlier, that residents don't have the physical or cognitive ability, or the social connections, to advocate for themselves.

DP: **In Australia, what is the philosophy behind the residential aged care sector, and has this proved to be successful?**

JI: The Aged Care Act 1997 promoted the notion of the free market philosophy for the residential aged care sector. Prior to 1997, the government funding allocated to the aged care sector directed that a substantial portion, approximately 70%, be allocated to staff salaries. Further, if the approved provider did not use those funds accordingly, then any residual funds were returned to the Federal Government.

  The Aged Care Act 1997, which is still in place, changed this so that approved providers would keep all their eligible funding irrespective of how much was expended on staff salaries. The regulations put in place at that time stipulated that the approved provider would ensure the aged care facility would have enough staff to deliver the care required by the resident. There was not a mandated model of care or a minimum staffing level. The notion was this would lead to innovation and encourage providers to be more efficient as they would be rewarded with greater profits.

DP: **Are there quotas for staff numbers?**

JI: There are no minimum staffing ratios mandated by the Federal Government, and there is no obligation to refund any unspent funding allocated for resident care. In my view the idea of a free market has failed, and could not have succeeded, because there is no empowered consumer, insufficient information to make decisions, and no transparency around how the facilities operate. Also, an older person usually requires residential aged care when they have had a traumatic and substantive life event – such as a major illness or injury. This combination of factors results in a resident who is powerless and at the mercy of a free market.

DP: **What you're telling me is the free market approach certainly hasn't done the aged care residents any favors. What has been the result of this approach for the providers?**

JI: The free market approach has benefited the providers. This is visible in changes within the aged care workforce. Over the past 20 years, there has been a steady reduction in the total number of qualified nurses employed in aged care; a substantial increase in personal care workers, who have very limited qualifications; and a greater proportion of casual employees. Each strategy reduced the economic costs to the provider in operating a facility and increased their financial profitability. Simply put, profiteering has become more prevalent in the aged care sector.

DP: **Are the issues you have discussed so far some of the factors that led to the 2018 Royal Commission into aged care being established?**

JI: Yes, these were the preconditions that led to widespread abuse, neglect, and suboptimal care of residents, the media exposés into aged care as well as widespread community concerns. The Royal Commission was extended on two occasions, releasing an interim report in October 2019, a special report on COVID-19 in late 2020, and the final report in February 2021.

DP: **What were the main findings in the Royal Commission's "Neglect" interim report?**

JI: The interim report, titled "Neglect," highlighted the major failings of the aged care system in Australia. Of particular note was the history of over 20 previous inquiries into the sector in the preceding two decades, of which little, if any, action had been taken by a government to address the core issues.

The findings were unsurprising in that they highlighted a lack of transparency and accountability at all levels throughout the sector. The report also highlighted widespread evidence of suboptimal clinical care, neglect, and abuse. The Royal Commission identified the contributing factors for these failures were an insufficient sized workforce; a workforce lacking the contemporary practice skills required to meet the needs of residents; and a lack of infrastructure to support the care of older people.

DP: **In your opinion, were there any other significant issues in the aged care sector?**

JI: One of the most glaring gaps was the intersection between aged care and health care. In Australia, the Federal Government is responsible for aged care and community-based health care. The State Government is responsible for the provision of acute hospital care.

While general practitioners are funded by the Federal Government, accountability for their clinical practice is through a separate professional medical regulatory body. The role of general practitioners, and the medical care of residents, is not addressed in the Aged Care Act 1997. As a consequence, we have a fragmented structure where we know that residents need ongoing health care, and the approved provider is not responsible for its provision. Instead, residents must rely on identifying and consulting with a general practitioner, who is not accountable to the aged care provider.

Another emerging trend in provision of medical care over the past decade is acute care hospitals developing in-reach programs whereby hospital staff attend an aged care facility to provide medical care. This initiative seeks to reduce the number of older people presenting to hospital emergency departments and provide care in place.

DP: **Did the Royal Commissions identify any major failings in residential aged care?**

JI: The Royal Commission highlighted two major areas in the interim report: one was on restrictive practice with a focus on the use of chemical restraint and the other related to the number of young people in residential aged care.

The definition of "young" was a person aged 64 years or less. This issue being young people with profound disabilities having no alternative option but to access residential aged care facilities for long-term accommodation. This matter has been problematic, and known to be so, for at least 15 years. In the early 2000s there were two Senate inquiries investigating the issue and potential solutions. As yet, it has not been addressed in any substantive way and is an example of the lack of accountability of government, as well as the senior public servants at the Federal Health Department.

DP: **Tell us more about restrictive practice in the aged care sector.**

JI: The subject of restrictive practice places a spotlight on the interactions between residents, families, general practitioners, aged care staff, aged care providers, the regulator, and the government. It is a microcosm of all that is wrong in residential aged care.

Restrictive practice in aged care settings has been, and remains, widespread in Australia and across the world. Again, in the early 2000s, the Federal Government released practice guidelines on how to reduce restrictive practices, and yet restrictive practice still flourishes, as identified by the Royal Commission.

Restrictive practice is an example of how a vicious feedback loop continues unabated as the harm impacts only the resident. The existing aged care system has entrenched and reinforced this poor practice. As mentioned earlier, a substantial proportion of older people in residential aged care have dementia, many with unmet needs leading to a person's behavior presenting as being unresponsive or aggressive.

The accepted and evidence-informed practice response to these behaviors are non-pharmacological interventions. This requires detailed and repeated assessment of the resident with a multidisciplinary team of health professionals, including medical and mental health expertise. Interventions require additional staff and more staff time to provide diversions and reassurance with the resident. Unfortunately, access to these specialized multidisciplinary team services is limited and obviously costly. Also, providing additional facility staff for the additional and ongoing care is limited and increases the provider's operating costs. As a consequence, what happens in practice at the facility level is the prescription of antipsychotic medications, rather than addressing the major systemic failures of the system.

DP: **Why would anyone prescribe an antipsychotic in these circumstances?**

JI: General practitioners have explained that they feel pressured to prescribe in order to maintain faith with the nurses, who are struggling to look after the older person with unmet needs. Nurses rationalize their requests with a valid concern about the threats to their own and other residents' health and safety and say they do not have time to provide the specialized care of one resident at the expense of the care for others. Further, their lived experience of requesting additional staff is rarely fulfilled, due to economic costs, creating a learned helplessness in staff.

Another common and powerful rationale is due to a misperception of the efficacy of antipsychotic medication. To the naïve observer, the vision of an aggressive and distressed person becoming calm after administration of an antipsychotic medication is a powerful reinforcement – what is poorly understood is that the calmness is due to sedation and not a therapeutic response.

DP: **What strategies would be needed to reduce the use of restrictive practice?**

JI: This is a systemic issue affecting the whole sector. Aged care providers would need to, first, improve their staff skills base through training, along with a commensurate increase in their salaries to reflect this expertise; second, increase the number of staff providing care; and third, develop models of care and support engagement of geriatric and gerontic specialists and allied health professionals to address the non-pharmacological approaches. This type of substantive change is obviously going to cost providers far more and would cascade through to the federal government for additional funding support.

Importantly, the regulator, who has been present throughout this epidemic of chemical restraint, has had very limited impact on addressing this issue. It highlights the gaps in the effectiveness of the accreditation process to identify, monitor, and address restrictive practice. This suggests an inherent limitation of accreditation which is not an efficient or effective mechanism to identify the nature of some types of clinical practice and that regulation in and of itself does not deliver a mature or high-quality human service.

DP: **Is there a role for government here?**

JI: Yes. The government hasn't really addressed the problem at its root cause. The approach has been relatively superficial, as a genuine approach to cease the use of restrictive practice requires substantive sector reform. This would include establishing new practice standards and guidelines; the provision of training to develop the skills in the medical, nursing, personal care workforce; supporting the providers with additional funding; and specifying the need to employ more staff to provide the upgrades in care. This would require a substantial investment into the aged care sector.

DP: **Has the Federal Government taken any effective actions in relation to restrictive practice?**

JI: I consider the Federal Government's responses to eliminating restrictive practice as largely being "workarounds" rather than directly addressing the underlying causes of the problem. Two initiatives from the government and regulator were introduced. First, a requirement for a person or their legal guardian's consent for administration of an antipsychotic medication. The concept and the process of obtaining consent is highly contentious, and some commentators consider it contravenes the human rights of the resident.

The second initiative was to improve the general practitioners' knowledge in relation to prescribing of antipsychotic drugs through additional education. This approach is a weak approach, as demonstrated by existing empirical research investigating how to change and sustain behavior change in health professionals.

The core or underlying issues remained unaddressed. The government and sector need to address the insufficient number of staff in a facility; an ill-equipped and trained workforce; and the lack of availability and access to highly specialized medical and allied health professionals who are experts in managing older people with dementia and complex needs behaviors.

DP: **So far, we have discussed the aged care sector prior to the pandemic. What would have happened next had COVID-19 not arrived?**

JI: Yes, we've discussed the situation leading into the end of 2019. As one would expect, the pandemic delayed the Royal Commission delivering its findings as planned in 2020. The reasons for delays are instructive as to the diverse impacts of the pandemic.

The initial delay occurred due to limitations in continuing to conduct "business as usual" due to the impact of public health interventions. These restrictions reduced staff ability to attend workplaces and led to closure of public hearings. Other delays occurred with diversion of existing resources to more immediate concerns that had to be addressed in the nation's emergency response to the pandemic. An additional delay was due to the government's request of the Royal Commission to examine Australia's aged care system response to the pandemic.

The Royal Commission's final report was tabled in parliament and released to the public in late February 2021. It is an extensive multi-volume review of the aged care sector with 148 separate recommendations, and each recommendation typically containing several subsections. The key recommendations include a new Aged Care Act that is resident centered, changes to the operations of the regulator, better clinical and corporate governance, improved transparency and reporting of performance, an expanded, better trained, and better paid workforce, and additional funding. If the recommendations are actioned by government, the aged care sector should improve.

DP: So, what happened globally across the aged care sector when the pandemic arrived?

JI: Well, little did any of us know that the cases coming out of Wuhan, China in December 2019 would dramatically alter the world. Australia had substantial, detailed planning and action around quarantine, limitation of travel, and equipping the health system to respond. The public health response was well established, co-ordinated, and has been remarkably successful.

Unfortunately, the more vulnerable groups at higher risk of infection and mortality were not given the necessary attention. Australia didn't measure up to, or deliver on, our potential to protect the residential aged care sector. The reason for this statement is that by the end of March 2020, we knew there were more than 350,000 cases of COVID-19 in over 100 countries across the world. There was media reporting and visual footage from Spain and Italy, as well as known outbreaks in France and England, where residential aged care had been particularly badly affected.

These should have served as a warning for what could happen in Australia and should have informed our pandemic response. In fact, the warning signs for residential aged care were evident in the initial epidemiological studies which had documented very high case fatality rates of approximately 20% in older people with multiple co-morbidities – in contrast the mortality rate was 1% for the general population. It was apparent to practitioners in geriatric medicine and gerontic nursing that the population characteristics of those dying from COVID-19 were almost identical to the people living in residential aged care.

There is no doubt that we should have identified the old and frail as the high-risk group, and yet the majority of the world did not and, as a consequence, was ill-prepared for preventing outbreaks and managing COVID-19 in residential aged care facilities.

DP: What effect did this early information about the high case fatality rate in older people with co-morbidities have on Australia's pandemic preparations for the aged care sector?

JI: As described earlier, Australia's residential aged care sector was already stressed and underperforming nationwide. The gaps in residential aged care sector, that were documented in the public domain, included poor infection control practices and an absence of a universal approach to infection control training.

When COVID-19 arrived in Australia, there were two major outbreaks in residential aged care facilities in New South Wales, which were another warning sign and another opportunity for learning. These occurred in April, at least three months before the second wave of the pandemic struck in Victoria, the second-largest state in the country, where over 650 people died in residential aged care. This accounted for approximately 75% of all deaths from COVID-19 in our nation.

When we compare Australia to other countries, numerically we have done extremely well, especially in the community setting and general population. Where we underperformed was in the residential aged care sector. Many of the deaths that occurred need not have happened, as we should have been better prepared – we could have been prepared if we had taken notice of the earlier warning signs. There were at least four substantive signals: in 2019 the interim report of the Royal Commission documenting a sector in crisis; in January 2020 with the initial epidemiological studies; in March 2020 with the international disasters in nursing homes; and in April 2020 with our own local outbreaks. We missed these opportunities to learn from others and to be better prepared – the failures occurred at every level of the system.

DP: Can you elaborate on what you mean by that?

JI: At the federal government level, there wasn't a cohesive national plan for managing residential aged care. While the public health response noted that residential aged care was a high-risk setting, there wasn't a specific strategy for the known and long-standing issues that would hamper an effective response.

There was not an acknowledgment nor strategy to adjust for an aged care sector that was already underperforming, lacking in staff, and inadequate infection control capabilities. Nor was there intersectoral coordination of the Federal Government, which is responsible for the aged care sector, with the States and Territories Governments which are responsible for infectious outbreak management and acute care hospitals.

A clear national plan of how to approach and respond to the pandemic in residential aged care was not published. The emergency preparation response was essentially delegated to the regulator and each of the individual providers.

Compounding the challenges was the regulator being in the stage of transformation at the time, integrating functions previously the domain of the complaints commission and the Federal health department. The regulator also didn't have the staff, or the expertise, required to support an emergency pandemic response. In addition, the pandemic management guidelines that the Federal government published placed the onus entirely on the individual aged care provider to prepare their facility and to protect the residents. It paid no regard to the commonalities of problems that would need to be addressed, the existing gaps in workforce and skills gaps, or the strength of the provider to negotiate with the State Health Departments and the hospitals and general practitioners.

DP: **What would have been required to formulate and agree a cohesive national plan?**

JI: At a national level, given that Australia is a federation of States and Territories, a cohesive national plan would have required agreement between the Federal, State and Territory Governments, the Federal Department of Health, the State and Territory Departments of Health and Public Health Response Units, the residential aged care providers, the acute hospitals, and general practitioners. An agreement should have outlined the roles and responsibilities of each during the pandemic.

DP: **Can you give us an example?**

JI: So, to give a hypothetical, let's consider a privately owned aged care facility in Victoria having an outbreak of COVID-19. The public health unit of the Victorian Health Department is responsible for oversight and managing the infectious outbreak; the approved provider is responsible for managing the day-to-day care of the residents; if the facility workforce is depleted due to illness or self-isolation, the Federal Government supplies additional staff through a surge workforce initiative; and access to acute care hospital management occurs through individual health services with oversight from another section of the Victorian Department of Health.

In addition, we have the general practitioners who may or may not be directly involved in the care of individual residents and are not accountable to the approved provider. Also, the approach to clinical care and willingness to visit on site at the facility varies between each general practitioner. There is also variation in access to, and the nature of, outreach medical services to residents through the public hospitals in their catchment.

On top of all of this, the regulator is also involved, both in terms of providing support in preparing pandemic response plans and in determining whether the facility is meeting the required standards. And so, you have the potential bizarre situation where an aged care facility is sanctioned for not being compliant with stipulated clinical standards of care, despite the fact that the Federal Government has instituted a surge workforce into that facility, and the approved provider may have been required to relinquish control of managing the facility.

DP: That sounds not only inefficient but also unfair. Are there other issues you have seen or heard about?

JI: Another curious hypothetical situation that highlights some of the boundary issues of responsibility is a large facility with multiple buildings on the State site has a localized outbreak in one self-contained section. The public health branch of the Health Department is involved where an outbreak occurs and technically has no responsibility for the other sections which do not have an infectious outbreak. So, unsurprisingly, this has created massive issues with communication and decision-making. Note, that I haven't yet mentioned who was actually in charge on the ground. This was a major issue and the lack of a clearly designated emergency response commander created delays in decision-making and suboptimal care. For example, who was managing the facility so that residents not infected with COVID-19 were still receiving personal and usual care; residents infected with COVID-19 were accessing clinical care; residents who were potentially exposed to COVID-19 were managed quarantined; staff healthcare needs and concerns were addressed; and families were updated about changes in the health status of loved ones

The multiple stakeholders and the lack of practical guidelines describing how each situation should be managed in a real-world setting created enormous confusion. And there were enormous amounts of complaints, from families who were not getting communication of whether a loved one had COVID-19, or whether their loved one was being transferred to a hospital.

DP: At the nursing home level, what were some of the more common issues that were encountered?

JI: What is disappointing is that we knew in March 2020 that there were at least three or four major and common problems for which residential aged care facilities needed guidelines. The most obvious guidelines that were needed included the details of lockdowns and restriction of visitors to facilities. The decisions about how this should operate were left to the individual approved providers. These could and should have been resolved with a standardized approach, following broad consultation across the country, and tailoring of plans for each State and Territory based on the level of community transmission. Instead, the 800 approved providers were left to their own devices.

DP: You're saying the lack of guidelines on these matters was a major failing. Was there anything else that really struck you?

JI: The optimal approach for managing residents with COVID-19 was lacking: specifically, the location of care. That is, whether residents should be cared for in place or transferred to hospital; identifying and standardizing the clinical criteria for transfer to an acute hospital; and identifying and supplying the clinical resources required if care in-place was to occur.

These are common and foreseeable matters that occurred across the world. Australia should have been better at resolving these pro-actively, early, and in a coordinated fashion, and this would have assisted in clarifying plans, and removing distressing, confusing situations.

Another issue was determining the optimal approach for residents who needed ongoing medical care but didn't have COVID-19. For example, appropriate management of people with dementia in circumstances and environments that are frightening because people are dressed in PPE with masks and muffled voice, families cannot visit, and the usual routine no longer exists.

DP: **Were there specific issues that arose in relation to the workforce in the aged care facilities?**

JI: We knew leading into 2020, and this was well documented by the Royal Commission, that we didn't have a sufficient aged care workforce, and the staff that were not sufficiently trained to meet pre-pandemic or usual care needs of residents.

It should have been obvious that the additional pressures of a pandemic would tip the balance to catastrophic failures. The workforce was inadequately prepared for the pandemic, staff education was largely missing or perfunctory in the areas required for emergency response "on the ground," and the arrangements for a surge workforce with aged care expertise were lacking.

DP: **What type of training are you referring to here?**

JI: The regulator implemented an online training course about how to don and doff PPE. This is of limited, if any, benefit as donning and doffing PPE is a complex cognitive and motor skill. It cannot be learned by watching someone; the learner only acquires the skill and competence by actual doing the task, that is frequent practice, with feedback to correct and reinforce. It also fails to send a message that COVID-19 is dangerous, that staff need to be meticulous, and that competence with the task is required. Staff must be trained and assessed to be competent and safe.

As such, the PPE training programs were not sufficient, and this was compounded by lack of clarity and detail in the infection control advice. A more effective approach would have been to provide robust infection control training using a "train the trainer" model, supported through a case management approach that clustered facilities into small groups across the country.

DP: **In addition to lack of training, what other characteristics of the aged care workforce impacted the pandemic response in this sector?**

JI: Pre-pandemic knowledge about the limitations of the aged care workforce were well and widely known. These known limitations were not well addressed. Specifically, that the majority, approximately two-thirds, of the workforce comprise personal care workers who have very limited training and many who do not speak English as their first language. In addition, their level of health and clinical literacy is consistent with their level of training: that is, low and perhaps best considered as negligible; well below the level of an enrolled nurse. And so, there was an unrealistic expectation that personal care workers were suddenly going to be transformed into workers able to complete some tasks that typically require the training of enrolled or registered nurses.

Another failing was the lack of presentation of essential information in a manner that was relevant to the audience. The aged care workforce often had to deal with highly technical, detailed information written more in a bureaucratic language or style. This was unhelpful to personal care workers. Information was not initially presented in different languages, nor did it explain to personal care workers what they needed to do at a practical level, in circumstances of extreme danger of COVID-19 in aged care.

Perhaps the more disappointing aspect was an apparent lack of compassion toward staff, with an absence of acknowledgment or reassurance around the risks to their own and family's health, and recognition that their role was essential to Australia's pandemic efforts. This was in stark contrast to acute hospital staff who were often referred to as "heroes" and their efforts recognized in tangible ways.

DP: How significant was the casualization of the workforce to the failings in the aged care sector?

JI: This was another aspect of the workforce known as to be problematic pre-pandemic. The increasing proportion of the casual workforce had been growing for a decade due to a combination of factors. That is, approved providers preferred this business and economic model as it potentially increased profits; and personal care workers being mostly female with care-giver responsibilities within their own home and family.

The impact of this casualization of the workforce led to more personal care workers having to work in multiple aged care facilities to generate a living income. During the pandemic we became very aware that people working in multiple places could increase the risk of transmission of COVID-19. A proactive approach to addressing these issues would have been beneficial; however, there were additional industrial relations issues that hampered the goal of having staff work in only one facility.

The combination of these factors, and the nature of the pandemic itself, resulted in a situation where you had a justifiably frightened workforce that wasn't being reassured or recognized for their value.

DP: What do you mean by "they were not recognized for their value"?

JI: Aged care workers were not considered "essential." In the early stages of COVID-19, doctors and nurses were given special treatment, including the provision of meals, and the "hotels for hero" that allowed them to stay close to work and to sleep in a hotel at no cost to them. Yet this was not available to aged care workers, and so we had a lack of societal level recognition about their true value.

DP: **What would you suggest in terms of providing cohesive, relevant guidance to this sector at a national level?**

JI: A better approach would have been a national aged care leadership group. This was eventually established, although not configured with the entire skill set that is needed. A national leadership group should have included representatives from the areas of public health, geriatric medicine, emergency management, acute hospital care, gerontic nursing, facility level nurse manager, general practitioner, personal care worker, resident and family, and human rights advocate. That's the configuration that you need for residential aged care.

This would be obvious if you actually know and work in aged care, because residential aged care is a microcosm of the whole world. The resident population incorporates individuals who are clinically stable and wishing to focus on quality of life; have a chronic illness and need active management; have a new and acute illness; require hospital care for illness; or who are dying and need palliative care. That is a very wide spectrum.

What was needed was a leadership group who knew and understood human rights and could provide a proportionate response for vulnerable older people in residential aged care. This was critical for informed discussions about the need for a lockdown, and how strict the lockdown should be. Those familiar with aged care would better understand how these interventions affect the quality of life of the residents, what demands are placed on the facility, and how to navigate the competing wishes and needs across the facility as a whole.

DP: **Were there any other gaps in terms of input into the national leadership group?**

JI: The lack of personal care and nursing staff representation was also a major gap. A successful emergency response requires regular input from the people who are having to do the work and implement the strategies. We needed people who knew how the day-to-day operations of a facility functioned, including the usual routine, culture of the organization, strengths and limitations of the workforce, and the ability to work as a team under stressful conditions. By knowing the actual conditions already in place, it's possible to tailor and prepare better for what is needed.

It is experienced nurse unit managers who know the residential aged care environment, know their staff, and know what needs to be done at a practical level. That's what was missing and, as a result, Australia had a top-heavy response that wasn't well coordinated, with chaos when outbreaks occurred, and political media spin messaging "everything is under control" without substantiation supported by objective data.

DP: **How satisfactory was communication during the pandemic, in relation to the aged care sector?**

JI: During the pandemic, there were regular briefings from Chief Health Officers across the country, and yet there wasn't a single briefing from an aged care sector representative. The absence of a trusted, non-partisan, and reputable aged care commentator or voice to explain what was actually happening, and to reassure residents and their families, was a major oversight. This was another gap in the overall pandemic response which, again, highlighted the lack of expertise or advisors on aged care into the public health efforts at the national level.

DP: What other suggestions do you have for improvement in managing nursing homes during a pandemic?

JI: The other approaches that should have been considered was case management through grouping of nursing homes and risk rating of nursing homes according to factors such as their size, according to residents accommodated, and history of regulatory non-compliance. This is a quick and simple way to stratify, while more sophisticated methods were developed.

It would have been useful to build communities of practice, whereby the nursing homes in a specific geographic region could meet with their local general practitioners and acute hospitals, to determine their collective resources and response. This could have been done relatively easily, with some guidance from a national aged care leadership group, and then locally implemented. These communities of practice could have gathered real-time information and feedback. This would provide detailed local level operational information about what was feasible and, where support was needed, to the national response.

The people who knew what to do at their nursing home in their region didn't have the authority to contribute to policy or weren't able to access resources they needed. This was a predictable result when there is a generic approach, decided centrally, and it is not nuanced to the diversity of regions and organizations.

DP: Is this a fairly typical issue in emergency situations?

JI: No. There was almost a complete disconnect between the central public health response that protected the community and that for the aged care sector. It was extremely disappointing to see it, particularly given Australia's reputation in emergency management of natural disasters, such as bushfires and drought, where there are far greater levels of cooperation and discussion from the top-down and greater representation of those most affected. Throughout all of this, there was no representation of residents; there was no one, apart from families through the media, speaking on behalf of what residents wanted and what they would tolerate. This was a major gap in our approach and remains so.

DP: Has the Royal Commission special report regarding the COVID-19 response in Australia accurately identified the issues in the aged care sector?

JI: The Royal Commission was asked to examine the COVID-19 response in Australia, but with very limited terms of reference. It was not asked, and therefore not able to look into, the root causes of the failures into the response for aged care. Instead, the Royal Commission was asked to advise on what could be done better in the future.

An additional concern is that the special report was completed and tabled before the second wave of COVID-19 in Victoria had resolved. In fact, the inquiry was occurring during the second wave, and as such was not able to consider how that was managed. Recall that the second wave was when the vast majority of aged care resident deaths occurred in Australia. So, in some ways it is a relatively hollow report: while it did highlight many of the issues raised, unfortunately it doesn't assist in better preparing us for future pandemics because of the limitations in terms of reference and timing.

DP: Have there been helpful, practical recommendations?

JI: The COVID-19 special report had five recommendations, which included the need for having a national plan specifically for the aged care sector; improving infection control practices; and improving staffing. It also recommended establishing better policies around some of the issues we have mentioned, for example around lockdown and transfer of residents to acute hospitals.

Of particular note was the recommendation describing the need for maintaining ongoing usual care to avoid functional decline in older people. This aspect was one of the hidden consequences of the pandemic. This aspect will come to light as we research and reflect over these experiences in the next 12 to 24 months. Perhaps an unanticipated consequence of focusing on the pandemic was the suboptimal care received by the residents who did not have COVID-19, as staff didn't have the time to maintain hydration, nutrition, exercise, and strength.

On reflection this was foreseeable, and we failed to prepare, being blinkered by concentrating solely on managing an infectious outbreak, and due to the guidance being presented from public health and infectious diseases experts. What we needed was a response that was tailored to the nursing home structures and functions.

While the public health and acute healthcare sectors had huge roles in the pandemic emergency response, it needed to be informed by an understanding of the usual operations of the aged care sector.

DP: Have there been other inquiries into the aged care sector during the pandemic?

JI: Yes, there have been a number of other inquiries, but these have related to individual nursing homes. Again, these were commissioned by the Federal Government and had restrictive terms of reference.

None of these addressed the bigger picture, instead focusing on how a nursing home was able to operate or respond. I think this approach was unfair, and essentially results in shifting blame solely onto the staff and management of the facility rather than the support systems that should have been forthcoming from health and aged care departments at jurisdictional and national levels.

DP: How significant were the physical characteristics of nursing homes in contributing to the severity of the impact of the pandemic?

JI: This was another major area where local knowledge of the sector could have contributed and informed response, with an understanding of the physical structure and layout of nursing homes. Most facilities are predominantly designed and built for residential style living, not for clinical care. As such, the facilities don't have the type of air-conditioning or ventilation system of an acute hospital, don't have the hand basins; have a high population density in the facility; and have shared communal living areas, shared bedrooms, and shared bathrooms.

There is not the space to separate staff from residents, and there is nowhere to store large volumes of PPE, equipment, and waste generated through infection control. There is nowhere to put the extra laundry coming through. So, some of those fundamental structures in the building, space, and equipment that are taken for granted in a hospital setting don't exist and become problematic in a nursing home.

DP: What happened in relation to screening of residents during the pandemic?

JI: The regular clinical screening of residents in nursing homes was an initiative which the sector advocated very strongly for. We designed a tool that was implemented and published in the academic literature. The importance of screening for early symptoms is an unfamiliar practice within nursing homes and, again, staff are not trained to perform the basic clinical measurement of residents' vital signs. These barriers of lack of experience, lack of knowledge, and lack of skills were only one part of the challenge.

Another barrier, and this was universal across the world, was that the screening clinical criteria for COVID-19 as applied to older people were largely wrong: wrong in that the clinical criteria assumed that older people have the same physiology, and the same pathophysiological responses, of a younger population. Specifically, older people don't mount an immune response or have a fever to the same extent as younger people. Older people do not often present with classical symptoms of a respiratory tract infection. When older people are unwell from any disease, they are more likely to present with a delirium, or changes in behavior, or changes in functional status. Older people may not have a rise in body temperature, and some may in fact have a drop with an infection.

So, in terms of understanding the pathophysiology of older people and applying these to screening guidelines for older people, the leading infection control organizations around the world got it wrong.

Also, expecting people with dementia to report their symptoms in a traditional way was an assumption presumably made through ignorance. The expectation that a person with dementia will be able to explain that they had a cough or a sore throat, and to volunteer that information, again shows a lack of thought or understanding of the at-risk population. Aged care practitioners understand that a person with dementia may explain their symptoms in a way that is not classical for an illness. This is considered basic or fundamental knowledge in geriatric medicine and gerontic nursing.

These, I think, were two of the biggest misses around the world. What they demonstrate is an ageist and discriminatory approach toward older people, and people with dementia, and a failure to include the aged care content experts in the emergency pandemic response.

DP: **So, in a nutshell, what do you consider the major problems were with the approach to managing the pandemic in the aged care sector?**

JI: Well, to recap, the unique characteristics of the resident population; the unique characteristics of the workforce; the physical structure of facilities; the nature of how a nursing home is managed in usual circumstances; and the failure to include aged care content expertise were contributing factors to the suboptimal approach to managing the pandemic response.

And so, at the end of it all, in my view, what we have is a response that was incredibly paternalistic; gendered and discriminatory in nature; and exhibiting enormous clinical narcissism. Evidence of the response being ageist included the lack of tailored screening guidelines to consider different presentations for older people who have the highest mortality risk, and the strategy that older people should receive healthcare "in place" rather than be transferred to an acute hospital.

DP: **Can you elaborate on what you mean by the response being "gendered and discriminatory"?**

JI: These are contentious ideas and lack objective evidence: a gendered response in that the majority of the workforce, and a majority of the residents, are women and as a society we do not pay attention to women to the same extent as men.

A discriminatory response is evident in breaches of human rights around the access to health care. This goes hand in hand with paternalism, the attitude of "we know what is right for you" without any true consultation about lockdown; whether residents chose to stay or leave the nursing home; what type of treatment and resources would be made available to residents; and whether the resources would be the same if a resident returned to living in the community.

DP: **So, you're effectively saying decisions were being made for residents, rather than with them?**

JI: Yes, paternalism overarches it all. The clinical narcissism is apparent in the absence of geriatric medical specialists, gerontic nurses, and residential aged care or nursing home managers being heavily involved and consulted in how to manage the situation.

There appears to have been an assumption that infectious diseases specialists, epidemiologists, public health physicians, and intensive care specialists were sufficient. I have no argument that these groups are essential and have the knowledge and expertise in an acute and public health response to the pandemic. However, I challenge the notion that they know how to manage older people in a nursing home. The general view, and it is wrong, is that the experts in medicine are those in high acuity services, in large academic centers, and that there is nothing complex about managing a nursing home which could be considered a step down from subacute inpatient wards in a hospital.

DP: Do you have a view on what aged care will look like in the future?

JI: The future of aged care is exciting and frightening at the same time. No one knows what the future holds. What we do know is the COVID-19 pandemic has uncovered an absolute failure in the system of aged care and nursing homes across the world. A key lesson is that these failings are not specific to an individual home or particular country; this is truly a global issue reflecting universal poor care for older people.

As such, this must reflect something very fundamental, at the core of society or human nature, for this same situation to unfold in the same way in so many countries. Is it our human nature that we do not value being old, and how do we determine the worth of a person? It draws us into the more existential question: am I only worth something in a democratic, capitalist society if I generate an income? And, once I get to 65 or 70 years of age, I have no worth and so, whatever I get from the community, I should be accepting of and happy with?

The second point is, whether this is an issue of ageism or is it the human instinct around survival, where we accept that survival as a species requires putting our resources into the next generations and beyond? These are existential questions, and I don't have an answer for those . . .

DP: As the current aged generation consider options for their future, what do you think their view will be of residential aged care?

JI: We know that the baby boomers generally do not want to go into nursing homes. We know at the moment, with the pandemic, that people in hospitals who are too unwell or frail to return home, don't want to go to a nursing home. The traumatic scenes and public disclosures of poor care have had an impact. So, there may be a substantial economic downturn in the financial viability of nursing homes as people don't want to live there anymore. On the opposite side of the coin is how we adjust to traumatic experiences: as people, we tend to forget or reinterpret these experiences pretty quickly. Perhaps in six or 12 months the visceral trauma will be forgotten, and we revert to our pre-COVID-19 approach.

What we do know is there is an overwhelming and clear preference for people to remain living in their own home. This requires increasing the level of community-based healthcare and social supports. If we had this in place pre-pandemic, the impact of COVID-19 would have been substantially less for older people.

What we have yet to determine is what is viable in the future. Is it possible to balance building and operating smaller nursing homes that are economically viable? Housing for 8 to 10 persons is the favored size; however, this eliminates some of the advantages that come with being larger scale, especially in terms of costs saving and being better able to have contingencies for workforce shortages.

And so, there are two different questions to answer. First, what is a viable size for a nursing home for residents, and the ability to secure sufficient staff? Second, what is a viable size for an approved provider to operate a nursing home and make a small profit?

DP: **What will the future look like for the providers of aged care homes?**

JI: I think that is still to play out depending on the inquiries that are happening, the potential for litigation, and what peoples' risk appetite will be. There's been an Amnesty International inquiry into aged care in the United Kingdom and Belgium; Sweden has had a separate COVID-19 inquiry by their regulator; Ontario, Canada, has an ongoing COVID-19 inquiry; and in the United States there have been damning reports come out of New York.

In Australia we have completed the Royal Commission special report; there is also an ongoing Senate inquiry; there are several civil class actions underway; and two coroners or medical examiner investigations being conducted. The issues are also being considered by the United Nations Human Rights Independent Expert on the enjoyment of all human rights by older persons.

The finding from these investigations will impact aged care both in terms of people's perception of risk and clarify accountability of who is responsible for delivering care.

The Royal Commission's final report noted up to 30% of residents have suffered through suboptimal care, neglect of personal care, and abuse. They made 148 recommendations for change, highlighting a contemporary aged care system requires a bigger, better trained, and appropriately compensated workforce. Other key initiatives include rewriting the Aged Care Act to be resident centered, ensuring a tougher regulator, having better representation of residents' views, and providing greater levels of funding.

DP: **We have heard some shocking stories of the ordeals residents and their families have faced during the pandemic, but we have heard less about the impact on staff. What are your views on this?**

JI: In addition to the pressures of working in an under-resourced and highly scrutinized sector, with additional multiple legal and judicial inquiry pressures, there is a moral or ethical dimension. Moral injury is increasingly recognized and has featured heavily around healthcare workers during the pandemic. The psychological hurt and harm that has occurred to families and residents is also likely to impact aged care staff. Seeing residents die, getting suboptimal care, feeling powerless to assist and receiving little support, and being pilloried by the community for the failures that are beyond their control will all harm staff.

I am expecting that as time passes, people will start to speak out about their experiences and more scandals of poor care will be uncovered. How this will influence the staff, and whether they wish to continue or leave the sector, remains to be seen. My view is we have created an environment where there will be a substantial staff shortfall due to moral injury.

DP: Learning from the pandemic, how could the provision of medical care be better addressed in nursing homes?

JI: How medical care is incorporated and delivered will need to be addressed. To operate an aged care facility for frail older people requires reliable, accessible, and optimal medical care. Despite this necessity, the medical care is not under the authority of, nor accountable to, the approved provider. This results in a major element in the functions of a nursing home being outside the locus of control of the approved provider.

In the future, a clinical model with a medical director will be necessary, along with nurse practitioners. The reform with potentially the greatest positive impact is having a gerontic nurse practitioner who understands older people and their pathophysiology, the operations of a nursing home, and how to harness staff into highly functioning teams. This is also beneficial as many of the therapeutic interventions needed in an aged care facility are non-pharmacological. And it is doable, especially in Australia. If we had 3,000 nurse practitioners, that is more than enough for one in each nursing home in Australia. There are strategies about how to recruit, train, and retain. The key step is long-term commitment from the Federal Government, and approved providers, both for the training and to provide security with those employment opportunities.

DP: In relation to infection control specifically, what do you think the future holds?

JI: The infection control standards will largely shift and become more aligned with what Hong Kong and other Asian countries did following the SARS pandemic. Better training, and better skills and resources for infection control practices, will obviously be needed.

DP: Given the experiences in the aged care sector during the pandemic, how important do you think it is to listen to the resident?

JI: The largest gap was a lack of respecting the human rights of older people and, I think, until that is addressed the sector will not be reformed or fit for purpose.

DP: Is there a role for aged care residents in reform of the aged care sector?

JI: Yes. The final part of the puzzle is finding a way that consistently engages and values the contribution of residents in the operations of a nursing home at a local, regional and national level.

DP: So, how might this be done?

JI: Some of the ideas for this could include implementing a clinical ethics committee in each nursing home that would provide a vehicle for that type of discussion. Again, that is not onerous or technically difficult to implement; it's just a logistical challenge that requires investment and resources.

Another option, which is a little more radical, is to provide a vote to every resident in every nursing home and to have them represented at Parliament by electing their own member of parliament. The number of MPs would be proportional to the population of residents. I doubt this would ever see the light of day but, having a network of residents that are able to be supported to put their point of view across on a monthly basis, through every home, and then centrally coordinated, is possible. It is also missing. And as long as that remains missing, I believe that no amount of restructuring or stricter governance arrangements will protect from another failure.

DP: **Is it realistic to think we could hear the voices of this vulnerable population?**

JI: We have seen examples of those that are vulnerable in the population being able to speak up and represent themselves. By being visible, it is easier for others to empathize and develop respect; that is what reduces their vulnerability. We have seen this with major movements in terms of equal rights, for example the suffragette movement and voting rights; the civil rights movement; those with HIV; and those with breast cancer who challenge the medical status quo to achieve better care. These are all examples of people who are directly affected being the ones leading the change. By standing up and showing society that they have an equal value and that they ought to have the same level of respect as everyone else, that they should be treated the same as everyone else. As long as residents are silent and invisible, then there is no identifiable group that is saying they are being treated unfairly and they are not being treated the same as everyone else.

So, if I were to advocate, and I am not a resident and I have a particular viewpoint, it is no more or less significant to another non-resident with a counter viewpoint. Having two academics argue about what life should be like in residential aged care is a pointless exercise and easily dismissed. We need to hear from the vast majority of residents as to what their life is like, and whether they feel they are being treated like the rest of the population in Australia. When we hear that regularly, then we know we are treating older people with the respect that we want for ourselves.

DP: **To conclude, what do you think are key considerations for law and policy reform for the aged care sector?**

JI: We have already covered many of these. To recap, these include starting with a new Aged Care Act that is based in human rights principles; better resourcing from the Federal Government; increasing the size of the workforce; improving the skill base of the workforce; greater transparency and accountability around the monitoring and performance of the sector; greater connection and representation of residents; better communication, collaboration, and partnerships between the relevant government bodies, hospitals, general practitioners, and nursing homes; preventing providers from profiteering;

ensuring funding allocated is expended on the resident; improved training in infection control; and evidence informed guidelines that are specific to the needs and circumstances of older people and nursing homes.

I would like to expand on two aspects that have become evident during the pandemic, and which have hampered delivery of a better emergency response. First, the propensity for the pandemic emergency response to be almost entirely top-down without consideration, involvement, or an understanding of the people and nature of their work. That is, the planning and implementation strategies were based on unfounded assumptions or idealized visions about how the aged care sector functions. This was dangerous as a complex sociotechnical system, like human services, has multiple layers starting with policymakers, government, health departments, regulators, nursing home owners, facility managers, staff, work tasks, and the resident. Effective pandemic planning requires understanding how "work" is done and the capabilities of the "people on the ground" – not a theoretical construct. My impression is almost all countries failed to involve the people in aged care with a genuine, practical understanding of day-to-day operations.

The second aspect is similar in the failure to appreciate the difference in behavior and motivations of how people would respond to the pandemic, and how the socioeconomic divide between rich and poor would manifest. Those making the emergency pandemic response plans at a national or jurisdictional level are public servants and senior health practitioners. They made assumptions that most people would follow the public health guidance without understanding the pressures on personal care workers, who barely earn enough to feed their family. This is another sad aspect of the pandemic – the huge divide between rich and poor, not only in terms of economics and health, but also in terms of a lack of understanding or empathy.

BOX 6.1   CORONA SHORT #10: SAMOA
DEBORAH, A TECHNICAL ASSISTANT FOR THE
MINISTRY OF HEALTH, PRAISES THE ISLAND'S
PANDEMIC READINESS

It's with some trepidation that I board the plane heading out of Melbourne, Australia, in early February 2020. There is news of a deadly virus in China, now spreading to other countries, and I am not sure how safe I will be on this flight, and whether other passengers or staff will be carrying the coronavirus, or sick with COVID-19, as we later learned to call it.

Hours later I arrive in Samoa, a beautiful South Pacific island where, a few years earlier, I was lucky enough to live and work as a volunteer for one year. I am returning to deliver some training at the Ministry of Health, and I can't wait to catch up with friends and colleagues.

The process for getting into Samoa isn't straightforward – they had recently experienced a measles epidemic and now there was a global pandemic threatening. In compliance with their border controls, I am required to provide proof of measles immunity together with a medical certificate, dated within three days of arrival, certifying I am free of fever, cough, and respiratory problems. The Samoans are doubling-down on protecting the island from further infectious threat.

I have all the required documentation and am questioned and temperature checked on arrival by workers clad in gowns, gloves, masks, and face shields. I am elated to see some of my friends as I clear border control. If you've never been to Samoa, you won't necessarily know how welcoming it is to arrive there, and how incredibly generous and thoughtful the Samoans are in their hospitality. Despite the tragic measles epidemic they had recently endured, the threatening pandemic and the local time being in the early hours of the morning, the arrivals lounge is vibrant with live, local, upbeat music, and we are greeted with smiles and friendly faces. And the warmth of the tropical climate, oh how I love that warmth!

The week flies by as I deliver the training to those charged with enforcing health laws on the island. The Ministry of Health building is opposite the main hospital, both multistory white buildings that are always a hive of activity – never more so than now. As always, the staff are enthusiastic and engaged in the training and, thankfully, with the island being free from the dreaded pandemic virus so far, we are not required to wear any PPE for the duration.

We work all day, with a break for lunch when we catch up on what has been happening since I was last there. At the end of each day, I enjoy catching up with friends, and feasting on delicious Samoan specialties including poke, *wahu* and swordfish, usually accompanied by fresh tropical fruit and a drink of *nue* – coconut milk straight from the coconut!

I see the Ministry of Health staff diligently monitoring the developing global pandemic, and the government tightly controlling their border to protect their people. I feel safe from this new coronavirus while I am in Samoa, as I have witnessed the stringent measures that are being taken to detect and contain any infectious disease. And, although I am sad to leave after only a week, I feel safe boarding the plane for my return flight, for the same reason. Samoa is free from coronavirus.

Meanwhile, I am returning to Australia, where there are 15 notified cases, across four States, including the State to which I am returning. On arrival, there are no temperature checks or social distancing requirements. I am uncertain as to whether I should wear a mask as a precaution; I know I am well, but I am not confident about anyone else. Needless to say, I clear the airport as quickly as I can and am relieved to make my way home. As a further precaution, I stay away from my parents and neighbors for a few days. I don't yet understand what this virus is about but, unlike Samoa, I know it has reached our Australian shores and I already sense it is a very real threat.

BOX 6.2   CORONA SHORT 11: NIGERIA
BASIL, A HUMAN RIGHTS LAWYER, SPEAKS OF
HOW HE CAN HELP WITH VACCINES IN IMO

They don't have similar COVID challenges in Nigeria. It is my understanding that the virus does not thrive in that hot weather. I am told that the only people who are getting it are staying indoors with air conditioning. If they had the colder Canadian weather, it would be disastrous. Generally, as a people, they think they are invincible, stronger than the virus; they are out and about and they don't wear their masks properly. I have to tell my brothers there how to wear them.

We have to convince people to get the vaccine. First, they do not make it in Nigeria so they have to rely on COVAX. And there is not a great choice because it is not made there. There are a lot of conspiracy theories about vaccines, way before COVID. They want to inject people to take their DNA, they want to implant them with chips through the vaccine, and religious leaders are very involved in spreading these false rumors. People have a lot of respect and regard for religious leaders. A lot of people I know have died. But there's a lot of carelessness, recklessness. They will never tell you someone dies of COVID because it will be contrary to perceived knowledge.

Vaccines are not plentiful to go around. There just is not a lot. A friend of mine went for two days to get it and on the second day there were only two vials left. No member of my family in Nigeria has got the shot yet. Even my mother who's 83. My uncle who paid my way through undergraduate education is in his 90s. He took other people to get their first shot. If there is someone whom they trust to tell them to trust the science, they will.

The enforcement of the ban on traveling does not work the same as some places. Nigeria is a stratified society, so the wealthier you are, the more you are able to travel even if they say there is no travel. A person who landed in Canada a while ago died of COVID just when he landed here. He had a certificate stating he was virus-free but they can fake that. The Nigerian politicians are known as lawbreakers – they don't believe the law applies to them. Our president does not believe in the Nigerian hospitals; he always goes to the UK for his medical treatment.

It is a matter of what's available. Ordinary people have to utilize the hospitals there, and the truth is that they are not well equipped. Our medical staff are well trained. They could thrive outside of the country, but it's for other reasons. It's a lack of equipment. There are a few hospitals that are trying to create a different narrative. But they are limited. The worst are the State hospitals – the human element is lacking. The money is lacking.

Wherever you have a society with corrupt factors, there are not resources to go around. They treat their family and friends first. They have the power to control vaccinations. There has not been a lot of uproar about people not getting the vaccine. Nigeria has over 200 million people. The first batch was

50–80,000. How are we going to get the vaccine to the majority of people with those numbers? But people don't care, they don't see it as a problem.

A couple of months ago there were demonstrations against police high-handedness. So people used that excuse to invade the politicians' homes. They found that those homes had vaccines stored inside. I have sent money through the local pastor who could get those vaccines for the people who are most in need. He identified them, and I send money so I could see them meet their needs. Everything in that society is political, and if you are not politically connected, you are not going to be protected.

Also, these are people who have to stay at home for weeks, doing nothing, and they will die of hunger if they cannot go out and get food. So that is how I can help.

Bibliography

Abrams, Hannah R. et al., *Characteristics of U.S. Nursing Homes with COVID-19 Cases*, J. Am Geriatr Soc, 2020;68:1653–1656.

Aged Care Financing Authority, *Eighth Report on the Funding and Financing of the Aged Care Industry*. Australian Government (2020), www.health.gov.au/sites/default/files/documents/2020/07/eighth-report-on-the-funding-and-financing-of-the-aged-care-industry-july-2020-eighth-report-on-the-funding-and-financing-of-the-aged-care-industry-may-2020_0.pdf (last visited Sept. 10, 2020).

Aged Care Quality and Safety Commission, *Guidance and Resources for Providers to Support the Aged Care Quality Standards*, Australian Government (2018), www.agedcarequality.gov.au/media/80036 (last visited June 2020).

Aged Care Quality and Safety Commission, *Guidance and Resources for Providers to Support the Aged Care Quality Standards*, Australian Government (2019), www.agedcarequality.gov.au/sites/default/files/media/Guidance_%26_Resource_V11.pdf (last visited Sept. 10, 2020).

Aitken, Georgia E. et al., *COVID-19 and Residential Aged Care: Priorities for Optimising Preparation and Management of Outbreaks*, Medical Journal of Australia, Dec. 9, 2020, https://doi.org/10.5694/mja2.50892.

Amnesty International. *As If Expendable: The UK Government's Failure to Protect Older People in Care Homes during the COVID-19 Pandemic*, Amnesty International (2020), www.amnesty.org/download/Documents/EUR4531522020ENGLISH.PDF (last visited May 11, 2021).

Anderson, Diana C. et al., *Nursing Home Design and COVID-19: Balancing Infection Control, Quality of Life, and Resilience*, J Am Med Dir Assoc, 2020;21:1519–1524.

Australian Bureau of Statistics, *Australian Demographic Statistics* (2019), Australian Government (2020), www.abs.gov.au/statistics/people/population/national-state-and-territory-population/latest-release (last visited Jun. 2020).

Australian Bureau of Statistics, *Disability, Ageing and Carers, Australia: Summary of Findings: A Profile of People Living in Residential Aged Care in Australia*, Australian Government, (2015), www.abs.gov.au/ausstats/abs@.nsf/Previousproducts/4430.0Main%20Features1042015?opendocument&tabname=Summary&prodno=4430.0&issue=2015&num=&view=2015 (last visited Oct. 24, 2020).

Australian Government, Department of Health, *Australian Health Sector Emergency Response Plan for Novel Coronavirus*, Australian Government (2020), www.health. gov.au/sites/default/files/documents/2020/02/australian-health-sector-emergency-response-plan-for-novel-coronavirus-covid-19_2.pdf (last visited Jun. 16, 2020).

Australian Government, Department of Health, *Coronavirus Disease 2019 (COVID-19): CDNA National Guidelines for Public Health Units*, Australian Government (2020), www1. health.gov.au/internet/main/publishing.nsf/Content/cdna-song-novel-coronavirus. htm (last visited Jul. 2020).

Australian Government, Department of Health, *Coronavirus Disease 2019 (COVID-19) Outbreaks in Residential Care Facilities: CDNA National Guidelines for the Prevention, Control and Public Health Management of COVID-19 Outbreaks in Residential Care Facilities in Australia*, Australian Government (2020), www.health.gov.au/sites/default/files/ documents/2020/05/coronavirus-covid-19-guidelines-for-outbreaks-in-residential-care-facilities.pdf (last visited Jul. 2020).

Australian Government, Department of Health, *COVID-19 Outbreaks in Australian Residential Aged Care Facilities: National Snapshot*, Australian Government (2020), www.health.gov. au/sites/default/files/documents/2020/09/covid-19-outbreaks-in-australian-residential-aged-care-facilities-11-september-2020.pdf (last visited Oct. 28, 2020).

Australian Institute of Health and Welfare, *Aged Care Data Snapshot-2019*, Australian Government (2019), www.gen-agedcaredata.gov.au/Resources/Access-data/2019/ September/Aged-care-data-snapshot%E2%80%942019 (last visited Jun 2020).

Australian Institute of Health and Welfare, *Factsheet 2018–19: Government Spending on Aged Care*, Australian Government (2020), www.gen-agedcaredata.gov.au/Topics/ Government-spending-on-aged-care (last visited Sept. 10, 2020).

Australian Institute of Health and Welfare, *Older Australia at a Glance*, Canberra: Australian Government (2018), www.aihw.gov.au/getmedia/7f3b1c98-c308-45c6-956b-b599893bdf33/Older-Australia-at-a-glance.pdf.aspx?inline=true (last visited Sept. 21, 2020).

AuYeung, T.W. et al., *COVID-19 and Older Adults: Experience in Hong Kong*, Asian Journal of Gerontology and Geriatrics, 2020;15(2).

Bielza, Rafael et al., *Clinical Characteristics, Frailty, and Mortality of Residents with COVID-19 in Nursing Homes of a Region of Madrid*, JAMDA, 2020;22:245–252.

Chatterjee, Paula et al., *Characteristics and Quality of US Nursing Homes Reporting Cases of Coronavirus Disease 2019 (COVID-19)*, JAMA Netw Open, 2020;3(7):e2016930.

Comas-Herrera, Adelina et al., *International Examples of Measures to Prevent and Manage COVID-19 Outbreaks in Residential Care and Nursing Home Settings*, International Long Term Care Policy Network (2020), https://ltccovid.org/wp-content/ uploads/2020/05/International-measures-to-prevent-and-manage-COVID19-infections-in-care-homes-2-May-1.pdf (last visited Jul. 2020).

Comas-Herrera, Adelina et al., *Mortality Associated with COVID-19 in Care Homes: International Evidence*, International Long Term Care Policy Network (2020), https:// ltccovidorg/wp-content/uploads/2020/10/Mortality-associated-with-COVID-among-people-living-in-care-homes-14-October-2020-3pdf. (last visited Jul. 2020).

COTA for Older Australians, *Industry Code for Visiting Residential Aged Care Homes during COVID-19* (2020), www.cota.org.au/policy/aged-care-reform/agedcarevisitors/.

Eagar, Kathy et al., *Australian Residential Aged Care Is Understaffed*, Med J Aust., 2020; 212(11), doi.org/10.5694/mja2.50615.

Gilbert, Gwendolyn L., *COVID-19 in a Sydney Nursing Home: A Case Study and Lessons Learnt*, Med J Aust, 2020, www.mja.com.au/journal/2020/covid-19-sydney-nursing-home-case-study-and-lessons-learnt.

Gnanasambantham, Kavitha et al., *Developing a Clinical Screening Tool for Identifying COVID-19 Infection in Older People Dwelling in Residential Aged Care Services*, Aust J Ageing (2020), https://doi.org/10.1111/ajag.12884.

Gorges, Rebecca J. and Konetzka, R. Tamara, *Staffing Levels and COVID-19 Cases and Outbreaks in U.S. Nursing Homes*, J Am Geriatr Soc, 2020, https://doi.org/10.1111/jgs.16787.

Guan, W-J. et al., *Clinical Characteristics of Coronavirus Disease 2019 in China*, N Engl J Med, 2020;382:1708–1720, www.health.gov.au/resources/publications/cdna-national-guidelines-for-the-prevention-control-and-public-health-management-of-covid-19-outbreaks-in-residential-care-facilities-in-australia.

Ibrahim, Joseph E., *COVID-19 and Residential Aged Care in Australia*, Aust J Adv Nurs, 2020;37.

Ibrahim, Joseph E., *Precis of Evidence: Exhibit 18–17 Witness Statement 12 August 2020 to Royal Commission into Aged Care Quality and Safety Hearing into Aged Care and COVID-19*, Australian Government (2020), https://agedcare.royalcommission.gov.au/media/28051.

Ibrahim, Joseph E., *Residential Aged Care: There Is No Single Optimal Model*, Med J Aust, 2018, www.mja.com.au/system/files/issues/208_10/10.5694mja18.00268.pdf.

Ibrahim, Joseph E., *Royal Commission into Aged Care Quality and Safety: The Key Clinical Issues*, Med J Aust., 2019, https://onlinelibrary.wiley.com/doi/abs/10.5694/mja2.50168.

Ibrahim, Joseph E. et al., *Meeting the Needs of Older People Living in Australian Residential Aged Care: A New Conceptual Model*, Aust J Ageing, 2020 Jun;39(2):148–155, https://doi.org/10.1111/ajag.12796.

Jain, Briony et al., *International Transferability of Research Evidence in Residential Long-Term Care: A Comparative Analysis of Aged Care Systems in 7 Nations*, J Am Med Dir Assoc., 2019;20(12):1558–1565.

Malikov, Kamil et al., *Temporal Associations between Community Incidence of COVID-19 and Nursing Home Outbreaks in Ontario, Canada*, JAMDA, 2020;22:260–262.

Mavromaras, Kostas et al., *National Aged Care Workforce Census and Survey: The Aged Care Workforce* (2016), www.gen-agedcaredata.gov.au/www_aihwgen/media/Workforce/The-Aged-Care-Workforce-2016.pdf (last visited July 2020).

McMichael, Temet M. et al., *Epidemiology of Covid-19 in a Long-Term Care Facility in King County, Washington*, N Engl J Med, 2020;382:2005–2011.

Ontario's Long-Term Care COVID-19 Commission, The Full Interim Recommendations Are (2020), www.ltccommission-commissionsld.ca/ir/pdf/20201023_First_Interim_Letter_English.pdf.

Ouslander, Joseph G. and Grabowski, David C., *COVID-19 in Nursing Homes: Calming the Perfect Storm*, J A Geriatr Soc, 2020;68:2153–2162.

Pappa, Sofia et al., *Prevalence of Depression, Anxiety, and Insomnia among Healthcare Workers during the COVID-19 Pandemic: A Systematic Review and Meta-Analysis*, Brain Behav Immun, 2020;88:901–907.

Rajan, Selina and Mckee, Martin, *Learning from the Impacts of COVID-19 on Care Homes: A Pilot Survey*, International Long Term Care Policy Network (2020), https://ltccovid.org/wp-content/uploads/2020/06/Learning-From-the-Impacts-of-COVID-19-on-Care-Homes-A-Pilot-Survey_June12.pdf (last visited July 2020).

Royal Commission into Aged Care Quality and Safety, *Aged Care and COVID-19: A Special Report*, Australian Government (2020), https://agedcare.royalcommission.gov.au/sites/default/files/2020-10/aged-care-and-covid-19-a-special-report.pdf.

Royal Commission into Aged Care Quality and Safety, *Final Report: Care, Dignity and Respect*, Australian Government (2021), https://agedcare.royalcommission.gov.au/publications/final-report.

Royal Commission into Aged Care Quality and Safety, *Interim Report:* Neglect, Australian Government (2020), https://agedcare.royalcommission.gov.au/sites/default/files/2020-02/interim-report-volume-1.pdf 2019.

Safer Care Victoria, *COVID-19 Screening Tool for Residential Aged Care Services*, www.bettersafercare.vic.gov.au/clinical-guidance/older-people/covid-19-screening-tool-for-residential-aged-care-services (last visited May 12, 2021).

Salcher-Konrad, Mamimilian et al., *COVID-19 Related Mortality and Spread of Disease in Long-Term Care: A Living Systematic Review of Emerging Evidence*, MedRxiv [preprint] (2020), https://doi.org/10.1101/2020.06.09.20125237.

The Senate Select Committee on COVID-19, *First Interim Report*, Australian Government (Dec 2020), www.aph.gov.au/Parliamentary_Business/Committees/Senate/COVID-19/COVID19/Interim_Report.

Stall, Nathan M. et al., *For-Profit Long-Term Care Homes and the Risk of COVID-19 Outbreaks and Resident Deaths*, CMAJ, 2020;192:E946–E955.

Stall, Nathan M. et al., *A Hospital Partnership with a Nursing Home Experiencing a COVID-19 Outbreak: Description of a Multiphase Emergency Response in Toronto, Canada*, J Am Geriatr Soc, 2020;68:1376–1381.

Tsai, Thomas C. et al., *Hospital Board and Management Practices are Strongly Related to Hospital Performance on Clinical Quality Metrics*, Health Aff (Millwood), 2015;34:1304–1311.

Willoughby, Melissa et al., *Mortality in Nursing Homes Following Emergency Evacuation: A Systematic Review*, J Am Med Dir Assoc, 2017;18:664–670.

World Health Organization, *Ethics and COVID-19: Resource Allocation and Priority-Setting*, World Health Organization, www.who.int/ethics/publications/ethics-covid-19-resource-allocation.pdf?ua=1 (Last visited Oct. 24, 2020).

Zhou, Fei et al., *Clinical Course and Risk Factors for Mortality of Adult Inpatients with COVID-19 in Wuhan, China: A Retrospective Cohort Study*, Lancet, 2020;395:1054–1062.

PART III
Security

7

INTELLECTUAL PROPERTY PROTECTIONS FOR VACCINES AND PPE*

Ana Santos Rutschman

Editors' introduction: Early in the pandemic there were reports of global shortages in personal protective equipment (PPE). Healthcare workers required PPE such as masks, gloves, and gowns to protect themselves and their patients from COVID, and yet there were insufficient supplies to meet the demand. In March 2020 the World Health Organization (WHO) responded by calling on "industry and governments to increase manufacturing [of PPE] by 40 per cent to meet rising global demand."[i]

In the meantime, there had been much work to develop a COVID vaccine and much discussion around the world about access to those vaccines. In early 2021, just over one year since the SARS–CoV-2 virus outbreak began, the head of the WHO declared the world was on the brink of a "catastrophic moral failure."[ii] He was referring to the issue of equitable access to vaccines across the globe: the "me-first" approach resulting in the richer countries dominating vaccine purchase at the expense of their poorer neighbors and the behavior of vaccine manufacturers in seeking regulatory approval in rich countries instead of "submitting their data to the WHO to green-light vaccine use globally."[iii]

While the rollout of vaccines commenced in some countries, such as the United Kingdom, the United States, and Israel, of which the latter was leading the world,[iv] others, such as Moldova, Ukraine, Georgia, and Armenia, had no access to the vaccine and no clear idea of when that might change.[v]

As our next author, Dr. Ana Santos Rutschman, explains intellectual property is a critical factor in the response to the pandemic and, more specifically, in the context of issues such as those highlighted above. For

DOI: 10.4324/9781003215769-11

example, the intention behind the mechanism known as COVAX is to prevent the apparently imminent catastrophic circumstances predicted by the WHO, by providing the means to promote global and equitable distribution of vaccines.

Dr. Ana Santos Rutschman can enlighten us on the legal and proprietary factors that might promote, or hinder, the research, manufacture and distribution of critical resources to combat COVID, such as vaccines and PPE. She is Assistant Professor of Law, Saint Louis University School of Law, Center for Health Law Studies, Center for International and Comparative Law. Dr Ana Santos Rutschman addresses intellectual property issues arising during the race to develop new treatments, vaccines and other medical technologies needed to address the public health problems posed by COVID-19. She highlights the two contrasting dimensions of the pandemic: on the one hand, the persistence of siloed approaches to R&D, technology transfer and allocation of health goods; and on the other, the emergence of countervailing collaborative efforts seeking to offset the progressive commodification of public health goods and overly proprietary traits of current innovation regimes. Which will prevail, only time will tell!

The COVID-19 pandemic from the viewpoint of intellectual property

The response to COVID-19 is indissolubly tied to intellectual property. In an increasingly globalized world in which infectious disease pathogens travel faster and wider than before, the development of vaccines, treatments and other forms of medical technology has become an integral part of public health preparedness and response frameworks.[1] The development of these technologies, and to a certain extent the allocation and distribution of resulting outputs, is informed by intellectual property regimes. These regimes influence the commitment of R&D resources, shape scientific collaborations and, in some cases, may condition the widespread availability of emerging technologies. As seen throughout this chapter, COVID-19 has exposed the shortcomings of ingrained reliance on intellectual property as a channel for the production and dissemination of medical technologies needed to address the problems posed by pandemics and epidemics. At the same time, COVID-19 has brought new life to countervailing efforts to explore legal and policy mechanisms to potentially offset some of the problems posed by the pervasiveness of, and shortcomings associated with, intellectual property dynamics.

In tracing the dual ways in which intellectual property has affected preparedness for, and the response to, COVID-19, this chapter highlights three features of contemporary intellectual property regimes and examines their impact on innovation(s) needed to address public health crises. First, it explores the incentives function of patent law and policy, which places considerable emphasis on market-driven investment in R&D on medical technologies. In so doing, intellectual property becomes one of the driving forces of the commodification of goods – vaccines, drugs or ventilator parts, for example – which are best understood as public health goods.

Second, the chapter illustrates how intellectual property has reinforced an ethos of siloed R&D, as illustrated by the COVID-19 vaccine race, which at the time of writing includes hundreds of separate vaccine development projects.[2] These siloes further extend into the allocative domain: with the development of medical technologies now largely steeped in proprietary frameworks, several countries have resumed the practice of reserving significant amounts of emerging technologies for their domestic populations,[3] thus curtailing the possibility of equitable transnational approaches to a global public health crisis. This approach is commonly known in the field of vaccines as "vaccine nationalism."[4] Nationalism skews the distribution of medical technologies developed during a pandemic, reducing opportunities for transnational coordination and, as seen below, tendentially limiting access to these technologies by populations in economically disadvantaged parts of the world.

The chapter ends nonetheless on a positive note, as COVID-19 has also made it abundantly clear that the legal infrastructure needed to address many of these problems is already in place. Early in the pandemic, several countries signaled that they would rely on intellectual property mechanisms to ensure broad and equitable access to medical technologies developed during (and possibly after) the pandemic, such as vaccines and treatments for COVID-19. These mechanisms embody different types of commitments to share intellectual property, data and knowledge.[5] At the allocative level, a significant number of countries joined an ad hoc vaccine distribution facility coordinated by Geneva-based international organizations. These efforts, albeit nascent and, in many cases, likely of a transient nature, constitute meaningful steps toward a better innovation ecosystem for medical technologies needed to prevent and respond to future pandemic.

Intellectual property before a pandemic

An often-cited purpose of intellectual property is its incentives function.[6] Patent rights, in particular, are partly regarded as catalysts for investment in areas traditionally considered risky and time- or resource-intensive.[7] Yet, literature and practice have long identified a growing number of areas in which this proposition does not fully account for current dynamics in innovation processes and the motivations of R&D players.[8]

Many health goods needed for pandemic preparedness and response are among those that tend to fare poorly if their development and production is primarily dependent on intellectual property incentives or other forms of market-driven forces.[9] Some of these goods might be scientifically complex and challenging to produce – for instance, a vaccine targeting HIV has yet to be developed, in spite of long-lasting R&D efforts – while others constitute relatively simple forms of technology – as is the case of ventilators, which were in short supply during the COVID-19 pandemic and for which there have been shortages in national stockpiles before pandemics occur.[10]

Because intellectual property incentives might strongly condition funding for R&D, some of these goods might remain undeveloped (or insufficiently developed) before a large-scale public crisis occurs.[11] This happens if the public health value of a particular good is hard to estimate, or if the anticipated return-on-investment is estimated as being insufficiently attractive from an economic perspective.[12] Preventatives like vaccines, which embody both of these problems, illustrate this dissociation between market incentives (including intellectual property) and public health goals. Vaccines are critical for the prevention of outbreaks of infectious diseases, yet their successful deployment translates into a non-event, or a limited public health crisis. Both outcomes are hard to quantify from the perspective of savings to health systems.[13] At the same time, most vaccine manufacturers do not expect significant return-on-investment for vaccines targeting emerging pathogens.[14] While there is a strong patenting culture in the field of vaccines as a whole,[15] the prospect of being granted a patent appears to be of limited importance in terms of catalyzing investment in pre-outbreak vaccine R&D.[16]

Dissociations between R&D priorities and public health imperatives tend to be cured (or at least lessened) by the occurrence of a pandemic or epidemic.[17] COVID-19 has illustrated this phenomenon in the form of concomitant R&D races to develop diagnostics, vaccines, treatments and other medical technologies. As these races unfold, the imprints of intellectual property are visible across different domains. The following section explores this shift in R&D approaches in the context of COVID-19, and highlights the persistence of proprietary approaches to the development, production and distribution of health goods needed during a pandemic.

Intellectual property and the silo culture during a pandemic

The COVID-19 pandemic ushered in a seemingly global race to develop treatments, vaccines and several other types of medical technologies. Yet, in spite of extraordinary goodwill and resource commitment toward expedited R&D, many of the efforts to produce these technologies still took place in siloed environments. While a pandemic or other form of large-scale public health crisis might temporarily solve some of the incentives and funding shortcomings registered in pre-outbreak periods, it does not fundamentally change traditional R&D dynamics. In particular, it does not do away with the siloed nature of R&D processes leading to the production of goods needed to respond to a borderless public health problem. This, in turn, breeds instances of duplication,

secrecy and lack of collaboration, active non-cooperation and inequitable allocation of R&D outputs.

Duplication, proprietary R & D and affordability issues

As an illustration of the siloed nature of pandemic R&D, consider the case of
vaccines. COVID-19 unleashed the most densely populated vaccine race in history: by late summer 2020, there were over 200 discrete vaccine development
projects across the world.[18] These projects varied in developmental stage, ranging
from pre-clinical studies to phase II and III clinical trials.[19]

As a general rule, a plethora of scientific approaches – combined with the
influx of numerous players – to a traditionally underpopulated and underfunded
field of R&D constitutes a welcome development. However, COVID-19 triggered what is arguably an overpopulation of the R&D field. Governments
quickly decided to prioritize a small number of vaccine candidates, funneling
public funding largely to a small number of selected candidates. For instance, in
the United States, Operation Warp Speed had narrowed down the field to five
vaccine candidates by early June 2020.[20]

That such a narrowing down of priority vaccine candidates should occur
is inevitable given both the nature of pharmaceutical R&D and funding constraints. Nonetheless, the enormous dispersion of resources and R&D attention
during the COVID-19 vaccine race – with the inevitable lack of coordination
and duplication of efforts it entails – also speaks to systemic shortcomings in the
development and production of health goods in periods of crisis.[21] R&D performance in response to pandemics or epidemics largely magnifies the structure
and dynamics of standard drug development, which is mainly firm or consortia-
specific, as well as based on patent-driven innovation processes.[22] As such, while
a pandemic temporarily triggers a spike in R&D funding and a compression of
R&D timelines, these are likely to result in overpopulated vaccine or drug races
that lead to wasteful duplication.

Concerns with duplication are not exclusive to vaccines. For instance, the
race to develop treatments for COVID-19 was also unusually populated, in terms
of the number of R&D players and products, as well as temporally. In late summer 2020, there were over 300 discrete treatment development projects, from
antivirals to monoclonal antibodies and plasma products.[23]

The duplication problem is further compounded by a general lack of collaboration among players participating in different R&D projects. Data, know-how,
and other forms of knowledge are not shared universally or made available in
meaningful ways, and in some cases – including the manufacture of goods critical for pandemic response and preparedness, like certain vaccines – can easily
be kept secret.[24] In sum, R&D in a pandemic continues to follow proprietary
models of innovation instead of tendentially collaborative approaches.

While problems of duplication and lack of collaboration are not solely attributable to the prevalence of an intellectual property-based R&D culture,[25] they

denote a certain generalized complacency with the commodification of vaccines, treatments and other public health goods. This commodification extends beyond the domain of R&D. Once developed and authorized or approved by regulatory agencies, like the US Food and Drug Administration or the European Medicines Agency, these goods might be made available in ways that effectively exclude some indicated populations from accessing them. Early on in the COVID-19 pandemic there were concerns with that excessive pricing of emerging vaccines and treatments, especially in the United States.

The first red flag happened in February 2020, when Secretary of Health and Human Services, Alex Azar, publicly stated that the government would not guarantee that COVID-19 vaccines would be priced affordably in the United States.[26] Secretary Azar explained the position of the government by alluding to a version of the incentives narrative alluded to in the previous section: "We can't control that price [of COVID-19 vaccines] because we need the private sector to invest."[27]

It should be noted that there are multiple legal mechanisms that would allow the government to guarantee the affordability of COVID-19 vaccines and drugs. Inventions that receive federal funding, as was the case of Remdesivir, are subject to march-in rights, which allow funding agencies to grant a license to other drug manufacturers in order "to alleviate health or safety needs" not reasonably satisfied by the patent holder.[28] Recently, scholars have made the case that provisions regulating government use of patented technologies – namely 28 U.S.C. § 1498 – can and should be used by the government to make or otherwise obtain a generic version of an excessively priced patented drug.[29] As Hannah Brennan and colleagues have noted:

> The government may negotiate a license in the shadow of its § 1498 power. Alternatively, the government may simply make or purchase the patented invention, leaving the patent holder to sue for damages if it is dissatisfied with the compensation offered. The present statute, like the 1910 Act, provides the only remedy available to a patent holder is reasonable and entire compensation; the patent holder may not seek injunctive relief.[30]

There are also legal mechanisms, unrelated to intellectual property, that would enable the government to promote the affordability of drugs, vaccines, and other emerging products needed to respond to the COVID-19 pandemic. In March 2020, the United States government used the Defense Production Act (DPA) to compel General Motors to start producing ventilators.[31] Many commentators argued that the government should use this pathway more extensively to obtain a broad range of products, from tests to N95 masks, and potentially beyond.[32] So far, however, the government has not done so.

The second red flag in this area occurred when prices were publicized for the first drug indicated for the treatment of COVID-19, an antiviral called Remdesivir.[33] In June 2020, Gilead – the pharmaceutical company holding patent rights over Remdesivir – announced that a full course of treatment (which takes place over five days) would cost $3,120 to Medicare, Medicaid and private insurers in the United States.[34] This price is 33% higher than the one charged to governments in other developed countries – which will pay $2,340, the same price tag supported in the United States by the Department of Veterans Affairs and the Indian Health Service, a division of the Department of Health and Human Services.[35] For developing countries, the company announced it would sell Remdesivir at a "substantially lower" yet unspecified price.[36]

Both instances – the general lack of a guarantee of affordability of COVID-19 vaccines, and the specific price tag for a COVID-19 treatment, considered steep by many commentators – illustrate one of the most significant problems associated with the ongoing commodification of public health goods. As R&D processes and distribution of these goods have been largely subsumed into overly proprietary rights frameworks, public interest considerations have been eroded – namely the public interest in broad, affordable access to vaccines, drugs and other goods needed to address the pandemic.

Proprietary rights and non-cooperative behaviors

Intellectual property may leave a different type of imprint on the response to a pandemic. COVID-19 provided an illustration of the possible chilling effects of a culture that places too much emphasis on the dynamics of intellectual property rights in the face of a situation of dire public health crisis.

Consider the following case. A hospital in Brescia, one of the Italian cities most affected by the COVID-19 outbreak, was rapidly going through its stock of valves needed to connect patients to ventilators.[37] After being unable to acquire replacement valves from the original manufacturer, the hospital turned to local engineers who were able to reverse engineer the valves and create a 3D-printable prototype, despite the original manufacturing company refusing to share the digital files containing the instructions to print the valves.[38] Through a partnership with local owners of 3D printers, the engineers were able to print 100 valves in a single day.[39] Moreover, while a valve from the original manufacturer had a price tag of over $10,000, the locally 3D-printed valves were produced at the cost of just over one dollar.[40] The partnership, however, refused to share the files containing instructions to print the valves with other companies, citing concerns about intellectual property liability for such distribution.[41]

This example illustrates how a web of intellectual property rights in an unsettled area of the law can detrimentally affect the use of life-saving medical devices during a pandemic. It is possible – in fact, likely – that several intellectual property violations occurred throughout the process that delivered valves to an overburdened hospital. These violations include the creation and use of the digital file, the printing of the valves and the printed valves. Had the engineers shared the files containing instructions for the 3D printing of the valves, further violations would in all likelihood have occurred.[42]

Currently, there is no legal mechanism to expeditiously and effectively compel transfers of intellectual property during public health crises when complex health goods are at stake. In spring 2021, several countries – including the United States – backed a proposal to waive intellectual property rights over COVID-19 vaccines altogether.[43] At the time of writing, the ultimate outcome of the proposal remains unknown.[44] Yet, it is worth noting here that passing a temporary waiver does not necessarily translate into greater availability of health goods for which pandemic demand vastly exceeds supply: suspending intellectual property-based obligations does not address the underlying issues of infrastructural limitations for vaccine manufacturing and shortages of raw materials that occurred during the COVID-19 pandemic. Additionally, waiving patent rights does not force the transfer of know-how and other valuable types of knowledge not captured in the information disclosed in patents.[45]

While these problems remain unaddressed for the time being, the COVID-19 pandemic has nonetheless prompted the development and implementation of several initiatives that seek to minimize some of the siloed effects of our patent-centric R&D culture. The chapter turns to these efforts in *Intellectual property collaborations* below, describing the patent pool created by the WHO and the Open COVID-19 Pledge.

Inequitable allocation of resulting goods

Pandemics pose global public health problems. Treatments, vaccines, and other medical technologies emerging from pandemic-induced R&D races might nonetheless be allocated in ways that are geographically and economically skewed.

No other area embodies this phenomenon more saliently than the development of COVID-19 vaccines – to the point that the expression "vaccine nationalism" is now firmly embedded into the popular discourse.[46] Vaccine nationalism can be defined as "efforts to influence the allocation of newly developed vaccines, or first batches thereof, to the detriment – often the exclusion – of other, generally poorer countries."[47]

During the early stages of the COVID-19 pandemic, several developed countries moved to reserve large numbers of vaccine doses for their domestic populations.[48] They have done so by entering into contractual agreements – often called pre-production orders – with pharmaceutical companies working on vaccine candidates in the more advanced stages of the R&D pipeline.[49] By mid-August 2020, the UK had placed orders for 340 million doses of vaccine, becoming the largest per-capita buyer in the world of COVID-19 vaccines.[50] The United States had placed orders with at least six vaccine manufacturers for 800 million doses of vaccine.[51] Overall, by late summer 2020, developed countries had placed pre-purchase order for over two billion doses of COVID-19 vaccines.[52]

At first blush this might appear consistent with contemporary notions of sovereignty and domestic public health agendas. In practice, unfettered allocation of vaccines through bilateral channels – such as pre-purchases contracts between governments and pharmaceutical companies – is bound to result in inequitable allocation of vaccines.

A recent study conducted by the Coalition for Epidemic Preparedness Innovations (CEPI) calculated that global manufacturing capacity for COVID-19 vaccines is between two and four billion doses by the end of 2021.[53] Given this estimate, contract bilateralism is likely to result in a disproportionate allocation of the first batches of emerging vaccines to countries that have the economic ability to negotiate pre-purchase orders. Conversely, indicated populations in developing countries – which have been deeply affected by COVID-19 – are likely to only be able to access a disproportionately smaller number of vaccines doses. Given the global nature of the pandemic, this split is inequitable toward populations in economically disadvantaged countries. Moreover, this form of nationalism runs counter to public health and epidemiological principles, which take a global (or at least transnational) approach to problems like COVID-19 rather than sovereignty-based responses to pandemics and epidemics.

Allocative problems like vaccine nationalism are not strictly intellectual property problems. Nevertheless, they derive from the same siloed and proprietary approaches to pharmaceutical innovation that intellectual property so often intensifies. As seen in *Pooled procurement*, there are ongoing efforts to curb vaccine nationalism, including the formation of a large-scale procurement mechanism (COVAX) aimed at the global and equitable distribution of COVID-19 vaccines.[54] Several countries, however, have declined to join COVAX.[55] Pursuant to its current policy of international isolationism, the United States is one of these countries.

Intellectual property collaborations

While the previous section documented different instances in which a silo mentality has prevailed over collaborative endeavors in the response to COVID-19, the ongoing pandemic has also originated a number of countervailing efforts aimed at fostering collaborations at the R&D and distributive levels. Some of these collaborations resort to well-known mechanisms in intellectual property history and practice (patent pools and pledges) to mitigate intellectual property-induced inefficiencies.[56] Others eschew purely nationalist approaches to the distribution of medical technologies emerging from R&D performed during the pandemic, through the creation of tendentially global models to finance and allocate health goods (procurement facilities, particularly in the field of vaccines).

Patent pools

In March 2020, the government of Costa Rica submitted a proposal to the WHO for the creation of a patent pool designed to cover a broad range of medical technologies:

> This pool, which will involve voluntary assignments, should include existing and future rights in patented inventions and designs, as well rights in regulatory test data, know-how, cell lines, copyrights and blueprints

for manufacturing diagnostic tests, devices, drugs, or vaccines. It should provide for free access or licensing on reasonable and affordable terms, in every member country.[57]

The World Intellectual Property Organization defines patent pool as "an agreement between two or more patent owners to license one or more of their patents to one another or to third parties."[58] Daniel Crane has aptly described patent pools as "a form of intra-industry social contract permitting the emergence from this Hobbesian war of each against all."[59] Patent pools focused on health technologies, or segments thereof, are not a new figure in the international landscape.[60] One of the largest and most well-known examples is the Medicines Patent Pool (MPP),[61] an organization created by Unitaid in 2010 to negotiate voluntary licenses for medicines needed in lower-resource countries (HIV, hepatitis C and tuberculosis).[62]

In addition to constituting an early response to time and demand-driven pressures on COVID-19 R&D pipelines, Costa Rica's proposal was partly fueled by concerns that health technologies emerging during the pandemic might be priced unaffordably for economically disadvantaged populations.[63] As implementation of the proposed patent pool began in the following months, the WHO further recognized that overreliance on intellectual property-based modes of innovation was unlikely to result in equitable access to health goods, even in periods of transnational public health crises:

> The COVID-19 pandemic has revealed the fallibility of traditional ways of working when it comes to equitable access to essential health technologies. This initiative sets out an alternative, in line with WHO's efforts to promote global public health goods, based on equity, strong science, open collaboration and global solidarity.[64]

The COVID-19 Technology Access Pool (C-TAP) was rolled out in late May 2020.[65] The goals of C-TAP are manifold. It aims to promote and accelerate the public disclosure of information critical to COVID-19 R&D through the sharing of gene sequencing research and clinical trial results.[66] It also advocates for the insertion of provisions into agreements mandating equitable distribution of COVID-19 treatments, vaccines and other emerging products, as well as the disclosure of clinical trial data.[67] It seeks to promote the licensure of these products to both large and small manufacturers and distributors. And, finally, it advocates for "open innovation models and technology transfer that increase local manufacturing and supply capacity."[68]

Patent pools like C-TAP are designed to reduce the risk and transaction costs associated with negotiating processes.[69] Moreover, they can potentially help speed up R&D timelines through their signaling function: R&D players (from scientists to institutional representatives to funders) know early on that a patent committed to the pool indicates that the underlying technology or method can be licensed, as opposed to substitutes or work arounds.[70]

Yet, patent pools are not without drawbacks. Participation in a pool is voluntary, often leading to limitations in terms of participants, their heterogeneity and the number and scope of pooled patents.[71] Additionally, patent pooling does not necessarily mean that distribution of, and access to, emerging innovations will automatically occur on an equitable basis. Agreements between licensors and licensees might be silent on pricing and distribution issues, which in turn might lead to the exclusion of indicated populations, especially in economically disadvantaged areas of the globe.[72]

To date, thirty countries and several international organizations have joined C-TAP.[73] While the numbers are somewhat encouraging, they showcase some of the inherent limitations of patent pools. In particular, some of the most salient players in pharmaceutical R&D have been reluctant to contribute patents to the pool.[74] After having commented favorably on other initiatives created to speed up COVID-19 R&D, the director general of the International Federation of Pharmaceutical Manufacturers & Associations expressed his views on C-TAP: "I don't quite see what the new initiative adds."[75]

Even against this backdrop, an important advantage of C-TAP is that it is part of a larger effort by the WHO and other institutional players in the international public health space to break down R&D silos and expedite both the development and the distribution of health goods needed to address the COVID-19 pandemic. In parallel with the formation of the pool, the WHO coordinated the creation and development of the Access to COVID-19 Tools (ACT) Accelerator, described as a "global and time-limited collaboration to accelerate the development, production and equitable global access to new COVID-19 essential health technologies."[76] As described in *Pooled procurement*, this collaboration is overseen by a network of international organizations and public health-oriented private organizations, including the WHO, the Wellcome Trust, the Bill and Melinda Gates Foundation, the World Bank group and the Global Fund.[77] The ACT Accelerator is divided into four pillars: diagnostics, treatments, vaccines and the strengthening of health systems.[78]

As seen above, the United States has by and large chosen not to embrace collaborative international frameworks in its response to the COVID-19 pandemic. The US Patent and Trademark Office has nonetheless created a voluntary program – Patents 4 Partnerships – to facilitate the licensure of patented technologies.[79] In its current iteration, the initiative focuses on technologies relevant to the response to COVID-19.[80] These technologies encompass patented products or processes "related to the prevention, diagnosis, and treatment of COVID-19, including, for example, personal protective equipment, disinfectants, ventilators, testing equipment and components thereof."[81] USPTO has made available a searchable platform – the IP Marketplace Platform[82] – that provides access to a centralized list of patents and patents applications.[83] As with patent pools, this mechanism seeks to reduce transaction costs and speed up R&D efforts during the pandemic. At the time of writing, there were over 300 patents listed as available for licensing.[84]

Neither the transnational patent pool model promoted by the WHO, nor the more modest experiment led by the USPTO, have fully displaced instances of nationalism and silo problems inherent to contemporary R&D processes. But these efforts – especially C-TAP in its tendentially global approach – illustrate the long-felt need for transactional intellectual property frameworks that do not adhere to strictly proprietary worldviews. In particular, they underscore and seek to address the tension between the nature of public health crises and scientific collaborations, on the one hand, and overly siloed R&D processes based on patent-protected health goods, on the other.

Patent pledges

Another pathway to promote the use of patented inventions consists in the adoption of yet another type of voluntary mechanism – the patent pledge.[85] Unlike patent pools, which signal a willingness to license proprietary technologies, patent pledges are structured around the non-assertion, or limited assertion or use, of patent rights.[86] As Jorge Contreras explains:

> [patent pledges] are commitments made voluntarily by patent holders to limit the enforcement or other exploitation of their patents. They are made not to direct contractual counterparties, but to the public at large, or at least to large segments of certain markets. And they are made without any direct compensation or other consideration.[87]

In recent years, patent pledges have become more common across several industries, from the automotive industry to computer software.[88] During the early stages of the COVID-19 pandemic, a group of legal scholars and scientists developed the framework for a COVID-specific pledge.[89] The Open COVID-19 Pledge (hereinafter the Pledge) was launched in March 2020 as "a commitment by holders of intellectual property to share their intellectual property for the purposes of ending and mitigating the COVID-19 Pandemic."[90]

Founding adopters of the Pledge included Facebook, Amazon, Intel, IBM, Microsoft, Hewlett Packard, and the Sandia National Laboratories.[91] The Pledge quickly amassed a wide-ranging portfolio of patents. For instance, NASA has pledged a patent covering 3D-printed respirators.[92] Fujitsu has pledged a patent covering disease diagnosis through automated software.[93] And Facebook has pledged US patent 20190163794, which covers systems and methods for the detection of contextual information indicative of misinformation.[94]

In addition to collecting and centralizing commitments from pledgors, the Pledge operates by providing different types of licenses. Developers of the Pledge created a set of standard licenses that can be adopted on an as-is basis by pledgors.[95] Additionally, the Pledge recognizes sets of requirements that should be met by non-Pledge licenses deemed either "compatible licenses" or "alternative licenses" vis-à-vis the terms of the Pledge.[96]

Standard licenses – for which there are two versions covering patents and copyrights and one covering patents only – address only essential contractual areas for technology licensure. They cover only five domains: grant and scope; time limitation; regulatory exclusivity; defensive suspension; and the inexistence of a warranty.[97]

"Compatible" licenses consist of licensing frameworks that "provide a set of minimum use permissions."[98] This group includes both pre-existing licensing frameworks that have been deemed to be consistent with the Pledge, such as the MIT license[99] and the Apache 2.0 license,[100] and licenses reviewed on a case-by-case basis and deemed to meet the overall requirements of the Pledge.

"Alternative" licenses consist of licensing frameworks that do not fit the previous categories, but which are nonetheless consistent with the Pledge.[101] These include the Creative Commons Attribution-ShareAlike 4.0 International license[102] and GNU's General Public License.[103] The Pledge has identified a set of terms that are not acceptable for a license to be deemed consistent with the spirit of the Pledge.[104] For instance, licenses cannot be granted exclusively for non-commercial uses, nor bear any kind of fees.[105]

This broad array of licenses allows pledgors to choose the specific contractual frameworks that best fit their interests. For instance, standard license OCL-PC v1.0 (covering both patents and copyrights) lasts "until one year after WHO declares the COVID-19 Pandemic to have ended."[106] Standards license OCL-PC v1.1 (covering both patents and copyrights) and OCL-P v1.1 (covering only patents) have the same default duration, but will not last "beyond January 1, 2023, unless otherwise extended by the Pledgor."[107] Pledgors may thus choose between an open-ended or a specific term. Similarly, while standard licenses are silent on indemnification,[108] other versions may contemplate the possibility of requiring "the licensee to indemnify the licensor for liability directly attributable to the licensee's actions."[109]

The breadth of health-related technologies encompassed by the Pledge, the multiplicity of flexible licensing frameworks it offers, and the compressed timeline in which it was implemented, set the Open COVID-19 Pledge apart from previous structured approaches to incentivize the licensure of patented goods – and especially of health technologies in a period of public health crisis. Perhaps more importantly, this effort shows how flexible licensing strategies can be used to promote technology transfer in furtherance of public interest goals *within* the dynamics of intellectual property. By maintaining their ownership interest while relaxing control of some of the sticks in their bundle of rights, pledgors adopt a different intellectual property strategy for a limited period of time that might result in the adoption of their technology – and potentially in valuable contributions to public health.

The intrinsically limited duration of the Pledge means that it cannot be used to assist in the pursuit of broader R&D purposes targeting pathogens likely to cause future pandemic or epidemics. It does, however, provide a blueprint for the development of similarly structured efforts in the upcoming inter-outbreak period.

Pooled procurement

The COVID-19 pandemic has prompted the creation of the COVID-19 Vaccine Global Access Facility (COVAX) to both finance the development of new vaccines and guarantee their equitable distribution on a global level.[110]

COVAX is integrated into a larger scheme – the vaccines pillar of the ACT Accelerator.[111] This pillar is designed to coordinate the development and distribution of COVID-19 vaccines from end-to-end. Three organizations oversee different segments of this end-to-end process. The Coalition for Epidemic Preparedness Innovations (CEPI), a public-private partnership that funds vaccine R&D targeting emerging pathogens,[112] coordinates the stages of development and manufacturing of vaccine candidates.[113] The WHO is the main driver for vaccine policy and allocative decisions.[114] And Gavi, a public-private partnership traditionally focused on the procurement of childhood vaccines for developing countries,[115] operates at the procurement and delivery-at-scale level.[116]

Overseen by Gavi, COVAX is a risk-sharing mechanism built into this network's procurement strategy. Participation in COVAX is open to any country wishing to join, subject to an advance commitment to purchase a certain amount of vaccine and a monetary or material contribution (the latter taking the form of vaccine doses).[117] In exchange, participating countries receive access to COVID-19 vaccines procured by COVAX once they become available, at a price negotiated between COVAX and individual pharmaceutical companies.[118] In early June, COVAX entered into the first of these procurement agreements with AstraZeneca, securing access to 300 million doses of vaccine.[119]

In this way, COVAX uses the same type of legal instrument that enables nationalistic allocation of vaccines – pre-production contracts – to further global governance of vaccines, while diffusing risk through resource pooling and attempting to maintain relatively low vaccine prices.[120]

The swift formation of COVAX and, more broadly, of the vaccines pillar of the ACT Accelerator, also speaks to the limitations of intellectual property as a push mechanism in incentivizing vaccine R&D. Moreover, COVAX denotes the need for complementary pull mechanisms accompanying intellectual property incentives and curbing the excesses of overly proprietary or nationalist approaches to pharmaceutical innovation, particularly during pandemic and epidemic crises.

Conclusion: intellectual property for the next pandemic

Many of the current approaches to pharmaceutical innovation during pandemics and epidemics rely on proprietary frameworks that are hard to reconcile with the public health demands posed by transnational outbreaks of infectious diseases. The COVID-19 pandemic illustrates these tensions through an accentuation of siloed modes of R&D, as well as the adoption of nationalistic approaches to the allocation of emerging medical technologies. While reinforcing the case for legal and policy changes ahead of the next pandemic, COVID-19 has provided a blueprint for interventions that might curb some of these siloed trends.

These efforts – from patent pools and pledges to procurement mechanisms – are nonetheless time-consuming and resource-intensive, in addition to being inevitably linked to geopolitical considerations. As such, when started during a pandemic, they constitute remedial modes of response, which are subject to accelerated timelines and practical constraints. Moving forward, the international community should direct attention, during the next inter-outbreak period, to the strengthening of some of these mechanisms – possibly turning some of the temporary initiatives described above, such as COVAX or pandemic patent pools, into more permanent structures.[121] These developments are needed not only to save time when the next pandemic occurs, but also to increase notions of equity and to promote dialogue centered on equity issues ahead of (inevitable) future crises triggered by emerging pathogens.

BOX 7.1 CORONA SHORT #12: CANADA JULIE, A MIDWIFE, NURSE AND MOTHER, DESCRIBES ATTENDING HOME BIRTHS DURING A PANDEMIC

March, April, and May of 2020 were panic times. I would have thought one of my colleagues would have taken advantage to take time off work – nobody has done that. It has been astounding. They have just kept pushing, picking up calls for others. But I will tell you there are so many layers for frontline medical workers who have children. For example, my son said, "Mom I hate it when I had to sit home and play video games while you are at work." I felt awful leaving them and having them fix their own meals. I don't know how other parents are doing it. I'm lucky in that my kids are older.

A while ago I worked with Médecins Sans Frontières in Congo. The major correlation was recognition of the value of maintaining the cold chain for vaccine integrity. I'm sure you've heard that some of these vaccines require minus 70 degrees storage. In Canada we are lucky with our climate. I don't know how they are going to pull that off in countries in Africa. That was what I was involved with, transporting vaccines for measles, mumps and rubella, keeping it cold for hours and days. On a motorcycle, a boat, on the back of a donkey . . . that's how it works there.

This pandemic couldn't come at a worse time. Or a better time. Ten years ago this would have stopped us in our tracks. Now, our natal classes are all virtual. Everybody is sitting in their house doing Zoom chats. We have had mothers tell us, "It saved my life."

We are following WHO standards but what we found was that psychosocially these people always appreciate face-to-face appointments. So Ontario Telehealth Network is doing the routine conferencing online; it's very secure. But a lot of our clients prefer telephone conferencing. I mean, they don't have to put on make-up and so on. For group activities they prefer video. That's received the most comment, though, in that most healthcare clinics are only inviting those receiving direct care into the clinic but not the support person.

In the summer of 2020, we were doing "parking lot visits." I brought all my equipment in my car and I'd conduct the chats about a person's care outside their house. The midwifery model of care involved home visits, specifically postpartum, so they didn't have to leave their homes with a young babe.

It's been a challenge for us. Wondering how we can safely go into people's houses not knowing if they were following the rules. We screened everybody carefully. We explained the dangers, putting others and their babies in harm's way. Most did not want to take that chance. Most stayed home. Some were choosing their midwives over anybody else for a home birth, even their grandmothers. That caused many hurt feelings on the grandparents' part.

So, everyone is swabbed and tested. We just assume everybody is positive. Same in the hospital. And we wear complete isolation gear, putting all PPE on to go into their home. And all off again when you leave. I don't have sterilizing equipment in my house or car. For home labor, I get out of my car in gown and mask, carry my equipment into their house. I don't eat or drink or use the bathroom in their house. Difficult for the longer births.

Notes

* This chapter benefited from early stage (virtual) discussions at the Singapore Management University Conference on Global Public-Private Law Approaches to the Covid-19 Pandemic and at the summer workshop series at Saint Louis University School of Law.

i Fadela Chaib, *Shortage of Personal Protective Equipment Endangering Health Workers Worldwide*, United World Health Organization News (Mar. 3, 2020), www.who.int/news/item/03-03-2020-shortage-of-personal-protective-equipment-endangering-health-workers-worldwide.

ii Staff Writers & AFP, *World Facing "Catastrophic Moral Failure" on Vaccines: WHO Chief*, News.com.au (Jan. 20, 2021), www.news.com.au/lifestyle/health/health-problems/world-facing-catastrophic-moral-failure-on-vaccines-who-chief/news-story/3c3a03ca5de2763bd69c29292339f16d.

iii *Id, ib.*

iv Will Ockenden, *Coronavirus Was Running Rampant in Israel: But a Swift Vaccination Program Is Having Dramatic Results*, Abc Health & Wellbeing (Feb. 7, 2021), www.abc.net.au/news/health/2021-02-07/covid-19-israel-vaccinates-half-population-against-coronavirus/13116696.

v Paula Erizanu, *Here in Europe's Poorest Country We Have No Vaccine to Argue over*, The Guardian (Jan. 28, 2021), www.theguardian.com/world/commentisfree/2021/jan/28/

here-in-europes-poorest-country-we-have-no-vaccine-to-argue-over?CMP=Share_iOSApp_Other.

1 See e.g. Milken Inst., *COVID-19 Treatment and Vaccine Tracker*, https://covid-19tracker.milkeninstitute.org (listing over 200 COVID-19 vaccine projects and over 300 COVID-19 treatment projects as of Aug. 25, 2020) (accessed May 4, 2021).

2 *Id., ib.* See also *infra*, **Duplication, Proprietary R&D and affordability issues.**

3 *Infra*, **Inequitable allocation of resulting goods.**

4 See e.g. Ana Santos Rutschman, *The Reemergence of Vaccine Nationalism*, Geo. J. Int'l. Aff. Online (Jul. 3, 2020).

5 These commitments were undertaken both by countries (C-TAP) and institutions, including private-sector R&D players (Open COVID-19 Pledge). See *infra*, **Patent pools** and **Patent pledges.**

6 See generally Stephen M. Maurer, *Intellectual Property Incentives: Economics and Policy Implications*, in Oxford Handbook of Intellectual Property Law (Rochelle Dreyfuss & Justine Pila, Eds.) (2018). See also Adrian Towse, *A Review of IP and Non-IP Incentives for R&D for Diseases of Poverty: What Type of Innovation Is Required and How Can We Incentivise the Private Sector to Deliver It?*, Final Report for the WHO Commission on Intellectual Property Rights, Innovation and Public Health (2005).

7 See e.g. Henry G. Grabowski et al., *The Roles of Patents and Research and Development Incentives in Biopharmaceutical Innovation*, 34(2) Health Aff. 302–310 (2015).

8 See e.g. Rochelle Cooper Dreyfuss, *Does IP Need IP? Accommodating Intellectual Production Outside the Intellectual Property Paradigm*, 31 Cardozo L. Rev. 1437 (2010); Amy Kapczynski, *Order without Intellectual Property Law: Open Science in Influenza*, 102 Cornell L. Rev. 1539 (2017).

9 See Ana Santos Rutschman, *IP Preparedness of Outbreak Diseases*, 65 UCLA L. Rev. 1200 (2018); Rutschman, *The Intellectual Property of Vaccines: Takeaways from Recent Infectious Disease Outbreaks*, 118 Mich. I. Rev. Online 170 (2020); Yaniv Heled et al., *The Problem with Relying on Profit-Driven Models to Produce Pandemic Drugs*, 7 J. L. & Biosci. lsaa060 (2020).

10 See e.g. Hsin-Chan Huang et al., *Stockpiling Ventilators for Influenza Pandemics*, 23 Emerging Infectious Diseases 914 (2017).

11 See Rutschman, IP Preparedness, *supra* note 9.

12 See Rutschman, *The Intellectual Property of Vaccines*, *supra* note 9.

13 *Id., ib.* See also Q. Claire Xue & Lisa Larrimore Ouellette, *Innovation Policy and the Market for Vaccines*, 7 J. L. & Biosci. lsaa060 (2020).

14 *Id., ib.* But see Ana Santos Rutschman, *Property and Intellectual Property in Vaccine Markets*, 7 Tex. A&M J. Prop. L. 110 (2021) (describing examples of commercially successful vaccines).

15 See Ana Santos Rutschman, *The Vaccine Race in the 21st Century*, 61 Ariz. L. Rev. 729 (2019).

16 See Rutschman, *IP Preparedness*, *supra* note 9.

17 *Id., ib.*

18 Milken Inst., *COVID-19 Treatment and Vaccine Tracker*, *supra* note 1 (listing 203 vaccine projects as of Aug. 21, 2020) (last accessed Aug. 25, 2020).

19 *Id., ib.*

20 U.S. Dep't Health & Hum. Services, *Fact Sheet: Explaining Operation Warp Speed* (Jun. 26, 2020); Stephanie Soucheray, *Operation Warp Speed Names 5 COVID-19 Vaccine Candidates*, Ctr. for Infectious Disease Research & Pol'y (Jun. 4, 2020).

21 World Health Org., *An R&D Blueprint for Action to Prevent Epidemics* 22 (2016).

22 See Heled et al., *supra* note 9.

23 Milken Inst., *COVID-19 Treatment and Vaccine Tracker*, https://covid-19tracker.milkeninstitute.org (listing 316 treatment projects as of Aug. 21, 2020) (last accessed May 4, 2021).

24 See W. Nicholson Price II et al., *Knowledge Transfer for Large-Scale Vaccine Manufacturing*, Sci. (Aug. 21, 2020).

25 See e.g. Ana Santos Rutschman, *The Mosaic of Coronavirus Vaccine Development: Systemic Failures in Vaccine Innovation*, Colum. J. Int'lt Aff. (Mar. 21, 2020) (noting the existence of "governance deficits in biopharmaceutical innovation systems").

26 See Nicole Wetsman, *Health Secretary Alex Azar Won't Promise That a Coronavirus Vaccine Would Be Affordable*, Verge (Feb. 27, 2020).

27 *Id., ib.*

28 35 U.S.C. § 203. See also Ryan Whalen, *The Bayh-Dole Act & Public Rights in Federally Funded Inventions: Will the Agencies Ever Go Marching In?*, 109 Nw. U. L. Rev. 1083 (2015).

29 28 U.S.C. § 1498; Hannah Brennan et al., *A Prescription for Excessive Drug Pricing: Leveraging Government Patent Use for Health*, 18 Yale J. L. & Tech 275, 301–302 (2017). See also Christopher J. Morten & Charles Duan, *Who's Afraid of Section 1498? A Case for Government Patent Use in Pandemics and Other National Crises*, 23 Yale J.L. & Tech. 1 (2020).

30 Brennan et al., *ib.*

31 See Aishvarya Kavi, *Virus Surge Brings Calls for Trump to Invoke Defense Production Act*, N.Y. Times (Jul. 22, 2020).

32 *Id., ib.*

33 See Gina Kolata, *Remdesivir, the First Coronavirus Drug, Gets a Price Tag*, N.Y. Times (Jun. 29, 2020).

34 See Matthew Herper, *Gilead Announces Long-Awaited Price for Covid-19 Drug Remdesivir*, STAT (Jun. 29, 2020).

35 *Id., ib.*

36 See Hannah Denham et al., *Gilead Sets Price of Coronavirus Drug Remdesivir at $3,120 as Trump Administration Secures Supply for 500,000 Patients*, Wash. Post (Jun. 29, 2020).

37 Dinusha Mendis et al., *3D Printing: How an Emerging Technology May Help Fight a Pandemic*, IPR Info (Feb. 25, 2020).

38 *Id., ib.* See also Anas Essop, *Hospital in Italy Turns to 3D Printing to Save Lives of Coronavirus Patients*, 3D Printing Industry (Mar. 18, 2020), https://3dprintingindustry.com/news/hospital-in-italy-turns-to-3d-printing-to-save-lives-of-coronavirus-patients-169136/

39 Mendis et al., *supra* note 37.

40 *Id., ib.*

41 *Id., ib.*

42 *Id., ib.*

43 Ann Danaiya Usher, *South Africa and India Push for COVID-19 Patents Ban*, 396 Lancet 1790 (2020); Thomas Kaplan et al., *Taking "Extraordinary Measures," Biden Backs Suspending Patents on Vaccines*, N.Y. Times (May 5, 2021), www.nytimes.com/2021/05/05/us/politics/biden-covid-vaccine-patents.html

44 Ana Santos Rutschman & Julia Barnes-Weise, *The COVID-19 Vaccine Patent Waiver: The Wrong Tool for the Right Goal*, Bill of Health (May 5, 2021), https://blog.petrieflom.law.harvard.edu/2021/05/05/covid-vaccine-patent-waiver/

45 Rutschman & Barnes-Weise, *supra* note 44.

46 See e.g. Adam Taylor, *Why Vaccine Nationalism is Winning*, Wash. Post (Sept. 2, 2020), www.washingtonpost.com/world/2020/09/03/why-coronavirus-vaccine-nationalism-is-winning/

47 Sam F. Halabi & Ana Santos Rutschman, *Viral Sovereignty and Vaccine Nationalism: Constructing the Post COVID-19 Vaccine International Order__* (forthcoming) (draft on file with author).

48 See Rutschman, *The Reemergence of Vaccine Nationalism*, *supra* note 4.

49 *Id., ib.*

50 Ewen Callaway, *The Unequal Scramble for Coronavirus Vaccines: By the Numbers*, Nature (Aug. 24, 2020).

51 *Id., ib.*

52 *Id., ib.*

53 CEPI, *CEPI Survey Assesses Potential Covid-19 Vaccine Manufacturing Capacity* (Aug. 5, 2020).

54 *Infra,* **Pooled procurement**.
55 See Donato Paolo Mancini & Michael Peel, *"Vaccine Nationalism" Delays WHO's Struggling Covax Scheme*, Fin. Times (Sept. 1, 2020), www.ft.com/content/502df709-25ac-48f6-aee1-aec7ac03c759
56 See Parts **Patent pools** and **Patent pledges**.
57 Letter from Costa Rica to the World Health Organization, Knowledge Ecology Int'l (Mar. 23, 2020), www.keionline.org/wp-content/uploads/President-MoH-Costa-Rica-Dr-Tedros-WHO24March2020.pdf
58 World. Intell. Prop. Org., Patent Pools and Antitrust – A Comparative Analysis (2014), www.wipo.int/export/sites/www/ip-competition/en/studies/patent_pools_report.pdf. See also generally Ryan Lampe & Petra Moser, *Do Patent Pools Encourage Innovation? Evidence from the Nineteenth-Century Sewing Machine Industry*, 70 J. Econ. Hist. 898 (2010); Robert P. Merges, *Institutions for Intellectual Property Transactions: The Case of Patent Pools*, in Expanding the Boundaries of Intellectual Property, Innovation Policy for the Knowledge Society (Rochelle Cooper Dreyfuss et al., Eds.) (2010); Carl Shapiro, *Navigating the Patent Thicket: Cross Licenses, Patent Pools, and Standard-Setting*, in Innovation Policy and the Economy, Volume I (Adam Jaffe et al., Eds.) (2001); Michael J. Madison et al., Constructing Commons in the Cultural Environment, 95 Cornell L. Rev. 657, 660–661, 681–687, 700–706 (2010); Jean Tirole & Josh Lerner, *Efficient Patent Pools*, NBER Working Paper No. w9175 (2002); Michael S. Mireles, *An Examination of Patents, Licensing, Research Tools, and the Tragedy of the Anticommons in Biotechnology Innovation*, 38 U. Mich. J. L. Reform, 141, 216–220 (2004).
59 Daniel A. Crane, *Patent Pools, RAND Commitments, and the Problematics of Price Discrimination*, in Working Within the Boundaries of Intellectual Property: Innovation Policy for the Knowledge Society (Rochelle C. Dreyfuss et al., Eds.) (2010).
60 See Peter K. Yu, *Virotech Patents, Viropiracy, and Viral Sovereignty*, 45 Ariz. St. L. J. 1563, 1599–1604 (2013) (describing the SARS patent pool); Brook K. Baker, *A Sliver of Hope: Analyzing Voluntary Licenses to Accelerate Affordable Access to Medicines*, 10 Northeastern U. L. Rev. 226 (2018); Esther van Zimmeren et al., *Patent Pools and Clearinghouses in the Life Sciences*, 29 Trends Biotech. 569 (2011).
61 Medicines Patent Pool, About Us, https://medicinespatentpool.org. See also Esteban Burrone, *Patent Pooling in Public Health*, in The Cambridge Handbook on Public-Private Partnerships, Intellectual Property Governance, and Sustainable Development (Margaret Chon et al., Eds., 2018); Krista L. Cox, *The Medicines Patent Pool: Promoting Access and Innovation for Life-Saving Medicines through Voluntary Licenses*, 4 Hastings Sci. & Tech. L. J. 293 (2012); Sandeep Juneja et al., *Projected Savings through Public Health Voluntary Licences of HIV Drugs Negotiated by the Medicines Patent Pool (MPP)*, 12(5) PLoS One (2017).
62 Unitaid, *The Medicines Patent Pool*, https://unitaid.org/project/medicines-patent-pool/#en (last accessed Aug. 28, 2020).
63 See Ed Silverman, *WHO Is Asked to Create a Voluntary Intellectual Property Pool to Develop Covid-19 Products*, Stat (Mar. 24, 2020), www.statnews.com/pharmalot/2020/03/24/covid19-coronavirus-costa-rica-intellectual-property/
64 World Health Org., *Solidarity Call to Action: Making the Response to COVID-19 a Public Common Good*, www.who.int/emergencies/diseases/novel-coronavirus-2019/global-research-on-novel-coronavirus-2019-ncov/covid-19-technology-access-pool/solidarity-call-to-action/ (last accessed Aug. 29, 2020).
65 World Health Org., *COVID-19 Technology Access Pool*, www.who.int/emergencies/diseases/novel-coronavirus-2019/global-research-on-novel-coronavirus-2019-ncov/covid-19-technology-access-pool (last accessed Aug. 29, 2020).
66 World Health Org., *WHO Director-General's Opening Remarks at the Media Briefing on COVID-19–29 May 2020* (May 29, 2020), www.who.int/dg/speeches/detail/who-director-general-s-opening-remarks-at-the-media-briefing-on-covid-19–29-may-2020.
67 *Id., ib.*
68 *Id., ib.*

69 See Muhammad Zaheer Abbas, *Treatment of the Novel COVID-19: Why Costa Rica's Proposal for the Creation of a Global Pooling Mechanism Deserves Serious Consideration?*, 7 J. L. & Biosci. 1 (2020). See Crane, *supra* note 59.

70 *Id., ib.*

71 See generally, Jorge L. Contreras, *Patent Pledges,* 47 Ariz. St. L.J. 543 (2015).

72 See e.g. Ana Santos Rutschman, *How "Vaccine Nationalism" Could Block Vulnerable Populations' Access to COVID-19 Vaccines,* The Conversation (Jun. 17, 2020), https://theconversation.com/how-vaccine-nationalism-could-block-vulnerable-populations-access-to-covid-19-vaccines-140689

73 United Nations, *COVID-19: Countries Support "One-Stop Shop" to Share Science and Research,* https://news.un.org/en/story/2020/05/1065132 (last accessed Aug. 29, 2020).

74 Chris Dall, *Pharma Execs Say Several COVID Vaccine Options Needed,* CIDRAP News (May 29, 2020). See also Ed Silverman, *The WHO Launched a Voluntary Covid-19 Product Pool: What Happens Next?,* Stat (May 20, 2020) (noting that "the pharmaceutical industry has dismissed the notion [of the patent pool], which underlies concerns that such a project is unlikely to succeed without widespread involvement").

75 *Id., ib.*

76 World Health Org., *The Access to COVID-19 Tools (ACT) Accelerator* (Apr. 24, 2020), www.who.int/publications/m/item/access-to-covid-19-tools-(act)-accelerator

77 World Health Org., *The Access to COVID-19 Tools (ACT) Accelerator,* www.who.int/initiatives/act-accelerator.

78 *Id, ib.*

79 U.S. Pat. & Trademark Office, *Patents 4 Partnerships,* https://developer.uspto.gov/ipmarketplace/search/patents

80 U.S. Pat. & Trademark Office, *About the Platform,* https://developer.uspto.gov/ipmarketplace/search/platform

81 *Id., ib.*

82 U.S. Pat. & Trademark Off., *IP Marketplace Platform,* https://developer.uspto.gov/ipmarketplace/search/patents

83 U.S. Pat. & Trademark Off., *About the Platform,* https://developer.uspto.gov/ipmarketplace/search/platform

84 *Id., ib.*

85 Contreras, *supra* note 71.

86 *Id.,* at 546.

87 *Id., ib.*

88 *Id.,* at 545–546. See also Jorge L. Contreras, *The Evolving Patent Pledge Landscape,* Ctr. Int'l Governance Innovation (Apr. 3, 2018), www.cigionline.org/publications/evolving-patent-pledge-landscape; Jonas Fabian Ehrnsperger & Frank Tietze, *Patent Pledges, Open IP, or Patent Pools? Developing Taxonomies in the Thicket of Terminologies,* PLoS One (Aug. 20, 2019); Elon Musk, *All Our Patent Are Belong to You* (sic), Tesla (Jun. 12, 2014), www.tesla.com/blog/all-our-patent-are-belong-you; Carey Gillam, *Monsanto Extends Pledge on Roundup Ready Soybeans,* Reuters (Jul. 8, 2010), www.reuters.com/article/monsanto-roundup/monsanto-extends-pledge-on-roundup-ready-soybeans-idUSN0824689420100709

89 See Matthew Bultman, *Scientists, Lawyers Create Coronavirus IP Pledge,* Bloomberg Law (Mar. 27, 2020), https://news.bloomberglaw.com/ip-law/scientists-lawyers-create-coronavirus-ip-pledge

90 See Open COVID-19 Pledge, *Frequently Asked Questions,* https://opencovidpledge.org/faqs/ (last accessed Aug. 30, 2020).

91 *Id., Make the Pledge to Share Your Intellectual Property in the Fight Against COVID-19,* https://opencovidpledge.org (last visited Aug. 30, 2020).

92 See *Id., NASA-JPL-3D Printed Respirators* (May 20, 2020), https://opencovidpledge.org/2020/05/20/nasa-jet-propulsion-laboratory/

93 See *Id., Fujitsu: Faster Disease Diagnosis Using Computer Software* (Jun. 3, 2020), https://opencovidpledge.org/2020/06/03/fujitsu-faster-disease-diagnosis-using-computer-software/; U.S. Pat. 20200118682, *Medical Diagnostic Aid and Method.*

94 See *Id., Facebook: Combating the Spread of COVID-19 Related Misinformation* (Aug. 11, 2020), https://opencovidpledge.org/2020/08/11/facebook-combating-the-spread-of-covid-19-related-misinformation/; U.S. Pat. 20190163794, *Contextual Information for Determining Credibility of Social-Networking.*

95 See e.g. *Id., About the Licenses,* https://opencovidpledge.org/licenses/ (last accessed Aug. 30, 2020).

96 *Id., ib.*

97 See e.g. *Id., Open COVID License 1.0 March 31, 2020,* https://opencovidpledge.org/v1-0/ (last accessed Aug. 30, 2020).

98 See e.g. Open COVID-19 Pledge, *About the Licenses,* https://opencovidpledge.org/licenses/ (last accessed Aug. 30, 2020).

99 See Open Source Initiative, *The MIT License,* https://opensource.org/licenses/MIT

100 See Apache, *Apache License, Version 2.0,* www.apache.org/licenses/LICENSE-2.0

101 See e.g. Open COVID-19 Pledge, *About the Licenses,* https://opencovidpledge.org/licenses/ (last accessed Aug. 30, 2020).

102 Creative Commons, *Attribution-Share Alike 4.0 International (CC BY-SA 4.0),* https://creativecommons.org/licenses/by-sa/4.0/

103 GNU Operating System, *GNU General Public License,* www.gnu.org/licenses/gpl-3.0.en.html

104 See Open COVID-19 Pledge, *About the Licenses,* https://opencovidpledge.org/licenses/ (last accessed Aug. 30, 2020).

105 *Id., ib.*

106 See e.g. Open COVID-19 Pledge, *Open COVID License 1.0 March 31, 2020,* https://opencovidpledge.org/v1-0/ (last accessed Aug. 30, 2020).

107 See e.g. Open COVID-19 Pledge, *OCL-PC v1.1,* https://opencovidpledge.org/v1-1-ocl-pc/ (last accessed Aug. 30, 2020).

108 See, *Open COVID License 1.0 March 31, 2020, supra* note 53 (last accessed Aug. 30, 2020).

109 *About the Licenses, supra* note 52.

110 See GAVI, Covax, The Act-Accelerator Vaccines Pillar, www.gavi.org/sites/default/files/document/2020/COVAX-Pillar- backgrounder_3.pdf

111 World Health Org., *The Access to COVID-19 Tools (ACT) Accelerator,* www.who.int/initiatives/act-accelerator

112 Coalition for Epidemic Preparedness Innovations [CEPI], *Our Mission,* http://cepi.net/about/whyweexist/

113 See Gavi, Covax, The Act-Accelerator Vaccines Pillar, *supra* note 110.

114 *Id., ib.*

115 Gavi, *About Our Alliance,* www.gavi.org/our-alliance/about

116 Gavi, Covax, The Act-Accelerator Vaccines Pillar, *supra* note 110.

117 *Id., ib.*

118 But see Ana Santos Rutschman, *The COVID-19 Vaccine Race: Intellectual Property, Collaboration(s), Nationalism and Misinformation,* 64 Wash. U. J. L. & Pol'y __ (forthcoming 2020) (draft on file with author) (criticizing the current allocative policy adopted by COVAX).

119 Gavi, *Gavi Launches Innovative Financing Mechanism for Access to COVID-19 Vaccines,* (Jun. 4, 2020), www.gavi.org/news/media-room/gavi-launches-innovative-financing-mechanism-access-covid-19-vaccines

120 Rutschman, *The Reemergence of Vaccine Nationalism, supra* note 4.

121 See Halabi & Rutschman, *supra* note 47.

8

HOW DO YOU SELF-ISOLATE WITH NOWHERE TO LIVE?

Carolyn Whitzman

Editors' introduction: For many years Japan has had a homeless population that sleeps in internet cafes.[i] For some who can't afford a home, this is a means of accessing affordable shelter, but when the pandemic struck, many of those cafes closed due to lack of business or pandemic-related restrictions. A survey by Japan's Ministry of Health, Labor, and Welfare revealed in 2017 that over 42% of Japan's homeless population was over 65, the first time that figure topped 40%.[ii] Today, in real numbers, there are 4,555 homeless people currently living in Japan, according to the latest figures of that ministry, from April 2019 and, of those, 1,126 live in Tokyo, the epicenter of Japan's COVID-19 outbreak.[iii]

This is the very group that is most at risk for COVID-19. In the UK, there are an estimated 30,000–40,000 people "sleeping rough" or in temporary housing. A COVID-19 Homeless Sector Plan has been devised to extend over £3.2 million of initial emergency funding to assist homeless people in self-isolating.[iv] Many of those people have significant underlying health conditions, and alternative shelter for those who are homeless are shared dormitory rooms, eating places, toilets, and bathrooms.[v] That raises significant concern about the impact of the pandemic on homeless people.

In Australia, early in the pandemic, a parliamentary committee on homelessness reported that, according to national census data from 2016, the national homelessness rate was 49.8 per 10,000 population, with Indigenous Australians significantly overrepresented.[vi] There was a concerted effort in capital cities to find shelter for those without a home. By utilizing empty hotel and motel rooms and vacant student

DOI: 10.4324/9781003215769-12

accommodation, there were remarkably positive results in a relatively short time frame. This instilled a belief in some that homelessness was indeed a solvable problem.

In this chapter, we introduce Professor Carolyn Whitzman, a passionate advocate and scholar in access to affordable housing. She is currently serving as 2019–20 Bank of Montreal Visiting Scholar in Women's Studies at the University of Ottawa. While in residence, she has undertaken Canadian-based research on scaling up women's housing and is working with the Canadian Housing Research Centre hub.

Dr. Whitzman served as Professor of Urban Planning at the University of Melbourne, Australia, for 16 years, where her research focused on affordable housing and women's safety in urban spaces. She is the author, coauthor, or editor of five books related to "the right to the city" from both a contemporary and historical perspective.[vii] She is also the author or coauthor of numerous book chapters, articles, and published conference presentations on affordable housing, children's independent mobility, women's safety, and disability rights. She frequently provides policy advice to local, state, and national government and to the UN, and has addressed the plenary session at the Habitat III Conference in Quito, Ecuador in September 2016.

In this chapter Dr. Whitzman demonstrates that some countries have already shown the way in providing cost-effective social housing, while others are lagging well behind. As she explains, by adopting and implementing strategies as those set out in this chapter, we would all do better in the next pandemic.

Introduction

COVID-19 is a health, social, economic, and political emergency. It is also a housing emergency.[1] In order to prevent the spread of COVID-19, governments across the world have asked and, in some cases legislated, that people "shelter at home."[2] As Leilani Farha, the former UN Special Rapporteur on the Right to Adequate Housing, has recently written: "Housing has become a frontline defence against the virus."[3] But for as many as 1.3 billion people, a third of the earth's urban population,[4] this basic precondition for health is denied. Inadequate housing conditions – where sick people cannot physically distance because of overcrowding, shared toilets are poorly maintained, or the pressure to pay rent forces people into working in unsafe conditions – have become means for community transmission.

In many countries, COVID-19 deaths have been concentrated in nursing homes, especially institutions run for profit. One study in the province of Ontario, Canada, where large-scale speculation in seniors' housing emerged during a neoliberal government in the late 1990s, has found much higher death rates in for-profit nursing homes:

> Southbridge Capital had outbreaks in nine of its 26 Ontario homes, and a 7.4 per cent death rate – more than 10 times that seen in public facilities. Investors in Southbridge Care Homes are promised a yield-based investment with "upside market gain." While those profits roll in, 176 people have lost their lives to COVID-19 in the firm's investment properties.[5]

Whether you are a frail senior in a nursing home; a foreign student trapped in Melbourne, Australia, sleeping in shifts because you are one of 15 people subletting a two-bedroom high-rise condominium;[6] a newly evicted older woman; one of 91,000 people living in encampments in California, United States, because living in a tent is safer than sleeping in a different shelter every night; an asylum seeker forced into an emergency shelter because you are unable to access public housing;[7] or one of the thousands of migrant workers in Singapore living in a crowded dormitory, your health is at greater risk. So too is the health of the people you contact as you line up at the food bank, pack meat or online purchases, or work on a construction site.[8]

With the growing realization that inadequate housing conditions can lead to increased community transmission, COVID-19 might prove a tipping point toward implementation of the right to adequate housing. More pessimistically, it might exacerbate existing trends, entrench systemic inequalities, and increase the risk of death in the next pandemic. This chapter will explore how either transformation might occur.

Pandemic housing responses in the past: a tale of three cities

By the beginning of the twentieth century, illnesses ranging from cholera to influenza were known to spread through microscopic particles passed between individuals. The new twin professions of urban planning and public health shared a belief that the housing conditions of the poorest people affected everyone. In the optimistic words of Engels:

> Capitalist rule cannot allow itself the pleasure of creating epidemic diseases among the working class with impunity; the consequences fall back on it and the angel of death rages in its ranks as ruthlessly as in the ranks of the workers.[9]

In 1918, Bloemfontein, a city of 31,000 people in South Africa, prided itself on its healthy upland breezes and self-perceived absence of slums, despite recent population growth from rural areas. But it was also on the main rail line from

Cape Town. Troop movement was one of the precipitating factors in rapid transmission of the initial wave of the Spanish flu in October of that year, with overcrowding and poor underlying health conditions leading to South Africa having one of the highest death rates in the world.[10]

Local political leaders immediately ordered a lockdown, with Black travelers banned from railroads and Black servants ordered to remain "at their master's house, as they are most susceptible and pass the infection to the whites."[11] Town leaders also swung into action to create temporary hospitals and isolation stations – for White residents only. Black people were forced to continue working, with ten carloads of laborers kidnapped and made to work as gravediggers and to live in the cemetery for the duration of the pandemic. Those who were "slow to return to domestic work or who could not show that their absence was due to the 'flu were prosecuted under the Master and Servants' Act."[12] Unsurprisingly, the local infection rate was 60%, and twice as many Blacks as Whites died in the epidemic. Some overcrowded areas with poor sanitation had death rates triple that of middle-class White areas, although statistics were not very well kept in Black neighborhoods that lacked access to health care.[13]

After the 1919 second wave, the Bloemfontein Town Clerk, unwittingly echoing Engels, concluded that "the poor take toll of the rich for the evil conditions under which they exist."[14] Local authorities moved quickly to relieve inadequate living conditions exposed by the virus – so long as the residents were low-income Boers and not "native." The municipality bought up newly discovered "slum properties" and upgraded them. An existing building was purchased and repurposed as an apartment building for single White women. Taking advantage of municipal ownership of large tracts of land at the outskirts of Bloemfontein, a working-class home-building program was expanded. When the Central Housing Board temporarily ceased funding these programs in 1921, the municipality raised a large loan from the South African Mutual Life Assurance Company to continue.

Housing quickly became a zero-sum game, where the gains of lower-income Whites were bought at the expense of the majority Black and "coloured" populations.[15] After the passage of the 1920 South African Housing Act, national building funds were made available to municipalities on condition that the new estates were racially segregated, with different access roads.[16] In Bloemfontein, cottages provided to "coloured" families were reallocated to lower-income Whites. By the mid-1920s, all of White Bloemfontein was served by a waterborne sewage system, while there was no provision in new Black ghettos for sewage removal other than by pail.[17] The intergenerational legacy of apartheid persists in terms of grossly unequal housing, health, and wealth outcomes – one factor behind South Africa's high COVID-19 infection rates.[18]

There were striking similarities thousands of kilometers north, in Sweden. There, the town of Östersund, with 13,000 residents, had one of the highest

Spanish flu death rates in that country, despite a salubrious position in the mountains and no acknowledged slums.[19] Although Sweden had remained neutral in World War I, armed forces were kept on alert, and Östersund was a garrison town with several military bases. Furthermore, a malnourished local population was overcrowded in cramped quarters, while wealthy tourists drawn by mountain views and restorative waters outbid local residents for housing. There were racialized inequalities as well: the indigenous Sami peoples had held their first national convention in Östersund in early 1918, demanding an end to discriminatory policies that forced them to live in temporary encampments.

When the pandemic hit, the town's bank director Carl Lignell withdrew funds provided by the national government without authorization and requisitioned a school for use as a hospital. Local authorities also moved quickly to quarantine suspected cases in their homes, where public health officers "discovered" whole families crowded in one-room wooden shacks.[20]

After 1919, the Swedish government declined to press charges against Lignell for his emergency fund appropriation and made tentative steps toward a more equitable social democratic model.[21] The end of World War I rent controls had led to widespread housing speculation, and tenant and labor activists developed their own low-cost alternatives. By the end of the 1920s, there were about 600 limited-equity housing cooperatives in the country, and today that sector represents 17% of all housing in Sweden.[22] However, this housing was aimed at relatively high-waged skilled working people, and low-income Swedes, including residents of Östersund, had to wait until the 1960s for the nation's transformative Million Homes Programme.[23] Sweden continues to have a high proportion of nonprofit rental housing, although it has fallen behind in recent years in affordable housing provision and rent control.[24]

In contrast to Bloemfontein and Östersund, where there was no direct involvement in World War I, the first wave of the Spanish flu reached Vienna in September 1918, just as it was losing the war. Thousands of refugees were streaming into a city that had already quintupled in population to two million over the previous half-century. Even before the war, in 1910, the city's workhouses accommodated over 60,000 people, more than 3% of the total population, including 7,000 children. No less than 95% of all the apartments lacked indoor toilets or sinks, and there was an average of ten people in the typical one-room apartments. Unsurprisingly, prewar Vienna had one of the highest rates of tuberculosis in the world.[25] Austria was particularly hard hit by the Spanish flu, with an estimated death rate of 1% of the population, much higher than Germany, France, or England.[26]

There was a wartime rent freeze and ban on evictions. After the fall of the Austro-Hungarian Empire resulted in a new constitution with universal suffrage, a social democratic municipal government was elected in 1919. Squatters built cabins and allotment gardens in the outskirts of the war-torn city; the municipality supported a cooperative brick and window manufacturing workshop to assist them. By 1931, the municipality owned a third of the land in the city, and any unused land incurred a heavy vacancy tax. A huge municipal housing program was funded by a progressive property tax: low-income renters paid 2% of assessed value, while luxury apartment dwellers paid up to 37%. The waiting list for new apartments prioritized those who were homeless or doubling up. The ground floor of new apartment buildings, designed by the best architects, included communal kitchens and laundries, kindergartens, libraries, and meeting rooms. By the time the social democrats were overthrown by fascists in 1934, 60,000 affordable homes had been constructed in a little over ten years.[27]

There are several lessons from the global pandemic a century ago that can inform current housing policy responses to COVID-19. First, although governments have known for well over a century that inadequate housing contributes to the spread of infectious disease, they often choose to ignore those most in need. Second, a more optimistic lesson is that governments, working with civil society, can act quickly and effectively to improve housing conditions during and immediately after a crisis. And third, none of the housing inequalities faced today – discriminatory housing outcomes for Black and Indigenous people, rich tourists seeking "vacation homes" outbidding lower-income households, and the persistent inability to provide adequate housing for those with the lowest incomes – are new. What might be new is a growing global movement toward the right to adequate housing and, along with that, a return to the basics of good housing policy.

The five basic mechanisms of good housing policy

Housing is as essential to individual lives and global sustainability as healthcare or education – a fact recognized by the UN Sustainable Development Goals.[28] But unlike healthcare and education, where basic provision has been increasingly guaranteed by most developed countries, housing has been increasingly left to the private market to provide, with minimal regulation to ensure adequate housing for all.[29]

Most of the twentieth century saw strong public housing provision by national and sub-national governments. In Singapore, 80% of post-independence housing was provided by the national government.[30] In Vienna[31] and Amsterdam,[32] the majority of housing was provided by non-speculative development, either municipally owned or community based. However, from the late 1970s onward, a global neoliberal turn took hold. In most of the world, public housing was privatized, and responsibility for provision of public and nonprofit housing was delegated to local governments without the fiscal or regulatory capacity to maintain or expand this stock. Unregulated and out-of-control speculation in major city housing markets led to price increases many times higher than household income increases (Figure 8.1).[33]

FIGURE 8.1 A public housing project in Vienna built in 1983 by artist Josef Krawina and architect Friedensreich Hundertwasser.

Source: Aolin Chen/Getty Images.

Note: It has different colored exteriors and features undulating floors, a roof covered with earth and grass, and large trees growing from inside the rooms.

Recognizing the human disaster governments have wrought

Homelessness, overcrowding, and growing intergenerational wealth disparities have blighted the lives of individuals, families, and communities, in rich as well as poor countries. Governments do not need to directly provide all housing, but they do need to steer effectively.[34] To do so, they must prioritize the needs and voices of those who are most marginalized.[35]

Collaborating within and among governments

This has three aspects. First is horizontal integration within scales of government; for instance, ensuring transit and social services proximate to housing requires collaboration between different departments or ministries of a government. Second, vertical integration between scales of government is necessary to ensure, for instance, that national affordable housing targets are not undercut by municipal zoning. And third, democratic governance between governments, nonprofits, and the private sector is necessary to ensure coordinated delivery of housing.

In three-tier governments like the United States, Australia, and Canada, the national government needs to provide strong steering through a strategy with common definitions and national targets. It also needs suitable funding, financing, and taxation mechanisms to ensure the right balance of housing supply at price points households can afford. Provinces, territories, regions, and states need to ensure that transit, as well as health and social infrastructure planning, including schools and community centers, support affordable housing targets. Local governments must be enabled to regulate and fund their own targets. Municipalities need to prioritize rapid construction of affordable housing in appropriate locations to address deficits and meet the needs of a growing and changing population. All levels of government should have a designated housing ministry, department, or authority.[36]

Legislating accurate definitions of "affordable housing" and "homelessness"

Only when legislating accurate definitions of 'affordable housing' and 'homelessness' is done can meaningful planning and measuring of progress be undertaken, consistently and comparatively.

In many countries, "affordable housing" is defined as a proportion of "average market price," which bears no resemblance to low-income households' ability to pay.[37] Household sizes vary, but low-income households are as likely to be a single mother with children as they are to be an individual.[38] It is better to start with three categories of household income, usually measured in comparison to average income within a metropolitan area or region (area median income, or AMI).

Very low-income households generally do not have paid employment and rely on pensions or other benefits totaling less than 30% of AMI. This category includes seniors, people with disability, and full-time single parents. Low-income households, earning between 30–50% AMI, generally rely on minimum wage jobs and are most likely to be in precarious employment, such as service sector workers. Moderate income households generally earn between 50% and 80% AMI, and often include "key workers" such as nurses and teachers. An affordable rent can be calculated using a short-cut, such as 30% of household income for rent and utilities, or using a more complex residual income approach: what is left for housing costs after other essentials, including food and transport, are paid.[39]

Adequate housing goes beyond affordability. Cheap housing is often located far from jobs and services like public transport or childcare, forcing households to buy cars and undertake long commutes. Homelessness is not simply living on the street but is the absence of safe and secure housing. Women are often under-counted in surveys of emergency shelters and those sleeping rough, but women-led households are far more likely to be living in unsafe, unaffordable, and overcrowded conditions. Women's homelessness has been exacerbated by an international spike in family violence associated with COVID-19. Women who are forced to remain in an abusive relationship in order not to lose housing or custody of their children are homeless. People forced to sleep in emergency shelters, including violence against women shelters, are homeless. Households "doubling up," sleeping on sofas or floors because of absence of other options, are homeless and are at increased risk of COVID-19.[40] Indigenous communities in settler societies like the United States, Canada, and Australia, which have been dispossessed of their ancestral land and isolated from their relationships to land, water, place, family, kin, each other, animals, cultures, languages and identities, are also homeless.[41]

Generating honest, transparent, and comparable needs assessments

Demographic data should be gathered regarding the number of households at various income categories, such as very low, low and moderate, but also average and high income, and their household sizes and characteristics, such as age, gender, race, and abilities. Then the proportion of those households that are experiencing inadequate housing must be calculated – housing that is unaffordable, overcrowded, far from necessary services such as public transport, and without private access to clean water or toilets. To the large deficit that inevitably results, there must also be added the net loss of affordable housing, as well as a projection of the housing needs of an increasing and changing population over the period covered by a plan, which is typically ten years. Deficit plus net loss of affordable housing plus projected population requirements equals housing need.

Regulating the right supply of housing at the right cost

Measures like capital gains tax exemptions for house sales, first-time homebuyers grants, and allowing zero down payment long-term mortgages simply incentivize housing speculation and increase risky levels of household debt.[42] In contrast, cities and regions can provide housing for all by specifying housing production targets at particular price points and tenures; ensuring an adequate supply of public and other nonprofit housing with ongoing subsidies to low-income households; providing low or no-cost land to nonprofit housing; limiting rent increases to inflation rates; and controlling speculation. To give one example, Hamburg, a German city with a population of a little under 2,000,000 and relatively high population growth, has an annual target of 16,000 new homes. This target is regulated through an agreement with the industry body for both private and nonprofit developers. Of this quantum, at least one-third must be subsidized nonprofit and another third must be private rental at a cost legislated by square meter. Developers who provide this "rule of third" in proposals obtain permits quickly and efficiently by the municipal housing department.[43]

Five pandemic-busting housing interventions

The current housing crisis was fueled by the financialization of housing: prioritizing profit over a basic human right and need. It predates COVID-19 and, as we now know, has exacerbated its impacts. In the United States, more than half a million people are reported to be experiencing homelessness on any given night. Those in congregate living settings like shelters, informal encampments, prisons, or nursing homes, with shared access to toilets and showers, not only have greater rates of mortality but are also generally very geographically mobile. For instance, many of the prisoners released during COVID-19 to reduce overcrowding in jails have no options other than shelters and encampments. This makes it more difficult to track and prevent transmission and to treat those who need care.[44]

Immediately acquire existing well-located properties

Several governments have rented or purchased properties such as hotels and short-term rentals left vacant by the precipitate drop in tourism to address homelessness. The Canadian province of British Columbia has purchased a 65-bed hotel in the capital, Victoria, in addition to two hotels with a total of 173 beds in the largest city of Vancouver, to provide permanent housing with social supports to those previously living in encampments.[45] In Portugal, where 90,000 holiday homes were left vacant as a result of COVID-19, the two largest cities, Lisbon and Porto, have rented a total of 2,000 central city apartments on two- to five-year leases for use as public housing. Lisbon banned the registration of new short-term rentals in 2019, reacting to the fact that over a third of central city apartments had already been lost to short-term rentals. Rents in the remaining stock had increased by almost 10% in the previous year alone.[46] In July 2020 in Barcelona, the city's housing department warned 14 companies, which collectively own 194 empty apartments, that if they hadn't found a tenant within the next month, the city could take possession of these properties with compensation at half their market value. These units would then be rented out by the city as public housing.[47]

The past 40 years have seen rapid dismantling of public housing systems. The UK alone lost 2.6 million municipally owned homes from 1980 until the "Right to Buy" program was discontinued in 2016.[48] It is eminently feasible for wealthy countries to act just as rapidly to reclaim affordable housing stock and end the large-scale homelessness created by bad political decisions. Finland's national Housing First strategy has ended chronic homelessness in that nation, providing 4,600 homes to formerly homeless people in the last decade, through a combination of acquisition of newly built shelters and conversion of emergency shelters once they were no longer needed. Although support services are still provided by the government, and short-term homelessness still occurs (e.g., shelters for women and children survivors of domestic violence), Finland spends 15,000 euros a year less per person housed, which frees up more funding for better public health.[49] As of late May, Finland had the second lowest rate of COVID-19 deaths in Europe, due to its National Emergency Preparation Agency that stockpiles medical equipment, initiating random antibody testing by April 2020, implementing dedicated contact tracing, and not having its most vulnerable citizens in overcrowded congregate housing.[50]

But the economic inequalities associated with COVID-19 may help generate homelessness faster than people can be re-housed, unless other actions are taken.

Stop Naturally Occurring Affordable Housing (NOAH)

In the United States, before the GFC, low interest mortgages and minimal deposits led to household debt increasing from 81% of GDP in 1984 to 260% of GDP in 2008.[51] From 2007 to 2011, 4.7 million households lost homes due to foreclosure and a million more to sales at less than value. Institutional landlords, who did not exist in the US single-family-rental market prior to 2010, grew to 25–30 companies with 260,000 single-family homes.[52] Even before COVID-19 the majority of renter households in the United States were paying an unaffordable amount, more than 40% of income. By July 2020, the number of Americans threatened by eviction because of the COVID-19 economic depression of the previous four months had ballooned to over 20 million.[53]

This story of huge firms concentrating billions of dollars in real estate, with expectations of high returns and a propensity to evict, is not unique to the United States. In Canada, it is estimated that for every social housing dwelling built between 2011 and 2016, 15 affordable private rental homes were lost – either through conversion to ownership, conversion to holiday rentals, or by institutional investors evicting tenants in order to vastly increase rents – a process known as "renoviction."[54] More than 6,000 eviction notices for non-payment of rent in the province of Ontario have been filed since COVID-19 hit in March 2020, even before an eviction ban was set to lapse in August 2020.[55] Real Estate Investment Trusts (REITs) and other large investors now own one in five apartments in Canada. In Ontario, where rent control no longer applies if the tenants vacate the property, REITs have been raising rents by up to 50% as they evict tenants.[56]

How can governments prevent homelessness and maintain affordable rental stock? The most direct method is supporting public and nonprofit providers to acquire existing rental buildings. More indirectly, measures can include strong eviction prevention, rent control, and retaining properties as long-term rental through banning conversions to holiday homes or home ownership. While many national and sub-national governments have temporarily suspended evictions and foreclosures, in most cases the unpaid rent or mortgage debts continue to accrue. This merely postpones large-scale homelessness until the temporary measure ends, even as unemployment remains high. Emergency financial support to cover rent and mortgage payments has been forthcoming in some parts of Canada (notably, British Columbia), Australia (notably, Victoria), and several European countries.

In the best practice scenario, emergency rent assistance would be supplemented by a longer-term rent freeze.[57] In Berlin, where 85% or 1.5 million households rent, the city government instituted a five-year rent freeze in February 2020, just before COVID-19 hit. The rent freeze was precipitated by a decade in which rents had more than doubled, while household income had not substantially increased. When the freeze ends in 2025, rents will not rise above the rate of inflation, which is about 1.3% per year.[58] When the German eviction ban ends in September, Berlin renters will be better protected from losing their homes, even if they are out of work. Similarly, Scotland's 2016 Private Housing Act gives municipal governments the authority to cap annual rent increases at 1% above inflation.[59]

Redress the imbalance of tax subsidy support for homeowners

Settler-colonial societies, like the United States, Canada, Australia, and New Zealand, stole Indigenous land. They then created a set of taxation and regulatory policies, including zoning, that promoted property ownership as necessary for security of tenure and wealth creation. This was especially lucrative for White settlers, who were able to protect their investments through restrictive zoning. In most of these societies, Black, Indigenous, and People of Color earn less and are in more precarious employment. They are also less likely to own property and more likely to be in rent or mortgage arrears due to COVID-19.[60] In contrast, cultures that supported rental housing through long leases, municipal land ownership, and a large stock of nonprofit housing, like Vienna, have enabled residents to be better able to weather financial and social shocks like the GFC and COVID-19, although racial inequalities, including in housing provision, still persist.[61]

Rapidly scale up the stock of non-speculative housing

Community land trusts (CLTs), nonprofit corporations that acquire and own land and housing for community benefit, arose from Black American activism around affordable housing in the late 1960s. They have worked well in both rich and poor countries where low- and moderate-income households cannot compete with speculative investors. Social purpose investment trusts can also assist in preserving affordable housing while using the equity and stable returns to invest in more land and properties.[62] In Montreal, Canada, Milton Parc is a CLT made up of 15 cooperatives and seven nonprofit housing providers that has provided housing for over 1,500 people on six city blocks for almost four decades. Since 2012, Vancouver's CLT has developed over 1,600 new homes and renovated thousands of existing homes.[63]

Governments need to end financial incentives to owning multiple houses for the purposes of speculation, such as Australia's tax system which allows home-owners to deduct losses on secondary properties, a tax loophole which, along with capital gains tax exemptions for house sales, costs the Australian economy almost 12 billion AUD a year.[64] British Columbia introduced taxes on vacant properties, along with a luxury home tax in 2018, which has led to annual revenues projected at 200 million CAD.[65] This new revenue stream allows the province to fund new affordable housing initiatives described earlier. Amsterdam has recently capped the sale price of new homes at below the current market average.[66] There are a range of mechanisms to support renters and curb housing speculation: banning conversion of rental properties to homeownership or short-term rentals; scaling up stock of non-speculative rental housing; applying surcharges for luxury homes and fines or seizures of vacant homes; capping new luxury investment housing in housing strategies; eliminating tax loopholes for homeowners; legislating the possibility of five-year leases; freezing or limiting rent increases to match inflation; and making evictions much more difficult. If these mechanisms were incorporated into housing strategies at all scales of government, rental housing would become much more "shock proof" and so too would the people living in that housing. Contract workers with lower capital could live more securely, with flexibility to invest any money saved by renting into other investments. Renting could become a real choice, rather than a one-way ticket to second-class citizenship and housing precarity.

Move toward a proactive approach

Incremental measures like re-zoning single-family properties to allow accessory units, inclusionary zoning and grants or loans for small-scale nonprofit projects will never bridge the affordable housing deficit, nor will they redress growing housing inequality. All government programs, from local to national, need to support affordable housing targets for various household incomes, sizes and types.

Once these targets are in place, there are many new technologies that allow rapid construction of inexpensive housing adaptable to an aging population. These range from modular housing to 3D printing. For instance, Vancouver has built over 650 modular homes with supportive services for homeless people in well-located areas in a little over two years, and Toronto has committed to construction of over 250 of these homes over the next year.[67] In Portland, 3D printers can now create code-compliant homes in 24 hours for $10,000, and Dweller, a start-up, is prefabricating tiny homes that homeowners can put in their yards and rent out, paying no upfront costs and keeping 30% of the rental income. In the UK, where nearly 50% of car parks are publicly owned, the company ZEDPods provides flexible, prefabricated multistory homes to build over surface car parks. Real estate firm JLL has identified 10,500 car parks that could accommodate 400,000 homes.[68]

These technologies could underpin a more collaborative approach between governments, nonprofits, and the private sector, one that is based on housing as a right rather than a commodity. As mentioned earlier, Hamburg's local government creates agreements with the development industry association that prioritize certainty over profit. Proposals that meet income-based targets and that improve the public realm are facilitated by the municipal construction coordination body with reduced development approval times, amendment of any regulations that impede inner city affordable housing construction, and subsidies for low-income units.[69] Vienna limits the profit that developers can make from home building but encourages development by providing construction financing at 1% for 30 years.[70]

Conclusion – choices for a healthier future

Homes have never been so important. With COVID-19, homes serve "not only as shelter and refuge, but also as workplace and school and gym and theatre and restaurant and bar and laundry and town square."[71] A stark political choice faces all governments and the citizens that elect these governments. The link between adequate housing and health is clear, effective policies and mechanisms known, costs and benefits calculable, and international law explicit. Business as usual will make things much worse. Whether we collectively save lives or destroy them is a matter of political will.

**BOX 8.1   CORONA SHORT #13: PHILIPPINES
FRENI AND FRED, EDUCATORS AND PARENTS,
RELY ON NATURAL CURES ON THEIR FARM**

Freni: At first during last year in March we were shocked. There were sudden changes in everything. Enhanced community quarantine was everywhere. Nobody was allowed to go out. So, a sudden change in lifestyle. If we obeyed everything they said, how will we survive? We followed our own protocol to keep ourselves clean. Our source of living is farming, so we are forced to go out. If we stayed in the house, afraid of what we cannot see, what will happen to our lives?

Fred: The government provided a little financial aid. But it is not enough for everyone. It was given to everybody, regardless. One time only. The economy is suffering, so instead of a national lockdown, there was a localized lockdown, on the street where the person with COVID lives. There were police on the street at all exits of our barangay. If you want to go for an appointment you need a medical certificate

---

and a pass from the municipality. On our farm, I have workers. Our place is in a very remote area. It is also a camping ground. We take in families – it is very helpful for them. COVID will not disturb the population of the barangay.

Freni: I believe if you are exposed to the sun, it is helpful, a healthy lifestyle and work and belief in God. At first, we used herbal medicines. My husband got sick and I thought he had COVID. But he could smell and taste. He was so weak but I did not use synthetic medicine. I only used steaming, putting coconut oil in the nose, mixing coconut oil with herbs in hot water. We have a lot of those herbs on our farm. Medicinal teas. We have trees – mahogany. They might laugh at us, but we are hugging those trees, asking them to give us energy. This is how we survive.

Fred: For one year we did not hear a lot about COVID. But then, the variant arrived. There were a lot of people around us who died. Those who suffered from stroke, diabetes, heart problems, dialysis went to the hospital and were diagnosed with COVID and they died. In the newspapers there are so many criticisms against our president. We are in the third world but Pfizer, and others, are made in the United States and Russia and so we are of less priority. I think the smaller countries are more able to handle the logistics of COVID.

Freni: The priests are telling people not to take the vaccine. I always consult the Bible. Why should we be afraid? Drink as much water as you can. In the barangay you see if people are not wearing a mask they are forced to do some physical punishment. If they do not do that, how can we get rid of this?

Fred: I am reading about the vaccine and it is used without any testing. We don't know the aftereffects. We read that some who got this vaccine died. People who are allergic to this medicine cannot be forced to take it. Filipinos are hard-headed people. There is a warning but still people go out so that is the problem with the Philippines. Because there are only three hospitals dealing with dialysis in our town, many people die. According to hearsay, even accidents turn out to be positive with COVID and they have to stay there.

Freni: Last October we were affected by four typhoons. It was harvest time. Everybody was depressed because you can see that the typhoon came at night so our rice was flooded. We could not get a good harvest and the problem is the price of the rice.

Fred: I made a proposal to the provincial government and we were able to put up drying machines, flat bed drying, in our area. The majority in the Philippines are doing 'farming by luck' – you are lucky when farming if there is no typhoon.

Freni: Do not listen to TV or radio about the pandemic. And God bless.

Notes

i Miwa Suzuki, *Japan's Homeless "Net Café Refugees" Seek Shelter Amid Virus Woe*, Jakarta Post (April 15, 2020).

ii Andrew McKirdy, *Japan's Homeless at Risk from Coronavirus Pandemic*, Japan Times (April 5, 2020).

iii *Id.*

iv Tony Kirby, *Efforts Escalate to Protect Homeless People from CIVID-19 in UK*, Lancet (March 26, 2020).

v *Id.*

vi Australia House of Representatives Standing Committee on Social Policy and Legal Affairs, *Interim Report on Homelessness* (October 1, 2020).

vii Titles include *Building Inclusive Cities: Women's Safety and the Right to the City* (Routledge 2013) and *The Handbook of Community Safety, Gender, and Violence Prevention: Practical Planning Tools* (Earthscan 2008).

1 Dallas Rogers and Emma Power, *Housing Policy and the COVID-19 Pandemic: The Importance of Housing Research during this Health Emergency*, Int. J. of Housing Policy 20(2). 177–183 (2020).

2 Leilani Farha, *COVID-19 Guidance Note: Protecting Residents of Informal Settlements*, UNHR Special Procedures (2020), https://reliefweb.int/sites/reliefweb.int/files/resources/75500.pdf.

3 Leilani Farha, *COVID-19 Guidance Note: Protection for Those Living in Homelessness*, UNHR Special Procedures (2020), https://cambodia.ohchr.org/sites/default/files/SR_housing_COVID-19_guidance_homeless.pdf.

4 Jonathan Woetzel et al., *A Blueprint for Addressing the Global Affordable Housing Challenge*, McKinsey Global Institute (2014).

5 Martine August, *The Coronavirus Exposes the Perils of Profit in Seniors' Housing*, The Conversation (July 23, 2020).

6 Asha Dow, *Slum Squeeze: Overseas Students Taking Turns to Sleep in Overcrowded Melbourne High Rises*, The Age (May 21, 2015).

7 UN Regional Centre for Western Europe, *COVID-19: How Do You Self-Isolate If You Have Nowhere to Live?* (April 3, 2020).

8 Amy Maxmen, *Coronavirus Is Spreading under the Radar in US Homeless Shelters*, Nature (May 7, 2020).

9 Frederick Engels, The Housing Option, published as a pamphlet (1872), reprinted by the Co-operative Publishing Society of Foreign Workers; quoted in Howard Phillips, *The Local State and Public Health Reform in South Africa: Bloemfontein and the Consequences of the Spanish 'Flu Epidemic of 1918*, J. Southern African Studies 13(2). 210–233, 210 (1987).

10 Howard Phillips, *The Local State and Public Health Reform in South Africa: Bloemfontein and the Consequences of the Spanish 'Flu Epidemic of 1918*, J. Southern African Studies 13(2). 210–233, 233 (1987).

11 *Id*, 212.

12 *Id*, 219.

13 *Id*, 220.

14 *Id*, 224.

15 *Id.*

16 Brandon Finn and Lindsay Kobayashi, *Structural Inequality in the Time of COVID-19: Urbanization, Segregation, and Pandemic Control in Sub-Saharan Africa*, Dialogues in Human Geography (2020), https://doi.org/10.1177/2043820620934310.

17 Leilani Farha, *supra* note 3.

18 Tim Cocks, *South Africa's Excess Death Rate above Normal, Suggests COVID-19 Toll Much Worse Than Official Figures*, The Globe and Mail (July 23, 2020).

19 Brian Melican, *How Spanish Flu Helped Create Sweden's Modern Welfare State*, The Guardian (August 29, 2018).

20 *Id.*

21 *Id.*
22 Hannu Ruonavaara, *How Divergent Housing Institutions Evolve: A Comparison of Swedish Tenant Co-Operatives and Finnish Shareholders' Housing Companies*, Housing, Theory and Society 22(4). 213–236 (2005).
23 Jardar Sorvoll and Bo Bengstsson, *The Pyrrhic Victory of Civil Society Housing? Co-Operative Housing in Sweden and Norway*, International J. of Housing Policy 18(1). 124–142 (2018).
24 Anna Granath Hansson, *City Strategies for Affordable Housing: The Approaches of Berlin, Hamburg, Stockholm, and Gothenburg*, International J. of Housing Policy 19(1). 95–109 (2019).
25 Wolfgang Forster, *80 Years of Social Housing in Vienna* (Vienna: Municipality of Vienna Housing Subsidies Department 2002).
26 Robert Barro, Jose Ursua and Joanna Weng, *The Coronavirus and the Great Influenza Epidemic: Lessons from the "Spanish Flu" for the Coronavirus's Potential Effects on Mortality and Economic Activity*, Center for Economic Studies and ifo Institute (CESifo): Munich (2020).
27 Tim Cocks, *supra* note 18.
28 United Nations, *Universal Declaration of Human Rights* (1948); United Nations, *UN Declaration on Social, Economic and Cultural Rights* (1966); United Nations, *New Urban Agenda*, UN-Habitat, Nairobi (2017).
29 David Madden and Peter Marcuse, *In Defense of Housing: The Politics of Crisis* (London: Verso 2016).
30 Sock Yong Phang and Matthias Helble, *Housing Policies in Singapore* (Singapore: Asian Development Bank Institute 2016).
31 Carla Weinzierl, Florian Wukovitsch and Andrea Novy, *Housing First in Vienna: A Socially Innovative Initiative to Foster Social Cohesion*, J. of Housing and the Built Environment 31. 409–422 (2016).
32 Arenda Jonkman, *Patterns of Distributive Justice: Social Housing and the Search for Market Dynamism in Amsterdam*, Housing Studies (2020).
33 Manuel Aalbers, *The Great Moderation, the Great Excess and the Global Housing Crisis*, International J. of Housing Policy 15(1). 43–60 (2015).
34 H. Brinton Milward and Keith G. Provan, *Governing the Hollow State*, J. of Public Administration Research and Theory 10(2). 359–379 (2000).
35 UN Special Rapporteur on the Right to Adequate Housing, *Guidelines for the Implementation of the Right to Adequate Housing*, Geneva, UN Human Rights Commission (2019), www.ohchr.org/EN/Issues/Housing/Pages/GuidelinesImplementation.aspx.
36 World Economic Forum, *Making Affordable Housing a Reality in Cities*, Geneva (2019).
37 Beibei Zhang, *Social Policies, Financial Markets and the Multi-Scalar Governance of Affordable Housing in Toronto*, Urban Studies (2019), https://doi.org/10.1177/0042098019881368.
38 Kaitlin Schwan et al., *The State of Women's Housing Need & Homelessness in Canada* (Toronto: Canadian Observatory on Homelessness Press 2020), http://womenshome-lessness.ca/literature-review/.
39 Matthew Palm and Carolyn Whitzman, *Housing Need Assessments in San Francisco, Vancouver, and Melbourne: Normative Science or Neoliberal Alchemy?*, Housing Studies 35(5). 771–794 (2020).
40 Carla Weinzierl et al., *supra* note 31.
41 Jesse Thistle, *Definition of Indigenous Homelessness in Canada* (Toronto: Canadian Observatory on Homelessness 2017).
42 Alan Walks and Brian Clifford, *The Political Economy of Mortgage Securitization and the Neoliberalization of Housing Policy in Canada*, Environment and Planning 47. 1624–1642 (2015).
43 Anna Granath Hansson and Christoph Kapalchinski, *Hamburg Fights Housing Crunch with Cooperation*, Handelsblatt (August 1, 2018).
44 Jack Tsai and Michal Wilson, *COVID-19: A Potential Public Health Problem for Homeless Populations*, The Lancet 5(4). 186–187 (2020).

45 *Province Purchases Howard Johnson and Buchan Hotels in Bid to Create Affordable Housing*, CBC News (June 24, 2020); *B.C. Government Buys Victoria Hotel to House the Homeless*, CBC News (May 15, 2020).

46 Victoria Waldersee, *Portugal's Airbnb Owners Resist Push to Low-Rent Housing*, Reuters (May 13, 2020).

47 Feargus O'Sullivan, *Barcelona's Latest Affordable Housing Tool: Seize Empty Apartments*, Citylab (July 16, 2020).

48 Alex Homer, *Right to Buy Homes Made £2.8m in Profit "in Weeks"*, BBC News (March 14, 2019).

49 Kathrin Glosel, *Finland Ends Homelessness and Provides Shelter for All in Need*, scoop.me (January 29, 2020).

50 Will Doig, *These Unsung Countries Are Vanquishing the Virus*, Reasons to Be Cheerful (May 22, 2020).

51 Robert Barro et al., *supra* note 26, at 52.

52 Francesca Mari, *A $60 Billion Housing Grab by Wall Street*, The New York Times Magazine (March 4, 2020).

53 Eric Levitz, *This Recession Is a Bigger Housing Crisis Than 2008*, The New York Times Magazine (July 13, 2020).

54 Steve Pomeroy, *Recovery for All: Proposals to Strengthen the National Housing Strategy and End Homelessness* (Ottawa: Canadian Alliance to End Homelessness 2020).

55 Victoria Gibson, *More Than 6,000 Ontario Tenants Could Face Eviction for Nonpayment of Rent during COVID-19, New Figures Show*, Toronto Star (July 25, 2020).

56 Martine August, *The Financialization of Canadian Multi-Family Rental Housing: From Trailer to Tower*, Journal of Urban Affairs 42. 1–23 (2020).

57 Konstantin Kholodilin, *Housing Policies Worldwide during Coronavirus Crisis: Challenges and Solutions* (DIW Berlin: German Institute for Economic Research 2020).

58 Douglas Broom, *This Is Why Berlin Is Freezing the Rent on 1.5 Million Homes*, World Economic Forum (February 27, 2020), www.weforum.org/agenda/2020/02/berlin-rent-freeze-stop-exodus/.

59 World Economic Forum, *Making Affordable Housing a Reality in Cities*, at 30 (2019), www3.weforum.org/docs/WEF_Making_Affordable_Housing_A_Reality_In_Cities_report.pdf.

60 See, for instance, Feng Hou, Kristin Frank and Christoph Schimmele, *Economic Impact of COVID-19 among Visible Minority Groups* (Ottawa: Statistics Canada 2020).

61 Steffen Wetzstein, *Assessing Post-GFC Housing Affordability Interventions: A Qualitative Exploration across Five International Cities*, International J. of Housing Policy (2019), https://doi.org/10.1080/19491247.2019.1662639.

62 Francesca Mari, *supra* note 52, at 17, 26.

63 Claudia Pedrero, *Community Land Trusts a Model for Community-Led Land Stewardship*, rabble.ca (April 19, 2019).

64 John Daley and Danielle Wood, *Hot Property: Negative Gearing and Capital Gains Tax Reform* (Melbourne: Grattan Institute 2016).

65 Rob Shaw, *B.C. Speculation Tax Figures Show Foreign Owners Hardest Hit as Expected Take Soars*, Vancouver Sun (July 11, 2019).

66 *How Can Europe's Cities Make Housing More Affordable?*, JLL (June 26, 2019), www.jll.ca/en/trends-and-insights/cities/can-europes-cities-make-housing-affordable.

67 Feargus O'Sullivan, *supra* note 47, at 3.

68 *Id*, 22, 29.

69 Anna Granath Hansson, *City Strategies for Affordable Housing: The Approaches of Berlin, Hamburg, Stockholm, and Gothenburg*, International J. of Housing Policy 19(1). 95–109, 102 (2019), https://doi.org/10.1080/19491247.2017.1278581.

70 Feargus O'Sullivan, *supra* note 47, at 25.

71 Megan Garber, *Homes Actually Need to Be Practical Now*, The Atlantic (March 29, 2020).

9

FROM CRISIS TO SANCTUARY

Prisoners in peril during COVID

Michael A. Crystal, Jacob Medvedev, and Peter Ketcheson

Editors' introduction: It seems just yesterday in COVID time that the world watched online as inmates in one of Italy's prisons clambered onto the prison roof during a riot. They were waving hand-painted banners begging for their release as the COVID-19 virus raged through the institution and infected the prisoners below. Those images from March 2020 record prisoners' struggle for the basic human right of security of the person. Italy's penitentiary system has created the perfect storm for pandemic spread: inadequate supply of masks and other PPE, no vaccine, inadequate testing, shared food and other necessities, and, by conservative calculation, 120% over capacity with over 61,000 prisoners and only 50,931 available beds.[1]

In America, reputedly the world's largest jailer at 2.3 million prisoners, inmates are packed into overcrowded facilities, living, sleeping, and bathing within feet – sometimes inches – of one another. The lack of basics such as soap, hot water, and clean towels mock the concepts of social distancing and sanitization.[2]

Canadians as well are assigning their corrections system a failing grade. As one investigation has clarified, "Prisons were never intended to be nursing homes, hospices, or long-term care facilities."[3] Macabre in its irony, some prisoners have since been called to action to make masks and hand sanitizers to ease shortages in the outside population, while those very labors in overcrowded spaces continue to threaten one of our most vulnerable populations.

Prisons do function like aged care homes in that they provide the coronavirus with optimum conditions for breeding. That environment reduces

DOI: 10.4324/9781003215769-13

to a mere wish list the recommended precautions of the WHO, the UN High Commissioner for Human Rights, the Centers for Disease Control in the United States, and the Parole Board of Canada. Two-thirds of Canadian federal prisoners who die of natural causes are under the age of 65, according to Canada's Correctional Investigator.[4] That statistic speaks to their vulnerability as a group to catastrophic health risks.

In this chapter we hear from three Canadians in the legal profession who examine how the judiciary and correctional authorities are responding to pressures to "decarcerate" during the pandemic, through either adjustments to bail conditions or considerations of early release. The authors propose that human rights challenges, such as the Italian prison roof riot, can be addressed with a more equitable long-term response: restorative justice. That sentencing option involves the offender's community in shaping a more idiosyncratic non-custodial resolution to meet the particular circumstances of each crime, victim, and offender. Their inspiration is a Dutch criminologist, Herman Bianchi, who advocated tirelessly for restorative justice. While that alternative to prison has been under public debate for several years, the coronavirus pandemic has created the defining moment to tip the balance of judicial and public opinion.

Introduction

Twentieth-century Dutch criminologist Herman Bianchi (1924–2015) was an opponent of mass incarceration. He viewed the criminal justice system as ineffective due to its emphasis on imprisonment rather than conflict resolution.[5] He saw the deficiencies of that system as particularly visible in the prison law context. Other scholars have identified the "continuing challenges to the scope of habeas corpus, a persistently dysfunctional internal grievance system, and a general reduction in the availability of legal aid"[6] as symptoms of an ailing criminal justice system. Bianchi advocated for the adoption of a restorative justice model, a system that would, in theory, more effectively protect the public interest and produce true justice by focusing on dispute resolution rather than imprisonment.

Putting Bianchi's model into action would likely require significant restructuring of conventional criminal justice processes. What has been missing is a precipitating event that would spur policymakers into action. In this chapter we propose that the COVID-19 pandemic (hereafter referred to as the "pandemic") is such an event. The crowding of inmates, lack of sufficient protective supplies, and insufficient in-house medical help have magnified the deleterious effects of the virus in prison populations. As a result, the pandemic has highlighted the potential consequences of defaulting to imprisonment and overpopulating detention facilities. At the same time, Canadian correctional authorities and jurists have embarked on wide-scale "decarceration" campaigns with the aim of lowering prison populations and thereby slowing the spread of the virus. In this way, the pandemic offers a second lesson: decarceration is possible. The question becomes: if mass incarceration is not *necessary*, then should society pursue it as the default option in the first place or is there potential for a wider acceptance of alternatives to detention?

Many criminal cases in Ontario decided during the pandemic underscore the flexibility of bail and sentencing principles, signaling that the law is adaptable to alternative means of obtaining justice. The contributors argue that decreased reliance on incarceration during the pandemic need not be restricted to the current disruption of conventional criminal procedures. Rather, the pandemic should serve as an opportunity to rethink how and when we choose to incarcerate for the long term.

This chapter consists of three sections: a summary of the pandemic's impact on Canadian prisons including prisoner infection and fatality rates; select bail and sentencing cases that illustrate how the pandemic has paved the way for the need to reconsider restorative justice as an alternative to mass incarceration; and a description of Bianchi's restorative justice framework, drawing particular attention to its compatibility with existing Canadian criminal law concepts.

COVID-19's impact on prisons in Canada

Although it is undoubtedly a universal scourge, the pandemic disproportionately threatens prisoners as they often lack "access to adequate health care and [are] unable to practise self-and-mutual protection measures."[7] A number of compounding factors expose prisoners to greater risk of severe illness and death. For example, persons in detention generally have a poorer health status than those who are not imprisoned.[8] Moreover, "ethnic minorities and socioeconomically disadvantaged individuals are differentially affected by both the criminal justice system and COVID-19."[9] Given the structural design of prisons that includes enclosed spaces without room for the recommended social distancing guidelines, widespread transmission of the virus is more likely to result in high infection rates similar to those recorded in nursing homes.[10] And while some are of the view that the prisoners are experiencing their "just desserts,"[11] the effects of the pandemic on prisoners are not confined to the four walls of their cells. COVID-19 outbreaks in jails and prisons have far-reaching impacts in surrounding communities because staff members and inmates return home, connect with those in the community, and thereby proliferate the virus.[12]

In view of the foregoing risks, there is ample incentive to find new ways to control the spread of COVID-19 in jails and prisons, not only to protect the best interests of those inside, but to also safeguard the best interests of society at large. The global pandemic has lifted the veil on our default instinct to incarcerate and has awakened us to the need for broader and more restorative responses to crime.

It is important to recognize that the pandemic is still a live issue a year after its outbreak. As such, the statistics that are presented in this section are only current to the time of this writing and are subject to change by the time this chapter is available to readers. Statistics from both federal penitentiaries and provincial jails evidence the gravity of COVID-19 outbreaks among prisoners. A study by the Canadian Broadcasting Corporation (CBC) conducted in July 2020 found that the incidence of COVID-19 in provincial and federal carceral institutions was up to nine times higher than in the general population.[13]

Correctional Services Canada (CSC), the administrative body that oversees the operations of federal penitentiaries, disclosed in September 2020 that 360 prisoners had tested positive from the 1,720 total tested across Canada prisons, representing an approximate 20% positive test rate.[14] That number included two COVID-19-related deaths.[15] By comparison, only 2.1% of COVID-19 test recipients in the Canadian general public had tested positive for the virus as of that date.[16] That disparity can likely be attributed to the unique risk factors faced by prisoners, such as their conditions of confinement and inability to social distance.

COVID-19 outbreaks have also been recorded at provincial correctional facilities. The aforementioned CBC study also revealed that as of 16 July 2020, 103 inmates and 51 staff in Quebec's provincial prisons had tested positive for COVID-19, representing an infected rate of approximately 11.80%.[17] In Ontario, as of the same date, 131 inmates and 31 staff members in provincial facilities had tested positive for the virus.[18] Those statistics emphasize that prisoners are disproportionately predisposed to catching the virus.

Canadian criminal law's response to COVID-19

To combat the pandemic's effects on prisons, Canadian correctional authorities have implemented various public health measures to curb rates of infection. Among the strategies, the CSC embarked on a large-scale decarceration campaign to minimize the population density of federal prisons to facilitate social distancing protocols. Whereas in February 2020, a month before the full brunt of the pandemic was felt in Canada, the Canadian federal prison population was 37,976, by April the number had dropped by 16% to 31,901.[19] In the same time frame, the provincial custodial populations across Canada declined from 24,085 in February to 18,181 in April, a decrease of 25%.[20]

By reducing prison populations, the CDC mitigated the number of people who would have otherwise been imperiled by the virus in penitentiaries. This raises the questions at the core of this chapter: if large-scale decarceration is possible in extraordinary circumstances, can it be applied in less turbulent times? Is there a *need* to default to incarceration when there are viable rehabilitative alternatives to imprisonment as seen during the pandemic? For Bianchi, the answer is a two-track approach to incarceration. On the first track, we should encourage alternatives to imprisonment that bring the offender and victim of crime together, such as community service, monetary compensation, and rehabilitative efforts. The second track, which is characterized by our traditional means of punishment, is left for those who are either ineligible for the first track on account of their violent nature or because they are simply uninterested in participating in it.

A line of COVID-19 criminal law cases in Ontario spotlights how the flexibility of bail and sentencing principles have been used to justify decarceration during the pandemic. In effect, such cases have dispelled the myth that mass incarceration is necessary. Instead, they signal the viability of alternatives to mass incarceration, such as Bianchi's restorative justice approach.

Bail cases

A fundamental principle of Canadian criminal law is that accused individuals are presumed to be innocent until proven guilty. Individuals are not typically detained while awaiting trial unless the detention is deemed warranted. As a result, unless their detention is ordered following a bail hearing, individuals are often released pending the completion of their cases on what is known as bail.

Bail under Canada's *Criminal Code*[21] (the "Code") will be denied if any one of three grounds for detention are met: the primary ground that the accused will not make all court appearances; the secondary ground that detention is necessary to maintain public safety; and the tertiary ground that mandates detention when it is necessary to maintain confidence in the administration of justice.[22]

In most cases, an accused person who has been denied bail at their initial hearing can bring an application for bail review.[23] If successful, the reviewing judge may vacate the initial bail court's detention order and release the accused individual pending trial.[24] However, a bail review judge does not have an open-ended discretion to vary the initial bail court's decision to detain the accused.[25] In fact, a bail review judge can only intervene in three instances: (1) where the initial bail court erred in law; (2) if the initial decision is clearly inappropriate; or (3) where there is new evidence that shows a material change in the circumstances of the case.[26] This chapter focuses on the third instance – where the reviewing judge finds a material change in circumstances. When that is found, he or she will undertake the bail analysis afresh to determine whether detention remains justified.[27]

With the advent of the pandemic, first instance bail courts and reviewing courts have had to recalibrate their conventional approaches to bail cases by having to now account for the overriding need to slow the spread of the virus in jails. Select bail decisions illustrate a flexibility on the part of the bench to consider novel arguments for granting bail.

The case of *R v JS*[28] provided the Ontario Superior Court of Justice ("ONSC") with its first opportunity to consider the implications of the pandemic during a bail review. The bail review was heard as Canada became engulfed by the pandemic. The accused had been charged with drug trafficking and was denied bail before the pandemic had reached Canadian soil due to tertiary ground concerns.[29] JS applied for a bail review on the basis that the initial bail hearing court erred and that there was a material change in circumstances.[30] Due to the newfound risk posed by the pandemic, along with the fact that two new proposed sureties had surfaced since the bail hearing, Justice Copeland held that there was a material change in circumstances that allowed him to review the bail court's decision.[31] Although the Crown agreed that there was a material change in circumstances, the Crown continued to oppose JS' release.[32] Nonetheless, Justice Copeland ultimately held that the newly proposed bail plan addressed the bail court's concerns and granted JS' release.[33]

It is clear that Justice Copeland's decision to release JS was based heavily on the existence of the newly proposed sureties. Nonetheless, it is important to note that Justice Copeland also found that the pandemic constituted a material change in circumstances that called for a review of the original bail decision. Moreover, the decision illustrated that the "greatly elevated risk" that the pandemic poses to inmates is a factor for courts to consider when determining if detention is justified on tertiary ground concerns.[34] This is because, as noted by Justice Copeland, "the practical reality is that the ability to practice social distancing and self-isolation is limited, if not impossible, in an institution where inmates do not have single cells."[35] As a result, *JS* set an early precedent that stands for the propositions that (1) individuals who were denied bail prior to the pandemic are entitled to apply to have their pre-pandemic bail decisions reviewed and (2) that courts are to consider the pandemic when determining if an individual should be denied bail.

In the case of *R v CJ*,[36] the ONSC continued its flexible approach to bail reviews. The accused was charged with 11 offences, including several counts of drug trafficking.[37] He had no criminal record and the bail review judge ordered the accused's release in accordance with a strict bail plan that included supervision by two sureties and ankle monitoring.[38] In his decision, Justice Conlan emphasized that the addition of electronic ankle monitoring to the proposed bail plan along with the "current state in Ontario of the COVID-19 health crisis . . . constitute[s] a material change in circumstances"[39] that allows for a review of the original detention order. Moreover, Justice Conlan took judicial notice of the fact that inmates are at greater risk of contracting COVID-19 than the general public:

> I also do not live in a bubble; it is incontrovertible that a jail setting is not conducive to the types of physical distancing and other safety measures being recommended by all of the health authorities to help protect oneself against the virus. To demand some "evidence" in support of that is, with respect to any contrarian view, unnecessary.[40]

While the judge recognized that the accused's charges were very serious, he stressed that bail considerations have to be tailored to fit the gravity of the broader circumstances:

> [T]his is not simply a mechanical exercise of checking boxes. It is much more nuanced than that. In the end, I do not believe that a reasonably informed member of the public would lose confidence in the criminal justice system if she discovered that a fairly young adult with no criminal record who proposes a very stringent bail plan with two residential sureties plus electronic monitoring, presumed to be innocent of the charges that he is facing, is released from the confines of a jail setting in the midst of a global health crisis having arrived, in spades, on our doorsteps in Ontario.[41]

The case of *R v TD*[42] provides another salient example of a decision where an accused, whose detention would likely have been warranted in the absence of the pandemic, was granted bail after accounting for COVID-19 considerations. TD had been arrested and charged with firearm and drug possession offences. In late 2019, he was denied bail and his detention was upheld in a subsequent proceeding.[43] Following the pandemic's arrival in Canada, Justice Barnes allowed TD's bail review application, ordering his immediate release with specified conditions.[44] In reaching this conclusion, Justice Barnes acknowledged that "real possibility of a COVID-19 outbreak in jail does not mean an automatic release from custody. Each case must be assessed on its own facts."[45] In the instant case, Justice Barnes concluded that the global pandemic "constitutes a material change in circumstances," allowing the Court to review the initial bail court's pre-pandemic decision to detain TD.[46] Ultimately, Justice Barnes felt that TD's new proposed bail plan, along with the newfound risks posed by the pandemic, justified the reversal of the bail court's decision.[47] While judges must always consider traditional bail principles, Justice Barnes underscored that the "practical effect of this global pandemic is that in some cases, persons whose detention is warranted absent COVID 19 concerns may be releasable because of COVID-19."[48]

Ultimately, the menace of the pandemic taken together with TD's newly proposed bail plan provided the Court with sufficient basis to find that TD's "continued detention [was] not necessary to maintain public confidence in the administration of justice."[49] In this way, *R v CJ*, *R v JS*, and *R v TD* illustrate that bail principles can be malleable under the extreme risks posed by a pandemic.

Appellate guidance regarding the impact of the pandemic on bail was provided in the case of *R v Kazman* ("Kazman").[50] In that case, the Ontario Court of Appeal ("ONCA") allowed a bail-pending-appeal application for an offender who was seeking leave to appeal to the Supreme Court of Canada ("SCC").[51] Justice Harvison Young echoed the caution that Justice Barnes had expressed in

R v TD: "[I] emphasize that this does not mean that bail will be granted in any case where COVID-19 is raised as an issue."[52] Nonetheless, in the instant case, Justice Harvison Young found strong basis for granting bail given that the appellant's health issues exacerbated the risks posed by the coronavirus.[53] As such, the Kazman decision lends further support to the notion that the pandemic has spurred judges to approach bail reviews with added flexibility, placing greater weight on factors such as age, health status, prior criminal history, and type of crime at issue.

Overall, the cases discussed here are noteworthy for having produced "near unanimous agreement that the COVID-19 pandemic constitutes a material change"[54] that allows for the review of detention orders made prior to the pandemic. A close reading of the decisions reveals another insight: the COVID-19 pandemic has caused judges to use the inherent flexibility in Canada's bail framework to consider offenders' circumstances holistically and fashion innovative terms of release that account for societal health and wellbeing alongside more traditional bail concerns. While these cases were decided in the context of a health crisis, the judges' reasoning does not expressly preclude the use of similar flexibility in the bail context once the pandemic ends.

Sentencing

As with bail cases, the pandemic's arrival in Canada has underscored the need for courts to leverage the inherent flexibility of sentencing principles to address the challenges posed by the pandemic.

Indeed, whereas in normal times emphasis might be placed on traditional sentencing objectives such as denunciation and deterrence, during the ongoing public health crisis we have seen a shift to placing more weight on inmate safety and offender rehabilitation. In effect, sentencing cases during the pandemic in Ontario have demonstrated that the sentencing calculus is flexible, adaptable to a global crisis, and amenable to restorative solutions. Consequently, the authors view the Canadian sentencing regime as one that Bianchi would have embraced for its flexibility.

In *R v Morgan*,[55] the ONCA confirmed that the pandemic qualifies as a "collateral consequence" that potentially exacerbates the impact of the sentence on the convict because of his or her particular circumstances. The appellant appealed his sentence of two years less a day. While all parties agreed that the sentence was appropriate at the time that it was imposed, on appeal the issue was whether the pandemic had subsequently rendered the sentence disproportionate to the offence because of the additional risks posed by the pandemic to those in detention.[56] Although the ONCA ultimately dismissed the offenders' appeal due to the leniency of the original sentence, the Court's characterization of the pandemic as a collateral consequence highlighted the need to account for the pandemic during sentencing. Overall, such holistic review of sentencing factors underscores the inherent flexibility of sentencing principles.

Justice Pomerance adopted a similar line of reasoning in *R v Hearns*[57] to account for pandemic considerations in sentencing. The accused was convicted of aggravated assault for having struck a woman in the head with a bat, fracturing her skull, and lacerating her scalp.[58] The Crown and defense counsel agreed on a joint submission for time-served coupled with a term of probation, which would ensure that the offender's time in pretrial detention would fulfill his sentence without the need for further incarceration.[59]

At the outset of the decision, Justice Pomerance noted that a sentence of time-served might ordinarily fall short of reflecting the seriousness and moral blameworthiness of the accused's offence.[60] However, with the pandemic as the backdrop, Justice Pomerance found it appropriate to depart from conventional sentencing reasoning and accepted the joint position by imposing a sentence of time-served.[61]

In reaching this conclusion, the judge took judicial notice of the fact that the global pandemic was disproportionately threatening inmates.[62] In anticipation of criticism that such flexible sentencing might be construed as a "get-out-of-jail-free card," Justice Pomerance emphasized that the "pandemic does not do away with the well-established statutory and common law principles."[63] Instead, Justice Pomerance held that the pandemic can alter the application of such principles: "It may soften the requirement of parity with precedent. The current circumstances are without precedent. Until recently, courts were not concerned with the potential spread of a deadly pathogen in custodial institutions."[64]

Justice Pomerance underlined that while the overriding proportionality principle of sentencing must be preserved, the fitness of sentences can be tailored to meet the unique circumstances of each case:

> COVID-19 also affects our conception of the fitness of sentence. Fitness is similar to proportionality, but not co-extensive with it. Proportionality dictates that the sentence should be no more than is necessary to reflect the gravity of the crime and the moral blameworthiness of the offender. Fitness looks at a broader host of factors. A sentence may be fit even if it is not perfectly proportionate. Fitness looks, not only at the length of a sentence, but the conditions under which it is served. As a result of the current health crisis, jails have become harsher environments, either because of the risk of infection or, because of restrictive lock down conditions aimed at preventing infection. Punishment is increased, not only by the physical risk of contracting the virus, but by the psychological effects of being in a high-risk environment with little ability to control exposure.[65]

For Justice Pomerance, the pandemic is precisely the kind of scenario that the SCC envisioned when it outlined potential justifications for deviations from the usual sentencing range in *R v Lacasse*:[66]

> There will always be situations that call for a sentence outside a particular range: although ensuring parity in sentencing is in itself a desirable

objective, the fact that each crime is committed in unique circumstances by an offender with a unique profile cannot be disregarded. The determination of a just and appropriate sentence is a highly individualized exercise that goes beyond a purely mathematical calculation. It involves a variety of factors that are difficult to define with precision. This is why it may happen that a sentence that, on its face, falls outside a particular range, and that may never have been imposed in the past for a similar crime, is not demonstrably unfit. *Once again, everything depends on the gravity of the offence, the offender's degree of responsibility and the specific circumstances of each case* [emphasis added].[67]

The underlying current of restorative justice in Justice Pomerance's reasoning came to the forefront in her call for a shared sense of humanity:

During these challenging times, people are being asked to call upon their sense of community, decency and humanity. That humanity must obviously extend to all individuals, including those incarcerated due to criminal charges or convictions [and] sentence. Where, however, a period of time served can address sentencing principles, *even imperfectly*, our sense of humanity tells us that release from prison is a fit and appropriate response.[68]

Justice Pomerance's humanistic approach illustrates how sentencing principles can be flexible when extraneous circumstances require them to be.

Resistance to overemphasizing the pandemic's effects

It is important to note that not all jurists have relied heavily on the purported flexibility of bail and sentencing principles when dealing with cases during the pandemic. There remains resistance to deviation from conventional criminal law reasoning due solely to the pandemic. Specifically, a line of cases in Ontario signals that not all judges will necessarily place an overwhelming amount of weight on COVID-19 considerations in fashioning their bail or sentencing decisions.

One example of such resistance can be seen in *R v Nelson*.[69] In that case, the accused was charged with several counts of robbery and illegal possession of firearms. Despite being released after a bail hearing, Mr. Nelson was later detained upon review due to secondary and tertiary ground concerns.[70] At his second bail review, the ONSC acknowledged that the pandemic was a factor in evaluating the tertiary ground and recognized that all inmates are at a higher risk of contracting COVID-19 in jail than they would be in the community.[71] Nevertheless, the ONSC detained Mr. Nelson largely because he was a relatively young man without preexisting health conditions that would have placed him at greater risk for COVID-19.[72] Justice Edwards found further basis for dismissing the application in the "seriousness of the charges, Mr Nelson's prior criminal record, [and] the weakness of the proposed plan of release."[73] As such, the *Nelson* case is an example of a decision where the court placed greater emphasis on traditional bail considerations as opposed to the challenges posed by the pandemic.

The approach taken in *Nelson* was repeated in *R v Jesso*,[74] where the ONCA dismissed an application for bail pending appeal. Justice Brown held that granting bail was not in the public interest, given that (1) the applicant posed a substantial risk to public safety as a sexual offender and (2) the appellant had not adduced evidence of outbreaks at his detention facility or that he had characteristics that made him all the more vulnerable to the virus.[75] In view of this, *Jesso* follows *Nelson* as another example where the court was reluctant to view the pandemic as a justification for the expansion of conventional bail principles.

There are also cases decided during the pandemic that illustrate Ontario courts' reluctance to stray from conventional sentencing practices due solely to the pandemic's presence on Canadian soil. An example of this is *R v McGrath*,[76] where the court set a high threshold for the relaxation of sentences due to the pandemic, limiting such flexibility to instances where detention would pose an exceptional risk to the accused's health. In that case, the accused was charged with a series of firearm-related offences.[77] The Ontario Court of Justice held that it would be inappropriate to reduce Mr. McGrath's sentence on the sole basis that the pandemic is present in Canada. The Court stressed that since Mr. McGrath was not elderly and did not have underlying health issues, he was no more vulnerable to the virus than those inmates who commenced their sentences prior to the illness' outbreak.[78]

Ultimately, Ontario's case law is not uniform in its treatment of the pandemic's implications for bail reviews and sentencing decisions. Decisions in those cases have not definitively indicated how much weight should be placed on COVID-19 considerations in reaching a decision. While some courts have relied heavily on the inherent flexibility of bail and sentencing principles to account for the unique threats posed by the pandemic to inmates, others have maintained their commitment to more traditional factors. Although a universal approach to bail reviews and sentencing is not likely to emerge until the SCC rules on a COVID-19-related criminal matter, at the very least, the pandemic has sparked a jurisprudential dialogue between levels of court concerning the potential expansion of traditional detention principles.

Herman Bianchi's restorative justice model

The advent of the pandemic has demonstrated – albeit, not unanimously – that sentencing and bail principles are inherently flexible, fit for recalibration to accommodate changing needs during times of crisis. Their flexibility has shown itself through the increased deference to decarceration during the pandemic as opposed to the historical default to mass incarceration during normal times. In effect, these events have shown us that decarceration is possible, which paves the way for future consideration of alternatives to detention practices. One alternative is the restorative justice framework proposed by twentieth-century Dutch criminologist Herman Bianchi. Under his proposal, those who have been released during the pandemic fall under the first track of restorative justice – individuals who are suited for alternative punishments that could potentially be served outside detention facilities. Conversely, those who remain in custody during the pandemic could likely be viewed as appropriate candidates for the second track of Bianchi's framework – individuals whose crimes are so severe and who show such a lack of remorse that they are ineligible for rehabilitative or community-oriented solutions.

Bianchi often cited a lecture he delivered at the University of Alberta with considerable unease. On the drive from the airport to the University, Bianchi (who had spent time incarcerated in a concentration camp during World War II) happened to spot the Edmonton Institution, a federal maximum-security prison located in the northeastern part of the city.[79] He was aghast that Canadians had the "evil taste" to build prisons that resembled concentration camps.[80] For Bianchi, the notion of watchtowers with heavily armed guards was odious and memorialized the sadism of the Nazis. It is not that Bianchi failed to accept the necessity of prison for society's most dangerous citizens: he did. However, for all other offenders, he advocated for a more thoughtful and restorative approach.

Two stories sum up Bianchi's theory that prisons should only be used as a last resort when there is no alternative. In the first story, Bianchi speaks of a friend whose son fell in love with a young woman. Sadly, there was another lover who, in a fit of pique and jealousy, murdered Bianchi's friend's son. Grief-stricken and unable to heal, the family of the deceased boy visited his murderer in prison. It was the first of many visits where they wept and prayed together. Ultimately, they reconciled, and the family was able to heal.[81]

In the second story, a woman came to Bianchi and asked him to visit her father, who was in a German prison for the kidnapping and murder of a child. The man was an engineer with no criminal past who abducted the child during Christmas time and demanded a ransom. Having received the ransom, he still murdered the young girl. Bianchi, after much pleading on the part of the inmate's daughter, went to see him thinking that the man was remorseful. He wished to engage him as an advocate for a restorative justice overture to the family of the deceased girl. Instead, he found an unremorseful man with no regret for what he had done to the little girl or her family. The inmate just wanted to complain about the deficiencies of the German prison system.[82] This story affirms Bianchi's position that prisons are only for the most dangerous among us. For other offenders, he recommended a more restorative justice approach, especially when the offender is amenable to the restorative approach. Such synergy, according to Bianchi, operates to facilitate both healing and reconciliation.

Bianchi understood the modern-day criminal justice system as having its roots in the Judeo-Christian religious tradition.[83] This led him to adopt a "homeopathic method" or approach to the concept of justice. Bianchi reasoned that if these practices rested on a diseased understanding of the Judeo-Christian foundation, then perhaps the disease could be cured by conceptions retrieved from the same tradition. Such thinking led him to the restorative notion of *tsedeka*,[84] a Hebrew word for justice whereby the offender and the community he wronged are reconciled.

By fastening his thinking to the notion of *tsedeka*, Bianchi set himself in opposition to the prevailing Western notion of justice as giving the offender his due punishment, first related by Aristotle and later developed by St. Thomas Aquinas.[85] Bianchi's difficulty with this commutative approach was that the accused got punished, while the victim got nothing. By contrast, in *tsedeka* both parties had to be engaged in a meaningful quid pro quo, where the victim received and the perpetrator gave; in this way, a proper balance was restored in the community, and most importantly, the offender was acquitted of his guilt.[86]

This last notion of *tsedeka* is not to be confused with that tired old trope that offenders who have served a sentence have paid their debt to society. For Bianchi, an offender serving a sentence in some remote prison is not acquitting himself of his guilt because it is done outside of the community. For true restoration to occur, according to Bianchi, there has to be a meaningful and motivated engagement between the violator and the violated. Such meditations led Bianchi to his seminal thinking on justice as sanctuary.[87]

In the sanctuary model, Bianchi sets out his notion of justice as a restorative process. The sanctuary model is not meant to replace the criminal sentencing law but to complement it as a parallel alternative. The wrongdoer and the wronged meet and work out a mutually satisfactory resolution to the criminal conduct. The traditional criminal justice process is stayed during this period. If a resolution cannot be achieved between them, the traditional means of criminal punishment will apply.[88]

According to Bianchi, to allow the perpetrator to complete his punishment in isolation from the community was to align his wishes with the particular sanction envisioned by the victim. The result is a restorative solution that heals the wounds created by the illicit conduct. Bianchi believes once this has occurred, an offender ought to be readmitted into society as a fully restored member of the community. The likelihood of this occurring in Bianchi's approach would appear to be greater than our current status quo because the community plays a dynamic role in formulating the sentence and so would be more acutely aware of its vested interest in the outcome.

On first glance, Bianchi's notion of restorative justice might seem incompatible with the deeply rooted notions of crime and punishment in Western criminal law. Indeed, Bianchi observed that Western criminal justice systems are dominated by legal positivism, resistant to progressive change and overly confident in the "moral power and expertise of modern legislation so as to assume that any law should in principle be considered good if properly handed down by a formal legislator."[89]

However, reforming the criminal law to align it with Bianchi's notion of restorative justice is not such a far-fetched concept. Elements of restorative justice have already made their way into Canadian criminal law in other forms, as evidenced by the development of separate courts for drug abuse and mental health issues. One of the most seminal changes arose with the case of *R v Gladue*[90] (*Gladue*), which reshaped traditional approaches to sentencing, bail, parole, and other areas of criminal law and procedure by requiring judges to consider several additional components of sentencing when the offender identifies as Indigenous.

In fact, Bianchi's proposal aligns with broader legislative and jurisprudential trends toward alternate forms of criminal justice that are gaining traction in Canada at the time of this writing. In February 2021, the Honorable David Lametti, the Minister of Justice and Attorney General of Canada, introduced Bill C-22[91] in the House of Commons. One of the overriding objectives of the proposed legislation is to repeal a number of the mandatory minimum sentences for certain offenses in the Code and *Controlled Drugs and Substances Act* ("CDSA").[92] Mandatory minimum provisions require minimum periods of incarceration for specific convictions. By removing such provisions, the Bill seeks to imbue the sentencing process with greater judicial discretion.[93] As a result, the Bill promises to empower judges to take a holistic view of the circumstances of each case rather than abide by rigid sentencing guidelines. The underlying aim of the proposed law is to prevent the administration of disproportionate punishments and to combat growing rates of over-incarceration.[94]

The Bill also proposes to expand the availability of conditional sentences, which permit offenders to serve parts of their detention terms in the community rather than in prison so long as certain conditions are met.[95] The availability of conditional sentences is limited by the various conditions that are enumerated in section 742.1 of the Code.[96] The Bill seeks to amend the foregoing section of the Code to eliminate various prohibitions on the availability of conditional sentences for specified crimes.[97] Overall, the Bill's proposals in favor of abolishing certain mandatory minimum provisions while also expanding the availability of conditional sentences echo themes similar to those we have seen in bail and sentencing cases during the pandemic as well as Bianchi's writing: incarceration does not have to be the default setting, and restorative justice is a viable alternative.

Further evidence showcasing the growing acceptance of restorative justice and alternatives to incarceration was seen in *R v Sharma*.[98] In that case, an Indigenous woman was sentenced to 17 months' imprisonment for importing cocaine in violation of the CDSA.[99] Among other things, Ms. Sharma challenged the constitutionality of elements of section 742.1 that limit the availability of conditional sentences.[100] The ONCA concluded that sections 742.1(c) and 742.1(e)(ii) produced disproportionate negative impacts on Indigenous people and held that the provisions were of no force and effect.[101] Pending the upcoming appeal at the SCC, *Sharma* is potentially a landmark precedent in Canadian sentencing law that – like Bill C-22 – signals a growing availability of alternatives to detention such as conditional sentences.

Overall, in much the same way that Bill C-22, *Gladue*, and *Sharma* opened the Canadian criminal justice system's mind to rethinking incarceration, the sentencing and bail cases are undergoing change during the pandemic. When viewed together, such legislative and jurisprudential developments indicate that the tectonic plates of Canadian criminal law are shifting away from carceral outcomes and more toward Bianchi's notion of restorative justice. They demonstrate that decarceration is possible and that prison need only be reserved for the most dangerous and unrepenting of offenders.

Conclusion

The COVID-19 pandemic has wrought havoc on prison populations. Due to the nature of confinement, prisons have largely been unable to put into action effective social distancing and sanitization best practices, which ultimately imperils the health and safety of those on the inside. In response to this grave threat, Canadian prison administrators and jurists have embarked on a wide-scale decarceration campaign. In particular, the justice system has relied on the inherent flexibility of bail and sentencing principles to increase reliance on alternatives to incarceration during the health crisis. In doing so, the pandemic has revealed a legal system capable of adapting to less incarceration and incorporating restorative justice measures in the right circumstances.

The pandemic is a teaching moment, an opportunity to consider whether restorative justice is a viable alternative to conventional criminal law practice now and in the future. Looking ahead, the recalibration of law in line with Bianchi's notions of restorative justice should not be limited to the duration of the pandemic. A mainstream embrace of alternatives to incarceration can potentially ensure that our prisons are better prepared to safeguard the health and safety of inmates in future transmissible health crises.

**BOX 9.1   CORONA SHORT #14: CHILE
LEONEL, TRAINING DIRECTOR FOR LEGAL
PROFESSIONALS IN SANTIAGO, RELIES ON
'RESISTENCIA'**

I work at the Justice Studies Center of the Americas, a nonprofit member of the Organization of American States. We work with all countries of Latin America training judges, prosecutors, professors, and lawyers to foster judicial reform in our country.

The pandemic changed our work. I tended to travel all the time for training and meetings. We were forced to convert all our training programs to online, very quickly. Thankfully, we were able to produce new materials and ideas. The pandemic led us to spread more information and access to justice at the same time, very useful given the situation. Also, the main impact of COVID on my job was that for the first time I spent more time at home. In 2020 I really enjoyed being here and able to devote time to home issues.

When the pandemic impacted my private life there was no time for sports, no opportunity to travel to Argentina to see my family, especially my little three-year-old niece. That was tough. But I tried to see the positive aspects. We tried to play sports in the square, but it was not the same. We were in lockdown in October 2020 and now we are in another lockdown. I am a very proactive person, so I have always had an interest in many activities at the same time. We now cannot be so selective. We need to be open-minded and explore all the avenues possible. We don't know what will happen. Not refusing options is my approach now.

In general, I support what the government has done. Maybe they have made mistakes in some cases, but I have to say we did well with the vaccine. We have 73% of the population with one dose; 55% with both doses. We are using four brands, Sinovac from China, Pfizer, Astra Zeneca, and now, since May, Canasino, another Chinese brand. In the beginning the Chilean government made a strong commitment to Chinese vaccines. Many people listened to the media that said the first dose of the Chinese brand was ineffective. So, the government had to produce clinical information to show that was not true. We are rationed. So, there was a fight between the different companies because some were saying the Russian vaccine was the worst, as used in Argentina, called Sputnik 5. We are negotiating for it in Chile.

Resisting is a word I would use to describe how we are coping. *Resistencia.* That's what I see in my family, friends, and colleagues at work. We are resisting with different tools. Being at home and not seeing the ones you love or resisting the fact your paycheck was reduced or you have a small business or trade that you cannot continue due to the impact of the virus. I also see that the idea of intelligence is involved. We need to be thinking of the pandemic and when or whether it will go away.

In terms of the economy impacting my life, Chile suffered a decline in 2020, the worst contraction in the last 40 years. Construction was affected; another is the tourist industry, hotels, and restaurants. In my daily life I saw places I used to go had been closed. Most of those will not reopen because the owners could not cope with the strength of the pandemic. I see most of my friends will have to think again about where they are going to work.

A very interesting question at this time is whether there is a role for law. Medicine is used to working with uncertainty. Not law. We see that with health professionals. Should people in law step back at this time? I was discussing this with my coworkers. The COVID crisis has exaggerated inequalities. It is important for judges to know that the person before them is a member of a gay or lesbian group that has been discriminated against and how COVID has influenced that. The law has a role to play in this context. We must bridge the gap between the context of their suffering and how law could be very aware of that and create spaces where judges can have a direct dialogue with them.

I do know that in Chile and Argentina the health workers are angry. At the beginning of the pandemic we were going out to clap our hands and say thank you. But then they are saying their conditions, salaries and infrastructure have not changed at all. We hear government saying "We are all in this together" but maybe not.

BOX 9.2   CORONA SHORT #15: CANADA
A JUDGE IN ONTARIO IS PROTECTED BY
'ACRES OF PLEXIGLASS'

Judges live a monastic life. We are used to cautious and restricted socializing, heightened concern about our safety and security, and the need to avoid uncontrolled expression of our thoughts and feelings in public. A colleague of mine likes to put it this way, "I was a much more interesting conversationalist and more fun to go out with – before I became a judge."

How has it been different since the pandemic? Trial judges are essential workers, so we still have to preside on cases and attend to other aspects of our jobs including pre-trial meetings, administrative work, and so on. The courtroom is equipped with acres of Plexiglass to separate us all, oceans of hand sanitizer, mountains of gloves, and an army of cleaners available at our beck and call in case anyone sneezes and a deep cleaning around the area is needed. We are all wearing masks or face shields or both. I've never seen or smelled the courthouse so clean.

As I open the door to enter, I am hit like a brick with the smell of disinfectant. It smells like a Swiss Hotel. A smiling young woman cleans the elevator buttons once every hour and spends the rest of her time wiping all the door handles. About half of our work is now done remotely to reduce the number of people attending the courthouse below the maximum dictated by the public health officials.

After decades of resistance, I have had to educate myself very quickly on the use of technology required to do remote work. I also have to teach remotely rather than in person. I feel very safe at work. I think someone would have to try very hard to catch COVID at our courthouse. It is now January 2021, and since March 2020 no one has caught this nasty virus at our courthouse. A small number have picked it up in the community, and they have been required to self-isolate for two weeks. Anyone who had contact with them has been warned, but also reassured that the correct protocols were followed. No one who has had contact with the carriers of this malevolent microbe at our courthouse has developed symptoms or subsequently tested positive. I am very grateful to the managers and administrators who organized all this in collaboration with the public health mafia. Other than a few minor inconveniences, my work life has not changed much.

As for my personal life, it is about the same, because I don't socialize much. Most socializing has always been generally quite stressful for me because I must be mindful to remain dignified in public, I can't let down my guard for a minute, and I have to be so careful about what I say and do. Once I was drinking ginger ale out of a large wine glass at a social event. Someone remarked, "Wow! What a big wine glass," and promptly tried to take a photo to put on the internet. It was during the time that a notorious judge was being tried before the Judicial Council for sexual harassment and public drunkenness. I quickly disposed of my wine glass before the photo could be taken and immediately left the event.

My home life is about the same as usual. I am not lonely because I am married with a family. I have to wear a mask if I go to the grocery store or pharmacy, which is a very minor inconvenience. The only thing I miss is that I cannot travel or spend time at small gatherings with close friends, and it is tricky to travel to other provinces and countries to be with family. But this is all temporary. Before the end of 2021 I should be able to see them again. I feel guilty, because I am having a much easier time than others. I am healthy. I am solvent. I am loved. I am busy writing articles and judgments. I am not bored. I am about as happy as I usually am.

Notes

1 Fatima Burhan, "Wider Steps Needed to Protect Prisoners' Health in Italy," Human Rights Watch (Mar. 20, 2020) www.hrw.org/news/2020/03/20/wider-steps-needed-protect-prisoners-health-italy#

2 Sharon Dolovich, "Every Public Official with the Power to Decarcerate Must Exercise That Power Now," The Appeal (Apr. 10, 2020) https://theappeal.org/every-public-official-with-the-power-to-decarcerate-must-exercise-that-power-now/

3 Government of Canada, "Aging and Dying in Prison: An Investigation into the Experiences of Older Individuals in Federal Custody," *Office of the Correctional Investigator*, www.oci-bec.gc.ca/cnt/rpt/oth-aut/oth-aut20190228-eng.aspx

4 Lisa Kerr, "Coronavirus in Prisons: How and Why to Release Inmates in a Pandemic," The Conversation (Apr. 21, 2020) https://theconversation.com/coronavirus-in-prisons-how-and-why-to-release-inmates-in-a-pandemic-136676

5 Herman Bianchi, *Justice as Sanctuary* (Oregon: Wipf and Stock Publishers, 2010) [Bianchi].

6 Adelina Iftene, Lynne Hanson & Allan Manson, "Tort Claims and Canadian Prisoners" (2014) 39:2 *Queen's LJ* 656 at 656 [Tort Claims].

7 United Nations Human Rights Special Procedures, "COVID-19 and Protection of Right to Life in Places of Detention" (2020), online (pdf): *Special Rapporteurs, Independent Experts & Working Groups* <www.ohchr.org/Documents/Issues/Executions/HumanRightsDispatch_2_PlacesofDetention.pdf> [United Nations] at 1.

8 *Ibid.*

9 *Ibid.*

10 Donald Berwick et al., "Protecting Incarcerated People in the Face of COVID-19: A Health and Human Rights Perspective" (May 1, 2020), *Health Affairs* www.healthaffairs.

org/do/10.1377/hblog20200428.846534/full/ *See also* Philip Sloane, "Cruise Ships, Nursing Homes, and Prisons as COVID-19 Epicenters: A 'Wicked Problem' with Breakthrough Solutions?" (2020) 21 *Journal of the American Medical Directors Association* 958.

11 For further discussion of the "just deserts" theory in American criminal law *see* John Sloan III and Langly Miller, "Just Deserts, the Severity of Punishment and Judicial Sentencing Decisions" (1990) 4:1 *Criminal Justice Policy Review* 19–38.

12 See for example, Naomi Thomas, "Jails Can Spread Coronavirus to Nearby Communities, Study Finds," *CTV News* (Aug. 4, 2020), online: www.ctvnews.ca/health/coronavirus/jails-can-spread-coronavirus-to-nearby-communities-study-finds-1.5050 160#:~:text=Jails%20can%20be%20a%20large/

13 Valérie Ouellet and Joseph Loiero, "COVID-19 Taking a Toll in Prisons, with High Infection Rates, CBC News Analysis Shows," *CBC News* (July 17, 2020) www.cbc.ca/news/canada/prisons-jails-inmates-covid-19-1.5652470 [CBC Pandemic Study].

14 Canada, Correctional Services Canada, *Inmate COVID-19 Testing in Federal Correctional Institutions September 25, 2020*, online: www.csc-scc.gc.ca/001/006/001006-1014-en.shtml [CSC].

15 *Ibid.*

16 Canada, Government of Canada, *Coronavirus Disease 2019 (COVID-19): Epidemiology Update*, online: https://health-infobase.canada.ca/covid-19/epidemiological-summary-covid-19-cases.html

17 CBC Pandemic Study, *supra* note 13.

18 *Ibid.*

19 Canada, Statistics Canada, "Changes in Federal, Provincial and Territorial Custodial Populations during the COVID-19 Pandemic, April 2019 to April 2020," (Aug. 12, 2020), www150.statcan.gc.ca/n1/daily-quotidien/200812/dq200812a-eng.htm [Stats Can].

20 *Ibid.*

21 *Criminal Code*, RSC 1985, c. C-46 at s 515 (10) [*Criminal Code*].

22 *Ibid.* at s 515 (10).

23 *Ibid.* at s 520.

24 *Ibid.* at s 520(7).

25 *R v St. Cloud*, 2015 SCC 27 at para 92.

26 *Ibid.* at para 121.

27 Gary Trotter, *The Law of Bail in Canada*, 3rd ed. (Toronto: Thomson Reuters, 2017) (loose-leaf revision 2020–3), ch 8 at 16–16.1.

28 *R v JS*, 2020 ONSC 1710.

29 *Ibid.* at paras 1–3.

30 *Ibid.* at para 3.

31 *Ibid.* at para 5.

32 *Ibid.* at para 4.

33 *Ibid.*

34 *Ibid.* at para 18.

35 *Ibid.* at para 19.

36 *R v CJ*, 2020 ONSC 1933.

37 *Ibid.* at para 3.

38 *Ibid.* at para 12.

39 *Ibid.* at para 6.

40 *Ibid.* at para 9.

41 *Ibid.* at para 8.

42 *R v TD*, 2020 ONSC 2654.

43 *Ibid.* at paras 1–3.

44 *Ibid.* at paras 1, 26.

45 *Ibid.* at para 6.

46 *Ibid.*

47 *Ibid.* at paras 15–26.

48 *Ibid.* at para 22.

49 *Ibid.* at para 25.
50 *R v Kazman*, 2020 ONCA 251.
51 *Ibid.* at paras 1, 21.
52 *Ibid.* at para 20.
53 *Ibid.* at paras 4, 16, 17, 21.
54 *R v SA*, 2020 ONSC 2946 at para 4.
55 *R v Morgan*, 2020 ONCA 27 [*Morgan*].
56 *Ibid.* at para 3.
57 *R v Hearns*, 2020 ONSC 2365 [*Hearns*].
58 *Ibid.* at para 1.
59 *Ibid.* at paras 8–9.
60 *Ibid.* at para 10.
61 *Ibid.*
62 *Ibid.* at para 11.
63 *Ibid.* at para 15.
64 *Ibid.*
65 *Ibid.* at para 16.
66 *R c Lacasse*, 2015 SCC 64 [*Lacasse*].
67 *Hearns, supra* note 57 at para 17 citing *Lacasse* at para 58.
68 *Hearns, supra* note 57 at para 24.
69 *R v Nelson*, 2020 ONSC 1728 [*Nelson*].
70 *Ibid.* at para 2.
71 *Ibid.* at para 34.
72 *Ibid.* at para 42.
73 *Ibid.* para 52.
74 *R v Jesso*, 2020 ONCA 280 [*Jesso*].
75 *Ibid.* at paras 37–38.
76 *R v McGrath*, 2020 ONCJ 192 [*McGrath*].
77 *Ibid.* at paras 1–2.
78 *Ibid.* at paras 41–42.
79 David Cayley, *Justice as Sanctuary*, davidcayley.com (Oct. 27, 2018), www.davidcayley.com/podcasts/2018/7/4/justice-as-sanctuary [Cayley].
80 *Ibid.*
81 *Ibid.*
82 *Ibid.*
83 *Ibid.*
84 Herman Bianchi and Harold Pepinsky, *Justice as Sanctuary* (Oregon: Wipf and Stock Publishers, 1994), p. 48 [Justice as Sanctuary].
85 Cayley, *supra* note 79.
86 *Ibid.*
87 David Cayley, *The Expanding Prison: The Crisis in Crime and Punishment and the Search for Alternatives* (Toronto: House of Anansi Press, 1998), pp. 317–329.
88 *Ibid.* at 324–329.
89 Bianchi, *supra* note 5 at 1.
90 *R v Gladue*, [1999] 1 SCR 688, 171 DLR (4th) 385.
91 Bill C-22, *An Act to Amend the Criminal Code and the Controlled Drugs and Substances Act*, 2nd Sess, 43rd Parl, 2021 (first reading Feb. 18, 2021) [Bill C-22].
92 *Controlled Drugs and Substances Act*, SC 1996, c 19 [*CDSA*].
93 Library of Parliament, *Bill C-22: An Act to Amend the Criminal Code and the Controlled Drugs and Substances Act–Legislative Summary (Preliminary Version)* (Feb. 26, 2021), online: https://lop.parl.ca/sites/PublicWebsite/default/en_CA/ResearchPublications/LegislativeSummaries/432C22E at 1–6 [Legislative Summary].
94 *Ibid.* at 1–2.
95 *Ibid.* at 6.
96 Criminal Code, *supra* note 21 at s 742.1.
97 Legislative Summary, *supra* note 93 at 7.

98 *R v Sharma*, 2020 ONCA 478 [*Sharma*]. It is important to note that application for leave to appeal to the Supreme Court of Canada was filed on Oct. 13, 2020. Leave was granted by the Supreme Court of Canada on Jan. 14, 2021.
99 CDSA, *supra* note 92 at s 6(1).
100 *Sharma, supra* note 98 at paras 1–4; Legislative Summary, *supra* note 93 at 7–8.
101 *Ibid., Sharma* at paras 180–185; *Ibid.*, Legislative Summary, *supra* note 93 at 8.

Bibliography

Legislation

Bill C-22, *An Act to Amend the Criminal Code and the Controlled Drugs and Substances Act,* 2nd Sess, 43rd Parl, 2021 (first reading 18 February 2021).
Controlled Drugs and Substances Act, SC 1996, c 19.
Criminal Code, RSC 1985, c. C-46.

Jurisprudence

R c Lacasse, 2015 SCC 64.
R v CJ, 2020 ONSC 1933.
R v Gladue, [1999] 1 SCR 688, 171 DLR (4th) 385.
R v Hearns, 2020 ONSC 2365.
R v Jesso, 2020 ONCA 280.
R v JS, 2020 ONSC 1710.
R v Kazman, 2020 ONCA 251.
R v McGrath, 2020 ONCJ 192.
R v Morgan, 2020 ONCA 27.
R v Nelson, 2020 ONSC 1728.
R v SA, 2020 ONSC 2946.
R v Sharma, 2020 ONCA 478.
R v St. Cloud, 2015 SCC 27.
R v TD, 2020 ONSC 2654.

Secondary materials: books

Bianchi, Herman, *Justice as Sanctuary* (Oregon: Wipf and Stock Publishers, 2010).
Bianchi, Herman & Harold Pepinsky, *Justice as Sanctuary* (Oregon: Wipf and Stock Publishers, 1994).
Cayley, David, *The Expanding Prison: The Crisis in Crime and Punishment and the Search for Alternatives* (Toronto: House of Anansi Press, 1998).
Trotter, Gary, *The Law of Bail in Canada*, 3rd ed. (Toronto: Thomson Reuters, 2017) (loose-leaf revision 2020–3), ch 8 at 16–16.1.

Secondary materials: articles

Berwick, Donald et al., "Protecting Incarcerated People in the Face of COVID-19: A Health and Human Rights Perspective", *Health Affairs* (1 May 2020), www.health affairs.org/do/10.1377/hblog20200428.846534/full/.

Iftene, Adelina, Lynne Hanson & Allan Manson, "Tort Claims and Canadian Prisoners" (2014) 39:2 *Queen's LJ* 656.

Sloane, Philip, "Cruise Ships, Nursing Homes, and Prisons as COVID-19 Epicenters: A 'Wicked Problem' With Breakthrough Solutions?" (2020) 21 *Journal of the American Medical Directors Association* 958.

Secondary materials: government documents

Canada, Correctional Services Canada, *Inmate COVID-19 Testing in Federal Correctional Institutions September 25, 2020*, online: www.csc-scc.gc.ca/001/006/001006-1014-en.shtml.

Canada, Government of Canada, *Coronavirus Disease 2019 (COVID-19): Epidemiology Update*, online: https://health-infobase.canada.ca/covid-19/epidemiological-summary-covid-19-cases.html.

Canada, Statistics Canada, *Changes in Federal, Provincial and Territorial Custodial Populations during the COVID-19 Pandemic, April 2019 to April 2020* (12 August 2020), online: www150.statcan.gc.ca/n1/daily-quotidien/200812/dq200812a-eng.htm.

Library of Parliament, *Bill C-22: An Act to Amend the Criminal Code and the Controlled Drugs and Substances Act – Legislative Summary (Preliminary Version)* (26 February 2021), online: https://lop.parl.ca/sites/PublicWebsite/default/en_CA/ResearchPublications/LegislativeSummaries/432C22E at 1–6.

United Nations Human Rights Special Procedures, *COVID-19 and Protection of Right to Life in Places of Detention* (2020), online (pdf): Special Rapporteurs, Independent Experts & Working Groups www.ohchr.org/Documents/Issues/Executions/HumanRightsDispatch_2_PlacesofDetention.pdf.

Secondary materials: newsprint & studies

Ouellet, Valérie & Joseph Loiero, "COVID-19 Taking a Toll in Prisons, with High Infection Rates, CBC News Analysis Shows", *CBC News* (17 July 2020), www.cbc.ca/news/canada/prisons-jails-inmates-covid-19-1.5652470.

Thomas, Naomi, "Jails Can Spread Coronavirus to Nearby Communities, Study Finds", *CTV News* (4 August 2020), online: www.ctvnews.ca/health/coronavirus/jails-can-spread-coronavirus-to-nearby-communities-study-finds-1.5050160#:~:text=Jails%20can%20be%20a%20large/.

Secondary materials: audio/digital media

Cayley, David, *Justice as Sanctuary*, davidcayley.com (27 October 2018), online: www.davidcayley.com/podcasts/2018/7/4/justice-as-sanctuary.

PART IV
Education and technology

10

WILL GOING ONLINE SAVE OR SINK THE TRADITIONAL UNIVERSITY SYSTEM?

William H. Dutton

Editors' introduction: As founding director of the Oxford Internet Institute at Oxford University in the UK, William H. Dutton has grave concerns for the economic devastation already caused by the online migration of university learning and the massive reduction in international student admissions. Recent events at many universities are playing out his fears. At Michigan State University, where Dr Dutton most recently headed the Quello Center in the Media and Information Department, executives announced, in January 2021, that the campus was closing and sports activities were canceled along with conference facilities and other expected perks of campus social life. The resultant loss was in the "tens of tens of millions of dollars."[1]

Earlier dire predictions warned of up to 200 university closures across the United States as the coronavirus accelerated.[2] Ten institutions in the United States have begun closure proceedings as of January 2021. Dr Dutton also addresses the larger questions of digital divides, corporate sponsorship, and the more personal choices to be made: which conversations and learning should be relegated to online? Does physical geography still matter online? And what are the costs to "social presence" and the "levelling off" effect of decisions to move online?

It's been over two decades since Dr Dutton left his position as a professor at the Annenberg School for Communication at the University of Southern California, where he served as president of the faculty, to launch the Oxford Internet Institute. At that time the internet was evolving from a practice training medium to a focus for social research and a tool for

DOI: 10.4324/9781003215769-15

real time classroom and online learning, a move not all college students welcomed. Dr Dutton's challenge at Oxford University was to take his experience in the early years of the study of information and communication technologies, and to introduce internet studies as a discrete multidisciplinary field of study for students at one of the oldest collegiate universities in the English-speaking world. Since then, he has continued to research and write extensively on the impact of the internet and the attitudinal and technological challenges it presents to our systems of education, politics, and social life.[3]

Interview with Martin Fellow, William H. Dutton, at Oxford University – November 2020

Elizabeth Kirley (EK): Bill, why are you so concerned for the survival of universities during this tumultuous time?

William Dutton (WD): I've spent my life in universities. So, I feel universities are my home. Now I think they are threatened as never before. They are suffering as a consequence of the pandemic.

EK: Are there skills you developed in America that can assist now that you are back at Oxford and in the midst of the pandemic?

WD: I have flipped back and forth across the Atlantic during my teaching, but I started my work in social sciences and communications technology back in 1974, when the internet was the ARPANET, and when you'd have to call people to tell them you had sent them an email. Since then, I have been focusing my research on the social and political implications of communication and information technologies, increasingly centering on the internet and social media and most generally – digital media.

The role of online learning and education has always been a fascinating topic for me. I was at the University of Southern California in the 1980s and 90s – for 22 years. One of the things I got involved with as President of the Faculty was helping the administration think about the university's move to online education in collaboration with other universities. At that time, online education was a new and exciting arena for campus-based universities to move into. The internet had proven already that it was surprisingly valuable for informal education, but it was not anywhere as far along as it is now. I became so engaged that I co-edited a book on this topic.[4]

Today informal education is incredibly dependent on the internet. If people want to know something about the coronavirus or status of the vaccines, for example, one of the first places they go to is the internet for information. In such ways, the internet and social media have become invaluable for informal education. However, we haven't figured out how to translate that transformational capability to the ways formal educational institutions, like universities, work. We essentially substitute online for offline practices that remain very similar. Computer-based systems and the internet had been used effectively in training, you know, like driver's education and where there's fixed content and its mainly transmitting information. But not in mainstream campus-based university education.

EK: **What did that look like in terms of control by the learner in the 1980s?**

WD: They had many forms of educational software, from enabling people to answer multiple choice questions, to participating in online forums. It's not that dramatically different from today, except for the more recent ubiquity of video communication systems like Zoom. Some of the very earliest test-based online educational programs at Oxford, for example, were philosophy courses. That might sound difficult, such as asking students, "What is the meaning of life? Discuss." But there could be great discussions among students that were open-ended and that enabled students and faculty to interact online.

EK: **So in the '80s I recall the Commodore 64 where you could play chess with the computer. There was no question that the computer controlled the game. In terms of education on campus when you were at USC, was control still in the hands of the university computer?**

WD: A great deal of it was – it was far removed from programmed learning, for example. More generally, universities wrote and shared their own in-house software for teaching and learning. IT staff took such pride in developing their own software and applications that a fundamental problem arose around 2000, with the emergence of the first commercial educational software, like Blackboard Inc. founded in 1997. You couldn't imagine it today, but people got fired from university IT staff because they refused to install commercial packages. It was a huge battle between the "open and free" software people, who did not want software to control its users, and administrators who preferred more closed and structured proprietary solutions bought right off-the-shelf.[5]

EK: **Was Blackboard more of a chat or message board?**

WD: Blackboard was an early "course management system" that enabled instructors to handle nearly all aspects of the course online, from uploading readings that they wanted to share with students, to managing discussions, exams, and grading. And because internet use was limited to a small number of students taking a course, the instructor could manage access to the material and discussion groups.

EK: **Could students participate from home or did they have to go on campus to login?**

WD: It was remotely accessible, not just a campus-only thing, but in the late 1990s, remote access was more difficult and slower than it is today. Its main use was on campus and in class. Instructors were using it even if they were teaching completely campus-based in person courses. They would use Blackboard as a way of distributing content; rather than having a book of readings, they would post the readings and syllabus on Blackboard for their class. At the turn of the century it was promising, and people envisioned systems like this would enable online education to take off dramatically and expand the scale of higher education.

And instructors envisioned there would be online lectures on certain standard and predictable topics. Why would it be limited to students at one university? So, we could call together the experts in subject "X" from top universities and we could have the best people we could find in all collaborating universities give and share lectures on their topics of expertise. I think it was very forward thinking and potentially what might well come about at some point in the future.

EK: At what point did it become more interactive, where the learner could ask questions synchronously rather than having to email the professor later?

WD: Well, emails are interactive and were around in the early 70s. The thing was, it was mainly academics that had some affinity for, and access to, computing. Early on it was the ARPANET, before it became the Internet. I remember in the early 80s showing my class "Here's the Internet," and "Here's things we can do on the internet, and here's a PC with various visual graphics material" linked to a bulletin board system that didn't use the internet at all but local phone lines. But none – not one – of my students wanted to use the internet. They thought it was too dull. It was just text and there was no color, no graphics, no sound equivalent to today. That changed over time with the development of the World Wide Web. The Internet was designed to share resources, and the Web was designed so people could share research, such as documents, across the world. The idea of sharing through the Internet and Web boosted that thinking greatly. And then came the browser.

When Mosaic and other browsers came about it became easy for any student to get access to information on the Web. It also gave colored graphics and the ability to have a user interface that looked like a local bulletin board and was exciting for the students. So, the internet, built on by the Web, and then the browser, went through continual developments. Browsers and internet platforms like Google perfected issues, like search and online video presentations, and made online education technically more feasible. The internet just continually gets better in many ways. It's arguable that, as it gets more user friendly, there's more "click" and "like" buttons and so it sometimes can dumb-down communication instead of pushing people to express themselves – using words even. As in social media with people "liking" videos and communicating only with emojis rather than communicating anything about a video in words.

EK: You might also have been leading the curve, Bill, in teaching communications.

WD: Exactly. We were supposed to be. But there's a real fundamental problem in getting people who are so involved with new tech that they think everybody knows this. It was sobering when I told students, "Here's some technology you can use," but nobody wanted to go on the internet because it just was not engaging to them at that time. Today, if you suggested "Would you like to use the internet for this or would you rather have a book or go visit your professor's office?" the question would be branded ludicrous, right?

EK: **I have noticed that universities, when recruiting faculty, promote library access as a feature. That might no longer be as appealing**.

WD: It is to me, but you are right. No, it's sad. I can remember my youngest daughter, when she was too young to even be thinking about college, she asked me for the definition of a word. I said, "Here's the dictionary, right here," and she said, "No that's alright." She wanted me to tell her, so failing that, she just turned and looked it up online. She left me holding the dictionary.

So, it was a cultural change. It was sad also for libraries. However, they are beginning to pick up and they are beginning to reinvent themselves to support group work and working with excellent computer access, exploiting their own unique holdings online, becoming hubs for networking communities, and more.

EK: **Bill, we can't overlook the fact that those who can afford them will have their iPhone and different devices in their home. There is a digital divide with that**.

WD: That's a very good point. I think it came to the fore most clearly with me in teaching campus-based courses where I realized that, increasingly, the students over time would not do the readings I suggested. Instead, they would informally go to search the internet and use their own sourced materials that were more easily accessible and that they thought were more interesting. So, I was battling with them and realized I couldn't control that and shouldn't. If they are inquisitive enough to look for material that they find of value, then I want to encourage that. But at the same time, I had to find ways of making sure that they were interested in material that I believed to be of more value for them to look at, even if it wasn't online.

EK: **So how did you do that?**

WD: Over time, thankfully, more articles, books and content of all kinds are online, and I have put the online version in the syllabus so they just have to click on that. You make it as easy as possible, so you really cater to that concern. Although I still read articles and buy books, the culture is changing. So, a student might not use a reference if it is not available online or if they have to pay for it. But I let them know that treasure troves of information are still not available online.

EK: **And some faculty seEK: out open access venues for their work**.

WD: Open access can be an ideological issue. I don't preach the use of open access because in practice the production of content still costs. Therefore, open access most often means that the author or institution rather than a subscriber pays those costs. This advantages the wealthier institutions and producers of information. So, I am happy to publish copyrighted material but also usually find a way for anything I publish to also be available in some form online, such as in a penultimate version, or as a working paper. There are many ways you can get material online while respecting copyright restrictions.

EK: **I became aware of the digital divide in the classroom when I asked students to do searches. They'd do it on their phone because it was cheaper to have a phone data plan without other expenses for the phone. Would you like to comment on that?**

WD: In the early stages of online access, students would use terminals at the university or in remote locations over a phone line hooked to an acoustic coupler. Then the PC revolution came along in the 1980s with the diffusion of low-cost portable computers that enabled more students to use computers in universities, generally their own laptop. Universities have tried to finance students to get their own computers, such as through a loan program. Many universities today have a loan program to buy a laptop computer if students don't own one. Nevertheless, some of the students who are most constrained financially don't want another loan; they borrowed money for their tuition, and/or for housing. And they think they can get by with their cell phone, their handheld device.

We have actually done some research on this issue. We are calling it the "mobile-only divide" where people believe they are fine with their mobile-only device. But we find that students, say in a first-year English composition class, are writing their composition on their handheld mobile device. And to me as an older person it's just absurd that people would think this is the best way to write. It's not. It's a myth. If we look systematically at what people do online, you can see real differences in what mobile-only users do, compared to those with multiple devices, including a laptop or desktop computer.

The typical person today has multiple devices. In the 1970s, the idea of even a household having a computer was an example of "blue-sky thinking." The idea that there would be a computer in the home was just not credible. Some futurists envisioned a big mainframe computer sitting near the furnace in the basement of a home. People would use it to control the home and whatever the bloody hell people would do. That was wishful thinking. Seriously, they didn't even *know* what the computer would do.

Today, many individuals have watches, game consoles, personal digital assistants. It's unbelievable and yet there are people who have no computer in the home besides their mobile phone. We did a study of distressed areas of Detroit and we found a lot of kids that had no access to computing besides a phone. Even if they had a laptop, they had to go to a neighbor's house for Wi-Fi access, so that they could share a broadband signal and do more online. Mobile-only and broadband access are real constraints.

EK: **What period was this Detroit study?**

WD: About three years ago. We have just published an article in the *Social Science Computer Review* about the mobile only issue.[6] It's very hard to show the differences in impact, but it became clear in the data that there is an impact, and intuitively I think anybody who has multiple devices knows there are limitations to the phone that handicap the mobile-only users.

EK: **Can you speak to the photo below?**

WD: It's a photograph of a student in Jakarta who is trying to participate in class during the pandemic using her mobile phone because the internet reception is weak. She is with other students but distanced, so there appears to be some social interaction possible (Figure 10.1).

EK: **In an article you wrote for *InterMEDIA*, you suggested that online education delivery does not necessarily relate to everyone logging on to a virtual classroom. Can you speak to how geography is tied into that?**

WD: My frustration was that there has been so much discussion over decades about whether executives should meet online or in person, or whether you should teach on or offline. And now in the context of the pandemic, we are still asking, "Is it possible to teach effectively online?" And in the aftermath of the pandemic, the question will become, "Should we teach online or offline?" and "Should this meeting be online or offline?"

I want to remind people that in the early 1970s Bell labs began to work with developing the Picturephone™ and University College London was

FIGURE 10.1   A student in Jakarta, Indonesia participates in online classes with her mobile phone and laptop during the pandemic.

Source: Jefta Images via Getty Images.

doing a series of socio-psychological experiments on teleconferencing for decentralizing business. In Britain, the question that drove experiments in the 70s was how to deal with the congestion in London. They wanted to move more employees out of London to reduce congestion in the city. Japan was dealing with the same issue – there it was called the Tokyo problem. Everybody wanted to work in the central core. Governments wanted to create business centers elsewhere – to distribute business and people in more decentralized ways.

The United States was also focused on substituting telecommunications for travel, but mainly in response to the 1973 oil crisis. So, in Britain, researchers conducted a variety of experiments where they organized meetings doing different kinds of information tasks face to face, on a video link, and then just by text, and so on. You can imagine the many different media you might use for meetings. The concept they developed was "social presence."[7] The concept is still used often by people. In a face-to-face talk you have the most social presence, that is, you have a stronger sense that you are really with a person and you can communicate and sense aspects of how those people feel and even what they are thinking, whether you are right or wrong. In video conferencing there's less social presence. You really only have a square view of the reality that you are seeing; and then in audio-only you have somewhat less presence, and then in text such as email, possibly the least social presence.

What's interesting is that researchers found that with many information transfer tasks, such as just exchanging information like, "What is your phone number?" or "How can I get a hold of you this weekend?" it is much more efficient to use a low social presence medium. Because if you stop by a person's desk and say, "I'd like to get your phone number," you probably should chat a little bit before asking them . . . probably say "Hello" and "How do you like the weather?"

EK: **Maybe this explains why some friends do not phone anymore. They don't want a call either because it's going to involve a time investment**.

WD: Yes, I bet you are often left leaving a message. That said, it's absolutely nuts to get a copy of my syllabus by face-to-face communication. But when you have a task that's affected by social presence, say you are negotiating your salary as the head of the bargaining unit, or you are trying to consider authorship of an article with your three coauthors, you might want to have social presence because certain things will be more salient. If I were the head of a department and you were a new faculty member, I would have the power in person to more effectively assert my positional authority. But if you were the most articulate member of the team and we met in person you'd probably win the day to become the first author. So, any information task that involves negotiating or bargaining among people, the outcome could be affected by whether you meet face to face or in a higher or lower social presence medium. And it's arguable that in some situations that seem like information-only tasks, there is still the element of social presence, as you suggested in your reference to friends' phone calls.

EK: **In the frame of the pandemic, when we are all social distancing, are we looking at an online conversation as face-to-face communication?**

WD: A video call grants higher social presence than email; it's the best we can do given we are located or even locked in different places. Timing and distance are the coordinates, given where we both are; this is the highest social presence we could have in this context – until we use even more immersive media closer to virtual reality. The point about social presence is that, if there were no constraints, we'd still want to think through "Do I really need to speak with someone face to face?" and "What can I relegate to online?" My *InterMEDIA* article[8] was arguing that you should locate yourself where you need to have face-to-face communication, such as being in the classroom with your students. Once the pandemic struck it was like, "We can just go online," as if they were equivalent. There may be times, such as in a pandemic when there is simply no choice. But we must remember that they are not equivalent, not either/or, lose or gain or a matter of choosing one over the other. For teaching, I think you should use the highest social presence medium possible – in person teaching. But if you can't be face-to-face, online is better than not meeting.

The biggest strategic benefit of getting online is that it changes who you can talk to. In that sense, it's brilliant. For example, we can meet each other online even during a pandemic. But another factor is if I'm teaching on campus, and am face to face, the students are more likely to at least act like they're paying attention to me even if they are not truly engaged. And I am more likely to be aware of whether they are paying attention, if they are bored or engaged, and if they get it. If I am online, it's much more difficult for me to feel I know whether they are even present. Are they are just checking their emails in class or are they truly engaged in the topic? And it's easier for me when the class is campus-based and there are ten of us around the table having a discussion. I can know who I should be calling on. I've taught online and I know it's more difficult to judge the ongoing social dynamics of the classroom. If I want to distribute the readings before class, however, it's a no-brainer that I would post it online.

EK: **Do you notice that with the "COVID method" where you can zoom into faces more easily you are able to spot whether the students are moving along with you more than with the large lecture hall?**

WD: I hope students realize that! Any medium can be used more or less effectively. The lecture hall is often used as an example of distance education because students can be asleep in the back of the room; there is such a low social presence. One of the very first psychology classes I took at the first university I attended in the 1960s was via television in a room with 300 students at 8 o'clock in the morning, AND the instructor had died years before this! Of course, the authors of most of our greatest books are no longer living, but we don't to go an auditorium at 8am to read their work.

I never took another psychology course as an undergraduate. It was like "Wow, why am I doing this?" Decades later, I can imagine students physically going to their university during the pandemic, finding that their course instructor is online, and thinking "Wow, why am I doing this?"

I fully understand that faculty and administrators are working overtime to deliver the best possible educational experience they can in the context of the pandemic. However, the ideal class has still to be a small tutorial class where students have to be awake and have to have read the material. Or one-on-one with a tutor in person. I don't think the one-to-one tutorial at Oxford is common now, compared to small group tutorials. But hopefully a one-on-one tutorial will remain the gold standard when the pandemic is no longer governing education.

EK: **So is that what you call "leveling off."**

WD: Well, that term is usually used in a very positive sense. Some technologies have an almost inherent democratic bias because they have a levelling effect. The telephone is probably the classic technology for "leveling," where you can talk to someone and reduce the social presence of someone's social position or relative influence. And email was very much like this. I remember in the early days of email, young people at a company who would email the president and get a reply and think "Wow." Well presidents figured out how to put a filter around them and have personal assistants filtering email, but technically it had this effect of enhancing the accessibility of people and putting people on a more equal footing. I mean even Donald Trump's use of Twitter as President had this effect, sort of a leveling effect with another Twitter user. It reduced his stature in a sense relative to others, despite what he said, but I think it just means that you can communicate with a person no matter what their position. This is good in the classroom, but teachers don't always want this, they want to be able to say, "You should be further along on this essay." They want you to pay attention. They don't want to be on the same footing.

EK: **That leveling issue deserves attention, though. I still receive emails that begin "Hey prof. . . ." At the undergraduate level.**

WD: That's likely to be the times but also in part a consequence of a leveling effect where people feel they can be chummy or informal. You must be giving off a sense you are one of the group. How do you manage that?

EK: **I actually use it as a teaching moment. We might not get to "high speech" and "low speech" discussion but . . .**

WD: I think that's very smart because you can then talk to a student about how that might not be the best approach.

EK: **I think students appreciate this; I teach law and besides course content you are training them about professional standards and behavior. They appreciate it. They might not be getting that elsewhere.**

WD: Yes, I'm sure.

EK: **So that is an issue for new educators, beginning in the craft, to know that by going online they are losing that authority to some degree.**

WD: But, of course, such a leveling effect could actually enhance communication and the ability to have a conversation, such as with your students. Nevertheless, the flip side to that is that a whole series of webinars do everything they can to technically enhance the authority of the speaker. They prevent anyone else from being seen or heard. They mute everyone, they shut off everyone's video unless they are called to answer a question, they disable sharing of screens so they don't get Zoom-bombed. But then the Webinar becomes a "one to many" lecture conducted in the dark. All is lost. The point of online media and class-based discussion is that it is *not* to be one to many, it is an opportunity for interactive communication at its best.

EK: **A major** COVID **problem is that they can't socialize in the normal way. It leads to all sorts of anxiety and other mental anguish**.

WD: In the UK, students do manage to socialize. I don't know how; they are not supposed to in groups of any scale. It is the subject of a lot of research. There is a sizable proportion of students who feel they don't need to comply. But most importantly it means the university is not functioning as it should. The whole idea is to be a learning experience in every situation. The pandemic has everyone thinking about the challenges of the classroom but, gee, the classroom is just one of the places where students spend their time at university, and not most of their time. And we are not thinking enough about socializing. The idea of going to a dormitory and being isolated in a room . . . that's so antithetical to the whole idea of a university enabling interpersonal learning. Now again, it's very difficult because there are so many pressures from government, health authorities, parents, and common sense to stay safe during a pandemic – I understand that. But then they should not be on campus, even if there are financial incentives for them to be on campus.

I can imagine some people thinking "Well, online education is the new normal. We'll have more of this." More is fine, but it has to be as a complement to campus-based education. A complement to the classroom, not a substitute.

EK: **I would think if universities don't address that, they are going to have lower enrolment. Have you observed that more people are taking a gap year, that they just pull out of the university experience altogether?**

WD: There is that. Some universities have found it is not as dramatic a downturn as expected. Partly because in the course of a pandemic there are relatively few jobs. Therefore, if you don't have a job, you might as well spend your time at university. It is less of a problem in the most prestigious universities. Some top programs have even seen more applications for entrance.

At the same time, it is a problem and an unknown problem. You don't know how many students didn't apply who could have been at the top of the ranks. And even small declines in enrolments can make a big difference. A lot of universities are not hiring faculty; they are not replacing faculty that leave. Universities are used to increasing incomes every year. And increasing costs. So going in the opposite direction is going to have an effect on the way people are thinking about keeping the university vital. We have to revitalize the university in a context in which there might be fewer resources and time lost by staying in place. One possible benefit is that the pandemic forced universities to openly confront how financially over-dependent they'd become on such things as housing, entertaining and feeding students.

EK: **So the educators are like frontline hospital staff. They've got their face out there; they are the front line of the institution. But the administration or the executives are going to have to figure out where we get this money. In your article you talk about how that's a critical challenge.**

WD: I want to second exactly what you said. The people who are teaching online, sometimes for the very first time, are excited. They spent their summers trying to rework their courses so they can be offered online. Many instructors must teach both online and offline so they can reach students face-to-face and for students who cannot make it physically they give an online version of that same session. They are deservedly proud of what they are doing. But they will not be successful in the long run. Thousands of teachers are instructed, "You will go online, and you will teach much of our class online" and a number of them do not want to go online, do not choose to do that, and they're sort of forced to do that. They have taught for decades and they don't have the training. If they get that kind of training, it's hard to be retrained after years of teaching in another manner.

Also, commercially available search tools like Google and Facebook are much easier to use and much faster than the tools developed and used by universities. They are having all those practical problems not meeting the expectations of students who are savvy internet users.

EK: **Students form Facebook groups, and we try to do breakaway sessions but none of that can replace the social interaction that is so necessary.**

WD: So true. You get inspiration from your fellow students. It's the social comparison, modeling, and the inspiration you get . . . it's just so much more difficult to get it online. I can literally see my online "friends" disappearing as I become more physically isolated. We communicate online primarily with those we meet in person.

EK: **I really hope we get smarter to recognize the other facets of education besides cracking the books, you know?**

WD: Yes. I think that's a big unknown . . . what impact this will have. But, likewise, the Presidents and Provosts and Deans are always writing letters promising that when this pandemic is over, we will all be snake dancing to the President's house. And you think, "Whoa, they are trying too hard with all these letters to students and their parents." To be in a position that they have to say that it's going to be okay, that we will still be in existence. I just don't know what consequence this is going to have on the university and its image, and our confidence in the university in the long run.

As we gain more control over the pandemic, we all need to remember and prioritize the value of in-person teaching and open interaction with peers and resources at campus-based institutions, augmented by online access to and from the wider world.

BOX 10.1 CORONA SHORT #16: ITALY
ERIC, FOOTBALLER AND TEACHER,
DESCRIBES THE EFFECTS OF LONG COVID

I was in a small airport in Rome. The baggage area was rebuilt as a test center and you could get in that queue or present proof you have had a test in the last 72 hours. You cannot sit next to anybody on trains and buses. Everybody is masked.

Airport police wave you into a test line if you say you haven't had one. A bit lax. It looked like a 10–15 minute wait after the test. I didn't care to linger, as you can imagine, I wanted to get out of airport fast.

The university in Italy is open, but the bars are closed and no indoor dining. No sports but otherwise operating. If you go up a hill where I am staying, and look around at the surrounding hills, you are looking at all lockdown territory. Everybody stays close to home unless they have to go somewhere to work.

Cities vary: Bologna is a mess, Naples is not good, but Florence is not bad. Everywhere was closed for Easter. I heard it's the reverse in the UK. Everywhere was open for Easter, then lockdown after.

I think I caught COVID. But once you have it, you cannot get tested. Unless you were at death's door you could not get tested or treated. Once you get it, why bother? I got a nose swab six months later and it was negative. I am just guessing that what I had was COVID based on the after effects. I'm pretty sure I have longtail COVID. I cannot hold my breath at all. At first I had a dry cough and fever, what felt like an ear infection that moved down my jaw. And the startling effect was riding my bicycle – if I tried for a burst of steam to go up a hill, I blacked out. I went blind and numb for a moment -numbness in my hands. It happened again on the soccer field. To be able to play at all you need to go through a full test, unless I play goalie.

Some students are running out of money. I got a flatmate because he was on his way back to his dormitory and they locked down that building so he's now with me. They just canceled everybody's keycard one night. If you were inside, you stayed in; if you were outside, you were locked out. Some authorities come by each day to drop off a bag of food. That's how it is. Everybody was completely broke but getting food packets. They gave them too much food so lots to go around. Students are locked in their rooms. But the majority of students have given up and left for home.

The economic is pretty well non-existent. My flatmate had to go out of the country to get work; a Canadian mate from the soccer team lost his job as shoemaker because there was no money to pay him. Employers could get reimbursed by the government but the red tape was so slow that it all kind of fell apart.

Another team member owns the local pizzeria – his landlord is on his case because he hasn't paid rent in four months. He got 5,800 euros from the government for the year. And part of that year he was shut down. A year ago, mid-May was the day you could go off your property and then two weeks later you were allowed to go into his pizzeria. So from July to October they could run at 1/3 to 1/5 capacity, and then the numbers went back up so they had to start all over again. The money is just not coming out of Rome.

Where I teach students keep masks on and instructors keep masks off in the classroom. Windows and doors are open at all times. There's spacing in the classroom. The real weirdness in the UK are the rules on closing pubs – they are not coordinated between England, Scotland, and Wales. So, students and those near the border would slip over to another country to visit the pubs.

BOX 10.2   CORONA SHORT #17: CUBA LEYSIS QUESADA VERA, DOCUMENTARY PHOTOGRAPHER, USES HER DAUGHTER FOR INSPIRATION IN FIGURE 10.2

My life revolves around the practice of art. My job as a documentary photographer is to expose and publish my photographs. As an artist I live from the sale of my works in exhibitions, to interested collectors or working in photography workshops.

With the arrival of the coronavirus, living from my job has been a bit more complex. Canceled exhibitions and workshops, closed galleries, suspended trips, social distancing or in my case long periods in quarantine, has meant a decrease in my earnings from the sales of my work. However, the financial help of family and friends from abroad has helped me cope with the pandemic and has prompted me to seek new ways of doing and communicating my work.

I live with my two daughters Mia and Avril; my greatest source of inspiration and the ones that make me face any challenge that appears. We live in Los Sitios, Centro Habana, a vulnerable and super populated neighborhood, in which the pandemic has had a negative impact since its inception. In the months of February and March 2021, our neighborhood was closed in quarantine due to COVID-19 infections, and it allowed me to document this process almost in its entirety. They were hard moments, of uncertainty, of queues, of confinement, of scarcity, which I tried to capture in the series. My neighborhood, my house, my daughters and my neighbors were my main collaborators. The photo taken of Avril and her friend training (Figure 10.2), was in my building, in this quarantine period, while they were training in a rustic gym to maintain physical shape.

COVID-19 has taught us to value family and friends much more, to have more responsibility and maturity in life. We have learned to face difficulties from another perspective and it has taught us that the most important thing is not the material but life. It has made us more human.

FIGURE 10.2   Avril and her friend are students at the National Ballet School, Cuba, and rehearse in the basement of their home during Covid-19.

Source: Leysis Quesada Vera (with support of Magnum Foundation New York).

Notes

1 See further, Rethinking College, PBS News Hour (5 Jan. 2021) reporting the announcement by Ohio Wesleyan University that, in order to save $12 million and stem revenue losses caused by the pandemic, it would permanently remove 20% of its faculty and staff and eliminate 18 of its major subjects. Many US colleges have been forced to refund student tuition and residence fees, cancel planned increases in tuition, increase financial aid for students, and incur considerable costs in on-campus COVID testing. Even prior to the pandemic, two- and four-year US colleges were experiencing a 2.5 million drop over the past ten years in student registration due, primarily, to rising costs in education.

2 Melissa Korn et al., Coronavirus Pushes Colleges to the Breaking Point, Forcing "Hard Choices" about Education, Wall St. J. (Apr. 30 2020) reporting "From schools already on the brink to the loftiest institutions, the pandemic is changing higher education in America with stunning speed."

3 Including several books: The Oxford Handbook of Internet Studies (OUP, 2013); Politics and the Internet in 4 volumes (Routledge, 2014); Society and the Internet with Mark Graham (OUP, 2014, 2019); and An Agenda for Digital Research (Elgar, 2020).

4 William H. Dutton and Brian D. Loader, eds., *Digital Academe: The New Media and Institutions of Higher Education and Learning* (London: Routledge, 2002).

5 A leading advocate of free software was Richard M. Stallman, *Free Software, Free Society: Selected Essays of Richard M. Stallman*, 3rd. Free Software FDN.

6 B. Reisdorf, L. Fernandez, K. N. Hampton, I. Shin, and W. H. Dutton, *Mobile Phones Will Not Eliminate Digital and Social Divides: How Variation in Internet Activities Mediates the Relationship between Type of Internet Access and Local Social Capital in Detroit*, 6 Soc. Sci. Comp. Rev. (2020).

7 See J. Short, E. Williams, and B. Christie, *The Social Psychology of Telecommunications* (London: John Wiley and Sons., 1976).

8 W. H. Dutton, *To Be or Not to Be Virtual: That Is Not the Question*, 48(3) InterMEDIA (2020).

11
CHATBOTS CAN TEACH US TO DETECT FAKE NEWS DURING COVID

Jacky Visser and Elena Musi

Editors' introduction: Would it surprise you to hear that false news spreads more widely than the truth? A research team in Massachusetts has suggested this is because "humans, not robots, are more likely to spread it."[1] Another study in 2019 of over 1,800 social media users found that young African media users (in Kenya, Nigeria, and South Africa) spend some time thinking about whether the information is true before passing it on.[2] Their decision to share it (even if they know it's untrue) depends on the topic and the type of message. The study also found differences between countries which might be important when thinking about how to prevent the spread of false information.

A third study by a Harvard University team found that among university students in six African countries, the most common motivation for sharing (mis)information, including health-related items, was a sense of civic duty or moral obligation.[3] In those cases, students felt compelled to alert friends and family "just in case" the information turned out to be true. Not doing so, in their view, could hurt their relationships.

Our guests for this chapter, Dr. Jacky Visser (JV) and Dr. Elena Musi, would agree that human-generated fake news has burgeoned on social media during COVID time, adding to our sense of uncertainty and confusion about who and what to trust. Dr. Visser is a professor at the Centre of Argument Technology at the University of Dundee, Scotland. He has devised a solution to enable students to take disinformation detection into their own hands: he uses chatbots, or argument technology, to train young learners to hone their critical literacy skills and the art of argument in order to detect fake news and false statements for themselves.[4] His methods were

DOI: 10.4324/9781003215769-16

developed from data gleaned from the BBC's radio debate program called "Moral Maze" that led to a suite of argument software tools so students could be assisted by algorithms to distinguishing fact from fallacies or opinion in the news they consume.

Dr. Elena Musi (EM) is a Lecturer in Artificial Intelligence and Communication at the University of Liverpool. Her expertise lies at the interface of theoretical and Applied Linguistics, Communication Studies and Artificial Intelligence. Dr. Musi has worked as the Language Engineer for Alexa in Italian in the Amazon Alexa Applied Modelling and Data Science team in Cambridge, Massachusetts. Before that, she completed a PhD in Linguistics and Argumentation at the Università della Svizzera italiana and was a postdoctoral fellow at the Center for Computational Learning Systems at Columbia University. She is currently principal investigator on a project examining "Being Alone Together: Developing Fake News Immunity."

ELIZABETH KIRLEY (EK): A good place to start is to define terms you both use in your research. If we consult the UNESCO Handbook for Journalism Education and Training, misinformation is information that is false but believed to be true by the person sharing it. Disinformation is known to be false by the person sharing it.
Now, Jacky, you discuss these concepts by distinguishing fact from fiction. I am fascinated by where you started with that discussion, what pulled you into that kind of pursuit.
Jacky Visser (JV): I think what pulled me in most is that reasoning and arguing about both fact and fiction are so central to the human condition, really. Without reason we would not have been the kind of species we are. And without the accommodation of reasoning and persuasion, being able to persuade each other and to deliberate, we would not have the kind of society we have. In every aspect of civil life, we make decisions, we deliberate, try to see the best options. And we try to back up all of it with reasons. At least that is the ideal situation.

We find often things don't work out in the ideal way. And that is because there are some other cognitive processes in the background that override people's inclination to reason objectively, neutrally. For example, people get persuaded not necessarily by reason but by who is saying something or whether they just had a nice cup of coffee or a bad one or whether they just had a good night's sleep or whether the text they are looking at has a photo of a puppy next to it. It's these things that tend to persuade people and I think that is fascinating. Also, we need to look at the kinds of mistakes people make and how we can really feel conviction about something that, upon reflection, we don't have good reasons for.

That all relates to distinguishing fact from fiction because it tends to be facts that deliver results. So, let's say you have a team of engineers and you want to know what the right way to building this aircraft is, then it's best to start from facts because if you build from fiction, it will either not take off or it will come down very quickly.

EK: **I see from your academic background that you deal in argumentation and reasoning. And yet I find your writing is very philosophical . . . which of those do you draw on most to get to the facts?**

JV: That's very difficult to get to. This area we deal with is inherently multidisciplinary. Looking at AI, for example, is a way of studying the human language and it's a way of building tools that have an effect on people and on society. On the other hand, studying argumentation and reasoning and communication can feed into the development of AI systems. Then for the rest it's fairly interdisciplinary because indeed you start from concepts from philosophy – logic, dialectic, rhetoric, philosophy of language – but what you are studying eventually is language use, communication. There is also a bit of psychology in the mix, what people are persuaded by. That also brings us to a bit of sociology to a degree – how people interact and relate to society at large. It's really broad. It's very difficult to look at argumentation and reasoning, fake news and misinformation just from a disciplinary position. The world doesn't really adhere to the boundaries of academic disciplines.

EK: **Elena, I note that on your website you reference theoretical and applied linguistics, communication studies and artificial intelligence. So, how you use those to distinguish fact from fiction?**

Elena Musi (EM): I found much of what Jacky was saying similar to my thoughts. But then I wanted to comment on the building of the airplane . . . it's true we have to start from facts there, from an engineering perspective, but without fiction we would probably never have airplanes. Because fiction is really the origin of creativity in lots of different ways.

My interest in the interaction between fact and fiction goes back to when I was reading Aristotelian *Rhetoric* in ancient Greek. What Aristotle says in the beginning is that the goal of rhetoric is investigating not what's true but what is similar to the truth. And then I realized that in studying linguistics the very essence of human communication is rhetoric. Why do we communicate? Because we want to make sense of reality. And we want to make sense of aspects of reality that are not evident to everybody else in the same way. And if you think about propaganda, it's all about making sense of reality, persuading people that that's the way to go.

And then I also realized that whenever we do have a crisis like this pandemic, it's actually involving fiction because, while there are some facts, what we are really interested in is fiction because there are predictions that we can't make, about when a vaccine's going to come out, about what type of symptoms are the real symptoms of COVID-19. So, what we are dealing with now is a sort of "post truth" environment where we do not have a lot of points of reference so facts do play a role. But at the end of the day there is a lot of fiction. Governments have to deal with fiction, giving us guidelines on how to behave in everyday life.

When I worked in industry to build conversational agents, and right now with chatbots, it's all about human-computer interaction. There are two aspects I find very interesting: understanding language and teaching software how to understand language and thinking about what type of language to create to achieve that. It's an interesting way of flipping the coin, let's say. The other aspect deals with users' perceptions of these types of entities because perceptions and attitudes are different when a computer is involved. It's not like having a human-to-human interaction. To say people like AI because they are able to simulate humans . . . there are lots of research results that show that is not the case.

EK: **Let's hope AI and agents don't soon get to the point where they can create their own fiction. Maybe they can already.**

JV: In a way they do. If we can say something is either fact or fiction full stop, and it's not a continuum, then in a way we already have those AI systems. Let's say chatbots that are producing and spreading fiction because that's exactly what fake news is. If we say, "fake news is non-factually true material that is made to look like a news report," this is exactly what automated systems are already producing.

EM: And then you might have fake news that is not necessarily entirely false but it's just misleading. So again, more complicated that just having completely fabricated information. Most of the time the triggering of fake news is still by humans. And 59% of fake news is not fabricated but contains pieces of misinformation, one of the results of the Reuters Institute analysis.[5]

EK: **In your work, do you talk about truth?**

JV: In a way, yes. But I try to focus on the procedural side. Regardless of the truthfulness of your starting point, your premise, you can apply reasoning. If unreasonable, we would label those "fallacious." In a way it's up to the people who are engaging in debate what they mutually agree on as their starting points. And then even if they choose a completely fictitious starting point, we can look at the procedural reasoning they employ and we can decide "Well, there's a logical fallacy here," or "OK you are saying this because there is an expert saying that too," but has that expert not been paid to give that opinion? Those kinds of things can be said even if the starting point is not true. And philosophically truth is difficult. What was considered true 400 years ago might not be considered true now by the majority.

For example, most people believe we live on a globe. Four hundred years ago it would have been accepted truth that the earth is flat. And now the truth is different.

EM: I agree with that. I think truth can be updated. Even scientific truth is updated. I agree the situation is difficult to understand in a distinct way. I think a more granular perspective is what we should take on to advocate for in our projects. When you work on news and information, defining truth is very difficult. You might have a piece of information that doesn't tell anything wrong in terms of facts; journalism might be a good example as it deals with new information and it can be perceived in a way that is actually false. It does not really correspond to what should be informative.

I can give an example. When I heard all this news about the link between blood type and COVID-19, that if you had a certain blood type you had higher chance of catching COVID-19, journalists were not necessarily conveying false information. It's simply that it was provisional, so you could not generalize. But a lot of people began to think, "OK, if I am this blood type, I really have to pay attention." It's the same situation with the idea that men are more at risk than women. That's the case in China but it turned out that there are fewer smokers among women than men, a factor that might have influenced that statement.

So again, the truth can always be updated. Especially where new scientific results arrive or if you look at more factors. What's going on here in logic is called abductive reasoning. Again, we are trying to make sense of reality, to get the best possible explanation for the facts that we have. So, this is also what's going on in the legal environment. You have some facts and you are trying to find the best possible explanation for them.

EK: **Fake news has become such a powerful force. How has that happened?**

JV: I guess fake news has been around a long time. There's one factor that makes it *seem* more prevalent. The fact that we are much more connected internationally. If there's a news article released in one place, we can easily hear about it in another part of the world. That is related to the idea that as a dissemination method, social media and the internet are creating an ideal environment for spreading fake news. Previously you might have needed to shout from a soap box and you might have reached a few people. Or you might print off a pamphlet and send copies around or get in a hot air balloon and throw them down but you wouldn't really reach too many people. Now, if you send out a tweet and you say something nice about the current president of the United States, he will retweet it and it will have an immediate audience of, say, a million. Which just makes it easier to reach people. I realize I am not really talking about the effect on the political environment. I have opinions on that but they are not based on any academic study. My impression is that we can see internationally that there is, over the past 10 years, a growing tendency to elect more populist leaders and there is a connection between populism and telling people what they want to hear. Often what people want to hear, to generalize, might not actually be the truth. So, I can see connections there but I haven't looked at that from an academic perspective.

EK: **So Elena, do you have an opinion on why fake news has become such a critical force in politics?**

EM: What I found interesting between fake news and politics as a whole is that fake news has been used as a weapon by politicians as a rhetorical strategy. So you have Trump saying "OK, that is fake news," and he is using that as a pejorative label to accuse media of working against him. Fake news becomes something else from its original meaning. It is used for self-defense.

Another aspect is maliciousness related to fake news. I was very scared when I realized that general conspiracy [theories] became so prominent and then acquired such political weight in the last election. In the end what unites people within a conspiracy is fake news. It is becoming a reality at the moment when they are supporting a specific candidate. Fake news becomes a speech act. If you have a particular interest in this you could refer to the Fake News Immunity Booklet which is accessible online.

JV: Yes, and I think we are also in an interesting situation where, on the one hand regarding political literacy, I would encourage everyone to look critically at where the story comes from. But it seems this has gone too far, there's a feeling that all ideas should be democratically decided and that all opinions carry equal weight.

EM: That's why we have, in the editorial system, a gatekeeping process, a screening of information and we try to prioritize what is disinformation and misinformation. So, if you are a journalist and you write the news you do have a code of principles and practice. You are liable if you spread misinformation.

EK: **Jackie, you recently published an article describing your use of AI to teach "reason-checking."[6]Can you describe how that works?**

JV: The reason-checking aspect is to counterbalance the fact checking. It appeared to us there are many ways people can be misdirected, misguided, persuaded to do things that are not good for them or others but that do not use false factual statements.

So as Elena was explaining earlier, it is very possible to start from true factual statements and still reason toward a suggestion or plan of action or other beliefs that aren't backed up by those facts. There is always a difference between correlation and causation: things can correlate and both of the things you are mentioning are the case, but if you start putting them together and drawing some conclusions, the reasoning is faulty in some way. So we were thinking that just looking at facts might not get you to the point you want to get to.

Now, about the difference between humans and machines, in spreading misinformation, disinformation and fake news. I think there has always been technology that would facilitate that. You could have a newspaper as a vehicle for spreading some misinformation but that newspaper is only reporting what you put in. Whereas now we have autonomous – let's call them bots – that have some agency by creating content. They produce articles by putting together some clever algorithms and some information that you can find online and construct some sentences and texts that are very difficult to distinguish from human-produced text. Much of that is faulty in its reasoning.

Nevertheless, there are some studies that show it is not those automated bots that create the greatest influence, as Elena pointed out. It seems there are three actors there: one is these kinds of bots that automatically produce disinformation; then we have people who maliciously try to put together some kind of fake news article to spread confusion or to further their objectives or the objectives of people who paid them; the largest effect can be found with a third group, people like you and me who are either not paying attention and sharing a news article that is not quite what it appears to be, or people sharing something because "Ah, it comes from my nephew and it's nice so we'll send it on." This group has a big effect on the fake news ecology and this is the group that we in Dundee have been focusing on.

Our challenge is how to instill some methodology of using critical literacy in those users so they learn how to see through the tricks and the magic, the narratives that might not quite work in their favor.

EK: **Your work at the University of Dundee involves using the Argument Web to help students recognize fake news**.

JV: There are two aspects to the Argument Web. First, it's an interconnected network of analyzed arguments. So, pieces of information that in some sense relate to each other by inference. The network contains claims with arguments "for" and "against" certain topics or propositions. And those arguments themselves have subsequent arguments, so in a sense all these pieces can be related to each other.

The more quantitative aspect of the Argument Web is what we might call a "software suite," a collection of software tools that interact with argumentation and debate, to measure it, quantitative metrics – so-called analytics – to get more insight into the most contested or central issues, to find out whether the claims that are being made are supported or not. There are also software tools that allow you to engage in a virtual debate with speakers from across history by combining what they said in previous debates, even though they might not necessarily have interacted with each other directly.

EK: **So you can have Plato in a dialogue with Aristotle, for example?**

JV: For example, yes. For that to happen there would be analyzed data in the Argument Web dataset from Aristotle's known debates, so as not to put words into his mouth or make the computer simulation say things Aristotle did not say. We would start from a known body of speeches or writings by Aristotle and then you as user could interact with that through argument technologies.[7] You could have Aristotle interact with analyzed texts of speeches actually delivered by Donald Trump or any speaker you choose whose data is saved in the Argument Web. You would then be able to apply your critical literacy skills to identify what kinds of reasoning patterns are being used by the speaker – persuasive or explanatory, for example, supported or based on fallacies. Using this method, the software also reveals where echo chambers are forming, in which people use fewer opinions diverging from their own, so that already held views or biases get reinforced.[8] Users are also able to identify the "backfire effect," the further entrenchment in one's views when presented with conflicting facts.

EK: **Then how can this assist us in recognizing fake news?**

JV: First of all there is the data side. The more analyzed data you have on something the more opportunities you have to bring them to the study of whatever news you are questioning. We can look in those data sets to see if there are particular characteristics we can identify as indicating fake news.

Equally on the software side, we have developed software tools like The Evidence Toolkit we used with the BBC. This is software that is part of the Argument Web to guide users through the steps to identify arguments in news articles, to understand what sort of underlying reasoning principles are used in those arguments. Then the user can see how to appraise those, recognize fallacies and bias. In this way we can help users assess fake news by developing educational software that shows them how to recognize good or bad arguments. Of course, bad argumentation does not equate fake news, but the instilled critical literacy skills can help identify it.

**BOX 11.1 EDITORS' COMMENT: A "LOW-TECH" EXPLA-
NATION OF HOW YOU ACTUALLY DO THIS**

So, for those of us who aren't strong on technical language and capabilities, this is what we did: using our computer or smartphone, we went to the website – http://fni.arg.tech

First, we read the information on the homepage and then clicked on "begin." We met animated characters who "talked" to us through text messages on the screen. We followed the instructions on the screen to engage in a discussion with the animated characters. Our responses were either by clicking on a box (e.g., "yes" or "no") or typing a text response into a box.

As we worked through various articles and, with guidance from the animated characters, we were instructed in how to review the articles for fallacies. We were also able to click on links on the screen to access other related information, such as a copy of the article that we were reviewing.

As promised, we found it very straightforward to use!

EK: **So Elena, when you're dealing with fallacy theory in your current project, are you doing something similar?**

EM: Yes, as Jacky was saying, during crisis situations such as COVID-19 you might be exposed to news that contains arguments that are structured but are nonetheless misleading. That is because the type of reasoning involved might be flawed. Or it might have been valid at one time but it has become outdated in light of new scientific discoveries. So, for example, if you heard Dr. Fauci, Director of the US National Institute of Allergy and Infectious Diseases, make the point in the first week of January 2020 that the coronavirus pathogen was not carried on water droplets from human breath, you would be dealing with false information, but not a deliberate case of fake news because he was not deliberately misleading his listeners.[9] An accurate method of COVID transmission had not yet been established.

That's why there are no automatic fact checkers able to recognize misinformation while there are some that can deal with the deliberate misleading involved in disinformation.[10] In lay terms, what robots are doing is leveraging a huge data set of true statistical claims related to COVID-19 as terms of comparison for claims to be fact checked. While such a system works for factual information, it does not for news reporting on government measures or predictions or evaluations of any sort: fact-checking such news implies having a complex knowledge base. For example, you need some deep expertise to identify whether the information presented has been cherry-picked while other available data might bring you to a different claim, especially when it comes to COVID-19. Even journalists might struggle with that.

Facing such a situation we decided to reverse-engineer the misinformation ecosystem using AI to teach humans how to become fact checkers themselves, learning critical skills in a communication environment through human-computer interaction. We started with a big data analysis of over 1,500 fact checks and analyzed them and came up with some statistically significant, fallacious ways of presenting news as well as their relation to sources. We built a heuristics or decision-making tool[11] to identify those fallacies and embedded it in a multi-agent chatbot where users can interactively learn this heuristics while fact-checking prototypical cases of misinformation.[12]

EK: **It's helpful to look at some examples of claims.**

EM: Most of the time you can find claims in the title of a news item. So "New Vaccine for COVID-19" or "Ibuprofen Complicates your Reactions to COVID-19."[13] We guide the users in the analysis of real news that has appeared in outlets or social media that's gone viral. So not just about fact checking news that's international or local but also across tweets, memes, or YouTube videos.

EK: **How would you get at memes?**

EM: One of the criteria for fact-checked memes is popularity on different platforms.

EK: **Does your recent project, "Being Along Together: developing fake news immunity" address these issues?**

EM: We have recently submitted a paper that sets out the theoretical and empirical starting points of the project, providing a workable definition for semi-fake news, namely news which does not contain fabricated information, but fallacious statements that make them misleading.

We are now working on a second paper showing how human-computer interaction, if effectively designed, can help the public acquire critical skills. In our Fake-News Immunity chatbot, users have the chance to engage through games with the thoughts of major philosophers and to interact with them while fact-checking. Besides providing an interactive and fast paced learning environment, human computer interaction reduces users' fact-threatening fears.

EK: **How do fact checking websites work?**

EM: Some fact checkers use ambiguous ratings such as mixtures which points to the presence of elements of both truth and falsity. Such a rating is not very informative when it comes to the misinformation triggers. Let's take two examples: Dr. Fauci's claim "there is nothing to worry about"[14] and another one about Italians stating they were able to see dolphins in the water again [during lockdowns to prevent COVID spread] implying that pandemic lockdowns had increased the presence of wildlife.[15]

As correctly flagged by staff at the fact checking website Snopes, both claims contain elements of truth and of falsity. However, the origin and the nature of the false information differs wildly. Claim #1 reports a quote wrongly attributed to Dr. Fauci: the sentence "there is nothing to worry about" is a misleading rephrase of his statement uttered on February 29th during the NBC morning talk show Today that, at that moment in time, "the risk is still low, but this could change." By neglecting the provisional tone of Dr. Fauci's assertion explicitly bound to the circumstances, social media posts from Trump's supporters have misrepresented Dr. Fauci's position. Claim #2, by contrast, gives voice to a nonlegitimate causal inference between the lockdown and a revitalized animal wildlife in Italy. Probably eager to come up with good news, social media users have reframed a simple correlation as a causation, falling into a post hoc fallacy.

EK: **Jacky, I understand your research has involved gleaning data from the BBC's radio program Moral Maze. Can you explain how you used them?**

JV: Sure. Moral Maze is a longstanding weekly radio program on BBC Radio 4 in which a moderator, panelists and guest experts discuss a morally divisive, ethically relevant issue. It's been about 10 years since Professor Chris Reid here at the University of Dundee started the relationship with Christine Morgan at the BBC because this debate show is really interesting from an argumentative perspective. It is a really well-structured, calm debate where people are well spoken, might interrupt each other occasionally but there are no real oratorical trickeries going on.

From a research perspective it is a very good source of data. There are two sides presented of a divisive issue with several experts setting out their argumentative case for why their view on the topic is correct and why the opponent's view is incorrect.

The software's computer code simulates debaters.[16] In Elena's experiments it's Greek philosophers. In ours, it's characters from the Moral Maze radio program. As a user of the Polemicist software you get to interact with this argumentative data through these virtual characters, these uhm . . .

EK: **Avatars?**

JV: Yes, in many ways they are avatars. Polemicist offers a way of traversing this data set. So it takes us back to the Argument Web where you have this interconnected network of propositions, of pieces of information that are themselves premises and conclusions of arguments. For example, if we have Melanie Phillips who is one of the panelists on the program, if her avatar makes a particular claim then you can ask her, through her avatar, why this is the case. It would respond with reasoning that the real Melanie Phillips advanced in the radio broadcasts. You could then respond, "Is it not the case that such and so" and you would introduce a counter argument. At which point you might want to bring in Matthew Taylor, another panelist on the show, through his avatar, to see what he has to say about it. So, you build up this different way of understanding the arguments that were made in the radio program.[17]

EK: **If you were participating in Moral Maze today within the COVID context, do certain moral questions suggest themselves? For example, the whole notion of the US leader announcing publicly to his constituents that he took the drug hydroxychloroquine which is traditionally used to prevent and treat malaria and unproven for safe use for the coronavirus? So, discussing with the heads of public safety and health the possibility of injecting bleach into the human body.**

JV: Yes, and sunlight. I must say it's been a while since I last checked out the Moral Maze myself, but I can't imagine they would not have done some episodes related to the pandemic. But generally they wouldn't look at such specific examples as with the Trump example – a particular press conference example. However, I can imagine they would do an episode on the morality of lockdowns for example. And then they would have famous experts that would have a leading role in the National Health Service (NHS) or is a mental health expert or someone representing the service industries. And they all bring their own perspective and they will debate issues from that perspective.

They tend to focus on more general topics. So, you could have an episode on the morality of vaccines and you could discuss whether it should be mandatory or not.

I see Elena is checking the program online.

EM: Yes, you guessed right, Jacky. They are debating the morality of vaccines. And there was a program on the issue of getting together with family for Thanksgiving (during the pandemic). There are lots of potential risks attached to such gatherings together with a new sense of guilt. Because if you are asymptomatic and you spend festivities with your family, you might spread the virus. Even if in the UK mass rapid testing has improved the scenario, there are still lots of moral questions on the table since the accuracy in detecting positive cases is low and a negative test shall not be considered a green light for visiting relatives in closed spaces.

EK: All good examples. Do you have other tools for students?

JV: Yes, we have developed the Evidence Tool Kit to assist students in developing critical literacy skills to deal with fake news. Again, it's similar to what Elena was describing insofar as they are using an educational software tool that is now in beta testing.

The Evidence Tool Kit is a piece of software we developed for the BBC as part of their 2018 Young Reporter project on fake news. It allows the user to pick a news article, and then takes the user by the hand through the steps to identify the reasoning structure in a news article and to see what types of arguments these are. So, it asks whether they rely on some expert or some statistical data or on some causal relations. Then the software prompts users to think about the critical questions they can ask to assess whether the reasoning makes sense.

For example, if we find the argument relies on an expert, we could look check whether that person is an expert in a relevant field. Or, is it an archeologist talking about vaccinations? We could also check whether the expert actually made that statement and said it at the relevant time Which goes back to the example you picked from Elena's paper about Dr. Fauci. He did actually say it, but that was February 2020. You can't hold him to that anymore.

The software also looks for any counter arguments in the news article. Many news organizations try to be balanced, to present arguments on both sides of the issue.

EK: **Jacky, can you speak to what you consider a very egregious false claim regarding COVID?**

JV: I would say the most egregious part is that they are made on camera, on the record, but are then being denied. There are no markers to indicate the comments about injecting bleach were a joke, for example. I would say the worst false claim there is to first say something and then deny ever saying it.

EK: **Elena?**

EM: There were a lot of conspiracy theories that were really quite browsable, but what I think was really surprising was the leading false claims that I was believing at the beginning.

I remember I was running in a park and was afraid of pigeons because we didn't know which animals were spreading the disease. I was paranoid. Actually, we know now that COVID-19 is not transmitted to humans from certain animals. Even though we know pets can get the virus. That was a misleading claim so I was a bit afraid of dogs and cats and pigeons.

I also remember the Gates conspiracy theory. It claimed that the government of Italy was calling for the arrest of Bill Gates. I was thinking "Wow, there's a lot going on there in terms of politics." It was a sarcastic comment by a minister that went viral.

I remember a fun one that I never believed in, that if you drink hot water with garlic you will not contract COVID-19. So there's is a mixture of vampire traditions going on with COVID-19 and zombies and so forth. It's very popular.

JV: It should help with social distancing!

EM: For sure, yeah.EK **Then there's the idea that if you are pumping gas or petrol and you have COVID it will re-order your DNA. Or that vaccines restructure your DNA.**

So, to wrap up, do you see your ideas reaching out beyond the academy to such entrenched groups in the United States as Q-anon?

EM: Yes, we hope to catch anti-vaxxers and conspiracy theorists. But it's possible that such groups do not want to spend their time playing with a critically thinking chatbot. But that is also why we have the communication environment to make it engaging. So, if you have people within your circle who are curious and they want to try it, one of our goals is wider knowledge transfer. So yes, potentially we'd like to change the mind of those conspiracy theorists. Whether this is going to happen, it's early to say. We'll see over the next months the numbers of people who pick up on this.

EK: **Can you give your impression of whether conspiracy theorists are more adopters than thinkers?**

EM: I think there are a plethora of factors which feature believers in conspiracy theories. There's for sure an element of confirmation bias. That is, conspiracy theorists don't really want to engage with critical thinking because it will go against their beliefs in a strong way. You can see it also in those who refuse to wear a mask when we get into a critical phase. It's difficult to generalize but one factor is just not being well informed. And 15% of the population seems not to be well informed in the UK according to statistics.[18] They are really infodemically vulnerable and it has increased during the last three months of the pandemic. I think it's because people are tired of feeling stress and danger and so they are trying to escape from that scenario. And so the best way to do that is to ignore the news and to just stay within your very small circle and try to forget about the situation.

EK: **Not much belief in the common good. Is it just that we are too tired to start thinking about these broader issues? COVID overload?**

EM: There's a real fear and also not just about health consequences of the virus. There's lots of people in the UK who have been furloughed for so long. That increases you fear about what's going to happen with the economy. Infodemic vulnerability also correlates to level of education.

JV: I want to make a slight counterpoint to Elena's comments. If you look at some other conspiracy theories, like flat earth, that somehow gains quite a bit of traction, as it turns out the people who engage with these conspiracy theories, and you can see this with the Q-anon people to a degree as well, they do actually spend quite a bit of time trying to assess the information they have and trying to find reasons for why their viewpoint is right and why what their opponents are saying is wrong.

So I don't think in all conspiracy theory cases it's a matter of disengaging critical faculties either out of pure laziness or lack of capability or just being tired of all the bad news. In some of these conspiracy theory cases people actually put in a lot of effort to try to reason about things.

I think there are some analogies between how people in various communities reason and are picking up on what their opponents are saying and what their allies are saying. This effect is enlarged by the current social media networks. Part of what you are seeing in your feed is selected by an automated algorithm that is partially trained by content that you have looked at in the past. Because there is an incentive for these companies to get you to keep on clicking on things. Many people like reading material they agree with. They are likely to stop reading things they don't agree with. And that creates these information silos and echo chambers where the feedback you are getting is more from information you . . .

EK: **Support?**

JV: Yes, that you like. It's corroborating your own thinking.EK **What do we make, then, of claims that are just so crazy? I go back to America**

again. When you look at the claim there is a child trafficking ring headquartered in a pizza outlet.

JV: At the moment, I think these ideas all come together with Q-anon people who believe Trump is going to drain the swamp. And there is a hedonistic cabal where they abuse and murder children to sustain themselves with the children's blood . . . yeah, how do people get there? It's mind boggling but also fascinating.

For example, there are journalists who go to meetings and talk to people who actually pull out fact sheets taken from websites. Just like with correlation and causation, if you pull together enough data, you will find correlation between things. And then if you are inclined to see patterns in such data (and humans are inclined to see patterns), that's how we've survived. Then, yeah, maybe you start believing these things. And you hear it from people in your online community and they have the same beliefs. So you become more and more entrenched.

One of the things Elena and I are each trying to do with argument technology and software tools is to make people less entrenched. One of the ways is to teach them more about critical literacy, critical thinking. There was a strong movement in critical thinking education in the 1970s and 80s. This is one of the reasons our Evidence Tool Kit worked so well with secondary school students. Children have a tendency to be less fixed in their belief systems. We want to teach people what tools they have at their disposal to determine what they should be believing. How to properly reason about things.

EK: **So this book is about outsmarting the next pandemic. Do you have any parting advice about how your discipline can help us respond in a smarter way next time?**

JV: I was thinking of my takeaway message more within the field of research we are working in. The main challenge is finding the balance between critically assessing the information that's coming in and still valuing the opinions given by experts. Because it seems that one of the things that is going wrong is that people are thinking that any opinion is as good as any other. If Donald Trump's opinion is that injecting bleach into humans could work, is that really any different than if Dr. Birks advises us to do so? Expertise has value. Maybe that's the main message. But we should also know how to assess those messages that are put forward by experts. That's a balance that seems to have been lost.EK **So the scientific method requires that, instead of leaping, you step forward cautiously and then test, test, test.**

JV: Yes, science is not always easy to consume. There's a real challenge there in how to present results so people will really listen and appreciate what's going on. In addition, I would say listen to the science critically. But that always means that to engage you need time, attention and critical capacity.

BOX 11.2 EDITORS' COMMENT: A SUMMARY OF REFORM SUGGESTIONS

Following further discussion with Jacky and Elena:

- we need government policy requiring that education curriculum in our schools include the development of critical thinking skills;
- the provision of robust advice to communication professionals, including journalists and those representing governments and medical organizations, on how to properly convey clear and accurate messages; and
- the development and deployment of software to train and support decision-makers in making better decisions.

These suggested areas of reform logically follow the discussion documented above. We can only hope this chapter, together with other discussion and debate regarding the proliferation of "fake news" and difficulties accessing clear, reliable information during the pandemic, will be the impetus for effective actions for reform across the globe.

BOX 11.3 CORONA SHORT #18: MAURITIUS DENNIS, OWNER OF AN OPTICAL RETAIL OUTLET, SPEAKS OF TOURISM

I came to Canada in 1971 from the small Island of Mauritius in the Indian Ocean. I went to the UK and, I was young, looking for a different adventure, so I asked to come to Canada. I got papers within two weeks because they needed immigrants back then. Very different from now. I met my wife here and she is from Mauritius too.

Nobody in Mauritius has the virus. It's a nice island and some distance from Africa and India so it can escape the virus. You have Mozambique to the west but not too close.

They have closed the borders so nobody goes in or out. I heard recently there is a cargo plane from India now bringing workers to Mauritius. They are building a subway system in the capital. There are a couple of cases now. They brought the variant from India. But I don't care what culture they are, we are all human beings.

Mauritius is importing the vaccine from India. And China and other countries are bringing it to Mauritius too. We've had a terrible colonial history, first the British and then the Portuguese and the French. But we are independent since the 1960s. Now Mauritius is in the top 10 countries of Africa in GDP. It is a rich country, I just don't know how rich.

Lots of British, lots of Europeans come as tourists. The numbers of COVID cases are low, except just lately there's been a spike. At the end of April. Nearly 100. I cannot go there now. From the beginning of March last year we were locked down, then we opened up, then we locked down again. It could be from any one of those changes.

We have lots of very nice hospitals. High numbers for the island. Private hospitals because people can afford to pay. They get different treatment from those who are poorer who get support from the government.

So far the supply of oxygen is pretty good. Unlike India, it's terrible there. And I am reading about cremation, it's very hard. I look at the TV, its heartbreaking.

The Prime Minister is probably doing the job. But it's a small island so lots of corruption. You don't see it, but it is there. Lots of politics around the pandemic. The main industry used to be sugar cane but not much now. Mainly the tourists now. And tea. But it's very expensive. People from China are coming and buying up the tea. So prices are going way up. Mostly they export tea now, getting a higher price. The economy is flat right now.

There is no government stimulus, everyone's independent. We have other difficulties too. Heavy rains for example.

So they know how to handle a medical emergency. You put everything in lockdown right away, so people can only go out if it's an emergency. Even to get groceries, you have to go by the alphabet. "A" families one day, "B" another. As a result, people cannot get enough groceries. But everybody who wants a vaccine gets it. There have been pandemics in Mauritius before but never like this. This is a very unique experience in my lifetime.

There are deniers for sure. It all depends on the mentality. Also, its religious. The leaders tell you not to go get a vaccine and so many don't go. The religious leaders are very influential. I say, even if the vaccine is no good, at least it's 50% helpful, so take it. Some are complaining but it's better than nothing.

Notes

1 S. Vosoughi, D. Roy and S. Arai, *The Spread of True and False News Online*, 359: 6380 Science 1146–1151 (2018).
2 Herman Wasserman and Dani Madrid-Morales, *An Exploratory Study of "Fake News" and Media Trust in Kenya, Nigeria and South Africa*, 40:1 Afr. Journalism Studies (2019).
3 Chikezie E. Uzuegbunam et al., *Spotting Hoaxes: How Young People in Africa Use Cues to Spot Misinformation Online*, Nieman Lab (June 2, 2021).
4 Jacky Visser, John Lawrence and Chris Reed, *Viewpoint: Reason-Checking Fake News*, 63:11 Comm. ACM (Nov. 2020).
5 J. Scott Brennan et al., *Types, Sources, and Claims of COVID-19 Misinformation*, Reuters Inst. (Apr. 7, 2020).

6 Visser et al., *supra* n. 4.
7 Such as the Polemicist application.
8 Id.
9 Nell Greenfieldboyce, *Scientists Probe How Coronavirus Might Travel Through the Air*, NPR (Apr. 3, 2020), reporting that, "Transmission of COVID-19 is through droplets, it is not airborne," according to Dr. Maria Van Kerkhove, the WHO's technical lead for COVID-19, speaking at a recent press briefing. "Therefore someone who has these small liquid particles that come out of their mouth, they travel a certain distance and then they fall so that's why we recommend the physical distance, to be separated so that you remove the opportunity for that virus to actually pass from one person to another."
10 Such as the Corona Fact Check. The website states: "CoronaCheck is a joint effort from the teams of Prof. Papotti at EURECOM and of Prof. Trummer at Cornell University. We automatically verify statistical claims with official data to fight misinformation about the Coronavirus disease (COVID-19) outbreak."
11 *Heuristics* can be defined as "mental shortcuts that can facilitate problem-solving and probability judgments. These strategies are generalizations, or rules-of-thumb, reduce cognitive load, and can be effective for making immediate judgments; however, they often result in irrational or inaccurate conclusions." An example is the maxim in advertising that scarcity of a commodity automatically makes it more desirable. See, *Why do we take mental shortcuts?* The Decision Lab website.
12 *See, for example,* News Immunity Chatbot website.
13 *See* David MacGuill, *'Everything Was Forbidden': Did Orwell's '1984' Predict COVID-19 Restrictions?*, Snopes (Dec. 2, 2020) for an example of a fake COVID-19 quotation attributed to George Orwell. This fallacy was uncovered by Snopes, a company created in 1994 that is identified as "the oldest and largest fact-checking site online, widely regarded by journalists, folklorists, and readers as an invaluable research companion."
14 Bethania Palma, *Did Dr. Fauci Say There Was "Nothing to Worry about" in Regards to COVID-19?*, Snopes (Apr. 14, 2020).
15 Bethania Palma, *Did Dolphins and Swans "Return" to Italian Waterways Amid COVID-19 Lockdown?*, Snopes (Mar. 20, 2020).
16 The Polemicist application is related to this program.
17 Dr Visser adds: "All of that is part of the Argument Web, with Polemicist as a software tool for dialogically interacting with the argumentative data from the Moral Maze. Our collaboration with the BBC presents an amazing opportunity to gather argumentative data, analyse it, and build interactive software."
18 Rasmus Kleis Nielsen et al., *Communications in the Coronavirus Crisis: Lessons for the Second Wave*, Reuters Inst. (Oct. 27, 2020) stating: "Offering a preliminary definition of the "infodemically vulnerable" as the subset of the public who consume little to no news and information about COVID-19 and say they would not trust it even if they did, allows us to provide a first estimate of the size of this group, which has grown from a small minority of 6% early in the crisis to a significantly larger minority of 15% by late August – an estimated 8 million people who are more at risk of being at best less informed and at worst un- or misinformed."

12

TECHNOLOGY'S GREATEST GIFT TO THE VOYEUR

Webcams in the K-12 classroom

David Guida

Editors' introduction: School closures around the world have left so many children and parents struggling with how to maintain learning. In many regions online learning is hampered by limited internet access and parents' relocation of their workplace to the home. Educational authorities often direct those same parents to serve as both teachers and motivators for their children. In some regions, the stress of such situations is heightened by lack of internet service and computer devices, irregular fees for learning resources by school administrators, or soldiers visibly patrolling the streets to enforce lockdown. Many students and parents are struggling.

Human Rights Watch has recorded a sampling of student experiences in Africa:[i]

- In North Africa, Moroccan student Nawal L. is offered online classes but instruction is not reliable: "Sometimes we don't hear from a teacher for the whole day, then he'd show up at 6 saying he didn't have enough internet credit." She added, "The physics teacher . . . just disappeared. . . . She just didn't give any class."
- Chéckina M., 13, in Kinshasa, Democratic Republic of the Congo, said she was given a study book by her school when it closed, but has had no further contact with her teachers. "I reread my old lessons. . . . I find math difficult to study at home."
- In Zambia, 15-year-old Natalie L. reports that the headmistress "came through the classes and told us to study on our own." Natalie finds that

DOI: 10.4324/9781003215769-17

> "It's been a little bit nerve-racking. Next year I have my [school leaving] examination . . ."

- In many schools in the Central African Republic, there has been no teaching for months. A mother of a six-year-old girl said she tries to get her daughter to do revision exercises, and three times a week they listen to classes on the radio. "But it is a program which is not specific for each level of class. It's too complex. . . . Our children have not had any support during this time of pandemic."
- Dekha A., 14, in Kenya, said her school sends revision papers to parents using WhatsApp twice a month. "A marking scheme is sent once the students have made an attempt and the papers are meant to be marked by the parents . . . The teachers do not communicate directly with us."

Girls face unique barriers during distance education. They are hesitant to go to their male teachers' homes as required in some locations. Family violence during lockdown also disproportionately affects young women. As a primary school teacher in Nairobi, Kenya, reported, "With the lockdown, all family members are staying in the house morning to evening. I have had some of the girls call to inform me that they are harassed by their fathers or uncles." In addition, girls are often expected to take on childcare responsibilities and household chores which further reduces their ability to keep up with their male classmates.

Uniquely affected are young students with physical or learning disabilities.[ii] Reporting from the National University Health System in Singapore, a research team concludes that developmentally disabled children "are especially vulnerable to the effects of the pandemic due to (1) greater healthcare needs, (2) dependency on community-based services and (3) mental health concerns."[iii] COVID-19 has also highlighted existing structural inequities for Indigenous children and their communities.[iv]

In this chapter, computer sciences teacher David Guida takes us to the Canadian online classroom, developed during the pandemic by district school authorities to enable teacher-supervised learning during lockdown. During several months of on-again, off-again school attendance, school boards have quickly devised a hybrid combination of classroom and online learning. Mr. Guida casts a critical eye on one disturbing activity enabled by Zoom, an American-based videotelephony and online chat software service used by most elementary and high school teachers in the province of Ontario.[v] That activity is the unauthorized webcam access to students' private lives and spaces gained by sexual predators. He argues that such activity is addressed by the *Criminal Code of Canada* as was shown in the pre-COVID-19 Supreme Court of Canada (SCC) decision in *Regina v Jarvis* (*Jarvis*). In practical terms, however, restricted movement of family members and reduced access to school authorities and social services means that reporting of such personal violations by young students has been significantly curtailed.

With the outbreak of the coronavirus in January 2020, and the announcement in March by the WHO that the spread of COVID-19 had reached pandemic proportions, educational authorities around the globe were involved in finding ways to continue educating young learners, while observing local health mandates for social distancing and other precautions to stem the viral spread. Many authorities chose online classes by requiring teachers to use videoconferencing interactive technology, such as Zoom, more broadly known as synchronous video education (SVE). The transition was met with considerable criticism in several countries for what one educator observed as "emergency triage learning slapped together on the fly."[1] As students and parents struggled to adapt to home learning while trying to keep parent-child boundaries, they might have been aware of the UN's assessment of the state of pandemic-era education as "a generational catastrophe that could waste untold human potential, undermine decades of progress, and exacerbate entrenched inequalities."[2]

This chapter examines whether the privacy protection afforded to complainants by the Canadian Criminal Code (*Criminal Code*) as applied in the pre-COVID-19 *Jarvis* decision is adequate or relevant to protect teachers and students now that teaching has migrated online with SVE technology. Although this is not a subject that is receiving much scholarly attention, online predation of teachers or students exists at this time as a very real possibility given that teaching and learning are situated in private homes and require the high technical capabilities of Zoom and other interactive telecommunication software provided by Canadian schools.

SVE technology is being used beyond the anticipated purposes of its creators, that is, within the home environment of teachers and students for educational purposes during a pandemic. This means that, despite the privacy protections enunciated in the Canadian *Jarvis* decision, the school's expectations of student behavior,[3] and the high professional standards expected of teachers under provincial *Education Act* legislation, regulation of surreptitious observation or recording of students by predatory teachers or other students for sexual purposes cannot be enforced effectively.[4]

Without law reform to address evolving cheapfake[5] and deepfake[6] technologies that can alter to a considerable degree the audio and video recordings once they have been completed, a student's "reasonable expectation of privacy" cannot be adequately protected. Further, the definition of "sexual purposes" cannot be ascertained at the time of observation nor in the indeterminate future.

Case study

The most relevant Canadian criminal case is *Regina v Jarvis*,[7] which focused on when and where a person will be held criminally liable for observing or recording others, without their knowledge, for sexual gratification. Ryan Jarvis was an English teacher at a Canadian high school. He used a camera concealed inside a pen to make surreptitious video recordings of female students while they were in the school's common areas and engaged in ordinary school-related activities. The majority of the videos focused on the faces, upper bodies, and breasts of female students. The students did not consent to such recording; in fact, they were completely unaware it was happening. A school board policy in effect at the time prohibited this type of conduct.

Jarvis was charged with surreptitiously observing or making "a visual recording of another person who is in circumstances that give rise to a reasonable expectation of privacy, if the observation or recording is done for a sexual purpose."[8] He was acquitted at trial because the judge was not satisfied that the recordings were made for a sexual purpose. The Ontario Court of Appeal upheld the accused's acquittal on other grounds, that the trial judge had erred in finding that the students were in circumstances that gave rise to a reasonable expectation of privacy. The case reached the SCC on the latter point in 2005.

The SCC convicted Jarvis, emphasizing that the entire context of the accused's actions should be taken into account, including the location of the complainant when observed or recorded; the complainant's lack of awareness of, or consent to, potential or actual observation or recording; the manner in which the observation or recording was done; the subject matter of the observation or recording; any rules, regulations or policies of the school or other authorities that governed the observation or recording; the relationship between the accused and the complainant; and the purpose for which the observation or recording was done.[9] It was held that this list of considerations is not exhaustive and not every consideration will be relevant in every case.

Expectations of privacy in SVE

Section 162(1) of the *Criminal Code*, as amended by Parliament in 2005, is ill-suited to addressing the privacy concerns inherent in SVE. Voyeurism, as it was conceptualized in 2005, was limited to viewing subjects with technologies such as binoculars, cameras or, in exceptional cases, pen cameras. Voyeurism is now enabled by ubiquitous webcams present in SVE classrooms. Accordingly, when Justice Wagner expanded the factors that must be considered in determining a reasonable expectation of privacy,[10] he could not have anticipated the myriad technologies, like those used in SVE, now available to students and their teachers in new learning environments.

Ontario school boards currently maintain that students, by participating in Zoom sessions, are implicitly consenting to the teacher's audio and video recordings of the lesson. That does not address the many ways that such digital data can be used. In other words, when participants are notified that a class session is being recorded by software applications like Zoom,[11] that does not mean the recording is the sole or authorized recording. For example, a meeting host has some ability to control sharing of screens and local recordings through the application. However, any student participating in the class, or uninvited third parties, can record any other student or the teacher on their own device. They can take screenshots or audio recordings of the entire class or individual students and post them on social media, either in their original format or as altered by software widely available online. Those activities might be undetected by class participants. Such capabilities render the consent or knowledge provisions of the *Jarvis* decision, and section 162(1) of the *Criminal Code* inapplicable. Those safeguards have not anticipated the dissemination capabilities of online sharing, nor the permanence of our images and actions once posted. Making a takedown or content moderation application to social media companies, whether granted or not, cannot erase material that has been reposted and shared instantly by social networks and third parties around the globe.

Screen sharing concerns

While a teacher is sharing information with students using the "screen share" function, any individual in the classroom can be focusing on another student's facial expressions, cleavage, or crotch, if they are captured within the field of vision. There are no effective methods of controlling such surveillance by other students or the teacher. That lack of control experienced by all SVE participants exposes them to random acts of voyeurism that are not addressed in the current legislation, which stipulates that subjects' privacy "can only be infringed if they are recorded or observed in a way that both causes [the subject] to lose control over their image and also infringes their sexual integrity."[12]

Further, *R v Jarvis* considers "the relationship between the person who was observed or recorded and the person who did the observing or recording,"[13] a factor that would be difficult to prove by anyone invoking the criminal legislation.

Indeed, as American psychology professor Mary Aiken contended as early as 2016, human behavior changes as it is translated to our online experiences. She warns that we can quite easily "stumble upon a behavior online" and immerse ourselves "in new worlds and new communities," thereby becoming "cyber-socialized to accept activities that would have been unacceptable just a decade ago."[14]

Further, Justice Wagner's use of *Charter* analysis in the *Criminal Code* context creates a counter-productive tension: whereas *Charter* values are meant to evolve over time, *Criminal Code* provisions are meant to stay fixed at the time of their enactment.[15]

Are screenshots and screen recordings "surreptitious"?

The *R v Jarvis* decision relied on the surreptitious nature of the accused's actions in using the technology of a pen camera, as was available in the early 2000s. Proving the accused acted "surreptitiously" involved establishing that the complainant had lost control of her image. Today's technology has vastly altered the notion of control. Proving today's voyeur is acting "surreptitiously" using standards of proof from the *R v Jarvis* era is less easy to establish given advances in technology. Until the technology and control of student screenshots and screen recordings can be better understood, determinations of their surreptitious nature cannot be reasonably made. Any SVE session or recording can potentially give rise to sexually purposed activities or intentions. A classroom session might be recorded either in screenshot or screen recorded form,[16] and then stored, undetected, for an indefinite period. This exposes all recorded participants to criminal victimization in the present, and to potential abuse in perpetuity, from both their peers and their teachers.

This can be seen in the 2019 case of *R. v. Trinchi*,[17] where the accused was found to have surreptitiously used an image from a webchat that he was conducting with his partner, with whom he was having a long-distance relationship.[18] Specifically, both were naked and both knew they were on video. Trinchi took a still photo of his partner from the live video stream, without her knowledge or consent, and later posted that image online. The judge of the ONCA used the *Canadian Oxford Dictionary* to define surreptitious information as that "obtained, done, etc. in secret or by stealth or by illicit means; clandestine."[19] The court determined that the accused had, by definition, acted surreptitiously, despite the complainant's knowledge that her nude image was being streamed over the Internet.[20] Using that definition, and *Trinchi* as precedent, the act of observing or recording student participants in SVE classes, while they are unaware that their images are being captured in screenshots, would qualify as "surreptitious."

The relevance of the *Jarvis* factors today

The non-exhaustive *Jarvis* factors for determining a participant's reasonable expectation of privacy are less relevant in today's online classroom. They are too broad to meaningfully measure a reasonable expectation of privacy and are diluted further by being pronounced "non-exhaustive" by the court.

Further, given the temporally and spatially indeterminate scope of online behaviors, factors such as "the relationship between the people involved"[21] are too mutable to prove. If a member of the vulnerable student sector were to record the screen of a classmate without his consent and then, years later, modify and distribute that screenshot, it would be difficult to attribute the source of the abuse, penalize the culprit, and remediate any damages.[22]

It can be argued that, since a recording needs to be surreptitious to qualify as voyeuristic,[23] the recordings conducted by SVE do not meet that test if participants are aware that they can be subject to screenshots and screen recordings by any participant at any time. Likewise, current mechanisms for conceptualizing voyeurism are unduly narrow and anachronistic. For example, asking whether a "video recording makes use of a zoom lens"[24] seems outdated, and less important, than effects achieved by today's ultra-high definition webcams. This is particularly so where the webcams are functioning in close proximity to participants, in spaces offering countless data about personally identifiable, sensitive information.

Current capability in image resolution

A further potential issue arises due to image resolution being so strong with current technology, and so widely available in digital devices. This enables new, previously unimaginable, crimes. For instance, security writer Bruce Schneier reported on how a cyberstalker in Japan was able to locate his victim by "enhancing the reflections in her eye and using that information to establish a location."[25] That capability reminds Schneier of the image enhancement scene in *Blade Runner* – that was science fiction but now, "image resolution is so good that we have to worry about it."[26]

One such worry is that "[t]he webcam may be technology's greatest gift to the voyeur," as cyber-psychologist Mary Aiken proclaimed in 2016.[27] Since then, webcam resolution has vastly improved,[28] to the point where the capture of any eye-movement, reaction and micro-reaction – both voluntary and involuntary – exposes body parts, either on purpose or accidentally, that are undetectable to other participants.

The role of large technology companies

Justice Wagner's finding that privacy is normative[29] subjects schools, which are supposed to be safe places,[30] to the privacy and security choices made by tech companies like Zoom. Lawrence Lessig's contention that "code is law," that tech companies' choices and code are more powerful than law,[31] is frighteningly astute at this moment in history, where an alternative to being physically in a school is achieved through computer hardware and software applications. Justice Wagner's use of the Criminal Code in *R v Jarvis*, as "an extension of the criminal law to protect . . . sexual integrity in light of threats posed by new technologies that encroach upon them,"[32] fails in protecting, or addressing, sexual integrity of SVE participants in today's K-12 learning environments.

Architectural dangers: the transition from bricks and mortar to virtual environments

There is also a problem with the architecture of applications, which is altering conceptions of privacy in K-12 education. Whereas educational systems can be built using the values within our normative tradition,[33] imposing platforms not designed for K-12 education can create an inconsistency with those values. The architecture and workings of applications like Zoom can evade or defy the law. Code will often undermine the law.[34] Technology's ability to transcend physical and temporal barriers parallels its ability to overrule law, as futurist Lawrence Lessig predicted when observing that "code is law."[35] Features that, in the physical space, would be mandated and enforced, are both optional and unenforceable in the virtual zone.

For example, in a physical classroom the act of taking a picture of a classmate, teacher, or student without their consent would generally be considered a privacy invasion. Filming that person with a high-definition camera, focused solely on the individual, without their consent, could also be illegal. However, proving the surreptitious nature of that act would be difficult because the individual would need to establish they had lost control of their image. Even explicit consent to bedroom recordings of intimate acts would be illicit if there was a loss of control by the subject. High-definition digital cameras, however, have capabilities that show the subject never had control in the first place.

By stepping aside and giving K-12 teachers and their students choices about how to conduct themselves online, the government and school boards are neglecting their role in protecting personal information and therefore increasing participant vulnerability, with potentially permanent effects. By allowing this to happen, government and school boards alike are giving software companies license to define privacy in the classroom.

The architecture of class video conferencing for K-12 solutions was not in place prior to COVID-19 school closures. The attempt to fit solutions to business problems for the vulnerable student sector risks, in the short term, exposing all participants to non-trivial risks, and giving technology companies the right to determine and shape the privacy and security values of K-12 education.[36]

Zoom's explosive growth as a result of COVID-19 has pushed the spotlight onto the application's privacy and security practices.[37] The application's functionalities and underlying technologies have alternated between offering strong and weak privacy and security.[38] Its functionality demonstrates that the architecture is a major driver of our youth's immature, and reactionary, privacy and security values.[39]

The Ontario College of Teachers, the provincial teaching regulatory body,[40] has identified technical glitches as one of the potential dangers of video conferencing with students. Its emphasis on glitches and teacher error belies the inherent dangers of SVE, and the inadequate functionality in place for keeping students safe.[41] It acknowledges that "[s]ome of the most popular video conferencing platforms were not created for educational purposes."[42] Accordingly, until a video conferencing platform addresses the unique challenges and risks inherent in the K-12 classroom, they should not be used with our young learners.

Sexual purposes in digital spaces

School boards have proposed that students dress appropriately while on camera. However, the opportunity to be on camera with a potential audience, makes acting in ways that will arouse attention more likely among young learners. The range of possibilities for student exhibitionism and mischief are limitless. Mary Aiken explains that this is part of students having fun; that students are acting as they would when gathering with their peers in person.[43] A cursory glance at TikTok, Instagram, or SnapChat applications (or other social media platforms popular with teens) shows that the vulnerable student sector might not be of sufficient maturity to conduct themselves in a manner that can be safely stored on others' hard drives or suspended in cloud databases.[44]

While there might be a general opinion that the vulnerable student sector has too much freedom in choosing how they appear on synchronous video, the conditions and capabilities that allowed Ryan Jarvis to engage in morally repugnant acts are now available to all participants of SVE. They are amplified by increasingly powerful technologies and are potential weapons for cyberbullying. Again, Mary Aitken describes the artful cyber-psychological torture that people, including children, are capable of exacting when armed with the proper digital tools.[45] In their hastily contrived return to online learning in response to COVID-19 school closures, school officials have not always adequately considered the *Safe Schools Act*.[46] For example, they are using tools that do not enable school principals or teachers to fulfill their legislative mandates to monitor and respond to bullying.

Voyeurism

While voyeurism can be approached as a crime, it is also a treatable medical disorder known as *scopophilia*.[47] Treatment of scopophilia gets into territories that are not addressed in the *Criminal Code*, nor accessible in Criminal Record Checks for a potential employer looking to discern whether a potential employee is addicted to pornography or inclined to voyeurism. "The Elephant in the Cyber Room," says Mary Aiken, is that pornography habits are startlingly common across all age groups.[48] Likewise, Ryan Jarvis's actions are symptomatic of our attention-based digital economy and a digitally voyeuristic culture.

As future generations grow in increasingly digital environments, long-term cyber-interactions could lead to online disinhibition effect, a psychological tendency of individuals to be "bolder, less inhibited, and judgment-impaired. Almost as if they were drunk."[49] That disorder can make the consequences of their actions feel less real. For Ryan Jarvis to stubbornly maintain, seven years after trials against him commenced, that while taking the videos "was wrong and it was stupid," he was not remorseful because he "didn't think anyone would get hurt,"[50] is to offer an excuse for future *Jarvis*-type actors. It also can blur the legal distinctions of voyeurism.

Classrooms full of (potential) criminals

The actions of teachers like Ryan Jarvis are of significant criminal concern and raise issues of potential legal liability for school boards.[51] The criminal intent to misuse SVE can exist in anyone with access to the session, either synchronously or through a recording, and with the requisite technological capabilities. To consider liability primarily through a unidirectional lens of teacher violating student, as in *R v Jarvis*, is to oversimplify the possible risks to vulnerable students in a classroom, both now and in the future. The Ontario College of Teachers, the Ministry of Education, and the average school official all focus on teachers who, like Ryan Jarvis, occupy a position of trust. If we apply the Routine Activity Theory ("RAT")[52] to the SVE environment, as suggested by Aitken, we can see that such criminal activity is equally likely to derive from the student population. RAT thinking maintains that, "when motivated offenders and suitable targets meet in the absence of capable guardians, crime is likely to happen."[53] Given that there are on average 20 students for each teacher, students represent more potential bad actors than teachers. That argument is strengthened when we consider that teenagers are more prone to vacillations of mood that can create cybersecurity risks, "exacerbated by the inexperience and naivete of youth."[54] Generally the savviest tech consumers in their families, and likely more savvy than their more senior teachers, teenagers are far more adept at conducting cyber abuses.[55]

It is a disturbing reality that there is a distinct lack of enforcement in SVE. Further, there are insufficient mechanisms for monitoring screenshots and screen recordings. These digital images can be used for any purposes, sexual or otherwise, without recourse. Increasingly, decision-makers of COVID-19 policy, in elementary and high schools, must be aware that their migration from bricks and mortar classrooms to SVE learning is strengthening the likelihood of voyeuristic crime.

Previously unimaginable risks: cheapfakes and deepfakes

As a result of new technological capabilities, our sensitivity to the information available in body images is changing. While Ryan Jarvis's videos were "focused on students' breasts,"[56] advances in facial recognition and deepfake technologies are just two of the advancing technologies that use facial data as their input, and which are increasing the sensitivity of high-resolution facial renderings. Jarvis's 32 videos of varying quality and control are relatively ineffectual when compared to the high-resolution,[57] continuous exposure, capable through hours of SVE. While Jarvis's focus on the students' breasts satisfied the legal test of voyeurism, faces are becoming a more volatile form of personal information that can be shared and manipulated. While speculation abounds about its veracity, a programmer claims to have built a program for identifying faces in porn and cross-referencing against social media, "with 100,000 identified so far."[58] Whereas breasts and anal regions are unlikely to be catalogued or cross-referenced across social media, and are therefore less identifiable, faces are becoming increasingly detectable and catalogable.[59]

A *deepfake* can be defined as a video that has been altered through some form of machine learning to "hybridize or generate human bodies and faces," whereas a *cheapfake* creates audiovisual manipulation through cheaper, more accessible software or by using "Photoshop, lookalikes, re-contextualizing footage, speeding, or slowing."[60]

Faces can be used in cheapfake and deepfake videos that can ruin lives and manufacture opportunities for voyeurism. In the now-outlawed *Reddit* forum called /r/deepfakes, deepfake enthusiasts advised each other on how to create deepfakes of their former classmates using various technologies.[61] Many strategies were shared, but the consensus was that the more high resolution photos one can use, the better quality it will be.[62] Of the roughly 15,000 deepfakes that are online (as of May 2020), 96% of them are sexual in nature and 99% of those involve women's faces being inserted into pornographic content without their consent.[63] One Reddit user said that they made a "pretty good" video of a girl they went to high school with, using around 380 pictures scraped from her Instagram and Facebook accounts.[64] SVE participants are able to capture far more than 380 pictures, likely of higher quality and facial detail. As the technologies for producing deepfakes grow, the number of videos produced is also likely to grow,[65] and the vulnerable student sector, including female teachers, is disproportionately more likely to be their subject.

Further, the authenticity of a video is not the primary catalyst for it going viral. Humans' propensity to believe what they see makes the authenticity of an image or video a secondary driver to the more viral qualities of negativity and salaciousness.[66]

Conclusion: privacy by design in virtual education

The criminal behavior examined in this chapter might never have come to light without the emergency transition of education to the online environment as demanded by the global pandemic. As government and school officials cannot predict what risks they are exposing students to in SVE, lower-sensitivity alternatives to the current full disclosure video model[67] should be used. In efforts to transplant the physical classroom to the virtual world, SVE participants are over-disclosing sensitive data, primarily biometric facial data, that are increasing likely to figure in cyber-based crimes like voyeurism, both now and in future applications of technologies. Schools must make mandatory least-revealing-means tests where the minimal, least-sensitive amount of data are transferred in synchronous learning to achieve the optimal level of education.

It is illegal to take pictures of others in schools without consent; this provision should be updated to include new capabilities and formats. Likewise, the same rationale against observing and recording people in schools that led to the conviction of Ryan Jarvis should be applied to the digital realm. However, since this cannot be enforced at present, it should be outlawed until more flexible legislation is enacted. With this type of behavior, perpetrated on minors, decriminalization is not an option. Justice Wagner's logic and deference to societal norms in the *Jarvis* decision no longer holds regarding SVE.

Further, law reform is needed to specifically address evolving cheapfake and deepfake technologies which are capable of altering audio and video recordings to a considerable degree. As stated above, until then, the "reasonable expectation of privacy" cannot be accurately ascertained, nor can sexual purposes be ascertained at the time of observation nor in the indeterminate future. Specifically, SVE should not be conducted until non–consensual, sexually purposed screenshots and video recordings of classroom interactions can be prevented. The continuance of education during the remainder of the pandemic must use less-sensitive modes of communication. Voice conferences or text chats are a few options.

Legislators must also examine the products of cheapfake and deepfake technologies currently available online to determine if law reform is immediately necessary to protect the privacy rights and reputations of vulnerable users. This must be done now, and as future, unimaginable technologies emerge. Reform is needed, and it is needed now.

BOX 12.1   CORONA SHORT #19: PAKISTAN SOPHIE, CO-OWNER OF AIR QUALITY BUSINESS IN KARACHI, CHANGES HER LIFESTYLE

I have a business that features Internet of Things technologies in Karachi. My principal supplier is in China. In January 2020 my agent placed the firm's annual order but by the end of the month there had been no reply. The Chinese contact reported that everything was closed and not expected to open until the first of March. I thought it was a joke – nothing in China ever closes down.

With the first case in Karachi the Pakistani government closed all schools. This upset my 16-year-old daughter who had yet to sit her final exams and graduate. My daughter insisted she was going to proceed as normal, especially with her graduation party.

The Pakistani government was reluctant to advise people on how to deal with the pandemic beyond dealing with it day-to-day. They were not centralizing information and even suggested that it was just the flu. Local politicians closed schools, then ordered full lockdown by 20 March 2020, but there was pressure from the federal government to reopen to stabilize the economy. It was general chaos. Most of Karachi's labor force are young, not rich, daily wage earners, with small homes they just return to each night to sleep. So difficult to keep social distance.

We closed our business early on. Our workforce are mostly recent graduates from across the city. The workplace was hot, air conditioning had to be turned off – a real melting pot. I told them to work from home even though my partner in Germany wanted to reduce staff or salaries. There was no revenue so the question was how to sustain the business for three months. I suggested minor cuts, up to 20%, and compensation later. A few workers left, some had no internet, unstable electrical capacity, no air conditioning. It was very hot. And so expensive for them to pay their own additional electricity. There were a lot of power outages as usual in summer. I gave all 15 of them flexible hours and created projects to keep them engaged so they would not seek other work. I also encouraged online courses as it was very tough for younger people to be stuck in their homes while some watched their siblings go out to work each day as demanded by their employers. When the first wave ended in August, they could not continue to work from home so a few came to work each day according to a rotation plan. Eventually they all came back.

People came to realize they had to change their lifestyle. The time at home had given them a chance to reassess what was important. Many still did not take the virus seriously – until a co-worker's father caught COVID and died. Up to that time some found it too uncomfortable to wear a mask and continually wash their hands.

In December 2020 we had to close down once again for a second wave. In my home, my husband, daughter, and I live on the main floor. My septuagenarian parents live upstairs. My mother found the adjustment particularly difficult as she was used to a maid for cleaning and cooking. She could no longer travel either, to see her other children in Winnipeg and in Norway. The streets of Karachi, a "24/7 city," were deserted.

Slowly we all took on different activities: my mother learned yoga and vegetable gardening and joined me for daily walks. Each evening I joined a friend for cycling, wearing a mask and scarf. There was not that rush to squeeze everything into the day. I started to have friends over if they wore a mask or visited outside. The air quality improved because there was almost no traffic. We call it "beautiful air." My daughter eventually had an online graduation ceremony. My yoga class moved online. I lost weight.

Now everyone is talking about what is important in life. Before eating out was taken for granted. Now it's quality time with the family. We have also developed hobbies, showing that there is so much to do with our time. So, just keep your close circle and let other things fall off the list. We have brought this on ourselves. Our people were living in cells, working 24/7. By the way, we have started a project to build and install air quality monitors across Karachi. Perhaps we will continue to have "beautiful air."

BOX 12.2   CORONA SHORT #20: CANADA CLAIRE, DRYCLEANER IN A SMALL TOWN, IS FORCED TO CLOSE HER BUSINESS

I own and run the only dry-cleaning business in a small town of about 6,000 people. When COVID was announced I had to close because we didn't know what we were dealing with. When our government included dry-cleaning in a list of "essential services," I decided to reopen to keep the business afloat. Our government had announced a onetime rent supplement which helped, but I also had to invest in some expensive precautions, such as a 10 by 4 foot plastic barrier across the main counter to keep the legal distance from my customers. I also keep a constant supply of hand sanitizer throughout the store. My mask is absolutely essential because I am in conversation with the customers all day and I handle their clothes. With all that, I still found I had to take on a second job to make ends meet.

I can't tell you how stressful it is to open to my customers and handle their soiled clothes every day. All I have to do is look behind me at the mounds of dry-cleaning hanging in a line, waiting to be cleaned, to feel a new sense of panic that this pandemic has caused. Do those clothes harbor germs? When people told me early on that they were just returning from foreign vacations or exotic locations, did that mean I was being exposed to the virus or foreign variants through their clothes? That worry is with me every day. We seem to know so little about the virus and how it is transmitted. I feel that as a business community we are ill equipped to deal with all the devastation we are seeing in the media.

COVID has taught me a lot. There is good news and bad news in the fact that my son and his wife have moved into the basement of our house to ride out the pandemic. I love having them and their three toddlers so close. But I can't see them and hug them for fear of exposing them to infection I might have picked up at work. Although I can hear them right below me in my home, I have not seen their faces for over a month. Each day, when their other grandmother arrives, goes downstairs and gives them a big hug, I feel the cost to me of this pandemic has been way too high.

Notes

i These accounts are detailed in Impact of Covid-19 on Children's Education in Africa, Human Rights Watch submission to The African Committee of Experts on the Rights and Welfare of the Child (31 August to 4 September 2020), online: <www.hrw.org/sites/default/files/media_2020/08/Discussion%20Paper%20-%20Covid%20for%20ACERWC.pdf>.

ii B. O. Olusanya, et al., "Developmental Disabilities among Children Younger Than 5 Years in 195 Countries and Territories, 1990–2016: A Systematic Analysis for the Global Burden of Disease Study" (2018) 6:10 The Lancet Global Health e1100–e1121. In 2016 it was estimated that, globally, 52.9 million children younger than 5 years have developmental disabilities.

iii R. Aishworiya and Y. Q. Kang, "Including Children with Developmental Disabilities in the Equation during This COVID-19 Pandemic" (2020) J. Autism Dev. Disord., https://doi.org/10.1007/s10803-020-04670-6.

iv Ryan Giroux et al., COVID-19 and Indigenous Children in Canada: What Can Paediatricans Do?, Canadian Pediatric Society CPS.CA (27 May 2021), online: <www.cps.ca/en/blog-blogue/covid-19-indigenous-children-in-canada-what-can-paediatricans-do>.

v Zoom functions on a cloud-based peer-to-peer software platform.

1 Paul W. Bennett, *End of Topsy-Turvy School Year: 5 Education Issues Exposed By the COVID-19 Pandemic*, The Conversation (6 June 2021).

2 *UN Secretary-General Warns of Education Catastrophe, Pointing to UNESCO Estimate of 24 Million Learners at Risk of Dropping Out*, UNESCO (5 August 2020).

3 For example, students are expected to avoid taking screenshots or screen recordings of other students or teachers.

4 For example in Ontario, *see further* "DUTIES OF A TEACHER" in the *Education Act* RSO 1990, c E.2 s. 264(1) where it is stated, "It is the duty of a teacher and a temporary teacher [. . .] (c) to inculcate by precept and example respect for religion and the principles of Judaeo-Christian morality and the highest regard for truth, justice, loyalty, love of country, humanity, benevolence, sobriety, industry, frugality, purity, temperance and all other virtues." These expectations are present both in teacher's private and public lives and are made particularly difficult to maintain by the prospect of SVE from teachers' homes.

5 Inexpensive, consumer-oriented software tools like Photoshop used to simulate individuals.

6 Advanced, specialist-oriented software tools based on machine-learning used to simulate individuals and human characteristics.

7 *R. v. Jarvis*, 2019 SCC 10, [2019] 1 S.C.R. 488.

8 Section 162.1 of the *Criminal Code of Canada, ("CCC")* states:

162.1 (1) Everyone who knowingly publishes, distributes, transmits, sells, makes available or advertises an intimate image of a person knowing that the person depicted in the image did not give their consent to that conduct, or being reckless as to whether or not that person gave their consent to that conduct, is guilty

(a) of an indictable offence and liable to imprisonment for a term of not more than five years; or

(b) of an offence punishable on summary conviction.

(2) In this section, *intimate image* means a visual recording of a person made by any means including a photographic, film or video recording,

(a) in which the person is nude, is exposing his or her genital organs or anal region or her breasts or is engaged in explicit sexual activity;

(b) in respect of which, at the time of the recording, there were circumstances that gave rise to a reasonable expectation of privacy; and

(c) in respect of which the person depicted retains a reasonable expectation of privacy at the time the offence is committed.

(3) No person shall be convicted of an offence under this section if the conduct that forms the subject-matter of the charge serves the public good and does not extend beyond what serves the public good.

(4) For the purposes of subsection (3),

(a) it is a question of law whether the conduct serves the public good and whether there is evidence that the conduct alleged goes beyond what serves the public good, but it is a question of fact whether the conduct does or does not extend beyond what serves the public good; and

(b) the motives of an accused are irrelevant.

9 *Jarvis, supra* note 7 at para 41.

10 *Ibid.*

11 *Recording Notifications*, Zoom Support (1 August 2020), online: <https://support.zoom.us/hc/en-us/articles/360000486746-Recording-Notifications>.

12 *Jarvis, supra* note 7 at 493.

13 *Ibid.*, at para 29.

14 Mary Aiken, *The Cyber Effect* (New York: Spiegel & Grau, 2016) at 105.

15 Jessica St. Pierre, *I Spy with My Little Camera: Voyeurism and Reasonable Expectation of Privacy after Jarvis*, Cty Carl. L. Assoc. (20 October 2019), online: <https://commentary.canlii.org/w/canlii/2019CanLIIDocs3877> at 5.

16 Screenshots are captures of a particular instance in time. Screen recordings involve both audio and video recordings of a screen.

17 *R v Trinchi*, 2019 ONCA 356.

18 *Ibid.*, citing the Jarvis case.

19 Katherine Barber, ed., *The Canadian Oxford English Dictionary* (Don Mills, ON: Oxford University Press, 2001) sub verbo "surreptitious."

20 *Trinchi, supra* note 17 at 2.

21 *Jarvis, supra* note 7 at para 29.

22 See Herbert Lin, *Attribution of Malicious Cyber Incidents: From Soup to Nuts*, Columbia Journal of International Affairs (9 March 2017), online: <https://jia.sipa.columbia.edu/attribution-malicious-cyber-incidents>. Attributing the source of a malicious act in the digital realm is difficult, especially when the adversary is technically adept.

23 "[Voyeurism] is committed when a person surreptitiously observes or makes a visual recording of another person who is in 'circumstances that give rise to a reasonable expectation of privacy.'" *Jarvis, supra* note 7 at 1.

24 *R v Rudiger*, 2011 BCSC 1397 at 76.

25 Bruce Schneier, *Images in Eye Reflections*, Schneier on Security (27 July 2020), online: <www.schneier.com/blog/archives/2020/07/images_in_eye_r.html>.

26 *Ibid.*

27 *Aiken, supra* note 14 at 105.

28 Surpassing our extrapolation from Moore's Law that technological capacity will double every two years.

29 *Jarvis, supra* note 7 at 68.

30 See *Duties of a Teacher, supra* note 7 at 300.0.1: "1. To create schools in Ontario that are safe, inclusive and accepting of all pupils. 2. To encourage a positive school climate and prevent inappropriate behaviour, including bullying, sexual assault, gender-based violence and incidents based on homophobia, transphobia or biphobia. 3. To address inappropriate pupil behaviour and promote early intervention. 4. To provide support to pupils who are impacted by inappropriate behaviour of other pupils. 5. To establish disciplinary approaches that promote positive behaviour and use measures that include appropriate consequences and supports for pupils to address inappropriate behavior. 6. To provide pupils with a safe learning environment."

31 Lawrence Lessig, *Code Is Law*, Harv. Mag. (1 January 2000), online: <https://harvardmagazine.com/2000/01/code-is-law-html>.

32 *Jarvis, supra* note 7 at 24.

33 *Lessig, supra* note 31.

34 *Ibid.*

35 *Ibid.*

36 *Lessig, supra* note 31.

37 Jordan Novet, *Zoom Has Added More Videoconferencing Users This Year Than in All of 2019 Thanks to Coronavirus, Bernstein Says*, CNBC (26 February 2020), online: <www.cnbc.com/2020/02/26/zoom-has-added-more-users-so-far-this-year-than-in-2019-bernstein.html>.

38 Public-interest technologist Bruce Schneier has been observing Zoom's evolution alongside Covid-19 developments, and it has been clear that their privacy and security policies

are changing daily. Bruce Schneier, *Security and Privacy Implications of Zoom*, Schneier on Security (3 April 2020), online: <www.schneier.com/blog/archives/2020/04/security_and_pr_1.html>.

39 Zoom announced that "In response to Covid-19, eye-tracking movements have been disabled." See *Attendee Attention Tracking*, Zoom Support (1 August 2020), online: <https://support.zoom.us/hc/en-us/articles/115000538083-Attendee-Attention-Tracking>. The fact that the functionality can be turned on and off irrespective of legal restriction, demonstrates Zoom's definitive role in defining privacy and security.

40 According to the *Ontario College of Teachers Act*, the OCT has the authority to decertify teachers for acts of *Professional Misconduct* under O Reg 437/97.

41 Teachers have a "Duty to Report" any concerns they might have of student well-being. This is a difficult responsibility to fulfill in SVE, as participants may ignore evidence of harm or abuse. *Duty To Report – Professional Advisory*, Ontario College of Teachers (2020), online: <www.oct.ca/resources/advisories/duty-to-report>.

42 *Ways to Connect with Learners Using Video Conferencing*, Ontario College of Teachers (2020), online:<www.oct.ca/-/media/PDF/video_conf_guidelines/Video_conference_guidlines_EN.pdf>.

43 *Aiken, supra* note 14 at 55.

44 Shilpa Das Gupta, *TikTok Is a Pedophile Magnet and Unsafe for Kids, Warns Cyber Security Expert*, McGill Media (25 January 2020), online: <https://life.gomcgill.com/tiktok-magnet-for-pedophiles-experts-warn-parents>.

45 Numerous cases of cyber-abuse exist. Very often former classmates are the perpetrators, for instance: "In November 2015, students in a small town of sixteen thousand were found to be circulating between three hundred and four hundred nude images of classmates as well as some eighth graders in the local middle school." *Aiken, supra* note 14 at 460.

46 *Safe Schools Act 2000*, R.S.O. 2000, c. 12.

47 *Aiken, supra* note 14 at 102. Aiken examines the case of prominent Washington DC Rabbi, Barry Freundel, who was sentenced to six and a half years in prison for installing a camera in a ritual bath to view women. She wonders, "What if Freundel had access to dozens of webcams?" Likewise, if Ryan Jarvis had access to high resolution videos of dozens of female students' chests and faces during SVE, his voyeuristic abilities would have been much more expansive.

48 *Aiken, supra* note 14 at 309.

49 *Ibid.*

50 Jane Sims, *Ryan Jarvis, London Teacher Who Secretly Recorded Female Students, Sentenced to Six Months in Jail*, London Free Press (28 August 2019), online: <https://lfpress.com/news/local-news/ryan-jarvis-london-teacher-who-secretly-recorded-female-students-sentenced-to-six-months-in-jail>.

51 The authors advise that "Well-drafted workplace policies prohibiting objectionable conduct may not only assist employers in setting workplace standards and expectations (and thus prevent many problems from arising) but also help to reduce an employer's risk exposure should wrongful conduct occur in the workplace." Tamara Hunter and Christina Badgley, "Case involving voyeuristic teacher leads to clarification of law relating to private vs. public places and provides valuable lesson for employers" *CanLiiConnects* (3 September 2019), online: <http://canliiconnects.org/en/commentaries/67430>.

52 *Aiken, supra* note 14 at 670.

53 *Ibid.*

54 Karen Levy and Bruce Schneier, *Privacy Threats in Intimate Relationships*, Journal of Cybersecurity (8 April 2020), online: <www.schneier.com/academic/paperfiles/Privacy_Threats_in_Intimate_Relationships.pdf> at 5.

55 *Ibid.*, at 6.

56 *Jarvis, supra* note 7 at 6.

57 Modern webcams used on videoconferencing platforms like Zoom generally produce video streams of sufficient quality to produce a believable deepfake, by using hundreds

or thousands of screenshots from a video stream, Samantha Cole, *People Are Using AI to Create Fake Porn of their Friends and Classmates*, Motherboard (26 January 2018), online: <https://motherboard.vice.com/en_us/article/ev5eba/ai-fake-porn-of-friends-deepfakes>.

58 Samantha Cole, *DIY Facial Recognition for Porn Is a Dystopian Disaster*, Vice (May 29, 2019), online: <www.vice.com/en_us/article/9kxny7/diy-facial-recognition-for-porn-weibo>.

59 See developments like Clearview AI's scraping of social media accounts for the purposes of building a facial recognition database. Benjamin Sobel, *HiQ v. LinkedIn, Clearview AI, and a New Common Law of Web Scraping*, Berk. Klein Ctr. Internet & Soc., Harvard University (21 April 2020), online: <https://papers.ssrn.com/sol3/papers.cfm?abstract_id=3581844>.

60 Britt Paris and Joan Donovan, *Deepfakes and Cheapfakes: The Manipulation of Audio and Visual Evidence*, Data & Society (September 18, 2019), online: https://datasociety.net/library/deepfakes-and-cheap-fakes/.

61 *Cole, supra* note 58.

62 *Ibid.*

63 Robert Chesney et al., *All's Clear for Deepfakes: Think Again*, Lawfare (11 May 2020), online: <www.lawfareblog.com/alls-clear-deepfakes-think-again>.

64 *Cole, supra* note 58.

65 Robert Chesney and Danielle Citron, *Deep Fakes: A Looming Challenge for Privacy, Democracy, and National Security*, California Law Review (14 July 2018), online: <https://ssrn.com/abstract=3213954> at 6.

66 Robert Chesney and Danielle Citron, *All's Clear for Deepfakes: Think Again*, Lawfare (11 May 2020), online: <www.lawfareblog.com/alls-clear-deepfakes-think-again>.

67 *Lessig, supra* note 31. Lessig shows that the choices we make in our tech-based disclosures have enormous implications. He refers to showing everything in a disclosure as a "one-card-shows all" approach, whereas "least-revealing means" tests are optimal for protecting users' privacy and security.

Bibliography

Books

Aiken, Mary, *The Cyber Effect* (New York: Spiegel & Grau, 2016), ebook.

Barber, Katherine, ed., *The Canadian Oxford English Dictionary* (Don Mills, ON: Oxford University Press, 2001) sub verbo "surreptitious".

Levy, Karen and Bruce Schneier, "Privacy Threats in Intimate Relationships" *Journal of Cybersecurity* (8 April 2020).

Case law

R v Jarvis, 2019 SCC 10.

R v Rudiger, 2011 BCSC 1397.

R v Trinchi, 2019 ONCA 356.

Legislation

The Constitution Act, 1982, Schedule B to the Canada Act 1982 (UK), 1982, c 11.

Criminal Code (R.S.C., 1985, c. C-46) s. 162(1).

Education Act, RSO 1990, c E.2, s. 264(1).

Professional Misconduct, O Reg 437/97.
Safe Schools Act 2000, R.S.O. 2000, c. 12.

Secondary materials: guidance

"Attendee Attention Tracking" *Zoom Support* (1 August 2020), online: <https://support.zoom.us/hc/en-us/articles/115000538083-Attendee-Attention-Tracking>.
"Duty To Report–Professional Advisory" *Ontario College of Teachers* (2020), online: <www.oct.ca/resources/advisories/duty-to-report>.
"Recording Notifications" *Zoom Support* (1 August 2020), online: <https://support.zoom.us/hc/en-us/articles/360000486746-Recording-Notifications>.
"Ways to Connect with Learners Using Video Conferencing" *Ontario College of Teachers* (2020), online: <www.oct.ca/-/media/PDF/video_conf_guidelines/Video_conference_guidlines_EN.pdf>.

Secondary materials: journal articles

Chesney, Robert and Danielle Citron, "All's Clear for Deepfakes: Think Again" *Lawfare* (11 May 2020), online: <www.lawfareblog.com/alls-clear-deepfakes-think-again>.
Chesney, Robert and Danielle Citron, "Deep Fakes: A Looming Challenge for Privacy, Democracy, and National Security" *California Law Review* (14 July 2018), online: <https://ssrn.com/abstract=3213954>.
Hunter, Tamara and Christina Badgley, "Case Involving Voyeuristic Teacher Leads to Clarification of Law Relating to Private vs. Public Places and Provides Valuable Lesson for Employers" *CanLiiConnects* (3 September 2019), online: <http://canliiconnects.org/en/commentaries/67430>.
Lessig, Lawrence, "Code Is Law" *Harvard Magazine* (1 January 2000), online: <https://harvardmagazine.com/2000/01/code-is-law-html>.
Levy, Karen and Bruce Schneier, "Privacy Threats in Intimate Relationships" *Journal of Cybersecurity* (8 April 2020), online: <www.schneier.com/academic/paperfiles/Privacy_Threats_in_Intimate_Relationships.pdf>.
Lin, Herbert, "Attribution of Malicious Cyber Incidents: From Soup to Nuts" *Columbia Journal of International Affairs* (9 March 2017), online: <https://jia.sipa.columbia.edu/attribution-malicious-cyber-incidents>.
Schneier, Bruce, "Security and Privacy Implications of Zoom" *Schneier on Security* (3 April 2020), online: <www.schneier.com/blog/archives/2020/04/security_and_pr_1.html>.
Sobel, Benjamin, "HiQ v. LinkedIn, Clearview AI, and a New Common Law of Web Scraping" *Harvard University – Berkman Klein Center for Internet & Society* (21 April 2020), online: <https://papers.ssrn.com/sol3/papers.cfm?abstract_id=3581844>.
Thomasen, Kristen and Suzie Dunn, "R v Jarvis – Location, Equality, Technology: What Is the Future of Privacy?" *CanLII Connects* (18 December 2018), online: <https://canliiconnects.org/en/commentaries/64964>.

Secondary materials: news articles

Cole, Samantha, "DIY Facial Recognition for Porn Is a Dystopian Disaster" *Vice* (29 May 2019), online: <www.vice.com/en_us/article/9kxny7/diy-facial-recognition-for-porn-weibo>.

Cole, Samantha, "People Are Using AI to Create Fake Porn of Their Friends and Classmates" *Motherboard* (26 January 2018), online: <https://motherboard.vice.com/en_us/article/ev5eba/ai-fake-porn-of-friends-deepfakes>.

Das Gupta, Shilpa, "TikTok Is a Pedophile Magnet and Unsafe for Kids, Warns Cyber Security Expert" *McGill Media* (25 January 2020), online: <https://life.gomcgill.com/tiktok-magnet-for-pedophiles-experts-warn-parents>.

Novet, Jordan, "Zoom Has Added More Videoconferencing Users This Year Than in All of 2019 Thanks to Coronavirus, Bernstein Says" *CNBC* (26 February 2020), online: <www.cnbc.com/2020/02/26/zoom-has-added-more-users-so-far-this-year-than-in-2019-bernstein.html>.

Sims, Jane, "Ryan Jarvis, London Teacher Who Secretly Recorded Female Students, Sentenced to Six Months in Jail" *London Free Press* (28 August 2019), online: <https://lfpress.com/news/local-news/ryan-jarvis-london-teacher-who-secretly-recorded-female-students-sentenced-to-six-months-in-jail>.

CONCLUSION

What COVID can teach

Elizabeth Anne Kirley and Deborah Porter

Why read this book now? Because this pandemic didn't have to happen – we need to understand why it did, and what went wrong. We need to be informed so we can hold our leaders, nationally and globally, to account. We hope, together, to prevent the next one.

We set out to consider the "big ticket" issues, identified by media coverage, that arose early in the pandemic. Several months passed before our analysis identified three indicators of pandemic readiness: first, countries with effective response showed national decisiveness from the top; second, an immediate, rapid response involved both testing and isolation; and third, sharing among the medical research community provided knowledge about the virus as it was acquired. Those indicators emerged from the work of our contributors who had been asked to identify the defining moment in their field that indicated change was needed. They also advised us on the best route to achieving those changes through law and/or policy.

The ingenuity of their suggestions constitutes a wish list for law and policy-makers, somewhat visionary and more inspiring than predictable: yes, we can support end-of-life choices for the critically ill in accordance with sound ethical, legal, and clinical principles (Chapter 2); and yes, we can birth babies safely during a pandemic (Chapter 3)

And our leadership must work on smoothing out supply chain disruptions (Chapter 4); must deal with disparities in mask wearing (Chapter 5) while dignifying the experiences and strengthening the security of those in long-term care (Chapter 6).

To promote such security and inclusion, we must encourage collaborative efforts to offset the commodification of public health goods (Chapter 7); work

DOI: 10.4324/9781003215769-18

on more creative ways to provide affordable housing for the homeless (Chapter 8); and rethink whether, in the criminal justice system, mass incarceration is truly a sounder resolution than restorative justice (Chapter 9).

And for sustainable quality education into the future, we must integrate online learning with equitable access to promote a holistic learning experience for university students (Chapter 10); optimize the use of artificial intelligence to rout out fake news (Chapter 11); and implement strategies to protect children from predators during online classes (Chapter 12).

Clearly, law and policy contribute to the means by which we can do better, but alone such means are not enough. Driving the intelligent choices set out by our contributors is the trust we hold in governments and their institutions, the courageous leadership shown by heads of state, the political and technological capabilities for data sharing across geopolitical borders, and, most essential, informed political will.

To consider how this has played out in the COVID pandemic so far, we look to two independent assessments in relation to the pandemic response of the World Health Organization (WHO) and, more broadly, the international community. The latter are reports of the Independent Oversight and Advisory Committee (IOAC) for the WHO Health Emergencies and the Independent Panel for Pandemic Preparedness and Response (IPPPR).

The World Health Organization

Handling of regional and global health crises traditionally begins and ends with the WHO. Since its postwar founding, WHO as a UN agency has attracted both praise and criticism for its response to international public health crises, including the 2003 SARS outbreak, the 2012 MERS epidemic, and now the 2020 SARS-CoV-2 pandemic. Criticisms focus on underfunding and consequent slowness in issuing advisory notices to its 192 member nations. Politicization of decision-making is another frequent complaint.[1] The WHO's strategic priorities are rooted in the UN Sustainable Development Goals, a set of 17 objectives for ending global poverty by 2030.[2] The economic fallout of this pandemic will undoubtedly necessitate UN and WHO concerted efforts to reduce its impact on this goal.

As the coronavirus began to emerge in China in late 2019, all nations looked to the WHO for an announcement that the outbreak was a Public Health Emergency of International Concern (PHEIC). The WHO made that announcement on 30 January 2020, a full month after Wuhan authorities had reported the outbreak to the WHO on 31 December 2020. WHO's director general then declared a pandemic on 11 March 2020; this signaled to national leaders that it was time to close borders to travelers and trade and introduce strict intervention to stop the spread.

About that time, the first committee to review the WHO's international pandemic response was struck: the Independent Oversight and Advisory Committee

(IOAC) for the World Health Emergencies Programme. The Committee consisted of nine members drawn from national governments, NGOs, the UN system, and academia with extensive experience in a broad range of disciplines. Members serve in their personal capacity to review whether the WHO is following its mandate.[3]

The WHO's pivotal role in the pandemic response includes

- preparing for emergencies by identifying, mitigating, and managing risks;
- preventing emergencies and supporting development of tools necessary during outbreaks;
- detecting and responding to acute health emergencies; and
- supporting delivery of essential health services in fragile settings.[4]

The IOAC's "Interim Report on WHO's response to COVID-19"[5] found general satisfaction that the WHO was meeting its mandate.[6] More specifically, however, it was found to have demonstrated inadequacy in both authority and resourcing to undertake the task of managing COVID-19 effectively. For example, early in the pandemic funding deficits caused delays in the provision of useful, fact-based guidelines and information to countries. The IOAC found:

> The delay between messaging at press briefings and putting out corresponding guidance on some key response elements such as the testing strategy, mask usage and managing personal protective equipment shortages, and the long-term virus suppression strategy, has given rise to uncertainty.[7]

The IOAC concluded that more intensive work is needed with Member States to improve and clarify risk assessments and corresponding alerts, and to give clout to the International Health Regulations for quicker action. They also recommended the WHO review existing tools for national and international preparedness, as well as the use of travel restrictions in the pandemic context; that it strengthen core WHO technical expertise; and that it define clearer roles and responsibilities for the director general, regional directors, and other senior staff with respect to emergencies.[8]

Now that over 18 months have passed and much of the world is battling variants and resultant surges in case numbers, there are two further reviews of importance. The first, the IPPPR, focused on the response of all Member States, not on the WHO mechanism itself. Specifically, it conducted a "comprehensive review of the international health response to COVID-19 and of experiences gained and lessons learned from that."[9] The second review was assumed by G7 members to assess the vaccine rollouts and shortages around the world and in particular the potential for COVAX intervention, as determined in the UK summit in June 2021.

The IPPPR presented two reports, the titles of which are telling: *COVID-19: Make It the Last Pandemic*[10] and the companion report *How an Outbreak Became a*

Pandemic – the Defining Moments of the COVID-19 Pandemic.[11] The correlation of the theme of leadership in both this book and those reports is strong endorsement for the need for a wide-ranging leadership review. Strong, collaborative, informed, transparent leadership makes a difference and, as we have discussed in this book, leadership gaps during a pandemic can result in catastrophic outcomes. It stands to reason, therefore, that quality leadership is essential to steering us out of this pandemic and preventing the next one.

Generally, the IPPPR reports determine that we should have seen the pandemic coming and we should have been ready. That is the clear message: "In spite of the warnings of pandemic risk and clear recommendations on what needed to be improved, the world had not taken these issues seriously."[12] The review committee found that attitude was due to limits imposed by the WHO's workforce capacity. In addressing such issues, the IPPPR, like the IOAC, made a recommendation to "strengthen the independence, authority and financing of WHO."[13]

With reference to the declaration of a PHEIC, the IPPPR found it to be ultimately inadequate. As it noted:

> The conclusion is that the alert system does not operate with sufficient speed when faced with a fast-moving respiratory pathogen, that the legally binding IHR (2005) are a conservative instrument as currently constructed and serve to constrain rather than facilitate rapid action.[14]

Even starting an investigation to ascertain the origins of the virus and its mode of transmission to humans, although recognized by the WHO as crucial due to "a risk of reintroduction of the virus in the human population and the risk of new outbreaks like the ones we are currently experiencing,"[15] seemed beyond its practical capacity. It wasn't until late March 2021 that the first official report of an independent team of scientists into the origins of the virus was released by the WHO. And this was only after calls from a number of countries and a request by the World Health Assembly to the WHO. Even then, the investigation was fraught with claims of inadequate access to essential raw data regarding the early cases, which again raises concern regarding the authority of the WHO.

The IPPPR claimed their recommendations "if adopted as a package will transform the international system for pandemic preparedness and response and enable it to prevent a future infectious disease outbreak from becoming a pandemic."[16] A lofty goal indeed, but one to which we should surely all aspire.

Regarding the response of Member States, is it time to consider specific, legally enforceable, obligations for their early reporting of potential outbreaks? Should these include the obligation to provide immediate access to information and facilities enabling an independent investigation into the origins of a virus and a moratorium on destruction of valuable evidence to inform that investigation? Should there be a mandated requirement for a timely and appropriate response by countries to a declaration of a PHEIC? And should any such powers vest in the WHO or another international body?

Also weighing in on the response discussion was the G7 summit with the theme "Our Shared Agenda for Global Action to Build Back Better." Despite many meetings across the globe held virtually, the relevant world leaders made a point of physically attending, demonstrating that the world was opening up once again to a united approach to recovery. Relevantly, the G7 Summit committed to supporting world vaccination. However, the commitment was limited: "Total G7 commitments since the start of the pandemic provide for a total of over two billion vaccine doses, with the commitments since we last met in February 2021, including here in Carbis Bay [Cornwall UK], providing for one billion doses over the next year."[17]

This was met with significant criticism as inadequate, including by the UN director general, Antonio Guterres. In noting more was needed, he warned that "if people in developing countries [are] not inoculated quickly, the virus could mutate further and become resistant to the new vaccines" and cautioned further that "We need a global vaccination plan. We need to act with a logic, with a sense of urgency, and with the priorities of a war economy, and we are still far from getting that."[18] This was reinforced by broader UN criticisms, echoing a widely held sentiment that "donat[ing] 1 billion COVID-19 vaccine doses to poorer countries lacks ambition, is far too slow and shows Western leaders are not yet on top of tackling the worst public health crisis in a century."[19]

Definitely room for improvement then.

The broader international pandemic response

There are many lessons we can learn from the COVID pandemic, and no doubt more to come. Key points include:

> *Strong, collaborative, informed, transparent leadership is imperative*: The catastrophic effects of the pandemic demonstrate that global leadership was lacking. As noted by the IOAC, the virus would not be defeated "without greater global solidarity and stronger multilateral cooperation"[20] and, in relation to leadership at a global level, that the "WHO cannot succeed without unified global political support during the next phases of the pandemic."[21] Along similar lines, the IPPPR found "coordinated, global leadership was absent. Global tensions undermined multilateral institutions and cooperative action."[22]
> Failure of leadership was also evident at a national level. According to the IPPPR, "too many countries took a 'wait and see' approach rather than enacting an aggressive containment strategy that could have forestalled the global pandemic."[23] And "February was a lost month of opportunity to contain the outbreak, even as the evidence of infections spreading globally was apparent."[24]
> *Pandemic preparedness and response are key*: A crucial strategy in preventing or combating a pandemic is pandemic preparedness and response.

This includes having a plan with a supportive legislative framework, effectively testing the plan, ensuring necessary equipment is on hand, and so on. Again, this was a significant area of leadership failure. As the IPPPR noted:

> While there have been concerted efforts in recent years to boost pandemic preparedness, they have fallen far short of what is required. Too many national governments lacked solid preparedness plans, core public health capacities and organized multisectoral coordination with clear commitment from the highest national leadership.[25]

To the contrary, "successful national responses built on lessons from previous outbreaks and/or had response plans which they could adapt."[26]

Of course, pandemic preparedness is costly. However, reluctance to spend on pandemic preparation is a false economy, as demonstrated by the cost of combating the virus. For example, "The US$72 billion estimated cost for preparedness corresponds to less than 1% of the total cost as we know it right now."[27]

Following the science is paramount: As noted by the IPPPR, successful countries "listened to the science, changed course where necessary, engaged communities, and communicated transparently and consistently."[28] In stark contrast, "Countries that devalued science, failed to build trust in their response and pursued inconsistent strategies found themselves continually lagging behind the epidemic and have seen the consequences in high rates of infection and death."[29] Sadly, there are all too many examples of this.

Combating the virus successfully isn't necessarily done best by the rich: While it might have been expected that well-resourced countries would generally respond more effectively, and successfully, to the pandemic, this wasn't necessarily the case. The fact of being a well-resourced country in itself didn't guarantee an advantage in combating the virus. As the IPPPR noted, "country wealth was not a predictor of success. A number of low and middle-income countries successfully implemented public health measures which kept illness and death to a minimum. A number of high-income countries did not."[30]

Supporting and protecting frontline health workers is critical: The devastating impact of the lack of leadership extended beyond unnecessary deaths in patients to the frontline health workers themselves. In many countries, those workers were completely overwhelmed, leading to physical and mental exhaustion. Worse still, the lack of PPE contributed to the high number of unnecessary deaths of these workers, at least 17,000 in the first year of the pandemic.[31] The tragedy of these deaths is at least twofold: the unnecessary loss of life and the depletion of the number of frontline workers essential to combating the pandemic.

Reliable, resilient supply chains are essential: A further significant issue that impacted us all in some way was the inability to access the goods we desired or needed. The impact of this was nowhere more profound than in the health sector. As the IOAC noted, "COVID-19 has overwhelmed health systems in several hard-hit countries, and the supply chain for personal protective equipment, testing kits and medical equipment such as oxygen treatment equipment and ventilators, is under immense pressure to meet global demand."[32] The impact on supply chains was also recognized by the IPPPR: "As COVID-19 spread into more countries, neither national nor international systems managed to meet the initial and urgent demands for supplies."[33]

It is a depressing story, and yet it is more than a story; it is the life we have been living since this pandemic started. Now, with an acute awareness of the many clear and tragic failures of leadership so far, what of the future? This pandemic is not over. And we know others threaten.

The future

The race is on – we must vaccinate the world population. This is considered essential to combating, and hopefully defeating, the virus. And yet, now we are seeing circumstances of unequal distribution of COVID vaccines that the WHO described as a potential "catastrophic moral failure," whereby the richer nations hoard the vaccines to the detriment of low-income countries.[34] And this despite the COVAX mechanism described by Dr. Seth Berkley, the CEO of Gavi, the Vaccine Alliance, as follows:

> The result of an extraordinary and unique global collaboration, with more than two-thirds of the world engaged – COVAX has the world's largest and most diverse portfolio of COVID-19 vaccines, and as such represents the world's best hope of bringing the acute phase of this pandemic to a swift end.[35]

As the IPPPR noted, "Vaccines were developed at unprecedented speed. . . . Now they must be distributed much more equitably and strategically to curtail COVID-19."[36] Only effective leadership can achieve this.

On a more positive note, in June 2021, there was a promising development, with the announcement by the WHO of the establishment of a consortium to develop and manufacture vaccines in South Africa.[37] This was lauded by Cyril Ramaphosa, the South African president, who also commented: "The COVID-19 pandemic has revealed the full extent of the vaccine gap between developed and developing economies, and how that gap can severely undermine global health security."[38] Only time will tell how effective this consortium, and perhaps others like it, will be.

As we move forward, there remain many unknowns: will we have to learn to forever live with this virus? Will we eventually find the origin of this virus? What does the future look like for those suffering "long COVID"? And, so it goes on . . .

But we can learn; indeed, we must learn. It is clear that strong, collaborative, informed, transparent leadership could have prevented or, at the very least, reduced the impact of the COVID pandemic. As we have experienced, the pandemic has been truly catastrophic at a global level. As at June 2021, according to the WHO data, there have been well over 181 million confirmed cases of COVID and almost 4 million deaths globally, though it is widely believed the actual death toll is well beyond the official statistics. And this doesn't take into account those living with "long COVID" – the serious chronic illness that continues well beyond the acute phase of the disease.

When the Spanish flu pandemic began in 1918, the 28th US president Woodrow Wilson failed to acknowledge the seriousness of the outbreak and take immediate, appropriate measures to detect, contain, treat, and eliminate the pathogen. As a result, by the lowest estimate, 21 million people died.[39] Over a century later and, at the outbreak of COVID, the 45th US president Donald Trump repeated those failings – all this despite the United States having developed a pandemic "playbook" and having a supportive legislative framework in place.

What we do know is that when a global crisis of this magnitude occurs, we share our fate. As this book draws to a close, and as we continue to respond to the current pandemic, the words of the IPPPR resound loudly:

> The world must learn from this crisis, and plan for the next one. Other-wise, precious time and momentum will be lost . . . now the world needs to wake up, and commit to clear targets, additional resources, new measures and strong leadership to prepare for the future.[40]

We simply must do better – we must learn to outsmart the next pandemic.

Smarter next time?

The prevailing wisdom is that a virus has no neurological capabilities, neither brain nor nervous system.[41] Therefore, it cannot remember or strategize as humans do. We know that our memories are encoded and stored in the neuronal networks of our brains. Forming memories is part of our cognitive processes. Remembering at both conscious and unconscious levels creates the foundation of our existence as individuals and as a society. Calling on those memories during a time of stress, such as the outbreak of a global health crisis, can help us to "anticipate and shape the future of our own well-being."[42]

Individual organisms or a collective ecosystem like the ocean contains encoded memories of its ancestors. Earlier ocean conditions are evident in the genetic information of its inhabitants, in their DNA and RNA that produce protein and other building blocks of life. An interdisciplinary team of researchers has formed the Ocean Memory Project[43] to explore the intersection of the ocean and memory, reaching way back to the substrate from which we all came. Its members point out that RNA-encoded genes, the only ones contained in the SARS-CoV-2 virus, have their ancient origins in the primordial ocean before jumping to land during the early evolution of terrestrial animals and plants. The ocean, then, "holds the memory of the earliest lineage of RNA viruses, one that eventually led to the coronaviruses that plague humans today."[44] It is hoped that, in future, similar collaborations can uncover more information on the involvement of viruses in a rudimentary cognition of their own, providing a window into how viruses "think." We might then have a glimpse into how to outthink them the moment we decipher their genetic presence.

In Chapter 1, we characterized the SARS-CoV-2 virus as an antagonist in a struggle for life against the human host it infects. While it is acknowledged that anthropomorphizing the pathogen is a contested approach, it is a useful device to consider how some biological discoveries have revealed that a virus has a formative link to human communication of memories at the cellular level. In 1995, for example, a research team determined that converting external stimuli to memory in the human brain involves a protein whose gene sequences, known as *Arc*, originated in ancient viruses or retroviruses.[45] Two subsequent studies have shown that *Arc* actually forms retroviral-like capsid structures to transfer our memory RNA between cells in the nervous system. This means that the host (you or me) has taken up a viral-like mechanism for communicating stimuli between the point of intake to the human brain for long-term memory storage. This is a completely novel way of cell-to-cell-communication, according to Travis Thomson, a neurobiologist from the University of Massachusetts. He advises that genome sequencing over the last decade has revealed that roughly half of the mammalian genome consists of DNA from transposon (elements that jump along the DNA strand) or viral origin.[46]

Viruses have shown themselves to be extraordinarily adaptive. Their rates of RNA sequence change are orders of magnitude greater than ours.[47] They display evolution in real time as they acquire antiviral drug resistance, maintain persistent infection through escaping immune system responses to infection, or, in the laboratory, rapidly adapting to different cell culture conditions, new receptors, and new hosts. SARS-CoV-2 has easily invaded such a major portion of the globe that nearly 90% of disease scientists studied by the journal *Nature* believe it is endemic at this point, destined to continue to circulate in pockets of the global population for years to come.[48]

In terms of strategy, once inside our bodies the virus prefers to target our nervous system cells. "Olfactory cells are very susceptible to viral invasion and are particularly targeted by SARS-CoV-2, and that's why one of the prominent symptoms of COVID-19 is loss of smell."[49] Damage to brain tissue might also be indicated by symptoms of dizziness, confusion, and stroke.[50]

For about 100 years, the scientific community has repeatedly changed its collective mind about viruses.

> First seen as poisons, then as life-forms, then biological chemicals, viruses today are thought of as being in a gray area between living and nonliving: they cannot replicate on their own but can do so in truly living cells and can also affect the behavior of their hosts profoundly.[51]

By limiting the study of viruses to nonliving species during much of the modern era of biological science, we have led most researchers to ignore viruses in the study of evolution. This pandemic has reignited curiosity about the coronavirus as a living and possibly thinking organism.

Unparalleled at this point in history is the convergence of two factors that enable our discovery of new paths to defeating SARS-CoV-2: the urgent willingness of the scientific community to share metadata and the new capabilities of artificial intelligence. As discussed in Chapter 1, that combination has produced within a few weeks the gene sequencing that informed treatment; the early availability of testing, tracking, and tracing software that hastened containment; and the approval of the first vaccine, Pfizer–BioNTech, within nine months of WHO's declaration of a global outbreak[52] – simply unheard-of timing in the annals of global infectious disease.

The fertile research environment can move quickly to uncovering our intimate relationship to viral infection at this time. We are at home, we have access to almost limitless data troves, and we are personally invested. SARS-CoV-2 has dropped the glove: will we pick up the challenge?

Notes

1 Daniel S. Goldberg, *Against the Very Idea of the Politicization of Public Health Policy*, 102:1 Am. J. Public Health 44–49 (Jan. 2012).
2 CFR.org Editors, *Backgrounder: What Does the World Health Organization Do?* Council for. Rel. (29 Jan. 2021).
3 Independent Oversight and Advisory Committee for the WHO Health Emergencies Programme, IOAC Committee, www.who.int/groups/independent-oversight-and-advisory-committee. Members bring experience from the International Federation of Red Cross and Red Crescent Societies, public health, the UN Commission on Information & Accountability for Women & Children's Health, health management and ethics, the USAID COVID-19 Task Force, and university research in infectious disease, and infection prevention and control.
4 World Health Organization, *What We Do*, WHO (2021), www.who.int/about/what-we-do/.
5 Independent Oversight and Advisory Committee for the WHO Emergencies Programme, *Interim Report on WHO's response to Covid-19*, IOAC (Jan.–Apr. 2020), www.who.int/publications/m/item/ioac-interim-report-on-who-s-response-to-covid-19.[IOAC Interim Report].
6 Id.
7 Id., 9.

8 Independent Oversight and Advisory Committee for the WHO Emergencies Programme, IOAC REPORT to the resumed WHA73/10, *Looking Back to Move Forward* (4 Nov. 2020), www.who.int/publications/m/item/looking-back-to-move-forward-ioac-report-to-the-resumed-wha73-10; Chandre Prince, *Independent Oversight Committee: WHO Needs Stronger Base of Finance and Authority for More Robust Pandemic Response*, Health Pol. Watch (25 May 2021).

9 The Independent Panel for Pandemic Preparedness and Response, *COVID-19: Make It the Last Pandemic* (2021), p. 8, https://theindependentpanel.org/mainreport/. [IPPPR Make it the last].

10 Id.

11 The Independent Panel for Pandemic Preparedness and Response, *How an Outbreak Became a Pandemic: The Defining Moments of the Covid-19 Pandemic* (2021), https://theindependentpanel.org/mainreport/. [IPPPR How an Outbreak].

12 Id., 11.

13 The Independent Panel for Pandemic Preparedness and Response, *COVID-19: Make It the Last Pandemic Summary Report* (2021), p. 5, https://theindependentpanel.org/mainreport/. [IPPPR Summary Report].

14 IPPPR, Make it the last, *supra*, note 9, 26.

15 World Health Organization, *Origins of SARS-CoV-2*, WHO (26 Mar. 2020), https://apps.who.int/iris/bitstream/handle/10665/332197/WHO-2019-nCoV-FAQ-Virus_origin-2020.1-eng.pdf.

16 IPPPR, Summary Report, *supra*, note 13, 4.

17 Carbis Bay G7 Summit Communique 2021 @ www.g7uk.org/.

18 Elizabeth Piper and Kate Holton, *"We Need More": UN Joins Criticism of G7 Vaccine Pledge*, Reuters Healthcare & Pharmaceuticals (13 June 2021), www.reuters.com/business/healthcare-pharmaceuticals/g7-donate-1-billion-covid-19-vaccine-doses-poorer-countries-2021-06-10/.

19 Id.

20 IOAC, Interim Report, *supra*, note 5, 11.

21 Id.

22 IPPPR, Summary Report, *supra*, note 13, 2.

23 Id.

24 IPPPR, How an Outbreak, *supra*, note 11, 22.

25 IPPPR, Make it the last, *supra*, note 9, 18.

26 IPPPR, Summary Report, *supra*, note 13, 3.

27 IPPPR, How an Outbreak, *supra*, note 11, 50.

28 IPPPR, Summary Report, *supra*, note 13, 3.

29 IPPPR, Make it the last, *supra*, note 9, 22.

30 IPPPR, Summary Report, *supra*, note 13, 3.

31 Id.

32 IOAC, Interim Report, *supra*, note 5, 3.

33 IPPPR, Summary Report, *supra*, note 13, 2.

34 British Broadcasting Corporation, *Covid Vaccine: WHO Warns of "Catastrophic Moral Failure"*, BBC WORLD (18 Jan. 2021), www.bbc.com/news/world-55709428.

35 Dr. Seth Berkley, *COVAX Explained*, Gavi: The Vaccine Alliance (3 Sept. 2020), www.gavi.org/vaccineswork/covax-explained.

36 IPPPR, Summary Report, *supra*, note 13, 3.

37 WHO News Release, *WHO Supporting South African Consortium to Establish First COVID mRNA Vaccine Technology Transfer Hub*, WHO (21 June 2021), www.who.int/news/item/21-06-2021-who-supporting-south-african-consortium-to-establish-first-covid-mrna-vaccine-technology-transfer-hub.

38 Id.

39 See, for example, John M. Barry, *The Site of Origin of the 1918 Influenza Pandemic and Its Public Health Implications*, 2:3 J. Transn. Med. (2004), stating that "The lowest estimate of the death toll is 21 million, while recent scholarship estimates from 50 to 100 million dead."

40 IPPPR, Summary Report, *supra*, note 13, 1.

41 Jonathan Jarry, *We Are All Mutants and So Is the Coronavirus*, McGill Off. Sci. & Soc. (16 Apr. 2020).

42 John Baross et al., *The Ocean Carries "Memories" of SARS-CoV-2*, Opinion, Sci Am. (15 Aug. 2020), www.scientificamerican.com/article/the-ocean-carries-memories-of-sars-cov-2/.

43 *Ocean Memory Project*, About, OMP, https://oceanmemoryproject.com/about/.

44 Baross et al., *supra* note 42.

45 W. Link et al., *Somatodendritic Expression of an Immediate Early Gene Is Regulated by Synaptic Activity*, 92:12 Proc. Natl. Acad. Sci. U.S.A. 5734–5738 (1995); M. R. Campioni and S. Finkbeiner, *Going Retro: Ancient Viral Origins of Cognition*, 86:2 Neuron 346–348 (2015).

46 J. Ashley et al., *Retrovirus-Like Gag Protein Arc1 Binds RNA and Traffics across Synaptic Boutons*, 172:1–2 Cell. 262–274.e11 (2018). Transposons are elements that can "jump" along the DNA sequence.

47 P. Simmonds, P. Aiewsakun, and A. Katzourakis, *Prisoners of War: Host Adaptation and Its Constraints on Virus Evolution*, 17 Nat. Rev. Microbiol. 321–328 (2019). https://doi.org/10.1038/s41579-018-0120-2

48 Nicky Phillips, *The Coronavirus Is Here to Stay – Here's What That Means*, Nature (16 Feb. 2021) describing a study by *Nature* of 100 immunologists, infectious disease researchers, and virologists.

49 Ana Sandoiu, *Covid-19 and the Brain: What Do We Know So Far*, Med. News Today (25 Jan. 2021).

50 Malorye Branca, *Early Details of Brain Damage in COVID-19 Patients*, Harv. Gazette (18 Nov. 2020).

51 Luis P. Villarreal, *Are Viruses Alive?* Sci. Amer. (8 Aug. 2008; 22 Nov. 2004).

52 *FDA Takes Key Action in Fight Against COVID-19 By Issuing Emergency Use Authorization for First COVID-19 Vaccine*, US Food and Drug Admin. (11 Dec. 2020), www.fda.gov/news-events/press-announcements/fda-takes-key-action-fight-against-covid-19-issuing-emergency-use-authorization-first-covid-19.

INDEX